THE RISE OF
GOLIATH

ADVANCE PRAISE FOR THE BOOK

'Demonetization and the GST were not the only disruptions that changed India. A.K. Bhattacharya provides a fresh perspective on many more such disruptive events that shaped India in the last seven decades. *The Rise of Goliath* presents a riveting account of these transformational moments.'—Nandan Nilekani, chairman and co-founder, Infosys, and founding chairman, UIDAI (Aadhaar)

'*The Rise of Goliath* uses the prism of disruptions to lucidly capture India's journey in the last seven decades. Equally illuminating is its prognosis for the disruptions that might take place in the coming decade.'—Vijay Kelkar, vice-president, Pune International Centre

A.K. BHATTACHARYA

THE RISE OF

GOLIATH

Twelve Disruptions That Changed India

PORTFOLIO
PENGUIN

An imprint of Penguin Random House

PORTFOLIO

USA | Canada | UK | Ireland | Australia
New Zealand | India | South Africa | China | Singapore

Portfolio is part of the Penguin Random House group of companies
whose addresses can be found at global.penguinrandomhouse.com

Published by Penguin Random House India Pvt. Ltd
4th Floor, Capital Tower 1, MG Road,
Gurugram 122 002, Haryana, India

Penguin
Random House
India

First published in Portfolio by Penguin Random House India 2019

ISBN 9780670091805

Typeset in Minion Pro by Manipal Digital Systems, Manipal
Printed at Replika Press Pvt. Ltd, India

www.penguin.co.in

MIX
Paper from
responsible sources
FSC® C016779

This is a legitimate digitally printed version of the book and therefore might not
have certain extra finishing on the cover.

For Jharna

CONTENTS

CHAPTER 1

THE MANY FACES OF DISRUPTION

The five years of the Narendra Modi government in India have given rise to an impression that the country has seen too many disruptions in a short period of time. There was demonetization, which many people believe was the mother of all disruptions, where 86 per cent of all currencies in circulation were declared invalid in one stroke. There was the Goods and Services Tax, or GST that promised to usher in a single indirect tax across the country, replacing over twelve different central and state-level taxes and a host of surcharges and cesses. There was also the Insolvency and Bankruptcy Code that ensured that promoters could lose their companies if they defaulted on repayment of loans from banks. Thanks to these disruptions, the economic landscape in India changed quite fundamentally in these five years. They have also given rise to the view that disruptions have been a hallmark of the Modi regime.

The basic premise of this book is that the Modi regime may have caused as many as three major economic policy disruptions in a relatively short period of five years, but disruptions per se have not been uncommon in India's journey of more than seven decades as an independent country. Indeed, it can be argued that India's journey as an independent country can be better understood if seen through the prism of disruptions. This book, therefore, will take you through a dozen such disruptions, starting right from India's Partition in 1947 to the launch of the GST in 2017. The list is not comprehensive. There will be legitimate scope for a debate on why a certain decision has been included as a disruption and why another disruptive decision has been excluded. The purpose of the book is not to present all the disruptions that India experienced in the last seven decades or so, but to indicate the nature of a few of these disruptions and how they made a difference to India's politics, society and economy.

It is also important to note that the disruptions captured in this book have played a significant role in the way India, like Goliath, has risen and grown in the last seven decades. Some disruptions have constrained the pace of India's change, while others have led India to a new trajectory of faster and rapid growth. Either way, the rise of this Goliath has been defined and shaped by these disruptions. Take away these disruptions and India's growth story could have been different.

The literature on disruptions tells us that disruptions are caused by both internal and external factors. Consequences of disruptions, however, vary depending on the nature and quality of internal or external forces. The next twelve chapters will check the validity of this argument and examine if all disruptions in India can be traced to endogenous or exogenous factors or whether some other factors were responsible for them. In the process, these chapters also answer many obvious questions about the dozen disruptions that changed India. Were all the disruptions sudden? Or did they represent an outcome of a series of developments? Were these disruptions always a planned effort or a culmination of events over which policymakers had little control? What was the politics and economics behind these dozen disruptions? Personalities behind disruptions are even more fascinating than the disruptions. Who were the key personalities directly or indirectly behind those disruptions? Some of them have played a key role in executing them, while some others may have just played along. Who were the protagonists of disruptions?

India's Partition in 1947 is the first disruption that we discuss in this book. It was a disruption about which many Indians as also their leaders were quite ambivalent. Could the leaders have delayed the country's freedom to prevent the partition of the country? Perhaps, yes. But it seems the top Congress leaders at that time were reluctant to take the risk of gambling on securing the country's freedom only as a united India. For so many years they had been leading a mass movement to throw the British out of the country that they feared any further delay in gaining freedom could be counterproductive and that might even be rejected by the people. There was, thus, an element of inevitability about accepting freedom with Partition. In any case, the idea of Partition had gained currency quite a few years before it actually happened in 1947. And when it happened, it had an impact on various fronts—on the nature of politics that would be practised in independent India and on the domestic economy and industry. The radio address of Jawaharlal Nehru on 3 June 1947 was what gave the first clear hints to the nation that India would soon become independent, but not as an undivided country. Was Nehru the only disrupter or was Mohammed Ali Jinnah, who pressed hard for the partition of India before the British could announce India's freedom, a bigger disrupter? Was Mohandas Karamchand Gandhi, too, in some ways a tacit disrupter?

The rise of *statism* is the second disruption that the Indian economy faced, and this became evident soon after Independence. The seeds of statism were, however, sown even before 1947. The Bombay Plan, a blueprint penned in the 1940s by leading lights of Indian industry such as Jamshedji Tata, Ghanshyam Das Birla, Kasturbhai Lalbai and Purshottamdas Thakurdas, envisaged a strong dose of government funding in key infrastructure sectors to revive the Indian economy to overcome the devastation of Partition, influx of refugees and communal riots. For India's private sector, that blueprint was a big jolt. The first industrial policy announced in 1948 confirmed that the private sector would only play a peripheral role. The state of the newly independent India would take over the responsibility of making investments in basic infrastructure and the production of a wide range of inputs for industrial activities. The launch of the planning process; the formulation of the Industrial Policy Resolution in 1956; Nehru's ideas of building huge public sector projects and showcasing them as temples of modern India; and the nationalization of the Imperial Bank of India along with a clutch of life insurance companies and the takeover of Air India, a successful commercial airline run by the Tatas till then, were all indications of how the disruption of embracing statism played out on Indian politics and economy.

Nehru allowed Indian agriculture, in sharp contrast to the statism of the industrial sector, to remain in the private sector. This was partly because of the obvious limitations of state capacity in undertaking agriculture in the public sector and partly because of the political risks of alienating farmers from the land—an automatic outcome of the state playing a bigger role in farming. Farmers and their rights to cultivate without any controls were part and parcel of India's freedom struggle. Nehru was obviously concerned that any state control over agriculture could upset farmers and militate against the spirit of freedom that the country had just secured for itself. Unsurprisingly, Nehru and, indeed, all his successors have not only let agriculture remain a private initiative but also kept it out of the reach of the organized corporate sector. An unintended consequence of this approach was the poor state of India's agriculture. The absence of organized farming also meant that Indian agriculture suffered from poor productivity and lack of technology. Farmers continued to remain poor, and unchecked population growth led to fragmented landholdings. This was a recipe for a food crisis. The disruption here was the acute food crisis the country experienced in the 1960s as also the Green Revolution that followed immediately thereafter. Apart from increased production, reducing the country's dependence on imports, the Green Revolution also led to a sharp increase in the use of hybrid varieties of foodgrain, which caused yet another disruption to the Indian economy. It was largely a positive disruption, but it also gave rise to income inequalities among the Indian farming community and laid the foundations of a support regime for agriculture in the form of minimum support prices and subsidies for inputs. This had its own adverse consequences for state finances.

Around the same time, i.e. from the late 1960s and the early 1970s, India experienced a stronger dose of statism, with the government deciding to nationalize a host of sectors such as banks, coal, petroleum and general insurance. Laws on the concentration of economic wealth and market dominance were introduced to tighten the government's levers of control on private industry. The economic disruption it caused in a wide range of sectors of Indian businesses and the economy was actually a response to a political challenge to the then government of Indira Gandhi. The Indira Gandhi-led government faced a challenge from a clutch of Congress leaders, who believed that she should act at their behest because they supported her candidature as prime minister. But Gandhi refused to be their puppet and instead came out with a raft of economic policies to firmly establish her leadership within her party as also in the government. Her response to this political challenge was to nationalize several industries to strengthen the role and sway of the public sector in the Indian economy and tighten laws on economic activities. The disrupter here was Indira Gandhi, aided and guided by some of her key advisers in the government. On the face of it, there was an economic rationale that Indira Gandhi presented to defend her decisions on the nationalization of banks and companies in a wide range of sectors, including coal, petroleum and general insurance. But dig deeper into the reasons for such decisions, and you will see how Indira Gandhi used nationalization as a tool for achieving her political goals of staying in power and isolating her opponents. Thus, the nature of statism in this phase was quite different in character and emphasis from the earlier round seen during Nehru's premiership.

Next in line of India's long list of disruptions was the *oil shock*. It was a disruption that was caused neither on Indian shores nor by Indian political leaders. It was triggered by a decision taken by the Organization of the Petroleum Exporting Countries (OPEC) to stop supplies of oil to the US and raise prices. It was an act of retaliation against US actions in support of Israel, which was at war with Syria in 1973.

India was a collateral damage as its dependence on oil imports was already huge. Its dependence on oil imports was its Achilles' heel and the cause of one of its biggest economic disruptions. It changed the way economic policy planning would be undertaken in the decades to come. India's economic policy focus shifted from one of import substitution to export promotion, wherein the new slogan was 'export or perish'. The reason was not far to seek. India needed precious foreign exchange to meet its requirement of oil imports, which also led to a gradual shift in its policies on trade and tariffs. An additional fallout was a new focus on oil exploration on Indian shores.

If the sharp increase in oil prices was a disruption triggered by developments outside India, the cause of India's next disruption was very much rooted in domestic political factors. And yet, the role of the increasing deterioration in India's economy in that disruption could not be underestimated. *The proclamation of Emergency* in 1975, which essentially abrogated the democratic rights of the people enshrined in India's Constitution, had its roots in the woes of the Indian economy that began with the oil shock of 1973.[1] Growing restlessness in large parts of north India, on account of unemployment, culminated into a political movement to unseat the then government. Indira Gandhi's response to that challenge was political. The declaration of Emergency was the biggest jolt to India's nascent democracy, and this turned out to be the strongest force for growing deep democratic roots in the country. This was a disruption that clearly had short-term negative outcomes but also made the voters more watchful and guarded against any tendency on the part of any political-party leader that threatened to abridge their democratic freedoms.

The celebrated *reforms of 1991* were also an outcome of a major disruption in the economy. The pursuit of growth through debt incurred by the government was among the factors that contributed to the twin shocks to the Indian economy. At one level, this resulted in the worsening of the imbalance in the Central government's fiscal situation. But at another level, the country's balance of payments, too, became unsustainable as its exports were not good enough to meet its rising import bill. What, however, led to the disruption of reforms was a combination of three forces: deteriorating balance of payments, growing fiscal indiscipline and increasing political instability. Each of the reforms in the areas of banking, insurance, aviation, telecommunications, trade policy and industrial policy changed India in a fundamental way.

Two political factors played a big disruptive role around the time the Indian economy was going through a crisis in the 1990s that led to reforms. It was an irony that the short-lived National Front government led by Vishwanath Pratap Singh in 1989 would be known less for its campaign against corruption, for which it was largely voted to power, and more for its decision to extend the scope of affirmative action or reservation of seats in educational institutions to backward communities in addition to those already reserved for scheduled castes and scheduled tribes. Both economically and politically, the acceptance of the recommendations of the Mandal Commission, a committee that was set up to extend the scope of reservation, caused a massive disruption. India's politics changed fundamentally from 1990, and its impact on the economy was no less significant. Politically, it was a big blow for the Bharatiya Janata Party, which relied on the Hindu vote bank that till then had a largely monolithic character. Reservation for backward communities splintered the Hindu vote into many smaller divisions, eliciting a bigger challenge for the BJP to use its community card. It could be debated whether the reservation politics led to the BJP's mobilization of Hindus to demand a Ram temple in Ayodhya or the other way around. Extending reservation for other backward communities led to further fragmentation of what was till then a largely monolithic Hindu vote bank. The BJP, therefore, found its Hindu vote bank fragmented into castes and galvanizing the entire community for electoral gains became a bigger challenge. Community politics was challenged by caste politics. Unsurprisingly, the agitation for demolishing the disputed structure at Ayodhya and the demand for building a temple there got a big push after the V.P. Singh government extended the scope of reservation in jobs and educational institutions by accepting the recommendations of the Mandal Commission. The rapid rise of the BJP was arguably an offshoot of the disruption caused by reservation. But in the end the country had to contend with the twin shocks of disruptions—reservation politics and the demand for a Ram temple at Ayodhya after the demolition of the disputed Babri mosque.

One of the key outcomes of the economic reforms of 1991 was seen in India's *telecommunications sector*. As the events unfolded, the rapid spread of telecommunications after the economic reforms fundamentally changed the way Indians led their lives or did business. The growth in telecommunications created more choices for consumers and ushered in the growth of a sector that also needed regulation.

The role of the government in the telecom disruption cannot be underestimated. While it brought about significant improvements in productivity levels in different sectors of the economy, the rise of telecommunications created a big challenge to producing skilled manpower and living up to increased expectations of improved governance.

At a structural level, the rise of India's telecommunications also had an indirect positive impact on the domestic economy. The spread of telecommunications across the country significantly improved efficiency in the delivery of a wide range of services. Productivity levels in the manufacturing sector went up. The market size for providers of goods and services increased with improved access to consumers through the rapidly growing telecommunications network available at falling tariffs.

India's *financial sector,* too, has witnessed a major disruption, even as the government tried to achieve higher growth through increased bank financing. Growth gets a boost if the pace of investments rises with the help of bank finances made available in plenty and at reasonably competitive rates of interest. Post-reforms India saw a dramatic rise in bank lending for projects, including many long-gestation infrastructure projects, which contributed to economic growth. But this also gave rise to the twin balance-sheet problem of the Indian economy, which was a reflection of the increasing indebtedness of Indian companies and rising levels of sticky assets or loans of Indian banks. This posed the biggest challenge for growth in the Indian economy. On the one hand, the banking sector was under increasing stress to lend more to the corporate sector for investments in new or existing projects. On the other, India Inc., which by now was groaning under the burden of huge debt and unable to repay its past loans, was reluctant to invest more as it was heavily indebted. Making the situation worse was the Indian industry's relatively low-capacity utilization level, which meant there was no urgent need for increasing investments to meet demand. The steps taken in quick succession to tackle this challenge included the legislation of the Insolvency and Bankruptcy Code and a massive bank recapitalization programme. The Reserve Bank of India (RBI) was empowered to force banks to refer indebted companies unable to repay loans to the insolvency process, even though the central bank's stringent norms for recognition of stressed loans and initiation of recovery proceedings had to undergo significant alterations after being challenged by the Supreme Court. On the whole, however, the enactment of the Insolvency and Bankruptcy Code meant that financial creditors (mainly banks) and operational creditors (vendors and suppliers of goods) could move specified courts to secure the recovery of their dues from companies that had defaulted on their repayment obligations. The recovery of such dues was ensured within a fixed time limit and often promoters of defaulting companies lost their companies to those who could repay the banks and take them over. Many stressed loan cases could not be resolved within the stipulated time limit, but the new law instilled a greater sense of discipline among borrowers, who realized that it was no longer possible to get away after not repaying their loan dues. At the same time, the stressed banks were recapitalized so that they could get back into the business of lending and some other banks were to be merged with each other. The net result of all these measures was a kind of disruption that India's financial sector had never seen in the past.

In terms of visibility and the abruptness with which it was implemented, *demonetization*, or the act of annulling almost 86 per cent of the country's total currency in circulation, has few parallels perhaps anywhere in the world. The disruption was engineered in November 2016 in a bid to attack black money, choke off sources of terror money and reduce the use of cash in transactions, hopefully leading to greater digitization. At the end of the nearly seven-week long exercise, however, it was still not clear if black money or terror-money sources were fully extinguished even though tax coverage had improved and there was less cash in the economy with more use of digital transactions. Looking back, demonetization was a flawed idea and its adverse impact on society, politics and the economy was widespread. There are those who believe that the government surprised everybody and took even its own ministers and senior officials unawares before announcing demonetization on 8 November 2016.

However, if you reflect on some of the decisions that the government took almost eight months before the actual announcement of demonetization, it would appear that this mother of all disruptions was not a sudden action. It only appeared to be a sudden action since the government had been planning it for at least eight months, in complete secrecy, before it was actually announced. Key officials in the central bank, the finance ministry and the prime minister's office were entrusted with the responsibility of planning demonetization. The inevitable question that arises is if demonetization was indeed planned many weeks before it was actually implemented, why did the government machinery mess up its execution causing widespread hardship and inconveniences? The disruption of demonetization was made worse by its execution.

In sharp contrast, the rollout of the *GST*, from July 2017, was a planned disruption and nobody could really quarrel with the logic or the need for introducing the new indirect tax regime. It was the most ambitious indirect tax reform that the Narendra Modi government has launched. Yet, nobody was in doubt even before its launch that its impact on the economy and businesses would be hugely disruptive. GST as a disruption posed many challenges at many levels—governance, public finance, fiscal reform, federal structure of the country and technology. How the pain of this disruption was managed and what new challenges and gains it creates for the Indian economy is a fascinating story of governance.

What kind of disruptions can be expected in the days to come? Of course, the disruptions of the future are difficult to anticipate. But there are some visible signs of what those disruptions could be. In the political sphere, there is a strong likelihood of an electoral reform that may combine the holding of the general and state elections at the same time. One mega election once in five years will also require other changes in the way governments are formed after the elections. 'One country, one language' is an idea whose implementation could cause yet another disruption. Its consequences could be far-reaching. Privatization of public-sector banks is a possibility and this would certainly cause a huge disruption, with economic and social consequences. Finally, the delimitation of electoral constituencies could be a disruption that could even strike at the root of India's continuation as one country in its current shape. But whether such changes will be actually introduced or these disruptions will remain only as ideas in the minds of some policymakers, only time will tell.

A few broad trends are noticeable in the kind of disruptions that have been captured in this book. Not all disruptions in the country have been adverse in their consequences. Even though they might appear to be adverse in the beginning, the long-term consequences of many of them have been positive. Take, for example, the disruption of the food shortage, the oil price increase or the balance-of-payments crisis that hit the Indian economy in the 1960s, the 1970s and the 1990s, respectively. Thanks to these disruptions, Indian agriculture today is far stronger, the Indian petroleum sector is more resilient (though its self-sufficiency continues to be a big cause for concern) and the economic reforms of 1991 have laid the foundations of a new India that could help ensure growth and development at a pace that was not seen earlier.

There is also an unmistakable linkage between disruptions and secrecy. Take, for instance, the manner in which Indira Gandhi nationalized fourteen banks on 19 July 1969 or Narendra Modi demonetized as much as 86 per cent of the country's currencies in circulation on 8 November 2016. Both decisions were planned in utmost secrecy and their announcement came as a surprise to many. But they were not actually sudden decisions. In the case of both bank nationalization and demonetization, the disrupters—Indira Gandhi and Narendra Modi—had engaged in deep and secretive consultations with their key advisers for weeks together before they sprang the surprise. So, at least two of the economic policy disruptions were planned in secrecy, but it would be fallacious to say that they were sudden.

Many of the disruptions also bring out the critical role played by the close network of advisers around the disrupter. This often raises the question on whether the disruptions could have taken place without the assistance of the close group of advisers. Would it have been possible for Indira Gandhi to have nationalized the banks without the kind of support and advice she got from her advisers like P.N. Haksar? Similarly, would a disruption like the declaration of the Emergency have been possible if Haksar had been around her in 1975? And could Narendra Modi have rolled out the GST without the support of his finance minister Arun Jaitley? The chapters on the various disruptions described in this book will provide some clues to answering a few of these questions.

What, however, is incontrovertible and beyond dispute is the close linkage between disruptions and decisive leaders. Whether it was Jawaharlal Nehru, Indira Gandhi, V.P. Singh, P.V. Narasimha Rao or it is Narendra Modi, each displayed elements of a decisive and forthright leadership in executing policies that have either tackled disruptions or contributed to disruptions. The following twelve chapters are ample testimony to this thesis. Enjoy the rise of this Goliath, marked as it is by disruptions.

CHAPTER 2

A TRYST WITH DESTINY

A few months after the birth of India and Pakistan in August 1947, Kishan Lal Thapar walked across the newly created international border between the neighbouring countries. It was a walk that Thapar still remembers. His father, a hygiene-conscious Punjabi who had a flourishing medical practice in Lahore, had decided to get him circumcised soon after his birth. The decision turned out to be an ordeal for young Thapar at the border checkpoint, and a reminder of what Partition meant for millions of Hindus and Muslims who had become refugees in the Indian subcontinent.

Communal fires blazed across the Indian subcontinent in the aftermath of Partition. Hindus felt aggrieved that they had to leave the newly created state of Pakistan while many Muslims decided to stay on in what came to be known as India. Hindu vigilante groups were active and deployed in full strength at the border checkpoints. Their goal was to make sure that only Hindus could cross the border to enter India. And the way of checking, at least men, was to see if they were circumcised. Humanity had sunk to low depths!

Thapar realized he would not pass that test easily and feared that he would be singled out as a Muslim faking to be a Hindu! The consequences could be fatal for him, Thapar quickly sensed. As the Hindu vigilante group subjected him to a thorough body search, Thapar intervened and showed through proofs of his birth certificate that he was born of a Hindu father and that it was only a medical advice that led to his circumcision. After many tense moments and heated arguments, Thapar salvaged himself. He and his family lost almost everything that they had built and nurtured in what is now Pakistan and the challenge of rebuilding life all over again was a daunting task. But the trauma of that single incident is still etched in Thapar's memory.

* * *

In 2002, Joga Jiban Chakraborty was back in Karoitoli village near Chandpur in what is now Bangladesh, after leaving it in the dead of night almost fifty-five years ago. Chakraborty's decision to go back to Karoitoli was prompted by his desire to see his village home that he left when he was barely sixteen.

After Partition, Chakraborty's ancestral village happened to fall in a territory in what then became East Pakistan. Along with his father and younger sister, he left the village, seeking safety and a new home across the border in India.

He remembered the warnings his father received from local Muslims, urging them to leave the village lest they were forced to physically eliminate them. The apparent act of mercy in the form of warnings—many other Hindu families had simply been killed without notice—was shown to Chakraborty's family because his father was a homoeopath and the local residents wanted to be kind to the man who had treated them when they were sick. Even so, Chakraborty's journey, partly on boat and partly on foot, was remarkable for the many raids from violent mobs who let them off only in return for money or a piece of jewellery.

On that morning in November 2002, when Chakraborty saw his village home, he found the Gaab tree (also known as Malabar ebony) still standing, its branches spread all around the house that was once his home. It was the same tree in whose branches he had kept himself hidden all night before he bid his childhood home farewell. The sight of the tree brought alive memories of the pain, trauma and fear of the future and of the challenges that lay ahead after his displacement from what he had known as his motherland.

The Stage Is Set

A radio address to the nation by two gentlemen, Jawaharlal Nehru and Mohammed Ali Jinnah, on 3 June 1947 settled the big question of how India would gain freedom from British rule.[1]

Just before the radio address, the British Viceroy Lord Mountbatten had laid bare the plan on how England would transfer power to India. The question on whether power would be transferred to a divided India or an undivided India had been raging for many months and the new plan showed that while Nehru's fears were confirmed, Jinnah's dream was coming true. Yes, India would gain freedom from British rule but not as one independent country.

A few months previously, on 20 February 1947, the British government had announced its intention of transferring power in British India to Indians by June 1948. It had then hoped that the major parties in India would work towards evolving a Constitution acceptable to all concerned.

But the statement on 3 June noted with some disappointment that the task of framing a Constitution for all had made little progress. Large parts of British India where the Congress leadership held their sway wanted independence from British rule as an undivided country, but areas where the Muslim League was dominant were keen that the country should be divided such that Muslims get a country for themselves. The delay in framing the Constitution for a new country was largely caused by this fundamental difference of opinion on how India would emerge after freedom from British rule—as a united country or a divided country. Thus, while representatives of the provinces of Madras, Bombay, the United Provinces, Bihar, Central Provinces and Berar, Assam, Orissa, the North-West Frontier Province, Delhi, Ajmer-Merwara and Coorg made progress in the task of framing a new Constitution, the Muslim League Party, including a majority of the representatives of Bengal, the Punjab, Sind and British Baluchistan decided not to take part in the Constituent Assembly that was entrusted with the responsibility of framing a Constitution for India after it became free from British rule.[2] The Constituent Assembly was set up after elections were held in August 1946. Members of the Assembly were elected by provincial assemblies. But after the elections, the Muslim League refused to take part in the process and that led to a deadlock, forcing the British government to explore the option of dividing India.

The British government set out its game plan under three broad heads. One, it reiterated its desire that the power to rule India be transferred in accordance with the wishes of the Indian people. But that task got complicated as there was no agreement among the Indian political parties on whether they would like to get freedom as a united country or after Partition as the Muslim League had desired. The reference was obviously to the growing differences between the leaders of the Congress and the Muslim League. Two, the British government made it clear that in the absence of an agreement[3] among the main Indian political parties on the transfer of power, it would take upon itself the responsibility of formulating a method that it deemed appropriate. Three, the British government had no intention of taking upon itself the responsibility of framing the Constitution for India. This responsibility in their view was to be undertaken by the Indian people, and the plan it outlined did not preclude the possibility of Indians deciding among themselves their future course. This did not rule out the possibility of different communities agreeing on a united India after freedom.

The reality before the British government was too stark to be ignored. It had to take care of the sentiments of both Hindus and Muslims before deciding on any course of action. It had no desire to disrupt the proceedings of the Constituent Assembly that had already begun its work in right earnest. But at the same time, it could not allow a Constitution to be enforced only in parts of the country willing to accept it. The options were clear: either the Constituent Assembly already set up and functioning was accepted by all or there would be another Constituent Assembly that would comprise representatives of areas not agreeable to participating in the consultations held by the existing Assembly or, in other words, those keen on forming a separate country.

The parts of British India that seemed to lack unanimity in taking part in the Constituent Assembly consultation taking place at the time—Bengal, the Punjab, Sind, North-West Frontier Province, British Baluchistan and Assam—provided a clue to the shape of things to come. The provincial legislative assemblies of Bengal and the Punjab were expected to meet in two parts—one would represent the Muslim-majority districts and the other the Hindu-majority districts. The die for India's Partition was cast.

When Jawaharlal Nehru delivered his radio address on 3 June, he was not his usual ebullient self. He laid bare his dilemmas at the prospect of the dream of united free India lying shattered but, regardless, did not flinch from justifying the need for independence at that point. He said with a heavy heart: 'It is with no joy in my heart that I commend these proposals to you, though I have no doubt in my mind that this is the right course. For generations we have dreamt and struggled for a free and independent united India. The proposals to allow certain parts to secede, if they so will, is painful for any of us to contemplate. Nevertheless, I am convinced that our present decision is the right one even from the larger viewpoint.'[4]

In sharp contrast, Mohammed Ali Jinnah delivered his radio address with a sense of triumph and the hope that the goal of achieving a separate Muslim state was to be realized soon. He appealed for peace and order, particularly to the Muslims in India, as he called for the need to 'galvanise and concentrate all our energies to see that the transfer of power is assisted in a peaceful and orderly manner'.[5] He left it to the Council of the All-India Muslim League to meet and decide on the proposal for a different constituent assembly for Muslims. There was little doubt that Jinnah made all the right noises about peace and orderly behaviour, but at the same time expressed his desire to move on with the creation of Pakistan.

Both addresses praised the manner in which Lord Mountbatten had dealt with the question of addressing the concerns of the people of India while deciding on the crucial question of how power would be transferred to the people of the subcontinent. The differences too were stark. Nehru spoke at length on how India would be guided by the belief and advice of Mahatma Gandhi, but Jinnah made no mention of Gandhi. Jinnah ended his short address with the words 'Pakistan *zindabad*'. Nehru ended his address with '*Jai Hind*'. That left nobody in doubt that the transfer of power by the British to India would result in the creation of two independent countries, India and Pakistan.

Two and a half months after the addresses by Nehru and Jinnah, British India was transformed into two independent countries—Pakistan on 14 August and India a day later. The event, by all reckoning, was a hugely disruptive moment in the history of the subcontinent. Writing in the *New Yorker* in June 2015, William Dalrymple summed up the trauma in these words:

> In August, 1947, when, after three hundred years in India, the British finally left, the subcontinent was partitioned into two independent nation states: Hindu-majority India and Muslim-majority Pakistan. Immediately, there began one of the greatest migrations in human history, as millions of Muslims trekked to West and East Pakistan (the latter now known as Bangladesh) while millions of Hindus and Sikhs headed in the opposite direction. Many hundreds of thousands never made it. Across the Indian subcontinent, communities that had coexisted for almost a millennium attacked each other in a terrifying outbreak of sectarian violence, with Hindus and Sikhs on one side and Muslims on the other – a mutual genocide as unexpected as it was unprecedented. In Punjab and Bengal – provinces abutting India's borders with West and East Pakistan, respectively – the carnage was especially intense, and savage sexual violence. Some seventy-five thousand women were raped, and many of them were then disfigured or dismembered.[6]

By the time—around early 1948—the two newly created nations settled down after suffering the trauma and disruption of Partition, between one and two million people had been killed in communal violence and as many as fifteen million people reported to have been uprooted.[7] Another estimate put the number of people killed in communal riots at between half and one million and those uprooted at over eighteen million people.[8]

While recounting the large-scale displacement and human misery in the wake of Partition, historian Vazira Fazila-Yacoobali Zamindar[9] mentioned an important issue that Partition had raised. The challenge of Partition was not restricted to the formation of two independent countries, with a transfer of people across the newly created border between India and Pakistan; the more formidable challenge lay in how the nation as community would be transformed into nation as citizens of the two states.

The Role of Gandhi

Partition was not a sudden disruption. The seeds of the idea that the Indian subcontinent could be split into two independent countries had been sown some years before the British transferred power to the leaders of India and Pakistan in August 1947. Who were the likely disrupters? Would Gandhi be considered a disrupter? Or, for that matter, Jawaharlal Nehru or Mohammed Ali Jinnah?

India's Partition was like no other disruption seen in the seven-odd decades of its existence as an independent country. Gandhi, Nehru or Jinnah may not have seen themselves as active disrupters, but they nevertheless— in different degrees—played roles that led to the disruption. Indeed, some may even argue that Gandhi was not a disrupter as he was firmly opposed to the idea of gaining freedom at the cost of India's Partition.[10]

And yet, one of the many ironies of Gandhi's life is that in spite of his not being a disrupter, history may judge him as having been one. Many argue that he was party to India's disruption that led to a large-scale dislocation of people and killing of several hundred thousands of people. Gandhi was opposed to the idea of gaining freedom from British rule without a united India. But as Jinnah's demands were getting more difficult and Partition looked imminent, Gandhi had no option other than to agree to Nehru's compromise formula. Freedom from British rule with a divided India was a lesser evil than no independence or a deferred date for wresting India free from the clutches of colonial power.

Jinnah's call for Direct Action Day to be observed by followers of the Muslim League on 15 August 1946 was a clear reminder to Gandhi that Partition had become inevitable. The communal violence and retaliation by both communities in Bengal and other parts of the country led to many deaths. And Gandhi from that date spent much of his time trying to soothe the hurt fabric of the nation severed and torn asunder by Hindu–Muslim communal tension and violence. Indeed, Gandhi was not part of the nation-wide celebrations that the Congress had organized in the wake of the country's independence from British rule. He was praying for Hindu–Muslim unity.

Yes, Gandhi had an indirect role in the disruption of Partition. Given his stature and the respect he commanded from the entire Congress leadership at the time, it would have been difficult for them to move ahead with the Mountbatten Plan for partitioning the country if only Gandhi had put his foot down. This remains one of the big unanswered questions of the history of the subcontinent. If Gandhi had opposed Partition and insisted on freedom from British rule only if the country remained intact—and there was no mass migration of people and no killing—would the disruption have been avoided?

There is a view that Gandhi's reluctance to stand in the way of what two of his most senior leaders—Nehru and Patel—were comfortable with was one of the reasons for his giving tacit approval to the Partition plan, even though he knew how disastrous and violent the consequences of the country's division on religious lines would be. Gandhi's role as a disrupter, therefore, has to be qualified. He could certainly have prevented the disruption, but his weak-kneed response to the Mountbatten Plan even as his two juniors—Nehru and Sardar Vallabhbhai Patel—agreed to it, was what led to India's most violent and costly disruption, one that changed the course of India's politics. Even seventy years after India's Independence, the country faces the consequences of that disruption. Writing in 2017, historian Sarah Ansari observed:

> Today, the two countries' relationship is far from healthy. Kashmir remains a flashpoint; both countries are nuclear-armed. Indian Muslims are frequently suspected of harbouring loyalties towards Pakistan; non-Muslim minorities in Pakistan are increasingly vulnerable thanks to the so-called Islamisation of life there since the 1980s. Seven decades on, well over a billion people still live in the shadow of Partition.[11]

Jinnah the Disrupter

Mohammed Ali Jinnah is an obvious suspect as a disrupter. A strong votary of nationalism, he nursed a deep suspicion about the Congress. He was a firm believer that the Muslim community's interest would never be protected or preserved in an India led by the Congress after the end of the British rule.

The irony, however, is that Jinnah, a lawyer by training and profession, began his political career as a member of the Congress. After studying at Bombay University and Lincoln's Inn, London, he started his own career as a lawyer, but also joined the Congress, although he did not occupy any leadership position. In 1913,[12] he joined the Muslim League, set up in 1906 as an outfit to voice the interests of India's largest minority, the Muslims. In just three years, Jinnah became the president of the Muslim League.[13] His first brush with the Congress was when Mahatma Gandhi returned to India and took charge of the party. Under Gandhi's leadership, the Congress in 1919 launched a movement of non-cooperation, whose chief goal was to mobilize Indians to boycott everything to do with British rule. Jinnah opposed the policy and on this ground resigned from the Congress. Till then, Jinnah had worked towards Hindu–Muslim unity and nurtured his image as one who could strengthen ties between the two communities. But his opposition to Gandhi's non-cooperation movement pushed him out of the Congress and closer to the Muslim League.

At the start of Jinnah's political career, there was no inkling that the young lawyer would soon turn so bitterly against the Congress. Inspired by the brand of nationalism that Gopal Krishna Gokhale promoted in Bombay, Jinnah saw himself as someone who could be one day called the Muslim Gokhale. In the few years he was associated with the Congress, Jinnah worked hard to ensure a better deal for the Muslims of India in political processes and participation in the freedom movement. He also built a reputation for himself as one who worked hard to achieve the political union of Hindus and Muslims. Gokhale even called him 'the best ambassador of Hindu–Muslim unity'. At Jinnah's instance, the Congress and the Muslim League began holding their annual sessions jointly. The Muslims got the promise of a significant concession from the British government in the form of a separate electorate for themselves in 1909, but the Congress always opposed this demand. Jinnah did not give up on a separate electorate for Muslims, and that remained one of his primary missions as a Muslim leader. But the holding of joint annual sessions by the Congress and the Muslim League, at least on three occasions, gave rise to a new hope of an understanding between the two parties. And indeed, a new pact was reached after the Lucknow joint session, according to which both the organizations would strive hard for constitutional reform as part of their demand for freedom.

It was some progress as far as the Hindus and Muslims coming together for a national movement was concerned. For the British, such unity was a cause for concern and a signal that if the unity got stronger, their colonial rule in India would be further weakened.

The rise of Mahatma Gandhi from 1914 onwards, particularly after the launch of the Non-Cooperation Movement in 1919, also coincided with the decline of Jinnah. Many Muslim leaders formed their own regional parties or saw reason to be part of the Congress movement. Jinnah also began to realize that his own political belief was increasingly becoming incompatible with that of the Congress leaders. He started distancing himself from the Congress and eventually left the party. During the 1920s and 1930s, Jinnah devoted himself to rebuilding the Muslim League and a more unifying cause for the Muslims to get together under the League umbrella. But those efforts did not yield much for Jinnah, who was often seen by many regional Muslim leaders as too nationalistic to protect and promote the interests of Muslims. Jinnah's image as someone who believed in Hindu–Muslim unity became a handicap for his political career. So crestfallen and frustrated had Jinnah become that he moved to London and began pursuing legal practice there. The Congress was on the ascendant during this period and became so dominant a force in the independence movement that it became more assertive, often underestimating Jinnah and his power to mobilize Muslims.

As talks for the formation of a national government gained currency in 1935, Jinnah saw it as an opportunity to once again try and reclaim leadership of the Muslim community in India. He returned from London and resumed his activities as a key leader of the Muslim League. Ironically, once again, it was a Congress mistake—arising out of its supreme confidence from its electoral victories in the 1937 polls—because of which Jinnah managed to stage a comeback to national politics. The Congress did remarkably well in the provincial elections of 1937, but the Muslim League also did well in the seats reserved for Muslims, not losing a single seat. But even then, the Congress flatly refused to form provincial governments in coalition with the Muslim League in areas where the latter had some presence. Thus, in all the six provinces, the Congress formed governments without the League. This soured relations between the Congress and the Muslim League further and just three years later, the League adopted its famous declaration at its Lahore meeting that demanded the partition of India and creation of the Muslim state of Pakistan.

The idea of a separate country for Muslims that could be named Pakistan had been mooted some years ago by Choudhry Rahmat Ali in his pamphlet *Now or Never, Are We to Live or Perish Forever?*, published in 1933. Ali at that time was a law student at the University of Cambridge and he presented his proposal for creating the state of Pakistan to the British and Indian delegates at the Third Round Table Conference held in London that year. While this idea found no takers at that meeting, it was to be picked up and adopted by the Lahore conference of the Muslim League seven years later.

The irony of Ali's initiative was that once Pakistan was born, he decided to settle down in the newly created state in 1948. But soon he had trouble with the new establishment as Pakistan Prime Minister Liaquat Ali Khan expelled him from the country after confiscating his belongings. Ali returned to London in October 1948 and died a lonely man in 1951.[14]

Even though Jinnah believed that Hindu–Muslim unity in an undivided India was possible, he realized that the structure under which this could be achieved was not acceptable to the Congress. He had always been a votary of a federation in which provincial governments enjoyed a reasonable degree of autonomy in administration and policy formulation. But he sensed that the Congress could betray the League. His feeling was confirmed by Nehru's speech in July 1946 qualifying the Congress's commitment to the Cabinet Mission plan for a three-tier federation for India, which would have meant that while the Centre would retain some powers, the states would have jurisdiction over many other issues, with the third tier looking after the rest. In such a system, Jinnah believed the Muslim League would have reasonable control over the administration of the second and the third tiers, taking care of the interests of the Muslims. With Nehru qualifying the Congress's commitment to this plan, Jinnah lost no time pressing for Partition, without any ambiguity.

In that sense, Jinnah was a disrupter. His earlier vision of promoting Hindu–Muslim unity and his belief that Muslims could live in a Hindu-majority India disappeared when it came to the crunch—the final years of the British rule when the deliberations over the modality and procedures for power transfer reached a critical stage.[15] Jinnah made it abundantly clear to all that he was for Partition, come what may and whatever be the consequences for millions of Indians living across the country in terms of relocation.

CHAPTER 3

MAKING THE BEST OF AN INEVITABILITY

Nehru was a central figure in the negotiations for India's Independence and, therefore, had a role in the final decision leading to Partition. The conventional opinion of him is of a leader who had a vision and who could look ahead of his time. However, the sequence of developments in the run-up to India's Independence presents a slightly more nuanced image of Nehru.

When the British government decided to send Mountbatten as viceroy to succeed Lord Wavell, the plan was to grant India its much-desired freedom from foreign rule by June 1948. That timetable, however, was completely upset after Mountbatten landed in India in March 1947 and reviewed the ground situation. And he decided that the British must leave by August 1947, instead of waiting for another ten months.[1] What brought about the sudden advancement of Britain's exit from India?

In early 1946, the Cabinet Mission plan had envisaged a three-tier federation for India. The Union government in New Delhi would keep foreign affairs, communications, defence and only those financial matters necessary for meeting the financial requirements of the Union. India after freedom, according to this plan, would consist of three broad territorial groups. The first group would include Hindu-majority provinces, the second group would consist of Muslim-majority provinces and the third group would include Muslim-majority Bengal and the Hindu-majority Assam. All three groups would operate virtually as autonomous states, but under a federation called India, with its Union government functioning from New Delhi.[2]

This was a plan that met with Gandhi's desire to have a free united India. Not surprisingly, the Congress leadership accepted the idea and so did the Muslim League, giving rise to a hope that India's freedom would not necessitate any partition. However, such hopes were dashed as the Muslim League took objection to a statement made by Nehru in July 1946. Nehru, perhaps reflecting his own concerns and those of many other senior leaders over the Cabinet Mission plan, said, according to one account, in a provocative speech that suggested that the Congress was not bound to any predetermined arrangement: 'We are not bound by a single thing except that we have decided to go into the Constituent Assembly.'[3] This infuriated Jinnah. It further fuelled his distrust of the Congress party,[4] which he feared would like to impose Hindu rule on the minority Muslim community in a free India. Jinnah felt that was a discreet repudiation of the Cabinet Mission plan. He convened a quick working committee meeting of the Muslim League. The outcome was that the League decided to walk out of the Cabinet Mission plan's three-tier federation of India after it was freed from British rule. Differences between the Congress and Muslim League got worse after Jinnah declared his resolve to observe 16 August 1946 as the Direct Action Day, which led to large-scale communal violence in different parts of the country. Jinnah's objective behind the call to Direct Action Day was to suspend all business and put pressure on the British government to yield to the Muslim League's demand to divide the country on the basis of religion and thereby pave the way for the birth of a Muslim-dominated Pakistan.

However, communal violence spread in the wake of the protest rallies organized by the Muslim League. Bengal witnessed the worst kind of killing and arson, with Muslims and Hindus staging pitched battles on the streets of Calcutta. Muslims became more determined in their resolve to have a separate country for themselves. Gandhi was unhappy with these developments and began his tour of the nation to douse the fires of communal unrest and restore Hindu–Muslim unity. He visited Noakhali in eastern Bengal, where Hindus had suffered hugely, and later visited Bihar, where Muslims bore the brunt of communal violence at the hands of the Hindus. At the heart of this flare-up was Nehru's July speech that became the trigger for Jinnah to call off the League's commitment to the Cabinet Mission plan. If the three-tier federation plan for India after freedom had gone smoothly, the disruption of Partition perhaps could have witnessed a different script.

There was another factor that contributed to the worsening of relations between the Congress and the Muslim League. The interim government, set up on 2 September 1946, was led by leaders of both the Congress and Muslim League. Communal violence, triggered by Direction Action Day launched by the Muslim League, continued even after the formation of the interim government. Even as those challenges were handled by the new government, the strained relationship between the two parties was showing in the performance and conduct of the top ministers in the interim government.[5] The home minister of the interim government, Vallabhbhai Patel, did not take kindly to fiscal proposals of the finance minister in that government, Liaquat Ali Khan, a member of the Muslim League. Deep and insidious motives were read into Liaquat Ali's budget proposals. The fiscal levies were meant for all industries, but Patel was deeply disturbed as Gujarati businessmen were seriously affected as well. In Patel, Nehru had found a new ally in his fight against the Muslim League.[6]

The Nehru–Patel relationship had a different aspect. As prime minister of the interim government, Nehru was closer to Patel than to Liaquat Ali Khan, who belonged to the Muslim League.[7] Thus, Patel's reservations against Liaquat Ali struck a sympathetic chord with Nehru. But within the Congress party, it was clear to all that Patel and Nehru were competing with each other to be the most favourite candidate to lead India after freedom. Both were vying for Gandhi's attention and sought his favour. Gandhi also made no bones about who his favourite leader was between the two. At the Bardoli meeting of the Congress to elect the party president in 1929, Gandhi chose to withdraw from the race after voting and transferred the votes cast in his favour to be counted for Nehru—an act that helped Nehru gain more votes than Patel.[8] Without Gandhi's partial act, Nehru would have been a poor second to Patel in that presidential race to lead the Congress. Patel did become the party president, but only two years later. The rivalry between Nehru and Patel within the Congress was a poorly kept secret. Yet, when Nehru saw the Muslim League spoiling the idea of India gaining freedom as a united country, he eventually played along with Patel in settling for the partition of the country, even though he was conscious of the mayhem it would cause.

In the final analysis, Nehru too was a disrupter in that he went along with the British plan for dividing India into two countries before granting it independence from its rule. He made a lot of public noise about his desire to gain freedom for a united India. But when it came to postponing the date for independence in the absence of a credible resolution of differences between the Congress and the Muslim League, he chose Partition, even though he was opposed to it at heart.[9]

Nehru as a disrupter was different from Jinnah as a disrupter. Nehru suffered from a lack of clarity on his approach to Partition. On the one hand, he was guided by his vision of a free united India wherein Hindus and Muslims lived in peace and harmony—a vision that he had inherited from Gandhi. But on the other hand, he was getting restless over the Congress's failure to bring the Muslim League and Jinnah round to accepting the terms on which the new united India would be constituted. The thought was that in the chase towards realizing the vision of a free united India, the goal of securing freedom from British rule should not get postponed almost indefinitely. In this regard, Nehru and Patel were more or less in agreement with the idea that popular aspirations for a free India, even if it is achieved after Partition, cannot be ignored.

In sharp contrast, Jinnah was clear that disruption or Partition was the only route that must be adopted for freedom from British rule. Jinnah was transparent about his disruptive motives. But Nehru was not that categorical. Partition—or the disruption to be caused by it—was the second best option, but nevertheless an option if the larger goal of securing freedom from British rule was to be achieved. Jinnah's brand of disruption was easier to gauge. The adverse consequences of Jinnah's brand of disruption were also easy to manage for one knew what he had hoped to achieve through Partition.

The Impact

The consequences of Partition were felt in many areas, and these consequences lasted for many decades after India gained independence. With Partition, India had to let go of a little less than a fourth of its total land area. Before Partition in 1947, the total land area of India was about 4.3 million square kilometres. With what was then known as East Bengal (which became Bangladesh from 1971) and West Punjab becoming Pakistan, an independent country, the total land area that went out of undivided India was about 1 million square kilometres. In other words, India after Partition saw 24 per cent of its total land area being hived off as a new country—Pakistan. This was perhaps the first and immediate consequence of the disruption caused by Partition.

The loss of land was painful for proponents of a free undivided India. It became more painful when they realized that Partition also meant less land per person in India and more land per person in Pakistan. The population pressure on India was already substantial and clear to its citizens in 1947. It got worse after Partition. The total population in undivided India was estimated at 390 million of which about 60 million went to Pakistan.

In other words, while India ceded close to a quarter of its land to Jinnah's dream, the population pressure in divided India increased as only 15 per cent of undivided India's population went to Pakistan. Even after taking into account the millions of refugees crossing the newly created borders—Muslims walking over to Pakistan and Hindus entering India—the population–land ratio for India did not get better. While Pakistan, too, had to face the problems of rehabilitating refugees from India, the pressure on India was more. In that sense, the Partition of India as a disruption has had one of the most widespread and long-lasting impacts on India's politics, society and even the economy.

One of the outcomes of Partition was that Kashmir became a part of India even though it had a Muslim majority. One reason was perhaps that in spite of having a Muslim majority, Kashmir had a Hindu king, Maharaja Hari Singh. Kashmir became a bone of contention when the British left India. The newly created state of Pakistan claimed control over Kashmir on the ground that it was a Muslim-majority area, while the Congress leadership did not wish to give it up; one of the reasons it cited was of course the fact that it was ruled by a Hindu king.

Kashmir is still a contentious issue between India and Pakistan. More than seven decades after Partition, the relations between India and Pakistan are still dictated by who should rule Kashmir. That is one measure of the nature of the disruption caused by Partition.

There were about 584 princely states in British India at the time of India's Independence, whose future dispensation was left to the rulers there.[10] Historian Ramachandra Guha, however, notes that the princely states at the time of India's Independence were fewer. He writes:

> One historian puts it at 521; another at 565. They were more than 500, by any count, and they varied very widely in terms of size and status. At one end of the scale were the massive states of Kashmir and Hyderabad, each of the size of a large European country; at the other end, tiny fiefdoms or *jagirs* of a dozen or less villages.[11]

Many of these princely states were not part of the major provinces and the presidencies under British control. Thus, while the British government decided to hand over these provinces and presidencies to the people of India, the decision on these 584 princely states was left to the individual rulers. An option was given to them to join either India or Pakistan. By the time the British left India on 15 August 1947, about a dozen of the princely states decided to join Pakistan. Congress leaders worked hard to convince the remaining princely states to join India.[12] That made sure that India's territorial integrity after Partition and Independence was by and large protected. Vallabhbhai Patel, Congress leader and India's home minister, played a crucial role in ensuring that these princely states signed on the Instrument of Accession that essentially meant that they gave up their sovereignty to be part of the Indian Union. The only thing that remained with them was their financial allowances and perquisites, known as privy purses. Three princely states, Travancore, Bhopal and Jodhpur, agreed to be part of India after initial resistance. Travancore and Bhopal wanted to remain independent, while Jodhpur debated if it should join Pakistan. Quick interventions by Patel and the Congress leaders helped change their minds and they joined India before 15 August 1947.

Three princely states—Junagadh, Hyderabad and Kashmir—posed different challenges for the Congress leadership. Junagadh was a Hindu-majority area in the Gujarat region, but its Muslim leaders had decided to join Pakistan after Partition. The Congress took serious objection to this and forced a controversial referendum, whose results were used to annul Junagadh's accession to Pakistan; it instead formalized the inclusion of the state in India. Similarly, Hyderabad ruled by the Nizam put up resistance against being part of India and decided to maintain its distinct sovereign identity. However, the Congress-led Indian government used persuasion and force to ensure the accession of Hyderabad as part of India. The Nizam was given a special status as a compromise formula. That left the issue of Kashmir.

What complicated the Kashmir issue was that although its ruler Hari Singh was Hindu, he was hesitant about joining either India or Pakistan. He was of the view that Kashmir could remain an independent state, joining neither Pakistan nor India. Significantly, Sheikh Abdullah, the leader of Kashmir's largest political party, the National Conference, and a popular leader of the Valley, had built a close rapport with the Congress leaders and was more inclined towards India. But Pakistan was also keen on taking over Kashmir, just as India was not comfortable about letting it either remain independent or align with Pakistan. Although Hari Singh signed a Standstill Agreement with Pakistan, which meant that status quo was to be maintained, the Kashmir issue remained unresolved when Pakistan and India were celebrating their freedom from British rule on 14 and 15 August 1947, respectively. What complicated matters was an invasion of Jammu and Kashmir by Muslim tribesmen in October 1947. The invasion from

Kashmir's western side was believed to have been inspired by Pakistan, although there is as yet no corroboration of whether Pakistan was indeed involved. A panicked Singh realized that he had no forces of his own to retaliate and sought help from India. The Indian leadership saw a sliver of hope in this situation and offered Singh assistance by dispatching Indian armed forces to Srinagar. The Indian authorities shifted the king to a safer place in Jammu, but before sending Indian troops to the Valley, it made sure that Singh had signed the Instrument of Accession to India. The Indian forces took a few days to push back the Pathan tribesmen. Even though Pakistan denied its involvement, the Indian government believed that Pakistan had a hand in the invasion and indeed saw that as the first incident of hostility with its new western neighbour. Later, when the Indian Constitution was adopted, Jammu and Kashmir was accorded a special status under Article 370, which granted autonomy to the state in all matters except defence, telecommunications and external affairs.

The man who played a stellar role in managing the accession of Jammu and Kashmir to India was Indian Home Minister Vallabhbhai Patel. Already, he had succeeded in persuading over 500 princely states to join the Indian state after Independence. The accession of Kashmir seemed like a major victory as it appeared that the Kashmir issue was settled for good. Indeed, in the early days after the deployment of Indian troops to thwart the Muslim tribesmen and freeing Jammu, Srinagar and the Valley, it seemed that India had scored a strategic victory in securing Kashmir for itself. However, the use of Indian forces in Kashmir and the manner in which the Instrument of Accession was signed almost as a quid pro quo for the deployment of Indian troops had international ramifications. To quell an international outcry, Nehru declared a ceasefire and referred the Kashmir issue to the United Nations for its arbitration with a clear hint of a plebiscite to determine whether Kashmir belonged to India or Pakistan, or it wished to be an independent country. There were concerns over the reference of the Kashmir issue to the UN and the prospects of a plebiscite. But ending all uncertainties, Kashmir decided to adopt a constitution in 1956 that declared it to be a part of India. The north-western part of the Kashmir Valley remained under Pakistan's control.

In the last seven decades or so, India and Pakistan have fought at least four open wars—in 1947, 1965, 1971 and 1999—and had many minor border skirmishes. In all these battles, the Kashmir issue always reared its ugly head. Pakistan continues to demand its suzerainty over Kashmir and India reiterates that Kashmir is its integral part. Neither Junagadh nor Hyderabad became a bone of contention with Pakistan in the wake of Partition. But Kashmir continues to defy any solution.

If India or the Congress leadership then had not insisted on Kashmir, it is possible that Kashmir would have either joined Pakistan or become an independent country. There is a strong growing opinion that believes that the problem of Kashmir that arose out of the Partition of India could have been resolved if only the Congress leadership in 1947 had acted more maturely. If Kashmir has caused so many wars between India and Pakistan, diverting away scarce resources that could have been used for development projects, was the trouble of retaining the princely state in the Himalayas worth it? India's defence needs over the years have been largely triggered by the Kashmir problem, with perhaps the largest chunk of the defence budget going towards arming the country against any attack from Pakistan. The World Bank, quoting data from the Stockholm International Peace Research Institute, points out that during 1960–2017, India's annual military expenditure never went below 2 per cent of its gross domestic product (GDP). It rose to as high as 4.2 per cent of GDP in 1987 and declined to 2.5 per cent in 2017. But the amount of resources allocated to meeting defence expenditure for a developing economy has remained huge.[13]

The Rise of Religion Politics

It is undeniable that the manner in which India obtained its freedom from British rule led to the rise of communal politics in the subcontinent. The Partition of India was driven by Jinnah's demand for a separate nation for Muslims. Jinnah believed that in no other way could the interests of Muslims as a minority community in India be protected. Leaders of the Congress, including Gandhi and Nehru, had wanted a free India without Partition. And even after it was clear that Pakistan would be carved out of India to make way for a separate country for Muslims, the Congress leaders refused to make India a country for Hindus only. That was perhaps one reason why a large number of Muslims decided to stay back in India, in a country that respected diversity and did not differentiate in its treatment of its citizens on the basis of their caste or religion.

In his address on 3 June 1947, Nehru made it amply clear to everyone that India was open to all, irrespective of their religious beliefs and practices. He said:

The united India that we have laboured for was not one of compulsion and coercion, but a free and willing association of a free people. It may be that in this way we shall reach that united India sooner than otherwise and that she will have a stronger and more secure foundation.[14]

For Nehru, India was a country for Indians. Jinnah, on the other hand, was focused largely on the Muslims in the speech he delivered on the same day. 'I cannot but express my appreciation of the sufferings and sacrifices made by all classes of the Mussalmans, and particularly the great part that the women of the Frontier played in the fight for our civil liberties,' he said. For Jinnah, his dream of creating Pakistan was close to realization, and he was worried primarily about Muslims.

Once Pakistan was a reality, Jinnah changed his tune somewhat. The opening address he delivered to the Constituent Assembly of Pakistan, as its president, in Karachi in August 1947 was remarkable. On three specific occasions during his short speech, made extempore, Jinnah talked about the values of secularism that he wanted Pakistan to cherish and promote. In the early part of his speech, he said: 'You will no doubt agree with me that the first duty of a government is to maintain law and order, so that the life, property and religious beliefs of its subjects are fully protected by the State.' In the middle of his speech, leaving nobody in doubt about what he was actually speaking about, Jinnah said:

If you change your past and work together in a spirit that every one of you, no matter to what community he belongs, no matter what relations he had with you in the past, no matter what is his colour, caste or creed, is first, second, and last a citizen of this State with equal rights, privileges and obligations, there will be no end to the progress you will make.[15]

Finally, Jinnah made a statement that must have surprised everybody, including those in the Congress. He told the citizens of Pakistan:

You are free; you are free to go to your temples, you are free to go to your mosques or to any other place of worship in this State of Pakistan. You may belong to any religion or caste or creed—that has nothing to do with the business of the state.

Such a categorical repudiation of governance or politics based on religion coming from Jinnah, the father of Pakistan created for Muslims, gave rise to hopes of a country that would become a modern state giving equal and fair treatment to people belonging to all religions.[16] But soon after, Jinnah died in 1949 and leaders of the new state of Pakistan backtracked on those principles enunciated by the man who had founded the nation. Pakistan became a country for Muslims, with hardly any place for those who did not practise Islam. India, on the other hand, gave to its people a Constitution that guaranteed equality to all irrespective of their religion. Its Preamble left no one in doubt that India was a 'sovereign, secular, democratic republic'.

And yet the nature of politics in India was influenced by what was happening to Muslims in India and what was happening to non-Muslims in Pakistan. Political discourse in India, in particular, changed quite dramatically. While the Congress continued to remain the flag-bearer of secular politics that envisaged that the state would treat all religions the same way, new political forces began to grow roots that thrived on the disenchantment among a small section of radical Hindus, who felt that if the Hindus in Pakistan were not treated fairly and equally, what was the logic of treating Muslims as equals in India? Political parties like the Jana Sangh, that drew their inspiration from the Hindu cultural outfits like the Rashtriya Swayamsevak Sangh (RSS), began to expand their footprint. The Congress leaders responded to such developments with an even more robust brand of secularism that Hindu fundamentalist parties dubbed as 'appeasement of the Muslims'.

The Partition of India thus led to the rise of politics over religion. One kind of disruption led to an even more divisive kind of disruption in India's politics. Over the years after Partition, politics in India has got polarized over religion. The rise of the Bharatiya Janata Party, which is an offshoot of Jana Sangh and owes its allegiance to the RSS, is ample testimony to how the question of Muslims has become central to India's politics. The demolition of the disputed Babri Mosque in Ayodhya in 1992, the demand for building a Ram Temple in the same complex and the assertion of the Hindu right to the exclusion of minorities, including Muslims, are all indications of how the religious basis of India's Partition is a factor that has not gone away. Instead, communal polarization has worsened and the social fabric in the country has continued to remain fragile and vulnerable to communal tension.

The irony of this is that even the views of the Congress, which stood for secular politics at the time of Independence and worked hard to avert Partition on the principle of communal harmony, have evolved over the last seven decades. Political fears of losing the Hindu vote bank to new outfits like the BJP have encouraged sections of its leadership to make moves that can bring them closer to the Hindus. Rajiv Gandhi's decision to allow a foundation ceremony to be held at the site of the disputed Babri Mosque in Ayodhya in 1989 or Rahul Gandhi's display of his visits of Hindu pilgrimage sites are signs of soft Hindutva. This is aimed at clawing back the Hindu vote base that the Congress may have lost to parties like the BJP or Shiv Sena.

It is clear, and deeply disturbing as well, that what the Partition of 1947 set off for India's politics over religion is still gaining salience and even strength, nor is it anywhere near losing its appeal among the masses or the political classes.

The Economy Partitioned

The impact of Partition on India's economy and business was even more telling. Business leaders of India were clear that the Partition of India would be better for the economy and business prospects.[17] This was in sharp contrast to the views held by a large section of the Congress, particularly Gandhi and Nehru, who felt that India should gain freedom as an undivided country. The business view was rooted in its hard assessment of the political and economic reality. The Muslim League made it clear that it would agree to independence as a united country only if the Cabinet Mission's plan to have a Centre with limited jurisdiction over defence, foreign affairs and communication was accepted and implemented. Indian business leaders believed that such an independent country would have a relatively weak Centre, which, therefore, would not be sufficiently empowered and resourceful in making the required quantum of investments in the country to revive an economy immediately after Independence. Hence, one of the reasons why Indian industry leaders, including doyens like Ghanshyam Das Birla, preferred Partition was because a divided India would facilitate the formation of a strong government at the Centre. This government would be then capable of and committed to taking the big investment decisions to provide the necessary infrastructure in the newly independent country and spur economic growth.[18]

A clear indication of the kind of disruption to the economy that Partition would cause was documented in detail by a report brought out by Homi Mody and John Mathai in 1945. Both were closely associated with the Tata group and differed with Nalini Ranjan Sarkar, another industry leader of the time, on the question of Partition. They opined that should a situation arise where an arrangement envisaging India's political unity was not acceptable to the Muslim community, the partition of India in order to end the stalemate should not be ruled out. *A Memorandum on the Economic and Financial Aspects of Pakistan*, the report prepared by Mody and Mathai, noted that Pakistan would be a viable economic unit if the partition were to happen after retaining the extant boundaries of the provinces. But if the partition were to happen based on the Muslim-majority districts, the consequences for Pakistan would be a disaster. They also maintained that if the country's growth objectives were paramount, it was necessary that the two countries after Partition must have cooperation between themselves, without which economic disaster would be a near certainty. In other words, they recognized that while political separation between the Muslim-dominated areas and the rest was advisable, economic cooperation between the two newly independent states was necessary to keep the economic engines in India in good shape. Thus, even after Partition, they wanted the two countries to have free exchange of raw materials and finished products, almost like a free-trade zone.

Given the political acrimony that preceded Partition, there was little chance of economic ties prospering between India and Pakistan. Since the Partition criteria were based on Muslim-majority districts, business houses remained largely immune to the consequences of Partition. Indeed, the Mody–Mathai report noted that if Calcutta were to remain part of India and not go along with Pakistan, the Muslim-majority districts of what was then known as East Bengal would be nothing more than economic slums. In other words, political separation of the country was favoured by big business as this would give them a strong centre that could invest in building infrastructure to revive the economy; the nature of the partition based on Muslim-majority districts ensured that the business houses remained largely unaffected. The plea for a free-trade zone type of cooperation between India and Pakistan was made because the business houses wanted their market reach to remain unaffected.

A look at the kind of industries that went to Pakistan and what remained in India after Independence is an indication that Indian business leaders preferred a partition based on Muslim-majority districts, which they believed would minimize the disruptive consequences of Partition on their businesses. C.N. Vakil notes in *Economic Consequences of Divided India, A Study of the Economy of India and Pakistan* that just about 10 per cent of the total industry of undivided India remained in Pakistan. In terms of employment in these industrial establishments, the 90 per cent of industry that remained in India after Partition accounted for over 93 per cent. With regard to joint stock companies and infrastructure facilities, India got the lion's share after Partition. Over 90 per cent of all units among the top industries like textiles, chemicals, cotton mills, silk, cement, sugar mills, match factories, paint manufacturers, heavy chemical plants and heavy engineering factories remained in India after Partition. Pakistan's share was 14–18 per cent of units in the engineering sector and rubber factories. And all the units in the following industries remained in India after Partition—jute mills, glass factories, paper mills, iron and steel establishments and automobile plants. Pakistan was a clear loser as far as getting a decent share in the industries that existed in undivided India was concerned. India's top business leaders proved to be highly discerning as they had sensed in advance that a political partition on the basis of Muslim-majority districts would deprive Pakistan of many industries and give India a head start, compared to its neighbour on its west and east. The advantages that Pakistan enjoyed after Partition—in having a lower population–land ratio and large chunks of fertile land in West Pakistan with a strong network of irrigation canal—were neutralized to a great degree as a consequence. And India's business leaders proved to be more perspicacious in ensuring that its business interests remained by and large intact. Indeed, by way of abundant caution, they advocated economic cooperation between India and Pakistan to facilitate free flow of goods and services across the newly created borders. That such cooperation did not fructify at all shrunk their market reach, but the way India got divided helped minimize the extent of the disruption that Partition could have potentially created for India's business leaders.

CHAPTER 4

A NEW ECONOMIC VISION

In July 1954, less than a decade after India's Independence from British rule, its first prime minister, Jawaharlal Nehru, went to Punjab to inaugurate the Bhakra-Nangal Dam, constructed on the Indian side of the Sutlej River.[1] At that time, the Bhakra-Nangal was the second highest dam in the world and showcased India's engineering prowess. Capable of generating about a million kilowatts of electricity, the dam's reservoir would also help irrigate over 7.4 million acres of land in the region. Nehru's inaugural address,[2] delivered in Hindi, would mark a significant turn in the way the government would become a key player in rebuilding India's economic infrastructure and industry after Independence.

Nehru compared the Bhakra-Nangal Dam to a temple or a mosque or a gurdwara. He said:

> As I walked around the site I thought that these days the biggest temple and mosque and gurdwara is the place where man works for the good of mankind. Which place can be greater than this, this Bhakra-Nangal, where thousands and lakhs of men have worked, have shed their blood and sweat and laid down their lives as well? Where can be a greater and holier place than this, which we can regard as higher?

The Bhakra-Nangal project, a government initiative, was described as a temple of modern India. Months later, Nehru would enunciate his government's new industrial policy, which would reverberate with the thoughts that he expressed at Bhakra—the desire to let state projects reach the commanding heights of the economy. He made a commitment to increase government investments in key infrastructure projects and fulfil what Indian industry leaders had desired even before the country freed itself from British rule.

Nehru's speech at Bhakra touched upon two other important issues. He compared the Bhakra-Nangal project with the setting up of universities. Places of higher education do not just meet the specific needs of the day but, more importantly, address the long-term goal of building storehouses of knowledge that help meet a country's growth aspirations. The Bhakra-Nangal project would thus meet the immediate requirements of irrigation and hydropower in the region, but it would also serve as a model of economic development in which the state would play a leading role. Nehru explained:

> Then again it struck me that Bhakra-Nangal was like a big university where we can work and while working learn, so that we may do bigger things. The nation is marching forward and every day the pace becomes faster. As we learn the work and gain experience, we advance with greater speed. Bhakra-Nangal is not a work of this moment only, because the work which we are doing at present is not only for our own times but for coming generations and future times.

For Nehru, the Bhakra-Nangal Dam also symbolized hope and the aspirations of a young nation that had just got freedom but was searching for the right model for economic development to address the challenges of poverty and growth. Thus, he said that the Bhakra-Nangal Dam was 'a landmark because it has become the symbol of a nation's will to march forward with strength, determination and courage'. The dam on the Sutlej River also inspired Nehru greatly. 'That is why, seeing this work, my courage and strength have increased, because nothing is more encouraging than to capture our dreams and give them real shape,' he said.

In just about two years, Nehru would bring about dramatic changes in India's economic policy space. He would also usher in the first phase of nationalization as his government would take over the majority ownership of the country's largest commercial bank, the biggest airline and a clutch of life insurance companies. Nehru would also unveil his government's first industrial policy framework—which would be independent India's first big economic policy document. It would also act as a major policy disruption for a nation that was beginning to come to terms with an increasing role for the private sector and the pursuit of a free-enterprise policy.

Harbingers of Change

There were early signs of Nehru's predilection towards a statist approach to ownership of key economic entities. The Bombay Plan, finalized in January

1944, had proposed state intervention in building infrastructure and basic industries after India's Independence. Titled 'A Brief Memorandum Outlining a Plan of Economic Development for India', it had the support of major industrialists of the time including Jamshedji Tata, Ghanshyam Das Birla, Shri Ram, Kasturbhai Lalbhai, Ardeshir Shroff and Purshottamdas Thakurdas. Most importantly, it enjoyed the support of Nehru.

To be sure, the Bombay Plan had not envisaged any dilution in the role of the private sector. But it believed that a national independent government would be required after the Second World War to make investments in critical infrastructure areas such as power, mining, metallurgy, transport and cement. The central role envisaged for the state enterprises had three layers—government control, government ownership and government management. The objective was to encourage all-round economic development, reduce regional economic disparities and build infrastructure in a way that the private sector could gain from increased productivity and cost advantages.

Indeed, the Bombay Plan was dubbed the 'non-official plan for the economic development of India, whose contribution to the First Five-Year Plan, framed in 1951, was substantial. The private sector had a significant role to play in the execution of the First Five-Year Plan. Of a total investment of Rs 3500 crore envisaged under the Plan, as much as 43 per cent was to have come from the private sector. While a few projects were to be compulsorily undertaken in the state sector, everything else was open to investment by private enterprises. The Industrial Policy Resolution of 1948, too, had provided for an adequate role for the private sector, raising the hopes of big business in the country that its role in independent India would not be curtailed and, indeed, may be enhanced.

The Nehru government had come out with what was its first industrial policy statement on 4 April 1948, less than a year after Independence. The statement's broad goal was to secure for the country a continuous increase in production and equitable distribution. It, of course, noted that the state must play a 'progressively active' role in the development of industries. How active was made clear when the resolution stated that the state would have the monopoly in setting up industries in arms and ammunition, atomic energy and railway transport. In addition, the state would be exclusively responsible for setting up new undertakings in six basic industries. An exception was made by clarifying that wherever the state found it necessary, it would set up industries in these six areas in cooperation with private enterprises. The private sector was free to set up industries in any area other than these nine specific areas, although the state reserved its rights to enter these areas as well, whenever it decided to do so.

The Industrial Policy Resolution of 1948 did cause some concern for Indian industry. Nehru's approach to the resolution was driven by his firm belief that the state must control strategic areas of the economy. Industry leaders were not happy with this direction, but they had little option as Nehru was not willing to concede ground on this issue to anyone else in the Congress and the government, such as C. Rajagopalachari, at that time the Governor General, or Vallabhbhai Patel, the home minister, who were opposed to such an expanding role for the state in the economy. While the government left a large segment of industrial activities open to the private sector, there was a sense in the policy that suggested that the state was not disinclined to enter any sector, if it so desired, in addition to the three sectors, where it had complete monopoly, and six basic industries, where the state could operate either on its own or in cooperation with the private sector. So, it was not entirely like the Bombay Plan, where the government would only set up basic infrastructure industries and leave open the rest for the private sector. The subtle shift in the government's economic policy focus could not be missed.

The framing of a law for industries was the next big factor that caused some consternation for big businesses in India, which were hoping to take full advantage of a vast market that had just opened up for them after Independence. The government's idea was to have a law through which it could regulate industrial activities. The name of the law was an indication of the mindset of those who were behind framing it. It was initially called the Industries (Development and Control) Act, 1951. Several business leaders, including the leading lights of the day like Ghanshyam Das Birla, were concerned over the spirit of the law, which was reflected in the use of a word that suggested that the government would control industry. After some consultation and effective persuasion, the Nehru government agreed to change the name of the law and called it Industries (Development and Regulation) Act. This, however, was only a cosmetic change. The bigger and more fundamental change was that through that legislation, industrial activities in the entire country were brought under the licensing regime, to be operated by the Union government. The law of 1951 empowered the government to regulate the way industrial development should take place. And the instrument for regulating was licensing. In many ways, this was the first clear sign of statism making itself evident in the country, and the licence raj had begun its long journey in the country—a journey that would come to an end only through an economic crisis and another disruption about forty years later.

Towards a Planning Commission

The setting up of the Planning Commission[3] in 1950 was in itself a major signal from the government on its intended economic policy course. The adoption of a planned economy model and the setting up of the Planning Commission were significant also because they left nobody in doubt about the dominant role assigned to the public sector in India's economic development. The Union Budget presented on 28 February 1950 announced the government's intention to set up the Planning Commission. The idea of the Planning Commission was controversial. It had met with resistance even from within Nehru's Cabinet. His finance minister, John Mathai, who had presented the Budget and had announced the government's intention to set up the Planning Commission, was opposed to the idea. Soon after presenting the Budget, Mathai resigned in protest. He said:

> I consider the Planning Commission not merely ill-timed but in its working and general set-up ill-conceived. The Planning Commission was tending to become a parallel cabinet . . . it would weaken the authority of the Finance Ministry and gradually reduce the Cabinet to practically a registering authority. The Planning Commission was totally unnecessary and in fact hardly qualified for its work . . . there was a general tendency amongst the various Ministries to disregard the authority of the Standing Finance Committee and that some of the greatest offenders were the Ministers directly under the control of the Prime Minister. When departures from accepted practice were approved by the Prime Minister, it has a demoralizing effect on other departments of Government.[4]

A fortnight later, on 15 March, the Nehru government adopted a resolution to implement its decision on the Planning Commission.

It was important to note that Nehru chose not to use the legal route to set up this body. This decision created a special status for the body since it had no statutory sanction. However, the Planning Commission was entrusted with the crucial responsibility of preparing and implementing plans across the country. Ironically, the absence of a legal foundation for the Planning

Commission was one of the reasons that facilitated a quick decision by the Narendra Modi government to abolish the Commission sixty-four years later and put an end to the system of periodic plans. In its place, the Modi government brought in a new think tank by the name of NITI (National Institution for Transforming India) Aayog. It is important to note that Modi, too, chose to set up the NITI Aayog through a Cabinet resolution, and not through the legal route.

In many ways, Nehru's decision to set up the Planning Commission through a resolution, without getting Parliament to approve it by framing a law, is a decision that defied governance logic. Here was an institution that was to usher in the most important change in the pattern of India's economic development by introducing a system of planning and adopting a socialistic model of growth. Yet, Nehru abstained from conferring legal sanctity on that body. An alternative explanation for Nehru's decision could have been that, being a visionary leader, he did not want to tie down his successors to a model of economic growth that was his preferred choice at that point in time. Indeed, if he had framed a law to set up the Planning Commission, governments that succeeded his would have had to get Parliament to repeal that law first before moving ahead with an alternative model of economic development. Narendra Modi would have had to wait a little longer to dismantle the Planning Commission and abandon planning. Thus, it is possible to attribute Nehru's decision to set up the Commission through a resolution of his Cabinet to his astute political thinking and concern for the flexibility in decision-making he wished to confer on his successors.

Nehru's vision for the Planning Commission was detailed and elaborate. Behind the setting up of the Planning Commission, he outlined a seven-point agenda. Thus, the Commission was given the responsibility to:

Make an assessment of the material, capital and human resources of the country, including technical personnel, and investigate the possibilities of augmenting such of these resources as are found to be deficient in relation to the nation's requirements;

Formulate a Plan for the most effective and balanced utilisation of the country's resources;

On a determination of priorities, define the stages in which the Plan should be carried out and propose the allocation of resources for the due completion of each stage;

Indicate the factors which are tending to retard economic development, and determine the conditions which, in view of the current social and political situation, should be established for the successful execution of the Plan;

Determine the nature of the machinery which will be necessary for securing the successful implementation of each stage of the Plan in all its aspects;

Appraise from time to time the progress achieved in the execution of each stage of the Plan and recommend the adjustments of policy and measures that such appraisal may show to be necessary; and

Make such interim or ancillary recommendations as appear to it to be appropriate either for facilitating the discharge of the duties assigned to it, or on a consideration of the prevailing economic conditions, current policies, measures and development programmes; or on an examination of such specific problem as may be referred to it for advice by Central or State Governments.

The mandate for the Planning Commission was elaborate, vast and all-encompassing. It was expected to not only prepare plans for the Centre, but also coordinate with states to help them resolve their economic policy challenges. More importantly, the Commission acquired the role of deciding on the pattern of allocation of Central grants and allowances to different states.

The political justification behind the setting up of the Commission showed the shift in Nehru's economic policy approach. The government resolution noted that the need for raising the country's standard of living through planned development was underlined as early as 1938—almost nine years before Independence, when the National Planning Committee was set up by the Congress. However, political developments and the beginning of the Second World War interrupted the work assigned to the Committee, although it did produce some useful papers. As the consultations over the formality of how India would gain its freedom from British rule made progress, the interim government of India set up in 1944 the Planning and Development Department, which swung into action without much delay and prepared reports on the nature of planned developments needed in India and, in particular, in the various provinces of the country. In less than two years of Independence, the Nehru government set up the Advisory Planning Board, which in 1949 reviewed the problems and challenges faced by planning in India and recommended the setting up of the Planning Commission to 'devote continuous attention to the whole field of development, so far as the Central Government was concerned with it'.

The Nehru government had also noted how the Centre and the state governments after Independence had started various developmental schemes, but the absence of necessary coordination and precise information about the availability of resources posed a big hurdle in their implementation. The overall view within the top echelons of the government was that there was a need for an organization that was free from the burden of day-to-day administration and could remain in touch with the government at the highest policy level to provide an objective assessment of the relevant economic factors needed for planning based on a careful appraisal of resources. Thus, the Planning Commission was born with the mandate that it would be headed by none other than the prime minister and would send its recommendations to the Cabinet of the Union government, freeing it from the hierarchical compulsions of routing its proposals through the normal channel that would have included the relevant Central ministries. At the same time, its relationship with the Union ministries and the state governments was carefully delineated so as to ensure coordination in policy. Not only was the Commission expected to work in close consultation with the ministries of the Union government, such engagement with the states was also one of the requirements. The states as well as the Central ministries were expected to implement the decisions that would be taken by the Planning Commission in consultation with the government.

CHAPTER 5

NATIONALIZATION AS THE NEW MANTRA

At the sixtieth session of the Indian National Congress, held in January 1955, Nehru outlined his government's new economic policy vision. He told the Congress workers that they should expect a departure in the government's economic policies from what was being followed soon after the country gained Independence. He said the government believed in economic development through five-year plans and a socialistic pattern of society. What did he mean by a socialistic pattern of society? The Planning Commission defined it as a system in which the basic criterion for determining the lines of advance must not be private profit but social gain, and that the pattern of development and the structure of socio-economic relations should be so planned that they result not only in appreciable increases in national income and employment, but also in greater equality in incomes and wealth.[1]

In the address, Nehru also talked about the need for 'substantially increasing production, for raising the standards of living and for having progressively fuller employment so as to achieve full employment within a period of ten years'.[2] This was nothing short of a revolution—an economic revolution bigger than any that had taken place in our times, Nehru said, realizing full well that what he was proposing to his party people would be hugely disruptive, and yet promising enough to make a qualitative jump in the state of the country's economy.

This was also when the First Five-Year Plan was coming to an end. The focus of the First Plan was on agriculture, price stability, power and transport against the backdrop of influx of refugees, severe food shortages and mounting inflation. Nehru set up the Planning Commission in 1950 and the First Five-Year Plan began in 1951. It turned out to be a successful Plan, influenced heavily as it was by the Bombay Plan, which had advocated a clear role for the private sector along with a focus on agriculture. Inflation was by and large contained, food availability was ensured and the refugees who came in after Partition were rehabilitated. Bountiful harvests in the last two years of the Plan period—in 1955 and 1956—helped achieve actual annual growth of 3.6 per cent, exceeding the target growth rate of 2.1 per cent.

But when Nehru spoke at the sixtieth annual session of the Congress in January 1955, he could not have been very satisfied with the performance of the First Five-Year Plan. The First Plan notched up healthy growth in the last two years with the help of good harvests, which is what partially explained Nehru's keenness to shift the focus of the Second Plan. He explained why the Second Plan would try to achieve both the aims of a welfare state and a socialistic economy. The creation of a welfare state required that the state would play a key role in promoting the economic and social well-being of its citizens. And a socialistic economy would entail government ownership of the means of production, assisted by government planning and income distribution. 'These can only be achieved by a considerable increase in national income, and our economic policy must, therefore, aim at plenty and equitable distribution,' he said. Nehru's belief in a socialistic pattern of society was complete. He once said: 'I will not rest content unless every man, woman and child in this country has a fair deal and attains a minimum standard of living.'[3]

The pains Nehru took to explain the concepts of a welfare state and socialistic economy show how conscious he was of the shift he was making in India's economic planning in just about a decade after Independence. He reasoned:

It is true that a socialistic economy must provide for a welfare state, but it does not necessarily follow that a welfare state must also be based on a socialistic pattern of society. Therefore, the two, although they overlap, are yet somewhat different, and we say that we want both. We cannot have a welfare state in India with all the socialism or even communism in the world unless our national income goes up greatly. Socialism or communism might help you to divide your existing wealth, if you like, but in India, there is no existing wealth for you to divide; there is only poverty to divide.[4]

Hence, Nehru argued that the objectives of achieving higher growth through increased investments would lead to a rise in production and in turn consumption to help achieve the goals of a welfare state and a socialistic pattern of economy. Apart from signalling a shift in the government's economic policy, this was a politically significant address as well. Nehru thought it was necessary to explain to the Congress leadership the spirit and mission of the Second Five-Year Plan so that he could convey to the large number of Congress workers and politicians, who were present at the annual session, the new direction of economic policy he was engineering and bring them on board.

Forging a New Framework for Industrialization

Already, the government had in 1948 decided to acquire a 49 per cent shareholding in Air India, which was till then a privately owned and privately run airline with domestic and international operations. The government's decision flowed out of Nehru's belief that at that stage of the country's economic development, the state must control strategic areas of the economy. Civil aviation was then considered to be a core transportation sector like the railways and the Nehru government wanted the state to take over the operations of Air India. The Tatas owned the airline and it was one of the companies in the Tata Group that its group chairman, J.R.D. Tata, was closest to. The 49 per cent stake sale to the government in 1948 still meant that the airline could be run by the Tatas as a private airline. However, in 1953, the Nehru government decided that Air India needed to be nationalized. Thus, through an act of Parliament, Air India's remaining private shareholding was acquired by the government. The Air Corporations Act of 1953 led to a lot of acrimony between Nehru and the founder chairman of Air India, J.R.D. Tata. The manner in which the airline was acquired left a bad taste not only for Tata but also for many other leading industry leaders of the day. It was not clear if the government would move ahead to nationalize more private-sector enterprises to gain control over key enterprises manufacturing goods or providing services in India. Of course, as a compromise, Nehru allowed J.R.D. Tata to continue to function as the chairman of Air India and that arrangement continued till 1977. But that decision had dealt a blow to private-sector initiatives. The message to private-sector industry leaders seemed to be that the government could take away or dilute the scope of their business if it wanted to, even if it was completely owned by them. Private players in India were taken aback by such an approach.

The next move was in 1956, which marked a watershed in India's economic history. A major shift in economic policies was being initiated. The Second Five-Year Plan was launched with a new focus. It was more ambitious as it aimed at an annual growth rate of 4.5 per cent. Compared to a growth target of 2.1 per cent for the First Five-Year Plan, the target was thus doubled for the Second Plan. Even when compared to the achievement of 3.6 per cent annual growth between 1951 and 1956, the Second Five-Year Plan's growth target showed that the government had shed its conservatism on the growth front. It decided to accord a lower priority to agriculture and instead laid greater emphasis on industrialization through the setting up of heavy and basic industries. The idea was to raise production, create more jobs and boost consumption and, thereby, create a virtuous cycle of growth and consumption leading to a welfare state that could take care of the basic needs of all its people. In order to achieve this goal, the Second Plan was unveiled and a new Industrial Policy Resolution was adopted—with the latter almost becoming the instrument to achieve goals set out in the former.

Indian business leaders were a little taken aback by this shift in the focus of the government's economic policy. They had hoped that while the Nehru-led government would make investments in building infrastructure, the private sector also would be given a free and bigger play in operating in all the remaining areas. Even before Independence, Indian industry leaders were engaged in consultation among themselves on the role of the government in the industrial sphere. The expectation then was that the Indian state after Independence would play an important role in the industrial sector. A view that was shared by G.D. Birla, J.R.D. Tata, Purshottamdas Thakurdas and Walchand Hirachand was that large-scale state enterprises would be necessary to develop the basic infrastructure in a country immediately after Independence. The private sector would not have the financial muscle to make such huge investments to build basic infrastructure.[5] But in all other areas of economic activity, the role of the private sector would be recognized and indeed it would be allowed to expand.

It was against the backdrop of such developments that Nehru made those speeches at the inauguration of the Bhakra-Nangal Dam and the annual session of the Congress party. The ground was being cleared for a policy shift to enable the state to play a larger role. The Industrial Policy Resolution of 1956 cemented those changes further.

The economic and political backgrounding of the 1956 resolution also showed a continuity in Nehru's thought processes on the need to achieve the goals of both a welfare state as also a socialistic pattern of economy—neither ignoring the importance of an investment-led rapid growth, nor underestimating the need for sharing those gains among the people of the country so that unemployment is eliminated and poverty is tackled.

The 1956 policy referred to the government's first industrial policy resolution adopted on 6 April 1948 and said:

> Eight years have passed since this declaration on industrial policy. These eight years have witnessed many important changes and developments in India. The Constitution of India has been enacted, guaranteeing certain Fundamental Rights and enunciating Directive Principles of State Policy. Planning has proceeded on an organised basis, and the First Five Year Plan has recently been completed. Parliament has accepted the socialist pattern of society as the objective of social and economic policy. These important developments necessitate a fresh statement of industrial policy, more particularly as the Second Five Year Plan will soon be placed before the country. This policy must be governed by the principles laid down in the Constitution, the objective of socialism, and the experience gained during these years.

The Industrial Policy Resolution of 1956[6] was also categorical about the need to accelerate economic growth, speed up industrialization, develop heavy industries, expand the public sector and build up a large and cooperative sector. These objectives were considered paramount because they would help provide more employment, improve living standards and raise working conditions for the masses. Along with those objectives, there were the goals of reducing disparities in income and wealth, and preventing private monopolies and concentration of economic power in the hands of a small number of individuals.

The Industrial Policy Resolution said: 'Accordingly, the State will progressively assume a predominant and direct responsibility for setting up new industrial undertakings and for developing transport facilities. It will also undertake State trading on an increasing scale.' But this did not mean that the private sector was completely ruled out from playing any role in industrial development. The private sector would be given the opportunity to develop and expand itself in the context of the country's expanding economy. But what would guide its growth was the principle of cooperation and need to allow the private sector to expand along cooperative lines. The private sector would, thus, play a secondary role that would be restricted only to supporting the government's major economic initiatives to be undertaken in the public sector.

Keeping this perspective in mind, the Nehru government's Industrial Policy Resolution classified industries into three broad categories—industries in the exclusive domain of the state; industries majorly run by the state, with the private sector playing a supportive role; and industries where most of the initiative had to be played by the private sector.

The Resolution made a special provision for small-scale sector units, which meant that the government would support these enterprises through differential taxation or by direct subsidies. The role of cottage and village and small-scale industries was recognized in ensuring speedy development of the national economy. By doing this, the government stayed true to its objective of striving to be both a welfare state on the one hand and a socialistic economy on the other.

For the public sector, Nehru wanted to decentralize wherever possible. He was also keen to ensure that the management in public sector stayed along business lines. Public enterprises were supposed to provide revenue for the State, which would also end up providing resources for further development.

'But such enterprises may sometimes incur losses. Public enterprises have to be judged by their total results and in their working they should have the largest possible measure of freedom,' the Resolution said. In other words, public-sector enterprises were to be given a special allowance if they incurred losses and a judgement call on them would be taken only after examining the pros and cons of their overall performance in terms of contributing to national economic development.

The same year of 1956 saw over 200 small insurance companies and provident societies being merged to give birth to a giant insurance entity called the Life Insurance Corporation of India. Lest the government's role in trading would get diluted, the government set up the State Trading Corporation with the mandate of exporting and importing a host of select commodities. One of its key responsibilities was to trade with the centralized selling and purchasing behemoths in the Communist countries, including the Soviet Union, the largest of them. In the import of many items, the STC was given complete monopoly, as in the case of cement. State control and state ownership of economic activities were slowly spreading their tentacles.

The First Phase of Bank Nationalization

That was not all; the government had begun taking over key institutions and entrusted their management and ownership with itself. Already in

1949, it had set up a financial institution —Industrial Finance Corporation of India—to provide long-term financing of infrastructure projects. In 1955, the government nationalized the Imperial Bank of India and rechristened it the State Bank of India (SBI). Imperial Bank of India till then was India's largest commercial bank, but its ownership was vested with private individuals. It was set up as a joint-stock company in 1921 and operated almost like British India's central bank till the RBI came into being in 1935 to assume those functions.

Immediately after Independence, however, India's first finance minister, R.K. Shanmukhan Chetty, had proposed the nationalization of the Imperial Bank of India, but the idea had few takers then and was opposed by none else than the then RBI Governor C.D. Deshmukh and industry leaders as well. Deshmukh had observed that if business and commerce were allowed to remain in the private sector, commercial banks, too, should be free to operate as private entities. However, within a few years, the mood changed. In November 1950, the Indian Parliament debated if the Imperial Bank of India needed to be nationalized so that more credit could be channelled to agriculture and cottage industries. But Deshmukh, who had by then become the finance minister, put his foot down.

The report of the Rural Banking Enquiry Committee, released during the same year, had added a new dimension to the debate over the ownership of the Imperial Bank of India. Its recommendation did not favour nationalization, but instead a reconstitution of its top management, an idea strongly resisted by those who were running the bank. A stalemate arose as the RBI and the Imperial Bank had failed to find a way out to resolve the tricky ownership question. Eventually, the report of the Rural Credit Survey Committee, finalized in the early months of 1953, recommended that the Imperial Bank of India needed to be brought under public ownership, a view that by now had the support of the then RBI governor Benegal Rama Rau. The Committee had recommended that bringing the Imperial Bank of India under public ownership should help the government entrust it with the responsibility for spreading banking facilities to the remoter regions of the country. To this end, the Committee recommended the formation of a new bank, to be called the State Bank of India, by amalgamating the Imperial Bank of India with the ten major banks associated with the former princely states. (The ten major state-associated banks were the State Bank of Saurashtra, Bank of Patiala, Bank of Bikaner, Bank of Jaipur, Bank of Rajasthan, Bank of Indore, Bank of

Baroda, Bank of Mysore, Hyderabad State Bank and Travancore Bank.) The SBI was to be the principal instrument for extending modern banking to the rural areas, and of linking it with the needs of cooperative credit and marketing institutions.[7]

Rama Rau did not agree to the views of the Rural Credit Survey Committee on amalgamating the ten major banks with the bank that would be set up after nationalizing the Imperial Bank of India. He believed that it was not practical to integrate all these banks at the same time. In a seventeen-page note he sent to the finance minister, he said that the Imperial Bank should be first taken up for reconstitution, and later, similar arrangements could be worked out for other banks. The recommendations of the Committee were hotly debated by the management of the Imperial Bank, parliamentarians and the RBI management. With the RBI governor supporting the move to nationalize the Imperial Bank, Nehru decided to initiate the necessary changes in the legal framework. Deshmukh, who had earlier opposed nationalization of the banking industry, acceded to the idea of nationalizing the Imperial Bank of India.

On 20 December 1954, Deshmukh released the report of the Rural Credit Survey Committee in Parliament and announced the government's decision to accept its recommendation on bringing the Imperial Bank under public ownership as 'the first step towards establishing an integrated commercial banking institution catering to the entire country. He also affirmed the government's intention not to disturb other parts of the banking system which would continue to remain in private hands.'[8] The government also imposed a condition that the state would at no time hold less than 55 per cent of the shares in the new bank. A legislative bill was moved in Parliament on 22 April 1955 to complete the process of nationalization and the bill was passed just after eight days on 30 April. When the SBI was born, the RBI held as much as 92 per cent of its shares; the remaining shares were held by private entities.

When the idea of nationalizing the Imperial Bank of India was mooted by Deshmukh, he had said that it was a decision based on economic, rather than doctrinaire, considerations. While moving the bill in Parliament, Minister of State for Revenue and Defence Expenditure A.C. Guha said the purpose of the new law was not just to take over the Imperial Bank, but to 'recreate our rural life, to vitalize and strengthen our peasantry, and to rejuvenate . . . rural areas'. Industry leaders like Lala Shri Ram were upset and issued statements opposing the idea of the nationalization. But Nehru remained unmoved in his decision. Fourteen years later, his daughter, Indira Gandhi, would take a far bolder and bigger step by nationalizing fourteen leading private commercial banks operating at that time in the country.

The nationalization of the life insurance industry in 1956, referred to earlier, was also one of the outcomes of the Nehru government's thinking on economic policy at that time. The Life Insurance Corporation of India absorbed as many as 154 Indian and sixteen foreign life insurers. In addition, it also absorbed seventy-five provident societies under its fold. The general insurance business, which provided insurance cover to various products and services, was allowed to remain in the private sector, although it was not clear why such an exclusion was made. Explaining the government's logic behind nationalizing life insurance, Nehru told Parliament: 'The nationalization of life insurance is an important step in our march towards a socialist society. Its objective will be to serve the individual as well as the state.'

A similar explanation was offered by the then finance minister C.D. Deshmukh when he piloted the legislative bill to nationalize the life insurance business in Parliament. Already, the government had created the Life Insurance Corporation of India after merging several small private-sector life insurance companies and bringing them under the ownership of the government. But now, Deshmukh was taking that process a step further. He said:

> Insurance is an essential social service, which a welfare state must make available to its people and the State must assume responsibility for rendering this service once it cannot be provided in any other manner . . . With the profit motive eliminated, and the efficiency of service made the sole criterion under nationalization, it will be possible to spread the message of insurance as far wide as possible, reaching out beyond the more advanced urban areas and into hitherto neglected, namely, rural areas.

This was not the first time that such reasons would be cited in India to justify the nationalization of an economic activity. Similar arguments would be offered to justify the nationalization of banks thirteen years later and under a different prime minister and more pressing political circumstances.

The Second Five-Year Plan: A Shift in Focus

The Second Five-Year Plan departed from the approach of the First Five-Year Plan, which ended in 1956. Nehru gave it a different push. Prasanta

Chandra Mahalanobis, an economist of repute and influence working with the ISI, was the moving spirit behind this plan. The plan focused on:

- rapid industrialization by setting up basic and heavy industries,
- a sizeable increase in national income to improve the standard of living,
- a large expansion of employment opportunities, and
- reduction of inequalities in income and wealth with a more even distribution of economic power.

It was an ambitious document at the time. It aimed at increasing the country's national income by 25 per cent in five years. The fuel for this rise in national income was to have come from a healthy dose of investments—the Second Five-Year Plan had projected an increase in the investment rate from 7 per cent of the GDP in 1956 to 11 per cent by 1961. It assumed that the rate of population growth would remain at 1.3 per cent and the capital–output ratio would be 2.3:1. The Plan relied a lot on heavy investments in the capital goods sector that yielded output over a longer period of time.

Overall investments in the Second Five-Year Plan at Rs 6,750 crore more than doubled from what it was in the First Five-Year Plan. The private sector's share in the total investments went up marginally to 46 per cent, compared to a share of 43 per cent in the First Five-Year Plan. But the most important shift in the Second Five-Year Plan was noticeable in the allocations of public investments in the industrial sector, aimed at rapid industrialization. In sharp contrast, the First Five-Year Plan focused on improving the capacity and infrastructure in the agriculture sector.

As the roll-out of the Second Five-Year Plan began, problems over its implementation began to surface. Food output had seen a smart recovery in the last two years of the First Five-Year Plan, thanks to good rains and a bountiful harvest. However, food production saw a decline during the period of the Second Five-Year Plan, resulting in a sharp rise in food prices. Inflation got worse because of the deficit financing that the government had resorted to. The cost estimates for all the heavy industrial projects that had been planned went awry.

The Second Five-Year Plan was also dependent a lot on large-scale imports to sustain the industrialization drive, but that led to a foreign-exchange shortage, dealing a blow to a Plan that was dependent on imports. It was soon clear that the investment allocations made for setting up the projects were not adequate and the government had to consider revising the size of the Plan. The projects were split into two categories—core projects, for which resources were prioritized, and other projects, which were placed on hold pending availability of funds. Inflation rising by 30 per cent during the five years of the Second Five-Year Plan was politically a big blow to the Nehru government; inflation was much less during the First Five-Year Plan. The growth target, at 4.3 per cent, was close to the target of 4.5 per cent. By that measure, the Second Five-Year Plan was not a complete failure.

The Mahalanobis model, which was expected to move the trajectory of the Indian economy to a new plane, failed to achieve the projected goal. Instead, the Indian economy was troubled by a set of problems that would continue to bedevil it for the next few decades.

The Chinks and Disrupters

Nehru will certainly be counted as one of the main disrupters who pushed India towards statism. He left nobody in doubt that he would advocate a policy of planned economic development. Leading lights of Indian industry at that time, including G.D. Birla and J.R.D. Tata, were not in favour of an economic policy that appeared to have been influenced by the model that Soviet economist Grigory Feldman had created for the planning exercise in the Soviet Union. But more than Indian industry leaders, the person who cast a more powerful influence on Nehru was Mahalanobis, who had set up the Indian Statistical Institute (ISI) and became a key adviser to the government. The close relationship between Nehru and Mahalanobis has few parallels in the history of economic policymaking in any country. A popularly elected leader was completely in thrall to an economist and the model of economic development he was propagating. In a rare display of how beholden Nehru was to the ideas of Mahalanobis, the prime minister visited the ISI campus in Calcutta (as Kolkata was known then) to inaugurate a new discipline of studies relating to planning for national development.

On 3 November 1954, Nehru was seated on the dais of the function organized at the ISI campus and Mahalanobis held forth on the rationale and virtues of the model of economic development that would eventually underpin the Second Five-Year Plan that would be launched two years later. In that sense, Mahalanobis was as responsible for the disruption caused to India's economic development pattern as Nehru. Indeed, given

Mahalanobis' central role in the formulation of the Second Five-Year Plan, he would be arguably a bigger disrupter than even Nehru.

The central message of the Mahalanobis model was to encourage investments within the country with the setting up of capital goods industries. This, as Mahalanobis said at the Calcutta campus of the ISI, would build the country's indigenous capacity to produce more capital goods, which in the process would boost investment and growth.

The consequences of Mahalanobis and his ideas endured for several decades in the sphere of economic policymaking in independent India. Barring a short period when Lal Bahadur Shastri as prime minister made an unsuccessful attempt at making an about turn on economic policymaking, statism as espoused by Mahalanobis continued for several years even after the underwhelming outcomes of the Second Five-Year Plan.

Indeed, the drive towards statism got a leg up in the succeeding years. For instance, it took almost seven decades before the Planning Commission was wound up and the model of planned development abandoned—by the government led by Narendra Modi in 2015. The roots of industrial licensing grew so strong that it took about four decades and a major economic crisis to force a major dilution in the licensing regime, dismantling the monopoly of the state sector in many areas of economic activity and removing licensing controls in most sectors. If it took about a decade for the Mahalanobis model to grow roots in Nehru's government, its gradual phaseout happened over more than two and a half decades after the country was hit by an unprecedented balance-of-payments crisis and fiscal indiscipline.

The consequences of the Mahalanobis model for India's political thinking and ideology were far more enduring and impactful. Grigory Feldman, the Soviet economist, had prepared the industrialization strategy of Joseph Stalin, who had ruled the Soviet Union from the mid-1920s to his death in 1953. It is widely believed, though without any official corroboration, that Feldman's ideas had influenced the thinking of Mahalanobis and that led to the shift in Nehru's economic policy approach. There was, however, a key difference between the situation in the Soviet Union and that in India: Feldman was asked to address through policy intervention the foreign exchange bottleneck in the Soviet Union and in India, by contrast, the foreign exchange bottlenecks occurred because of the implementation of the Mahalanobis model with its discrimination against exports. Nevertheless, the idea of the state leading the industrialization efforts through the use of scarce foreign-exchange resources for funding projects and meeting rising consumption demand appealed not just to Nehru but to a host of other socialist leaders and those belonging to the Left political parties in India.

Thus, even though there were flaws in the Mahalanobis model, as they became evident from the outcomes of the Second Five-Year Plan, Indira Gandhi, who succeeded Nehru after a short interregnum of about eighteen months, continued to espouse the same principles for a couple of more decades. At another level, the influence of the Left political parties on governance was hardly on the wane. Left leaders continued to provide ideological sustenance to the idea of the state leading the industrialization efforts in the country at least till the 1980s.

Heads of the government were either influenced by such Left-oriented thinking or were not strong enough to usher in a change in the direction of economic policy, departing from the path pursued by the nation's first prime minister. It was only the crises in the late 1970s and the 1990s that led to a gradual dilution in the government's approach to state-led industrialization efforts.

The final departure from the statist policies happened in the 1990s, and the nail in the coffin of state-led planning processes was driven by the Narendra Modi government by the end of 2014 when the Planning Commission was wound up and the pursuit of a socialistic pattern of the economy was finally thrown into the dustbin. But that statism in India's economic policymaking held such a long sway is an indication of how a disruption initiated in the early years after India's Independence had a long-lasting impact on the economy.

CHAPTER 6

FROM SHIP TO MOUTH

An indication of how serious India's food crisis in the 1960s was could be had from the way Prime Minister Indira Gandhi responded to a note from one of her senior civil servants sometime in May 1967. Her newly appointed secretary in the prime minister's secretariat (which was rechristened Prime Minister's Office [PMO] later in 1977), P.N. Haksar, brought to her attention the serious shortage in the availability of rice in the country.[1] India was dependent not only on wheat imports from the US but also on imports of rice from Burma (as Myanmar was known then). It was noticed that there were no rice shipments from Burma for the whole of April. This could have caused major problems in different parts of the country and food shortage could be politically explosive. Gandhi wrote to General Ne Win of Burma requesting him to resume rice supplies to India to help avert hardships for the people of India. A major drought had pushed foodgrain output in 1965–66 down to just about 72 million tonnes, a steep fall of about 19 per cent over the output in the previous year. More worryingly, the dip in output was steep in rice—about 9 million tonnes, with its output falling to just about 30.5 million tonnes in 1965–66. In 1966–67, foodgrain output had marginally improved to 74 million tonnes, but was nowhere near a level to obviate the need for emergency imports to meet domestic demand.[2]

India's continued dependence on imports of wheat and rice to meet domestic demand for these cereals was a major policy challenge, with serious economic and political consequences for the government. Not surprisingly, a major agrarian unrest had gripped the country a little later in the year. Poor peasants and tea-garden workers in and around Naxalbari of West Bengal were mobilized by a few Maoist ideologues to raise their voice against repressive landowners and demanded a share in the land they held beyond the statutory ceiling. Landowners retaliated and in one such incident assaulted a sharecropper. This triggered widespread protests in the area that led to violent clashes and forced acquisition of land and even confiscation of foodgrain by militants. On 23 May 1967, a few peasant militants killed a police inspector, Sonam Wangdi.[3] The law enforcement agencies responded quickly, with the might of the state backing them. Two days later, the police killed nine tribal women and children.[4]

What started as agrarian distress was now a full-blown political crisis, with the peasant militants seeking guidance from the neighbouring China. The Chinese state-controlled media gave the development ample publicity. A month later, on 28 June, Peking Radio broadcast news of the unrest in India and a few days later, in the first week of July, the *People's Daily*, an organ of the Communist Party of China, described the developments as 'a revolutionary storm of Indian peasants in the Darjeeling area'. The movement spread to other neighbouring states of Orissa and Andhra Pradesh and even Bihar. A few months later, the movement spread further and Assam, Kerala and Punjab were not spared from its grip.

A government note[5] prepared in October 1969 analysed the causes and nature of the agrarian tensions prevailing in the country at that time. The report sowed seeds of the idea of land reforms, and Gandhi's subsequent attempts to undertake land reforms drew their inspiration from this report.

Famine, Food Shortages and Policy Response

Availability of food was not a strikingly new problem for India. Memories of the Bengal famine of 1942–43 were fresh in the minds of Indians when they gained independence in 1947. Nobel laureate Amartya Sen recounted in 1998 in one of his essays published in a Bengali weekly how he was haunted by the stories of poor families during the famine making do with just the starch left over after cooking rice. Even to get a few drops of that starch there would be long queues outside homes of relatively well-off people during those days. The Bengal famine claimed over two million lives.[6]

There have been academic debates over whether the famine was caused by the shortage of food or the inability of the distribution system to make food available to all the people in the country. In *Poverty and Famines: An Essay on Entitlement and Deprivation*, Sen argued that famines in India were not due to a shortage of food, but to 'exchange entitlement failures', which take place when workers are unable to exchange their labour for acquiring food. During the Bengal famine, agricultural labour was the worst affected because their ability to exchange their labour for rice or food was seriously undermined.

When the monsoon fails, one of the consequences, apart from a drop in farm output, is a decline in demand for farm labour. This leads to an increase in supply or availability of farm labour at a time when the demand for such labour has declined. Consequently, wages are depressed, undermining the ability of landless labourers to exchange their labour for wages. Such a drop in exchange entitlement for landless labourers, who dominate Indian agriculture, results in financial impoverishment and inability to buy food. The economist's approach to such a problem is to introduce food-for-work programmes so that landless labourers can use such facilities for earning in the form of food from the labour they do in such programmes, usually launched by the government. The absence of such food-for-work programmes can aggravate the effects of a decline in food output and prevent it from degenerating into a famine.

Whatever be the reason for such famines in the past and the logic for the government to launch food-for-work programmes to mitigate the adverse impact of sharp drops in food output, the stark reality was that India could not feed its entire population of 300 million when it became a free country in 1947. Restrictions were in place on the number of people who could be invited to wedding feasts. In ordinary circumstances, no more than thirty people could be fed during a wedding.

M.S. Swaminathan, the father of India's Green Revolution and the man who steered India's farm policies from the early 1960s and continued to influence policies in the post-Green Revolution period as well, makes no secret of the country's poor agricultural infrastructure. In an essay he wrote in 2012,[7] he wrote about India's agricultural conditions in 1947 in these words:

> Hardly 10 per cent of the cultivated area had assured irrigation and the average consumption of NPK (nitrogen-phosphorus-potassium) fertilisers was less than one kilogram a hectare. The average yield of wheat and rice was about 800 kilogram per hectare. Mineral fertilisers were mostly applied to plantation crops; food crops got whatever organic manure farmers could mobilise.

India's precarious food situation had a political aspect as well. Recognizing India's food crisis, Prime Minister Jawaharlal Nehru decided to visit the US in October 1949 and meet President Harry Truman to request help for India to meet its food scarcity situation. While Nehru received a rousing welcome from Truman, there was no actual progress in securing food supplies from the US, which had surplus wheat. While the Indian side argued that in spite of the green signal from Truman, bureaucratic procedures came in the way of a final decision on wheat supplies to India from the US, there were also suggestions that the US had sought to impose some policy conditions before wheat could be supplied to India. The Indian side decried such attempts to link food aid to secure some policy changes in the recipient country. The Americans, however, defended their stance arguing that no specific request for food aid had actually been received from India during Nehru's visit. At the end of Nehru's visit, there was no agreement between India and the US on wheat supplies and India's food situation remained precarious.

Nehru made yet another attempt at securing wheat supplies from the US in 1950, when a specific request for food aid was communicated to Washington. India's ambassador to the US, Vijayalakshmi Pandit, submitted a formal request to the US for supplying two million tonnes of wheat to India. Truman, according to senior journalist Inder Malhotra's account,[8] was cautious but did his best to get a US law passed to accept the request for food aid from Nehru. His caution arose from his own assessment that the US Congress would not easily pass the proposal. This was because Truman knew full well that US Congress leaders did not approve of India's policy of non-alignment and also its friendly ties with China at that time. In spite of that, Truman sent the bill to the US Congress and even tried to secure the support of the Republicans.

Opposition to food aid for India came not just from the Congress, but also in equal measure from the House of Representatives. It was a different world, where India had few sympathizers in the US, where the political leadership would even wonder why India would not tap Pakistan for importing wheat to meet its shortage. Pakistan's agriculture was in better shape at that time than India's. This was largely because the more fertile western part of Punjab, which also benefited from the world's most extensive irrigation canal networks at that time, had gone to Pakistan. Jawaharlal Nehru was extremely distressed by the US's dilly-dallying on a request that was of critical importance for India and it was a question of Indian people going hungry and facing another famine so soon after the Bengal famine of 1942.

Malhotra quotes B.K. Nehru, who was at that time the minister for economic affairs at the Indian embassy in Washington, on a gripping conversation between Vijayalakshmi Pandit and Sam Rayburn, Speaker of the House at that time. Rayburn was also under the impression that India's reluctance to import wheat from Pakistan was because of a rivalry between 'a Hindu India' and 'a Muslim Pakistan'. Pandit had to correct that impression and told Rayburn that India was not a Hindu India, and it had more Muslims than did Muslim Pakistan. After that conversation, the US tone changed somewhat. A statement from Prime Minister Nehru, where he said that India would prefer two million tonnes of wheat from US as a loan and not as a gift, also helped improve the situation.

Within days of that statement, the US Congress passed the India Emergency Food Aid Bill to provide two million tonnes of wheat, valued at that time at $190 million, and all of that came to India as a loan. President Truman signed it into a law on 15 June 1951. But there was no celebration over the decision in India as everybody knew of the tortuous path the agreement had gone through. It was a deal that showed India's fraught relations with the US as much as it brought to light India's doddering food economy and its inability to feed its own people. Americans were also unhappy over the fact that while the US food shipment decision was not widely appreciated in India, there was much jubilation and applause over the Soviet Union's decision to send wheat to India at around the same time although it was of a much smaller quantity.

In spite of India's political travails with wheat imports soon after its Independence, the government of the day did not refocus its energies to bring about a comprehensive policy change to raise the agricultural sector's capacity to produce adequate foodgrain and feed its people. The first two Five-Year Plans, of course, lay emphasis on expanding the area under irrigation and on fertilizer production. But they did not make any significant impact on India's foodgrain output in the two Plan periods. In 1950–51, the output of wheat, rice and pulses was estimated at 50.83 million tonnes; it increased after ten years of planning to 82.02 million tonnes in 1960–61. This was a compounded annual growth rate of less than 5 per cent, not adequate to meet the growing demand for basic necessities of the Indian people who had just got independence and believed that true freedom would arrive for them when they attained freedom from hunger as well. Thus, import of foodgrains kept rising in this period. Net import of cereals and pulses was estimated at 1.39 million tonnes at the end of the First Five-Year Plan in 1956, and more than doubled to 3.49 million tonnes in 1961 by the time the Second Five-Year Plan ended.

Why did India's planners ignore its agriculture? Economist Deepak Lal, who was part of the Planning Commission in the late 1960s, has an explanation. In his short note on economics in India in the *New Palgrave Dictionary of Economics Online*, Lal[9] puts the blame on the model of development framed by Prasanta Chandra Mahalanobis, who was the inspiration behind the first two Five-Year Plans and was one of Nehru's most trusted economists. Lal concluded:

> An implicit assumption of the Mahalanobis framework was that agriculture could be left alone, merely being a source of 'surplus labour' and of the limited savings and foreign exchange for the heavy Industrialization strategy. By the mid-1960s, this neglect had led to a severe food crisis. The transformation of agriculture, which until then had been seen largely as a means of promoting equity through land reforms, then became a matter of debate.

In other words, the policy of treating agriculture only as an instrument of redistributing assets and resources through land reforms boomeranged on the Indian economy as inadequate farm output caused food shortages increasing the country's reliance on imports.

Lal's analysis of Indian agriculture also reveals three broad trends that hurt the Indian farmers' productivity and economic well-being. One, the package of initiatives to address the ills afflicting Indian agriculture did not see any major change over the years. They were largely focused on improving irrigation networks and ensuring increased availability and use of fertilizers, supply of better seeds and enhancement in land tenures. Indeed, the availability of improved irrigation networks was a big boon for India's agriculture after high-yielding varieties of seeds were introduced in the late 1960s, without which the goals of attaining self-sufficiency in agriculture would have remained unrealized. But the policy framework was not alive to fresh developments in agriculture and, therefore, could not come up with appropriate policy responses.

Two, the government chose to rely on such empirical research work on India's agriculture that showed an inverse relationship between farm sizes and productivity per hectare. Such research showed that productivity levels were found to be higher in smaller farms than the large ones. This finding, Lal argues, was used to push through land reform policies to give rise to small, family-labour-based peasant farms, which in turn would promote equity and efficiency. An improvement in the productivity of agriculture was cited as the economic rationale for land reforms resulting in smaller landholdings. In the process, the government ignored other studies that challenged such arguments.

And three, the shift in the industrial policy approach in the 1950s that introduced a *licence-permit raj* extracted a huge price for India's agriculture. Such policies, Lal, argues, implied a heavy tax on agriculture. 'From 1965 efforts were made to correct this by price supports to farmers, which led to an improvement in the terms of trade. But this changed again in the 1980s with growing but inefficient input subsidies becoming the main form of supporting agriculture,' Lal noted. A combination of price support schemes and input subsidies was what the government pursued over the years to help Indian agriculture, paying less attention to the need for increasing basic investments in the sector and encouraging greater use of technology for productivity gains.

Even after the economic reforms of 1991, there was no noticeable shift in the government's policy approach to agriculture. On the contrary, it got worse. Instead of improving rural infrastructure, amending laws that placed curbs on marketing of farm produce and increasing investments to ensure linkages of Indian agricultural crops with the markets through food-processing supply chains, the governments only brought in band-aid solutions. These included putting higher minimum support prices and even palliatives like waiving agricultural loans. Some feeble efforts in the right direction were made, but they were too few and far between. The government tried to create the infrastructure for agricultural marketing and amend the marketing laws for agricultural produce to provide farmers the freedom and choice on the question of selling crops, but no real headway was made in that direction.

The debate over the years has also shifted to the launch of an income support scheme for farmers and even a universal basic income (UBI) scheme. However, with a huge burden of subsidies already in place, such debates have been hijacked by concerns over fiscal consolidation. Governments at the Centre or in the states have been wary of introducing such income support schemes. Withdrawing existing subsidies would be unpopular and, therefore, the government has shown extreme reluctance to even phase them out. Thus, an income support scheme without eliminating the existing subsidies would increase the overall burden on the exchequer, making the states fiscally broke. Such fears came true just before the 2019 general elections. The Narendra Modi government's Budget for 2019–20, announced just before the general elections of 2019, launched an income support scheme for small and marginal farmers with landholdings of less than 2 hectares or about 5 acres. However, the scheme has imposed a huge burden on the government's fiscal capacity—as large as about 0.36 per cent of India's GDP. And since the new support scheme has come without abolishing or phasing out some existing farm subsidy schemes, the financial burden on the Indian government will be harmful for its overall capacity to undertake the much-needed developmental expenditure in many other areas of the economy. In addition to the problems arising out of the additional fiscal burden, the income support scheme (about Rs 6000 per farmland holding below 2 hectares) suffered from another major flaw: the support scheme benefited only those who owned land and ignored a vast number of landless farmers or farm workers growing crops on land parcels belonging to the landowners. In that sense, the Central government's income support scheme suffered from the same problem that had dogged the Rythu Bandhu scheme (Agriculture Investment Support Scheme) in Telangana, as per which the state government would offer Rs 4000 per acre per farmer every season to help them purchase farm inputs like seeds, fertilizers and pesticides and pay for farm labour. In Telangana, too, the scheme excluded those who did not own land. The challenges of maintaining land records and verifying them before disbursing the money to the land-holding farmers were even more daunting in a country where land records were poorly kept in many states. But the tendency to offer more such palliatives to Indian farmers has only increased over time. One of the first decisions taken by the Modi government after the BJP's thumping victory at the 2019 general elections was to extend the coverage of its income support scheme (PM Kisan Samman Nidhi Yojana) to include all farmers irrespective of their landholding size. Universalizing the income support scheme for all farmers was part of the BJP's election promise and it meant an increase in the government's annual expenditure from Rs 75,000 crore to Rs 88,000 crore.

CHAPTER 7

A NEW EXPERIMENT BY INDIRA GANDHI

In May 1967, why was Indira Gandhi desperate to seek help from the Burmese head of state for an early dispatch of rice to India? She knew that she could count on only a few countries with close ties for securing food aid for India.

The Indian economy was yet to recover from the adverse consequences of a war with Pakistan in 1965, soon after which she assumed charge as prime minister in January 1966. Lakshmi Kant Jha, Gandhi's secretary, shared with her that the plan to devalue the Indian currency against the US dollar was ready. This move was going to revive exports, which would revive the economy and boost growth.

By the end of March that year, Gandhi was in Washington for a two-day official visit to the US. By the look of it, her visit was a success as she hit it off very well with the US President Lyndon Johnson.

Pranay Gupte's account[1] of the visit in *Mother India: A Political Biography of Indira Gandhi* shows that Johnson was simply charmed by Gandhi. In two unusually warm gestures, not only did Johnson walk her down after the talks between the US and India from the White House to Blair House, where she was staying, but he also decided to join a dinner hosted by the Indian ambassador, B.K. Nehru, although he was not scheduled to attend it. On her part, Gandhi did everything she could to please the Americans. She had stopped criticizing the US for its role in Vietnam during her trip and had broadly agreed to devalue the Indian currency. In return of the wheat and project aid that she had sought from the US, she also agreed to Johnson's proposal to set up the Indo-American Education Foundation with the help of the rupees that it had accumulated from the proceeds against its wheat shipments to India under Public Law 480, or PL 480. The Foundation was to undertake research in education in India. Gandhi's approval of the proposal was a big concession to the Americans as their earlier attempt at getting the previous two prime ministers (Nehru and Lal Bahadur Shastri) to agree to this proposal had failed.

Gandhi realized the enormity of the impact of her move to come closer to the US. To balance it, perhaps, she scheduled a stopover at Moscow on her way back to New Delhi. Soviet Prime Minister Alexei Kosygin noted the warming up of relations between India and the US. However, he graciously committed to continuing all Soviet assistance to India as provided for under the existing agreements between the two countries. Such an assurance proved to be crucial.

In the next few weeks after her return, however, Gandhi realized that she had been actually spurned by the US. She had pleaded for 12 million tonnes of wheat and $435 million in loans from the US but what Johnson agreed to was to send only 3.5 million tonnes of wheat and approve $900 million in project aid to India. Kosygin's gesture of continued Soviet assistance during her trip had helped secure the Indo-Soviet relationship that was almost on the verge of collapse after Gandhi's meetings with Johnson in March 1966.

As domestic politics heated up over India agreeing to the US setting up the Indo-American Education Foundation and the impact of the devaluation of Indian currency by over 57 per cent—from Rs 4.76 a dollar to Rs 7.50 a dollar—Gandhi decided to stage a retreat from her pro-US stance. What also complicated the situation was the way the shipments of the promised wheat were held up because of the red tape, and the Johnson administration was simply not able to address the delays. Gandhi decided to change course and resumed her criticism of the US actions in Vietnam and also withdrew her government's support to the proposal on the US setting up the Indo-American Education Foundation. That was in July 1966.

It was a short honeymoon with the US. While food aid was what prompted Gandhi to engage with the US a little more favourably, her disenchantment with the US also led to the unfolding of a new series of measures that charted a new direction of India's economic policy.

The Green Revolution

M.S. Swaminathan, India's most renowned agricultural scientist and the man who would later play a crucial role in ushering in the Green Revolution in India, explained the stagnating agricultural output and the challenge the country was facing from a different but more relevant point of view. The focus during the ten years of the first two Five-Year Plans was on improving the irrigation network in the country and on raising fertilizer production, but little attention during this period was paid to the need for improving farming practices and the productivity of Indian farmers. Agricultural scientists during that decade were simultaneously experimenting to assess the response of rice and wheat varieties to the application of fertilizers and the spread of irrigation facilities. Wheat and rice varieties grown by most farmers were noticed to have tall and thin straw. The overwhelming opinion of experts was that Indian farmers should have the benefit of wheat and rice seed varieties that would produce plants that have short and stiff straw. Tall crops also suffered from another disadvantage. In the event of a storm or windy rain, they were more likely to be flattened and damaged compared to shorter plants.

Early efforts at boosting farm output saw scientists exploring cross-breeding of plants that would address the issue of crop height. Dr K. Ramiah, a rice scientist, suggested in 1950 that the country should experiment with the crossing of the japonica varieties of rice with the indica rice varieties. Japonica varieties had to be imported from Japan and the indica varieties were available in plenty in India. The objective of the cross-breeding programme was two-pronged—to gain the advantage of higher productivity from the Japanese varieties and benefit from the hardiness and adaptability of the Indian strains. Japonica varieties had an average yield of over five tonnes in a hectare of land compared to only about one tonne to two tonnes for the indica varieties. Research and experimentation on these lines had begun in the early 1950s at the Central Rice Research Institute in Cuttack. However, the indica-japonica rice hybridization programme did not make much progress as some genes to develop semi-dwarf varieties of rice were available in the 1960s from Taiwan and the International Rice Research Institute in the Philippines.

A similar pattern of research and experimentation followed so that wheat cultivation in India could improve its yield. The per hectare yield of wheat with the existing crop varieties in India used to be as low as two tonnes per hectare. Soon after the Second World War, research on the semi-dwarf wheat plants with a high-yield potential had led to the development of a new variety in the US by the name of Gaines. The average yield for the newly developed varieties had reached as high a level as 10 tonnes per hectare. Around the same time, Dr Norman Borlaug, who was working in Mexico, obtained the seeds containing these dwarfing genes and began work on developing a new variety of dwarf wheat crops. The key difference between the Gaines variety and what Borlaug was working on was the time of the year when these crops would be cultivated. The Gaines variety worked well during winter, but not in spring. Borlaug, on the other hand, was working on a variety that would be suited for India's rabi crop.[2]

In 1959, Swaminathan approached Borlaug to explore if his semi-dwarf wheat varieties could be used under Indian conditions to improve wheat output. It was a partnership that resulted in a disruption for Indian agriculture that was largely positive in its impact—the Green Revolution. Borlaug wanted to acquaint himself with the growing conditions in India and visited India in March 1963. Recalling those days, Swaminathan writes:

> We tested the material at locations all over North India during the rabi season of 1963. The multi-location trials revealed that the semi-dwarf wheats of Mexican origin could yield four to five tonnes a hectare, in contrast to about two tonnes a hectare of the tall Indian varieties. It became clear that India had the tools with which to shape its agricultural destiny.

Mere success in the trial of hybrid semi-dwarf varieties of wheat was not enough to bring about the desired transformation of Indian agriculture in terms of its output levels and productivity. A blessing was the appointment of Chidambaram Subramaniam as the minister of agriculture and food in July 1964. Subramanian gave the idea of spreading the cultivation of the high-yielding varieties his full support, along with the adequate provision of irrigation and mineral fertilizer. The outcome became evident in 1968.

In 1968, Indian farmers harvested about 17 million tonnes of wheat, surpassing by a long margin the previous highest output level of 12 million tonnes recorded in 1964.[3] 'Such a quantum jump in production and productivity led Indira Gandhi to announce the "Wheat Revolution" in July 1968,' Swaminathan wrote in an article in 2012 to celebrate the development of India's agriculture to a level where the state could guarantee food availability for all through a right-for-food programme. The desire to improve production and productivity in other crops led to an expansion of the programme to use hybrid, high-yield varieties for other crops like maize, jowar and bajra. With the assistance of the Rockefeller Foundation, Indian scientists worked on developing hybrid and high-yielding seeds and succeeded in introducing new varieties in wheat, rice, maize, jowar and bajra in 1967. Indian farmers also became more yield-conscious, which was perhaps the most durable gain of the Green Revolution.

The Other Side of the Green Revolution

Not everyone, however, looked at the Green Revolution the way Swaminathan did. Ashok Mitra was certainly one who didn't. Between

1966 and 1970, the Agricultural Prices Commission (APC) got a new chairman in Mitra, who would later become the finance minister in the West Bengal government with Jyoti Basu as the chief minister. This was also the time when Indian agriculture was going through a crisis and the shortage situation was overcome through the launch of the Green Revolution. Mitra, however, had a different assessment of both the need for the Green Revolution as also of its impact.

In his autobiography *A Prattler's Tale: Bengal, Marxism, Governance*,[4] Mitra was quite forthright about the ill-effects of the high-yielding variety of seeds that contributed to the Green Revolution in the country in the late 1960s. 'The men in power had become aware of the varieties of "high-yielding seeds", the Ford Foundation was sending teams of scientists and technologists to explain to Indian politicians and civil servants how the country's agricultural sector could be transformed through the application of such seeds,' Mitra wrote.

The argument against such a high-yielding variety of seeds was that these alone were not enough to sustain agricultural growth. Equally important was irrigation, pesticides and sufficiently large holdings of land so that irrigation efforts could be undertaken without much difficulty. Mitra believed that the success of the Green Revolution by the use of such high-yielding variety of seeds also meant a big boost to rich farmers since such cultivation was possible only on large landholdings owned by them. While small farmers could be left out of the benefits that would accrue through improved earnings, Mitra stated, 'Rich farmers who participated would also receive adequate loans from the government, thereby enabling them to have access to high-yielding seeds and other necessary inputs including irrigation water in the right amounts.' In short, the Green Revolution was not an egalitarian experiment and was biased in favour of rich farmers. Since the focus of the Green Revolution was to increase productivity and yield, rich farmers with larger landholdings benefitted more than the small or marginal farmers. Marginal landholdings have indeed trebled in the four decades after the Green Revolution. Consequently, more than 85 per cent of operational landholdings in the country are below 2 hectares or with small and marginal farmers. Such farmers cannot reap the full benefits of high-yielding varieties of seeds that need better farming practices and the use of fertilizers, which are outside the reach of most of them. Not surprisingly, 85 per cent of Indian farm households earned 9 per cent of total farm income, while the rest cornered as much as 91 per cent.[5]

Mitra's regret is that the benefit of the Green Revolution was restricted not just to a sharp rise in output from large landholdings owned by the rich farmers. Inequality in the farm sector increased with rich farmers becoming richer even as poor and marginal farmers became poorer. Worse, the rise in farm output was quickly followed by demands from rich farmers for higher minimum support prices from the government so that they could hold up the market prices to help improve their earnings. The APC was specifically mandated to fix the minimum support prices of all these crops so that the farmers did not lose out on account of a fall in prices, which was quite likely after a sudden spurt in output and availability in the market. Around the same time, the government also asked the APC to devise a mechanism for announcing minimum support prices for these crops.

The minimum support prices were used to procure foodgrains from the farmers. This was aimed at ensuring remunerative returns to farmers. At the same time, the policy was expected to help the government build sufficient stocks in its godowns, which could be used if there was a shortage on account of crop failure in any year. However, the dilemma that arose was that if the minimum support prices had to be raised to provide remunerative prices to farmers, the prices for crops to be sold under the public distribution system too had to go up unless the government stepped in with higher subsidies. Thus, the Green Revolution saw a section of farmers prosper with higher output and increased earnings. However, new challenges arose before the government in the form of keeping a check on food subsidies and ensuring that the marginal farmers were not left out of the overall improvements in the farm sector.

On how the rich farmers benefitting from the Green Revolution behaved, Mitra's commentary is instructive:

> Wherever I went, I noticed the growing clout of the rich peasantry. They were in possession of the largest land-holdings, the best of the high-yielding varieties of seeds were being provided to them, and the government gave them the requisite irrigation facilities besides power, fertilisers and pesticides at subsidised rates. Their average cost of production should therefore have been lower than that of farmers who remained without these benefits. But few amongst the rich farmers and their lobby would accept this argument.

The acute food crisis the country faced in the 1960s caused a huge disruption to the political system as also to Indian agriculture. It also paved the way for the Green Revolution. But Mitra's assessment shows that the Green Revolution caused another disruption that created greater inequalities in Indian agriculture. The success of higher foodgrain output led to the government ignoring the more fundamental problems of the farm sector—its need for more investment, better technology and market linkages to secure better returns for farmers' produce.

Challenges of the Green Revolution

Like any other disruption, this shift in the way Indian farmers began looking at farming also threw up fresh challenges. There were criticisms that the use of hybrid high-yielding varieties encouraged greater use of fertilizers and chemical pesticides, which were harmful for the environment. Also, as mentioned earlier, many believed that Green Revolution tended to bypass poor farmers who had small landholdings. Thus, the benefits of the technological disruption in Indian agriculture were cornered by rich farmers or *kulaks*. To a great extent, there was merit in and justification for such criticisms. This surely called for more policy intervention so that there was no concentration of economic power among the few rich farmers. Years subsequent to the Green Revolution have seen this conflict in policymaking in evidence from time to time, without any successful resolution of the issues and dilemmas arising out of them.

The recollections of Surinder Sud, one of India's most well-informed commentators on Indian agriculture, about the food crisis of the 1960s and the subsequent Green Revolution tells a riveting story of how Indian agriculture went through a dramatic phase of change. For Sud, the advent of the Green Revolution was a direct outcome of a combination of global politics and domestic shortages. According to him, 'The ship-to-mouth food economy of India those days triggered the desire for self-sufficiency and the Green Revolution.' With human rights violation in Vietnam and Lal Bahadur Shastri's criticism on the US role in the war, the shipments of wheat under the PL 480 programme were diverted to other destinations. This aggravated the food shortage situation in India. Of course, the Soviet Union came to India's rescue and the food situation was not allowed to get worse. But so precarious was the situation that Shastri exhorted Indians to give up on one evening's meal in a week to save food consumption and reduce the country's dependence on imports.[6] Restaurants across the country were asked not to serve evening meals on all Mondays.[7] With the consequences of India's war with Pakistan being felt on the economy,

Shastri coined a new slogan that underlined the critical role of both the soldier and the farmer—*Jai Jawan, Jai Kisan.*

Three persons played a critical role in India's food economy in that phase. M.S. Swaminathan, who was at the time doing research at the Indian Agricultural Research Institute (IARI), Norman Borlaug, who was the director at the International Wheat and Maize Research Institute, or SYMMIT, in Mexico, and C. Subramaniam, who was at the time minister for food and agriculture in the Union government. Swaminathan and Borlaug developed dwarf varieties of wheat plants. The big advantage was that such plants would not be easy victims of storm or rain.

In addition, the new varieties responded well to fertilizers and irrigation, thereby increasing the yield. What's more, the nutrition of the plants shifted from the stems to the grains, which meant more wheat output. The first round of shipments of these newly developed varieties were delayed and led to delayed planting in India. Borlaug flew down to India and made some critical suggestions like adding more fertilizers and introduced a concept of 'gap filling', which essentially meant that seeds were planted even in areas where they had earlier gone dead. The output from these varieties was substantially higher than the traditional ones.[8]

Enter the third protagonist of Green Revolution—C. Subramaniam. On receiving reports of a huge increase in output from the new varieties, Subramanian wondered why the country was not importing large quantities of seeds of the new varieties for distribution across farms in the country. Once the scientists gave their go ahead, Subramaniam ordered for the import of 18,000 tonnes of seeds for the new dwarf variety of wheat—the largest ever consignment of seeds to land on Indian shores. As soon as the seeds landed in Indian ports, they were dispatched to different agricultural research institutions and universities so that they could undertake further research and ensure that they adapted to Indian conditions.

Two institutions came up with the adapted varieties based on the imported seeds—the Punjab Agriculture University (PAU) in Ludhiana and the IARI in Pusa, New Delhi. PAU called the seed Kalyan and IARI named it Sona. A mongrel variety was produced from both these seeds and this was called Kalyan Sona. It is the Kalyan Sona variety of seeds that made the Green Revolution in the late 1960s a reality. Of course, the credit for the sharp rise in output should not just go to these seed varieties, but also to many other factors like the availability of supporting infrastructure including irrigation, fertilizers and an effective minimum support price mechanism. This is also why Punjab benefitted most from the new varieties of seeds—its farmers had larger landholdings and enjoyed an extensive network of irrigation through tube wells and a functioning procurement system along with a minimum support price mechanism. Sud recalls that in 1972 the country had a surplus wheat production to the tune of almost eight million tonnes. A country that suffered from chronic food shortages and had rarely focused on the need to create storage facilities was suddenly up against a problem of plenty. School holidays, scheduled for the summer months, were advanced and the surplus wheat was stored in the school classrooms in different districts of Punjab.

The Green Revolution also put a lot of pressure on the government's capacity to procure, store and distribute foodgrain. The Food Corporation of India—which had been set up in 1964 to undertake price support operations to safeguard the interests of farmers, distribute foodgrain across the country and maintain a safe level of buffer stock for national food security—was asked to pull up its socks and expand its operations to reap the full benefits of the Green Revolution.

There were socioeconomic implications for farmers as well. Jat Sikh farmers, who so far had remained in the background and had a relatively low ranking in social hierarchy, gained hugely from producing more foodgrain and earning higher returns on their investments in cultivation. The pre-eminence of non-Jat Sikhs in the social hierarchy was challenged by Jat Sikh farmers, who now were becoming rich. Mechanization of farming was another direct consequence of the Green Revolution. With more earnings from higher produce, farmers were encouraged to introduce mechanized farming, and this led to an increase in the use of tractors in a big way. The propagation of the Kalyan Sona variety of seeds for growing wheat had another impact on the dining tables of Indians. The rotis, made out of imported wheat from the US under PL 480, had a reddish colour and, therefore, were not favoured in most Indian homes. In contrast, the wheat produced from Kalyan Sona was ideal for rotis. Their colour was amber, not red, and similar to the grains of desi wheat. More importantly, they were tastier than the rotis produced with US wheat.

The verdict on the disruptive impact of the Green Revolution on Indian agriculture is best summed up by what Norman Borlaug said in 2000: 'Increased food production, while necessary, is not sufficient alone to achieve food security. Huge stocks of grain have accumulated in India, while tens of

millions need more food but do not have the purchasing power to buy it.'[9]
Kathryn Sebby of the University of Nebraska, in her research paper on the
impact of the Green Revolution on small farmers in India had this to say:

> The lack of a stable agrarian system in India has made it difficult for
> Green Revolution technology to impact everybody positively. This is
> because of a rigid social structure, which makes it difficult for those
> without money to improve their social conditions. Those with more
> money (and therefore more land) can afford the seeds and chemicals
> necessary to compete in the Green Revolution market. Farmers with
> less money cannot afford to buy the necessary technology and resort to
> money-lenders to purchase on credit. They then find themselves in debt
> and paying exorbitant interest rates. They buy the technology on credit
> to keep up with large farmers and stay competitive in the market, but
> the debt alone negates any possible financial success they can achieve by
> adopting Green Revolution technology.[10]

This is a sobering thought. The Green Revolution certainly bailed India out
of a tight food situation in the 1960s. But it did not bail Indian farmers—
particularly small and marginal farmers—out of their existential problems
in farming and reaching their produce to the marketplace.

In sharp contrast to statism in the sphere of industrial and economic
policies, Nehru allowed Indian agriculture to remain in the private sector.
Not only Nehru but all his successors have allowed agriculture to remain
a private initiative and have kept it out of the reach of the organized
corporate sector. Indian agriculture thus suffered from poor productivity,
lack of technology and a marked absence of reforms of laws on marketing
for agricultural produce.

Many farmers remained poor, and unchecked population growth led to
fragmented landholdings. This was a recipe for a food crisis. The disruption
here was the Green Revolution that essentially resulted from the adoption
of hybrid varieties of foodgrain, mostly cross-bred strains, and the use of
inputs like water, fertilizers, plant-protection chemicals, including pesticides
and weedicides, and improved agronomic practices. But its benefits did not
flow to all sections of Indian agriculture. Of that there is little doubt. A look
at the preponderance of small and marginal farmers with landholdings of
less than 2 hectares, estimated at about 85 per cent of all the landholdings
in the country, and the growing agrarian distress becoming a political issue
in almost every election since the Green Revolution are ample proof of that.

CHAPTER 8

THE ERA OF NATIONALIZATION

The second phase of nationalization of economic activities in the country began under the prime ministership of Indira Gandhi. It caused no less disruption than the first round of nationalization in the 1950s. But this time there was a crucial difference. The second phase of the rise of the State had deeper political roots.

Gandhi's turn towards statism was as much influenced by her political compulsions as by the company of her close advisers during her first stint as the prime minister from 1966 to 1977.

On the one hand, she had to counter the old guard in the Congress, which, in the garb of the Syndicate, was trying to put all kinds of political pressure on her to gain the upper hand in the leadership of the Congress. The Syndicate was led by K. Kamaraj, former chief minister of Madras; Neelam Sanjiva Reddy, a strong leader from Andhra Pradesh; Atulya Ghosh, president of the West Bengal unit of the Congress; S.K. Patil from Maharashtra; and S. Nijalingappa from Karnataka. The Syndicate was opposed to Morarji Desai for ideological reasons—the former were opposed to the pro-business leanings of the latter. When Nehru died in 1964, the Syndicate was active in ensuring that Desai could not become the next prime minister. Instead, the Syndicate propped up an alternative in Lal Bahadur Shastri, a mild-mannered leader from Uttar Pradesh, who kept a low profile even as a minister in Nehru's Cabinet. However, the Syndicate received a jolt when Shastri showed he was his own man and led the country as prime minister, with strong determination and a clear direction, for about eighteen months. The Syndicate was active again when Shastri died suddenly in January 1966. Desai was the claimant again, but this time too, the Syndicate put up Indira Gandhi as an alternative to Desai in the belief that Nehru's daughter would remain beholden to it and would be guided by its advice. However, like Shastri, Gandhi decided to wrench herself free from the influence of the Syndicate and opted for an economic policy course that would present her as a leader with firm conviction in a socialistic pattern of society. The Syndicate believed that Gandhi would become a puppet in their hands, but Gandhi decided through her actions that she was not going to be led by it. Indeed, she even appointed Desai to be her finance minister, almost as a signal to the Syndicate that she would have a person in such a key position even though he was not favoured by it.

On the other hand, she saw the need to build her political base by winning the support of the Young Turks, or the relatively young members of the Congress, who wanted the party and the leadership to take economic steps that could achieve social justice and equity. She could achieve both the goals by the nationalization of key economic activities, which indeed marked the first few years of her prime ministership in a prominent way.

Few people had heard of the Congress Forum for Socialists Action or CFSA in the first few years of its formation in 1962. The group was set up with a handful of senior Congress leaders and was led by Gulzarilal Nanda, who was a man of great integrity and associated with the country's labour movement. It had the blessings of then prime minister, Jawaharlal Nehru, who summed up the mission of CFSA in the following words:

> The Forum is meant to spread socialist ideas and outlook among our people. More specifically, it is meant to help the study of various aspects of socialism in order to give an intellectual background to our people's thinking. This is welcome because there is [a] great deal of vagueness in our thinking.[1]

Apart from holding a few seminars, the CFSA was not very active in the first five years of its existence, until April 1967, when a few young Congress leaders like Chandra Shekhar, Mohan Dharia, Chandrajit Yadav and K.V. Raghunatha Reddy got together to revive the activities of the Forum and press for the adoption of socialistic economic policies.

The outcome of such initiatives became evident at the All India Congress Committee (AICC) in New Delhi in the last week of June 1967. Just four months previously, the fourth general elections had been held and the Congress under Indira Gandhi managed to retain its power at the Centre. However, it had a reduced majority, thanks to a substantial drop in the number of Lok Sabha seats under its belt. It got 283 seats, down from 361 in the 1962 general elections. There were widespread protests over growing inequality, agricultural distress and rising inflation. The Congress's performance in the state Assembly elections was worse, as it lost seven states, where different political parties gained power defeating the Congress. The ten-point economic policy that was adopted by the AICC was a response to the electoral reverses the Congress had faced.

A Strong Political Trigger

Behind the decline of the Congress in the 1967 elections was the economic consequence of the decision that Gandhi had to take immediately on assuming prime ministership in 1966 after Shastri's death. Shastri died soon after India fought a war with Pakistan, whose adverse economic consequences were as devastating as the shortage-ridden food economy that had dogged the country for the preceding few years. The US had turned off the tap for financial aid for India. The country's dependence on food imports and the foreign-exchange shortage left Shastri with no option other than a devaluation of the Indian currency. In return, the US not only offered more help but also leaned on the International Monetary Fund (IMF) to favourably consider a request of financial accommodation for India. Lakshmi Kant Jha, secretary to Prime Minister Shastri, had already prepared a blueprint for economic policy liberalization that could be introduced once some economic stability was restored with financial assistance from the US after the currency devaluation.

Shastri, however, faced some internal opposition to the idea of devaluing the Indian currency. His finance minister, T.T. Krishnamachari, did not see eye to eye with him on this issue. The only option left for Shastri was to effect a reshuffle of the finance portfolio. Krishnamachari was replaced by a relatively unknown Congress leader Sachin Chaudhury and the calculation was that the new finance minister would be on board the controversial issue of devaluation. As events in the subsequent years of the 1960s would show, there would be another reshuffle of the finance portfolio—in 1969. Gandhi would divest Morarji Desai of the finance ministry just before she took an equally controversial decision on nationalizing fourteen banks. Two finance ministers were sacrificed by two prime ministers in the space of three years.

With Chaudhury in North Block, the decks were clear for devaluation. Chief Economic Adviser I.G. Patel and RBI Governor S. Bhattacharya left for Washington to hold consultations with the IMF and inform them of the government's plan to devalue the currency. Everything was going on smoothly so far. But in January 1966, Shastri, who had gone to Tashkent to hold talks with his Pakistani counterpart, died. The devaluation plan had to be put off.

Gandhi assumed charge of the government on 24 January 1966 and her secretary, Jha, apprised her of the plan to devalue the currency. Gandhi held a round of consultations with economists and her advisers to decide on the quantum of devaluation. In April 1966, she visited Washington to gauge for herself the likely impact of the decision. At the end of the visit, she was convinced by the US and IMF administrations of the assistance she would get after going through devaluation. Many Congress leaders were not convinced and the decision to devalue the Indian rupee by over 57 per cent from Rs 4.76 a dollar to Rs 7.50 a dollar set off a chain reaction in the economy with higher import costs raising the inflation rate as a consequence. Remember that India was hugely dependent on imports of crude oil and petroleum products to meet its energy needs. India's imports of petroleum and petroleum products spiked by 19 per cent from $84 million in 1966–67 to $100 million in 1967–68. On top of that, the promise of assistance from the US took its own time to materialize and another drought hit the Indian farm-economy. India's opposition to the US role in Vietnam complicated the situation as US President Lyndon Johnson used delaying tactics in sending foodgrain shipments to India.

The Indian economy was in a perilous state; so critical was the situation that the Indian government had approached the IMF to seek temporary help under the latter's compensatory financing facility. In 1966–67, India received a net assistance of $130 million from the IMF and following it up with another IMF dose of $32 million in 1967–68. A sharp drop in foodgrain production in the country led to an increase in food imports—up from $676 million in 1965–66 to $868 million in 1966–67. Imports had shot up from $2.87 billion in 1965–66 to $3.25 billion in 1966–67 but stabilized at a lower level of $2.75 billion in the following year. What, however, caused concern was the tepid rise in exports even after devaluation. Merchandise exports rose from $1.65 billion in 1965–66 to $1.77 billion in 1966–67 but again declined to $1.68 billion in 1967–68. It was becoming clear that the devaluation move without accompanying measures to improve efficiency and productivity levels had failed to deliver. It did not take much time before devaluation was blamed, and Gandhi became the target of attack even within the Congress. She had used her personal political capital to go for devaluation and turn towards the US and the IMF for help. She felt let down by her policy advisers and even the US. On her way back from a trip to the US, she took an impromptu decision to visit Moscow, capital of the Soviet Union. Soon after, she virtually junked the note on reforms that Secretary Jha had prepared for implementation. An idea that was attempted in a half-hearted manner failed to yield the desired results and then it was given a bad name and junked. The Indian economy was taking a fresh turn thanks to a combination of political and economic developments.[2]

Gandhi felt herself besieged by a variety of challenges from within the Congress party and outside. The general elections were to be held in February 1967. If the Congress won fewer seats in the Lok Sabha and lost some states, the economic situation in the wake of devaluation and the worsening food scarcity situation played a significant role.

A Survival Strategy

The push for the ten-point agenda for action, unveiled by Gandhi at the AICC session in New Delhi in June 1967, came largely from leaders like Chandra Shekhar and Mohan Dharia, who were members of the CFSA.[3] Chandra Shekhar was a socialist politician from Uttar Pradesh, but had joined the Congress in 1968. Dharia belonged to Pune in Maharashtra and was a Congress leader. Both came close to Gandhi and provided her socialistic policy inputs, but had turned against her as she turned authoritarian, leading to the imposition of the Emergency. Both were detained in jail during the Emergency.

The ten points of the new economic policy revealed Gandhi's shift towards the Left. Some of those points were aimed at achieving social control of banks, nationalization of general insurance, introduction of state trading in import and export, state trading in foodgrain, expansion of cooperatives in processing and manufacturing industries, effective steps to curb monopolies and concentration of economic power in light of the monopolies commission report, provision of minimum needs to the people, restrictions on unearned increase in urban land values, a plan for a rural works programme and quicker implementation of land reforms and removal of privileges enjoyed by princes and ex-rulers of states that had acceded to the Union of India during Independence in 1947.

The clout of the CFSA was on the rise even after the adoption of the ten-point economic policy at the New Delhi AICC session. In particular, leaders like Chandra Shekhar and Mohan Dharia made no secret of their disenchantment with the government's failure to prevent the growing concentration of wealth among a few industries and to ensure a more equitable distribution of resources of the weaker sections of society. In

August 1967, Gandhi, under advice from her secretary, P.N. Haksar, set up a committee to investigate if large industrial houses secured undue advantage over others in the grant of industrial licences and whether they got a larger share of these licences. The committee (the Industrial Licensing Policy Inquiry Committee) was to address the CFSA's concerns that the existing industrial licensing system had made large industrial houses larger and created monopolies in the process. Expectedly, the Committee's findings endorsed the CFSA's fears. The political ground had thus been laid for the eventual legislation to curb the growth of monopolies and concentration of wealth in a few industrial houses. This was the political background to how the Monopolies and Restrictive Trade Practices (MRTP) Act was passed by Parliament later in 1969, which essentially curbed the growth and expansion of any company that had an asset base of over Rs 20 crore. Accordingly, all such expansion plans would be subjected to closer scrutiny by the government before any fresh licences could be granted to them.

By July 1969, Indira Gandhi presented yet another document at the Bangalore session of the AICC. It was called 'Note on Economic Policy and Programme'. That was 9 July. The document went well beyond what the ten-point economic policy agenda that was circulated at the New Delhi AICC session almost two years ago. It talked about the need for land reforms and steps to curb the concentration of economic power in the hands of a few industrial groups. Interestingly, the idea of bank nationalization had not yet entered the thought process of the Congress leadership even at that time. The discussion was still focused largely on social control of banks and how it could be made more effective. Bank nationalization as a natural follow-up measure to social control of the banking sector was only an idea then—at best a suggestion from the country's prime minister, and nobody had thought then that Gandhi would take just another ten days to announce the biggest disruption for India's banking sector—the nationalization of fourteen banks. There could be no doubt about the enormity of its impact on the Indian economy.

Bank Nationalization as a Trump Card

It is not that Indira Gandhi's government had been slow in implementing its June 1967 idea of enforcing social control on banks. On 14 December 1967, Morarji Desai, who was then deputy prime minister and finance minister, told the Lok Sabha that the government had plans to introduce a legislative bill on social control of banks. This bill was to facilitate the reconstitution of the boards of directors of banks, prohibit advances or guarantees to directors and to the companies in which they were interested. The Bill was to also facilitate the acquisition of the business of a particular bank by the government, if the bank defaulted in complying with the provisions of the new law and the directives issued under it. The RBI, it was pointed out, would enjoy additional powers to ensure the new law's enforcement.

It was clear from Desai's clarifications in the lower house of Parliament that he had some concerns over the negative impact the new law would have on the business of banking. He said that the most important objective of the law was to ensure that there was no favouritism towards any group or firms on the question of sanctioning loans. *The Hindu*, in a report published on 15 December 1967, stated the following:

> Stating the Indian banking system had attained stability and strength over the last 15 years, Mr Desai expressed the confidence that the implementation of the social control measures would lead to a positive reorganisation of the banking system on sound lines and enable it to fulfil the role that was required of it.[4]

A year later, the law to enforce social control on banks was passed by Parliament, and it came into force on 1 February 1969. While introducing the Bill in Parliament, which after passage came to be known as the Banking Laws (Amendment) Act, 1968, Desai said that the aim of the scheme of social control was 'to regulate our social and economic life so as to attain the optimum growth rate for our economy and to prevent at the same time monopolistic trend, concentration of economic power and misdirection of resources'.[5] The objective of the new law was to ensure more equitable distribution of the banking system's resources and the allocation of adequate loans to priority sectors like agriculture, small-scale industry, the public sector and the self-employed. A national credit council, chaired by the finance minister with the RBI governor as vice-chairman, was set up to determine the norms for flow of credit needed for different sectors of the economy. Even as the newly set up Council got down to the task of overseeing the allocation of loans, Gandhi decided to go for the next move: nationalization of banks. The objective of the National Credit Council was to ensure adequate credit availability to needy sections of society and it left the ownership patterns of the banks unchanged. The move to nationalize banks was also to ensure that bank credit was more easily available to the sections of society that needed it the most, but the government decided to achieve that goal by giving itself more power and acquiring the banks.

What happened on 9 July at the Bangalore AICC session had a definite impact on the developments that took place between 16 July and 19 July. The political logic of that move was as important; the government believed it to be its economic policy imperative.

In the normal course, officials like the finance minister and RBI governor should have mattered a great deal in the way developments took place in 1969 with regard to bank nationalization. But what really transpired in the month of July was somewhat different. RBI Governor L.K. Jha had earlier ensured that the RBI put its best foot forward in reaching the goals outlined under the scheme for social control of banks. But he was not greatly enthused by the idea of nationalizing banks. I.G. Patel was the special secretary in the economic affairs department of the finance ministry. He too was not excited about the idea of bank nationalization. Patel was considered to be close to the finance minister, Morarji Desai. By this time Desai had become a sworn political rival of Gandhi. On the other hand, Gandhi became more reliant on a group of advisers and bureaucrats led by her secretary in the prime minister's secretariat, P.N. Haksar.

After 9 July, relations between Gandhi and Desai had grown too bitter for either of them to tolerate each other. On 16 July, Gandhi divested Desai of the finance ministry portfolio and took charge of the ministry herself. It was a move that appeared to have had a two-pronged objective. One, Gandhi had made up her mind on bank nationalization, which Desai was not happy about. Two, she might have been also acutely aware that the nationalization move would be able to help her win popular support, and secure her credentials as a leader keen on bringing about social and economic equity through government policies. She might have also wanted to get the powerful groups within the Congress, including those who were part of the CFSA on her side. And she also would have believed that the move would marginalize as also side-line the powerful Syndicate leaders, Desai and even her home minister Y.B. Chavan. In any case, she did not want the credit for bank nationalization to be shared with anybody else, let alone Desai.

Thus, on 17 July, she gave the green signal to her secretary, Haksar, to make preparations for nationalizing a clutch of banks. No numbers were given as to how many of them had to be nationalized. Such details were left for Haksar to work out. She also wanted the entire preparations for bank nationalization to be completed in utmost secrecy. She would not consult RBI Governor L.K. Jha, who happened to be in New Delhi that day. She would not consult her special secretary in the Department of Economic Affairs, I.G. Patel, though she and Haksar thought highly of him as an economist and an economic administrator. The reasons for this secrecy was that she had two more political goals to be achieved before she could take everyone by surprise with the decision on bank nationalization.

One, she wanted Desai to quit the government before she could reveal her plans. Two, she wanted to get the ordinance to be signed by her trusted Vice-President V.V. Giri before 20 July. Giri had been officiating as the president since May that year when the President Zakir Hussain died. Now elections were to be held for the next President of India. Gandhi was trumped by the Syndicate leaders, including then Congress president Siddavanahalli Nijalingappa, who also wanted their candidate to run for the post of the President. Sanjiva Reddy was the Syndicate's nominee as the Congress candidate. Gandhi had endorsed the candidature of Reddy but had an alternative plan ready with the help of Giri. She wanted to outwit the Syndicate by allowing Giri to contest the elections as an independent candidate, but for whose candidature she would ensure all her followers supported him.

Once Haksar got the go-ahead from Gandhi to work towards bank nationalization, he talked to D.N. Ghosh, who was then a deputy secretary in the banking division of the economic affairs department in the finance ministry. It was late at night of 17 July that Ghosh[6] got a phone call and he drove down to Haksar's residence on Race Course Road, only to be told that he had to prepare the legislative draft and the ordinance to enable the government to announce bank nationalization by 19 July. In his book, No Regrets, Ghosh writes that he and Haksar discussed the pros and cons of the bank nationalization move till late that night. Ghosh had another round of meeting with Haksar and Gandhi in South Block on Friday, 18 July. Till then, neither the RBI governor nor the top officials of the finance ministry were aware of the move that would fundamentally change Indian banking.

Jha and Patel were brought into the loop only by the evening that day, after Desai quit the government subsequent to being divested of the key finance portfolio. This was an insult to a senior leader of the party and Desai had little option other than quitting Indira Gandhi's council of ministers. There were no guesses on who succeeded Desai as the next finance minister. Gandhi appointed herself as the finance minister, which was an additional charge for her. The entire evening that day Ghosh and other senior officials worked late into the early morning of Saturday at the RBI guesthouse and completed the draft ordinance and the law to give effect to bank nationalization. The Cabinet met at 5 p.m. and passed the proposal. A couple of ministers raised questions over the compensation package for the private-sector entities which would lose control of those fourteen banks, but those doubts were addressed and Ghosh had to be summoned to explain the logic of the package to the ministers. Once the Cabinet passed the proposal, Ghosh ran to Giri, who was waiting for the Cabinet's recommendation and gave his seal of approval. Gandhi addressed the nation over All India Radio and announced her government's decision to nationalize fourteen banks.

About forty-seven years later, on 8 November 2016, another Indian prime minister would speak to the nation on television and announce an even bigger disruption—annulling about 86 per cent of the country's currency in circulation in one stroke and replacing them with new notes.

What Indira Gandhi told the Lok Sabha on 21 July 1969, two days after promulgating the ordinance on bank nationalization, encapsulates the political justification of her decision. Referring to the 1956 Industrial Policy Resolution, she said:

> Nearly 15 years ago, Parliament approved that we should set before ourselves the goal of a socialist pattern of society. Since then Government have taken several measures towards the achievement of this goal. Public ownership and the control of commanding heights of national economy and of its strategic sectors are essential and important aspects of the new social order which we are trying to build in the country. We regard this as particularly necessary in a poor country which seeks to achieve speedy economic progress consistent with social justice in a democratic political system one which is free from the domination of a few and in which opportunities are open to all.[7]

The decision to nationalize banks was challenged in the Supreme Court, whose verdict in February 1970 was a temporary setback for Indira Gandhi. Actually, the verdict had upheld the acquisition of the fourteen banks and the legislative rights of Parliament in taking such a step, but it had declared invalid the principles and procedures used to determine the amount of compensation to be paid to the shareholders who had been divested of those institutions. But since the compensation formula was an integral part of the overall law on nationalization, the apex court had to strike down the entire legislation. The government, however, reworked the compensation formula and Parliament passed a new legislation to make it a law on 31 March 1970.

It was a unique junction where India's economic policy disruption coincided with a political disruption. Gandhi had made up her mind that after the 1967 general election setback, where the Congress lost as many as seventy-eight Lok Sabha seats, she must isolate the Syndicate Congress consisting of old-guard leaders of the party that included K. Kamaraj, Neelam Sanjiva Reddy, Atulya Ghosh, S.K. Patil and S. Nijalingappa. On the other hand were the CFSA leaders who were putting pressure on Gandhi to bring about socialistic economic policies that ensured greater economic and social justice for poor people in particular. Gandhi wanted to kill two birds with one stone—come out with a big-bang policy that addressed the concerns of the CFSA and, at the same time, take the initiative away from the Syndicate Congress leaders. Divesting Desai of the finance minister's portfolio, which eventually forced him to quit the government, propping up and supporting Giri to become the next President by defeating the official Congress candidate, N. Sanjeeva Reddy, and bank nationalization were part of the same grand plan of Indira Gandhi in 1969. In the end, Gandhi succeeded in her mission and benefitted politically from both these disruptions. For Gandhi and her very close advisers, bank nationalization was not a sudden decision. They were aware of the direction of economic policy as far as the financial sector was concerned. Social control of banks was just the beginning in December 1968 and its culmination was bank nationalization in less than a year.

A Nationalization Spree

Next in line for nationalization was coal mining, one of the oldest industries in the country. Commercial coal mining began in the late eighteenth century. Sumner and Heatly of the East India Company started operations in the Raniganj Coalfields in 1774. But the growth and development of coal mining was slow initially as there was not much demand for coal in the domestic economy. The launch of steam locomotives in 1853 triggered an increase in the demand for coal. Annual coal production quickly rose to about 1 million tonne and further to about 6 million tonnes by 1900. Around the time India became independent in 1947, the country's coal production had increased five times and reached 30 million tonnes. By the time India's coal production, largely in the private sector, rose to about 40 million tonnes in 1956, a major policy shift took place. The Nehru government set up the National Coal Development Corporation (NCDC) and it brought under the newly set-up organization all the coal mines owned by the Indian Railways, which needed a stable, reliable and uninterrupted supply of coal for running its locomotives. NCDC was the first step in independent India to undertake planned development of the coal industry. At around the same time, Singareni Collieries Company Limited (SCCL), which had begun operations in 1946, was acquired by the Andhra Pradesh government. Subsequently, SCCL became a joint undertaking with the Indian government owning 49 per cent shares and the Andhra Pradesh government owning the remaining 51 per cent. The state's footprint over the country's coal sector had thus expanded.

The year of 1956 also saw the announcement of the Industrial Policy Resolution, which had listed coal and lignite among the seventeen industries mentioned in Schedule A. This did not mean that the government would nationalize the coal industry. Nor should it have created any fears in the minds of the private sector that at some point in time the government could nationalize the existing private coal-mining units. The growth in these Schedule A industries, including coal mining, would be led by the State, but it did not preclude the continuation of the private sector in these industries and even growth within their existing ownership structure. Only four industries, mentioned in Schedule A, were to be government monopolies, requiring the government to take them over. These were: railways, air transport, arms and ammunition and atomic energy. The Industrial Policy Resolution had stated that Schedule A would include industries, 'the future development of which will be the exclusive responsibility of the state . . . All new units in these industries, save where establishment in the private sector has already been approved, will be set up only by the State.'

The Industrial Policy Resolution of 1956 thus did not preclude the expansion of the existing privately owned units, or the possibility of the State securing the cooperation of private enterprise in the establishment of new units, when the national interests so required. In addition to having exclusive control over the railways, air transport, arms, ammunition and atomic energy, the government was also of the view that the State must have adequate capacity in these two critical areas of transportation infrastructure—air transport and railways. It, of course, added the proviso that whenever cooperation with private enterprise was necessary, the

State could ensure, either through majority participation in the capital or otherwise, that it has the requisite powers to guide the policy and control the operations of the undertaking.

The nationalization of the coal industry or indeed of general insurance or of oil companies was not mandated by the Industrial Policy Resolution of 1956, and what drove such initiatives under the government in the early 1970s was largely a political calculation. These steps bolstered the position of Indira Gandhi in the Congress party as also in the government. The government narrative was somewhat different to justify the nationalization of the coal industry. The government continued to maintain that the growing demand for coking coal from the steel industry called for a big push to intensify the exploitation of coking coal reserves. However, the government of the day was of the view that the private sector in charge of the coking coal mines did not have recourse to the huge capital resources to make necessary investments to boost production. The government was also a little wary of the reported instances of unscientific mining practices and the poor working conditions of labour in many of the private coal mines. A combination of such factors was cited in support of the government move to go in for coal nationalization.[8]

In 1971, coking coal mines were nationalized and two years later non-coking coal mines were also taken over by the government. 'In October 1971, the Coking Coal Mines (Emergency Provisions) Act, 1971 provided for taking over in public interest of the management of coking coal mines and coke oven plants pending nationalisation,' stated a note from the ministry of coal.[9] By 1973, the government had nationalized all coalmines except those run by the Tata Iron and Steel Company and Indian Iron and Steel Company which were exempted because they were captive suppliers to their own steel plants.

The government's explanation for coal nationalization cited two reasons.[10] The international oil market had turned volatile, followed by the oil price shock of 1973. This forced the government to re-examine its energy options. A Fuel Policy Committee was set up for this purpose. The Committee's recommendations suggested, among other things, that coal should be developed as the primary source of commercial energy in the country. The second reason was rooted in the government's assessment that the existing coal miners, largely in the private sector, were not making the investments in the coal sector critically needed to sustain its growth to meet the rising demand. Steel and mines minister under the Indira Gandhi government, Surendra Mohan Kumaramangalam, justified coal nationalization on the ground of conserving the scarce coal resources of the country by striving to achieve five specific goals: halting wasteful, selective and slaughter mining; planned development of available coal resources; improvement in safety standards; ensuring adequate investment for optimal utilization consistent with growth needs; and improving the quality of life of the workforce.

There is, however, strong reason to suggest that the manner in which coal nationalization was implemented was reflective more of the Gandhi government's political expediency than the reasons that Kumaramangalam had cited in his defence of coal nationalization while delivering many of his Parliamentary speeches. Before joining the Congress, Kumaramangalam belonged to the Left, having been a member of the Communist Party of India. He wielded considerable influence over Gandhi and her economic policies. A powerful orator and a strong believer in the idea of nationalization and a socialistic pattern of society, Kumaramangalam joined the Congress in 1967 and remained loyal to Indira Gandhi, when the Congress split in 1969. Two years later, he fought the Lok Sabha elections in 1971 from Pondicherry and won the seat. He became the steel and mines minister soon after his election and held that position till he died in an Indian Airlines air crash in 1973. Kumaramangalam's stint in the government is also the period when Gandhi had gone into overdrive with her policies on nationalization and increased state control over economic activities.

While Kumaramangalam had provided detailed justification for coal nationalization, independent researchers found many holes in his arguments. A research paper, written by Rajiv Kumar and published in the *Economic and Political Weekly* in 1981, argues how the nationalization move could have been triggered by the government's need to manage a crisis in the coal industry rather than give shape to its socialistic policy goals. And the blame for the crisis in the privately owned coal industry would largely fall on the government's policies that affected the mining units. The government, after all, had been exercising all kinds of controls over pricing, production, compensation norms and safety measures for the coal mining industry from 1944 onwards. Kumar's thesis was that nationalization of coal mining was 'forced upon the government by a complete breakdown of the industry, resulting from a collapse of profitability in the organized sector and its inability to continue mining in the prevalent market conditions. The reasons for such a collapse were the actual causes for nationalisation.'

The reasoning put forward by Kumar, who is now the vice-chairman of NITI Aayog, the Narendra Modi government's think tank that replaced the Planning Commission, would give a new dimension to the debate over the nationalization of the coal industry. This argument's validity, however, does not take away from the political reasons for which Gandhi had gone ahead with nationalization. There is no gainsaying that nationalization was hugely disruptive for the coal industry, which till then was largely in the private sector.

Once their coking coal assets were taken over by the government, private miners read the writing on the wall and began transferring their plants and equipment outside the purview of their coal enterprises for fear of losing them in the next phase of nationalization. Kumar calculates that the private miners had left a total debt of Rs 300 crore at the time of nationalization of non-coking coal mines in 1973.

Kumar's conclusion provided a new perspective to coal nationalization. Contrary to the widely held belief that coal nationalization was part and parcel of Indira Gandhi's political vision of ushering in a socialistic pattern of society, Kumar's numbers showed how the move to nationalize actually bailed out private miners, who were already under financial stress. It could be argued that coal nationalization was not just an instrument of Gandhi's socialism, but a cleverly disguised financial rescue operation to help private coal miners.

CHAPTER 9

POLITICS OF ROBIN HOOD

At around the same time as the coal industry was nationalized, the government initiated yet another move that disrupted domestic as well as foreign companies that may have had some interest in investing in India. On 19 September 1973, the Indian Parliament took two significant legislative decisions. One, it repealed an earlier law, the Foreign Exchange Regulation Act (FERA) of 1947, and passed an amended version of FERA of 1973, with more stringent provisions and wide-ranging powers for law-enforcement agencies, including the ability to arrest chief executive officers, senior officials of companies or even industrialists for violation of the rules under the new statute.

The 1947 version of FERA had been aimed at imposing controls on the use or dealings in coins, bullion, securities or payments in foreign exchange in a situation where there was a foreign-exchange shortage. However, the enforcement of this law turned out to be lax and, on the basis of a 1972 Law Commission report, the Indira Gandhi government brought in a new and more stringent version of FERA in 1973. It made the RBI the regulator for all transactions in foreign exchange by individuals or companies. Its objective was to conserve foreign exchange and optimize its use in a situation of shortage. The new law imposed restrictions on a host of transactions, including on import and export of certain currencies, illegal payments in foreign exchange, payment settlements in other countries, holding of immovable property outside India and establishment of businesses in India and acquisition of immovable assets in India by foreigners or foreign entities.

How disruptive the move was could be gauged from the fact that soon after its enforcement from 1 January 1974, it was mandated that companies would have to bring down their foreign equity to below 40 per cent and those that wished to keep it above that limit must get specific clearances from the RBI. According to estimates, as many as 881 companies had applied to the RBI for an exemption to the FERA norms on a 40 per cent cap on foreign equity, but only 150 companies were allowed to exceed the ceiling. Others had to dilute their foreign shareholdings to below 40 per cent or pull out of the country. By 1977–78, as many as fifty-four companies applied to exit India and nine more followed suit in 1980–81, according to an estimate made by Prithwiraj Choudhury and Tarun Khanna in *Charting Dynamic Trajectories: Multinational Enterprises in India*.[1] While this caused major turbulence for foreign companies that had invested in India, it was a bonanza for many Indian businesses and investors, who used the opportunity to pick up shares of many companies that had to offload their shares in the Indian market to dilute their foreign shareholding and comply with the FERA norms.

But the overall impact of the FERA move was negative on the business environment in India. Coming as it did just four years after the enforcement of another highly restrictive law on monopolies, it became clear that Indian businesses were receiving a raw deal from a government that was overzealous in asserting its socialistic credentials and helping Gandhi, its leader, secure her hold within the ruling Congress party. To be fair, the roots of the law to curb the concentration of economic wealth grew sometime before Gandhi assumed charge as the prime minister in 1966. In May 1964, the government led by the newly elected prime minister Lal Bahadur Shastri had set up the Monopolies Inquiry Commission headed by Justice K.C. Das Gupta. In his report, Gupta noted how the concentration of economic power in a few industrial houses was a bane for the Indian economy. That report was with the government in October 1965. Shastri, however, took no action on that report.

After Shastri's sudden death in January 1966, Indira Gandhi led the government and soon found herself beleaguered by political pressures from the Syndicate, a powerful section within her own party. There was a simultaneous need for her to guide economic policies in a way that could establish her as a pro-poor and pro-people leader at a popular level. This goal was easy to achieve if her policies could be presented as instruments that were tough on big business. On 18 December 1969, the Indian Parliament passed the Monopolies and Restrictive Practices Act that effectively imposed an asset ceiling on industrial houses at Rs 20 crore. Any further expansion by an industry which was already above that cap would be subject to government clearance. Among the other key objectives of the new law were: control of monopolies, the prohibition of monopolistic practices and of restrictive and unfair trade practices.

Another move that helped bolster Gandhi's pro-poor and anti-rich image was her government's decision to abolish the financial benefits that former rulers of provinces and states enjoyed after they had acceded to the Union of India in 1947. These benefits were granted to the rulers and princes of these provinces when the then home minister Vallabhbhai Patel had negotiated with them in 1947 for joining the Indian Union. There were more than 500 such princes and rulers who were granted these benefits, called privy purses, and these were guaranteed under Article 291 of the Indian Constitution. The annual quantum of the privy purses would vary depending on the ruler. For instance, the ex-ruler of Mysore was given an annual privy purse amount of Rs 26 lakh, followed by the ruler of Hyderabad at Rs 20 lakh, the rulers of Travancore and Jaipur at Rs 18 lakh each and the ruler of Patiala at Rs 17 lakh. There were also many other former princes, who would get as low a compensation as Rs 5000 a year.[2]

The practice of paying privy purses to the former rulers of these provinces was an easy target for Indira Gandhi to enhance her image as a prime minister who had strong socialistic leanings and who would not hesitate to strike at the roots of royalty and their privileges. Even before Gandhi, attempts were made to do away with privy purses, but its abolition would have required an amendment to the Constitution. Undeterred, Gandhi went ahead and moved a Constitution amendment bill to scrap the system of the privy purses for former rulers and princes in India. She did not succeed the first time. While the Lok Sabha passed the bill, it was defeated in the Rajya Sabha in 1969. Two years later, Gandhi once again moved the bill to abolish privy purses to amend the Constitution and justified the need for such a step to reduce the government's revenue deficit, which had come under pressure. By the end of 1971, both the houses of Parliament passed the Constitution amendment bill to end the system of privy purses.

Gandhi had successfully converted what her critics described as a breach of promise made in the Constitution into an action that would seemingly bring about social equity and egalitarianism. Her popularity was on the rise, and her position within the Congress party was almost unassailable. The Statement of Objects and Reasons, accompanying the Constitution Amendment Bill, succinctly captured both her political and social goals behind the abolition of privy purses:

> The concept of rulership, with privy purses and special privileges unrelated in any current functions and social purposes, is incompatible with an egalitarian social order. Government have, therefore, decided to

terminate the privy purses and privileges of the Rulers of former Indian States. It is necessary for this purpose, apart from amending the relevant provisions of the Constitution, to insert a new article, therein, so as to terminate expressly the recognition already granted to such Rulers and to abolish privy purses and extinguish all rights, liabilities and obligations in respect of privy purses. Hence this Bill.

With that law, the 26th Amendment to the Indian Constitution, Gandhi reaped a political benefit from an action that actually annulled a privilege that her father, Jawaharlal Nehru, had granted to more than 500 rulers of provinces in pre-Independence India.

More Nationalization

Three more industries were taken over during this phase of Indira Gandhi's turn towards socialism: General insurance, textiles and the petroleum industry. The ten-point economic policy note that Gandhi had circulated at the June 1967 AICC session had underlined the need for nationalizing the general insurance industry. This was perhaps one of the easier decisions for the Gandhi government to implement. The life insurance industry had already been nationalized in 1956.[3] At that point, general insurance was deliberately not nationalized on the ground that it did not have any direct impact on the people and had more to do with business and industry. That thinking, however, changed as Gandhi was battling a new political reality she was confronted with.

The British had set up the first general insurance company in Calcutta in 1850 and it was known by the name of Triton Insurance Company Ltd. In the following 120-odd years, the general insurance industry spread its roots across the country and there were more than 100 private companies offering general insurance policies to businesses and individuals by the time the Gandhi government decided to nationalize them. That was in 1973. All these companies were amalgamated and grouped into four companies—the National Insurance Company, the Oriental Insurance Company, the New India Assurance Company and the United India Insurance Company. A holding company overseeing all these companies was incorporated in 1972 by the name of General Insurance Company, or GIC.

A similar exercise was undertaken for private-sector textile mills that had gone sick. The number of such financially insolvent mills rose to 103 by the end of 1972-73 and the government decided to bail them out by acquiring them in the hope that these could be revived and lakhs of jobs saved. By December 1974, the Sick Textile Undertakings (Nationalization) Act was notified whose purpose was to acquire and transfer these sick textile undertakings under a newly created state-owned entity. The objective of the law was to reorganize and rehabilitate sick textile undertakings so as to 'subserve the interests of the general public by the augmentation of the production and distribution, at fair prices, of different varieties of cloth and yarn, and for matters connected therewith or incidental thereto'. The total compensation paid to the owners of these 103 textile mills was estimated at about Rs 46 crore.

The Takeover of Oil

The third big nationalization effort initiated by the Indira Gandhi government in this phase pertained to the petroleum industry. Oil companies in India were controlled mostly by American and British companies and their dominance continued till at least the end of the 1950s. The Industrial Policy Resolution of 1956 had clearly indicated that the petroleum sector would be the exclusive preserve of the State and all future expansion and development in this sector would be undertaken by the public sector. However, the domestic oil sector required technical collaboration from Western firms to undertake development on its own. The nature of British and American oil companies was such that India did not expect any technical assistance from them in this area. The option that India exercised was to tie up with the Soviet Union and Romania for developing its oil sector. But collaboration with the Soviet Union in the oil sector did not continue beyond a point, partly because the US companies decided to extend a helping hand and partly because the Soviet technologies had their own limitations in certain sectors of the oil industry. For instance, Soviet expertise in offshore oil exploration and production was far less advanced than that available in the US.

The strained relations between the Indian government and the foreign oil companies operating in India owed their origins to the realization of the Indian political leadership that the country was far too dependent on the latter. India's oil industry was effectively controlled by a few foreign oil companies like Burmah-Shell, Standard-Vacuum and Caltex. The writing was on the wall for these foreign companies when the Indian government gave vent to its intentions—first in the industrial policy of 1948 and later in 1956—that the State would like to see all new facilities in the petroleum industry to be set up in the public sector.[4] The foreign companies realized their days in India were numbered. However, in spite of the change in the policy, India remained tied to a colonial oil-supply system in which India could import its petroleum products only from Sterling-area countries, which meant India had to make payments in dollars or pounds. Recognizing the hardships in paying for oil in dollars, India considered the option of reaching out to the oil companies to explore the feasibility of setting up a refinery in the country to reduce India's dependence on imports of petroleum products. However, there were not too many takers of this approach within the country. Many experts advised the government that reaching out to foreign oil companies and requesting them to set up refineries in India would not bear fruit.

However, the foreign companies operating in India had expressed their willingness to set up two refineries in the country provided that they could sell the products at a price that was 10 per cent higher than the price at which they would be available in the international market. That was in 1949. For good reasons, the Indian government spurned such offers and the relations between the foreign oil companies and the Indian government reached a new low.

Two years later, international developments in West Asia changed the foreign oil companies' minds once again. Iran, where these foreign companies had a huge presence, decided in 1951 to nationalize the British Petroleum-controlled oil refinery in Abadan, Anglo-Iranian Oil Company, and expelled other Western companies from other oil refineries in the city. Supplies of petroleum products to India from Sterling areas (markets with which India would trade using Pound Sterling as the currency) became a problem and the Western companies also feared that in such a situation Iran might make inroads into the Indian market. Burmah-Shell and Standard-Vacuum decided to extend an olive branch and set up a refinery each between 1954 and 1957 near Bombay. Another refinery was being built by Caltex in Visakhapatnam.

Even after the setting up of these refineries, the relations between the Indian government and the foreign oil companies saw no significant improvement. The first note of discord surfaced over the crude oil discovered in 1953 at the Naharkatiya oilfield near Dibrugarh in Assam.[5] The government was keen that the crude oil from Naharkatiya must be processed under a joint production arrangement with Burmah Oil. In other words, Burmah Oil was denied the exclusive rights over refining or marketing of the oil from Naharkatiya. Burmah Oil retaliated and suspended all exploration activities in India. This decision was prompted by the government's thinking that such oil assets should be exploited in the state sector as part of its policy on developing the hydrocarbons sector keeping in mind the strategic goal of building domestic capacity in this area. Burmah Oil, on the other hand, was naturally disappointed as it felt cheated out of an asset it wanted to exploit and through that expand its presence in the Indian market. The second note of discord arose out of the government's charge against the foreign oil companies regarding the pricing of the imported oil. The government said the foreign companies were charging a price for imported oil that was much higher than could be justified by any yardstick. Complicating the situation further, these oil companies were not in favour of refining the Soviet crude oil that the Indian government had by then begun to import at relatively better and easier terms. With impatience with the foreign oil companies running high as they were not too keen on either expanding their refineries capacity in India or training Indian engineers for refineries, the government decided in 1958 to set up Indian Refineries Limited in the state sector, which in the next few years was able to set up, with Soviet and Romanian assistance, new refineries at Noonmati near Guwahati in Assam, Barauni in Bihar and Koyali in Gujarat. Making life more difficult for western foreign oil companies in India, the government told them that no permission would be granted to them to build new refineries in the country unless they agreed to offer the Indian government a majority shareholding in them. It became clear that just as oil influenced global politics, the reverse also was true in India.

It was under these circumstances that the government decided to set up the Indian Oil Company in 1959, with the primary objective of supplying petroleum products to Indian public-sector enterprises to meet their demand. Gradually, its role expanded and it was entrusted with the responsibility of selling petroleum products of state refineries. After a short period of relative stability, the domestic oil market was once again disrupted by a price war triggered by the foreign oil companies in India. This was in August 1961. The foreign oil companies were uncomfortable with the rapidly rising imports of oil by India from the Soviet Union and undercut prices quoted by Indian Oil, which retaliated with even lower prices. As a result, it was faced with margin pressure, made worse by its storage problems. The western foreign oil companies soon realized that it was a losing battle as the government of the day had decided to side with Indian Oil Company as it was driven by the national considerations of allowing an Indian company to secure and preserve its dominance in the market. The government also placed a cap on the foreign companies' marketing share, which was linked to their share in the domestic refining capacity.

The early 1960s saw further consolidation of Indian oil companies and marginalization of the foreign oil players. Indian Refineries Limited, with its three refineries, was merged with Indian Oil Company in 1964. The merged company was rechristened Indian Oil Corporation, which now was in the business of both marketing petroleum products and refining oil. The primacy of Indian Oil Corporation was also ensured with the government deciding that all future refinery ventures would have to sell their products through its marketing network. Not only that, the government prohibited imports of crude oil and petroleum products by private companies and made IOC the exclusive agency for importing petroleum products, including crude oil, and distributing them to other refineries or companies in the Indian market. It was becoming clear that closer ties with the Soviet Union and India's increasing reliance on oil imports from that country led to a set of economic policies that gave rise to state controls in more areas of the economy, including the oil sector. If Western oil companies had to set up refineries in India, they had to partner the Indian government. Thus, in 1963, the Indian government, Phillips Petroleum Company of the US, and Duncan Brothers & Company, an Indian firm, joined hands to set up Cochin Refineries and started refining oil from 1966. Similarly, Madras Refineries (later renamed as Chennai Refineries) was set up in 1965, where the Indian government had a share of 74 per cent, with AMOCO of the US and National Iranian Oil Company of Iran, holding 13 per cent shares each.[6]

The frosty relationship between foreign oil companies and the Indian government continued even in the early 1970s. Nevertheless, foreign oil companies maintained their dominance in the Indian oil sector until the mid-1970s. As explained earlier, many minor problems arose in the way these foreign oil companies were operating in India. There were irritants arising out of their pricing policies and the margins of profit they were hoping to earn from their operations in India. But there was a new trigger in October 1973, when the OPEC decided to cut oil supplies to the US and Western countries and jacked up global crude oil prices.

One of the consequences was the Indira Gandhi government's decision to nationalize the three foreign oil companies that were still operating their refineries in India. The response from the foreign oil companies was of shock as their worst fears of growing Soviet influence on the Indian economy were coming true. They also apprehended that the Indian government would continue to adopt socialistic policies. Caltex and Esso were quick to decide on leaving India as a market, but Burmah-Shell explored the options of staying on in the Indian market even as a minority partner in the ventures that had been launched in the country. The government did not accept the proposal. On the other hand, Caltex and Standard-Vacuum faced their own internal organizational challenges and were quick to quit India, though they retained their linkages through crude oil supplies.

The first to go was Esso, which had a 26 per cent stake in Hindustan Petroleum. In 1974, the Indian Parliament passed the Esso (Acquisition of Undertakings in India) Act, 1974, that would allow the government to take over the assets and business run by Esso Eastern Inc. The stated objective of the takeover was to ensure coordinated distribution and utilization of petroleum products marketed by Esso Eastern Inc. in India. Burmah-Shell was the next company to exit when a similar law was passed in 1976. A year later, in 1977, another law was passed by Parliament to nationalize the businesses of Caltex—the third foreign oil company to be affected by the government's nationalization drive.

On 28 November 1975, The New York edition of the *New York Times*[7] carried a small news item that brought out how India had said goodbye to foreign oil companies. Datelined New Delhi, the report filed on 27 November 1975 stated:

> The government announced today that Burmah Shell, the British-owned oil company in India, would be taken over at the start of the new year. An agreement, signed last night, provides for 100 per cent acquisition of the company, the largest foreign oil operator in India, which owns a 6-million tonne refinery and a vast network of gasoline stations. The take-over is the second of a foreign oil company here. An Exxon subsidiary was taken over by the Indian Government two years ago. Burmah Shell would be paid adequate compensation, official sources said as was Exxon. Negotiations for the take-over of Caltex, the third oil company here, would begin soon, they said. But with the acquisition of Burmah Shell, the government brings under its control 95 per cent of the entire petroleum industry in the country.

There is little doubt that Indira Gandhi was the primary force behind the series of disruptions that were unleashed in just about six years from 1969 to 1975. The economic disruption they caused in a wide range of sectors of the Indian businesses and economy was actually a response to a political challenge to Gandhi. A potential political disruption was averted through economic disruption that delayed by at least a couple of decades India's eventual turn to private enterprise and competition. But the sustained manner in which Gandhi used economic policy disruptions to achieve political goals will have few parallels. What is remarkable is that she managed to get around her a set of key advisers who helped execute her ideas and offered justification for the steps she took during those years. While those advisers had reasons to believe in the economic merit of the steps they endorsed like nationalization of banks, Gandhi chose to adopt them initially for her own political survival and then to strengthen her position within the Congress and the government.

The importance of the influence of people like Kumaramangalam and Haksar, as well as the ideological force exerted on her by political leaders like Chandra Shekhar, is difficult to ignore. Once those influences were over or when these personalities ceased to hold any sway over her or when she saw that the potential political benefits of such Left-of-Centre economic policies were on the wane, Indira Gandhi looked like a different political leader. She lost little time in abandoning those policies on nationalization and state control. Instead, she embraced more market-friendly economic policies. When she returned to power, after the Emergency, and again assumed charge as prime minister in 1980, her economic policies changed direction, ushering in the first phase of liberalization, encouraging foreign investment, moderating import duties and relaxing industrial licensing policies. Gandhi's nationalization drive was the outcome of a political necessity and the influence of her political colleagues and advisers.

CHAPTER 10

INDIA'S NEW DISRUPTION

For most Indians, 19 October 1973 does not ring a bell. But this was the day when a decision taken by twelve members of the OPEC fundamentally altered the way India would manage its economy for all times to come. That day at Vienna, OPEC decided to place an embargo on oil exports to the United States and raise prices of crude oil. In six months or so, oil prices spiked by over 300 per cent. The primary reason for the OPEC countries placing an embargo on exports of oil to the US was because the latter had intervened in the West Asian war between Israel on the one hand and Syria and Egypt on the other. The US intervention tilted the balance in the war in favour of Israel. The OPEC decision was a retaliatory move.

India, among many other countries, was a major sufferer. Its dependence on crude oil imports to meet its energy requirements was almost 65 per cent. Even after the OPEC embargo was lifted, oil prices remained elevated. A new uncertainty in the global oil economy was introduced. Whenever OPEC, which accounted for a large chunk of global oil production and exports, decided to cut supplies or production, prices shot up. The disruption to the Indian economy was huge. Fresh from a victory in its war with Pakistan, which led to the creation of Bangladesh, India was politically resilient. But its economy was a victim of global oil politics played by OPEC.

The decision of OPEC in 1973 was its first big action since its formation in 1960. Five oil producing and exporting countries—Iran, Iraq, Kuwait, Saudi Arabia and Venezuela—had signed an agreement in Baghdad in September 1960. OPEC's mission was to 'coordinate and unify the petroleum policies of its member countries and ensure the stabilisation of oil markets in order to secure an efficient, economic and regular supply of petroleum to consumers, a steady income to producers and a fair return on capital for those investing in the petroleum industry'.[1] Shorn of the jargon and niceties of the phrases used to describe its mission, OPEC was essentially meant to galvanize joint action from the major oil-producing and -exporting countries to secure higher prices for a raw material they knew was finite and would not last long. Hence, they recognized the need to raise the price of crude oil so that they could make the most of their non-renewable natural resources.

The idea of regulating oil supplies in order to protect the producers' income was so appealing that by 1962, three more countries—Qatar, Indonesia and Libya—joined OPEC. And by the time OPEC took that momentous decision to impose an embargo on oil supplies to the US in October 1973, four more countries—the United Arab Emirates, Algeria, Nigeria and Ecuador—had joined the group. Four more countries joined OPEC—Gabon in 1975, Angola in 2007, Equatorial Guinea in 2017 and Congo in 2018—but in 2016, Indonesia suspended its membership for the second time since it joined OPEC in 1962. With fifteen member-countries, OPEC by now controlled over 42 per cent of the world's total oil supplies, 61 per cent of total oil exports and 80 per cent of proven oil reserves. During the early years of its existence, OPEC did not have much of a say or role in the way international crude oil prices behaved. But things began looking up during the early 1970s, when first the international demand for crude oil went up and simultaneously the domestic production of oil in the US declined.

Two sets of developments, no less significant in terms of their potential for causing major international disruptions in the world economic order, had led to the further hardening of oil prices. In a dramatic move, US President Richard Nixon decided in 1971 that he would take the dollar off the gold standard. This was a reversal of a policy that the US had adopted in 1944 in the wake of the Bretton Woods arrangement that among many other things also led to the creation of the World Bank and the IMF to restore economic order and fuel growth in the aftermath of the Second World War. On 15 August 1971, after a couple of days of intense consultation with his economic advisers and senior officials of his government, President Nixon announced what is by now known as the Nixon shock or the New Economic Policy.[2] It marked the start of a process to end the Bretton Woods system of fixed exchange rates, which had come into being after the end of the Second World War.

What did the Bretton Woods system seek to achieve? It had envisaged a system where the external values of foreign currencies would be fixed in relation to the US dollar. And the US dollar's value would be expressed in gold at the price of $35 an ounce, fixed by the Congress. In less than two decades, the dollar became overvalued.

This was because a surplus of the US currency—caused by its foreign aid, military spending and foreign investments—created an untenable situation wherein the US did not have enough gold to cover the volume of dollars in circulation globally if measured against a gold price of $35 an ounce. Two of Nixon's predecessors had made valiant attempts to support the dollar and keep the Bretton Woods system alive. John Kennedy and Lyndon Johnson had introduced various measures to achieve the same goal of supporting the dollar and protecting the Bretton Woods system, but had not achieved much success. Some of their steps included the imposition of curbs on foreign investments and foreign aid, in addition to reducing the outflow of dollars. But the dollar's volatility increased as the foreign currency markets sensed that the situation on the ground would someday force the US government to go for a devaluation of the greenback.

Nixon's address on 15 August 1971 was historic.[3] Underlining the need for the US to focus on the challenges in a post-Vietnam world (America had by then taken the first steps towards gradually ending its involvement in the war in Vietnam), Nixon listed out a three-point agenda: 'We must create more and better jobs; we must stop the rise in the cost of living; we must protect the dollar from the attacks of international money speculators.'[4] What followed were tax cuts, a ninety-day freeze on prices and wages and delinking the dollar from the gold standard. Several rounds of negotiations followed between the US and industrialized countries over the question of the dollar's exchange value and after a couple of rounds of devaluation, six countries belonging to the European Community agreed in March 1973 to tie their currencies and jointly float it against the US dollar. This move once again indicated the moving away from the Bretton Woods system of fixed exchange rates and embracing a floating exchange rate system.

Switching the dollar off the gold standard essentially meant that countries could not any longer redeem their dollar held in their reserves in gold. With the dollar being linked to gold under the gold standard policy, anyone holding dollar reserves could actually get from the US an equivalent amount of gold at a pre-determined exchange rate. Once the dollar was off the gold standard, there was a panic reaction from those who had held huge dollar reserves on the understanding that these were equivalent to gold in value. The delinking of dollar from gold, thus, led to an unusual spurt in the demand for gold and its price spiked, even as the value of the dollar went down.

Members of OPEC were hurt in a different way. The international price of crude oil had been kept in the dollar and since the exchange value of the dollar had come down, exports of OPEC countries suffered in terms of a lower unit value realization. Indeed, so steep was the decline in the value of the dollar that the OPEC countries even mooted the idea of pegging the price of crude oil to gold, a move that did not have too many takers and was eventually dropped.

A second blow to the OPEC countries came from a series of disturbing geopolitical developments in West Asia. A war between Israel and Egypt—also known as the Yom Kippur War—broke out in October 1973. Egypt, with the assistance of Syria, launched a massive attack on Israel. Around the same time, OPEC countries' oil ministers were meeting in Vienna. In the early days of the war, Egypt and Syria seemed to enjoy an upper hand as Israel found it difficult to respond to the attack. The equation changed somewhat with the US helping Israel with the airlift of arms and military assistance coming in from the Netherlands and Denmark. By 17 October, Israel had regained lost ground and both Egypt and Syria were facing difficulties. Two days later, the US President sought congressional approval of $2.2 billion in emergency military assistance for Israel. That perhaps was the proverbial last straw on the camel's back. On the very same day, OPEC decided to use, for the first time, oil pricing as a political weapon to counter the US and its allies. An embargo on exports of oil to the US, Israel and to their allies was announced, followed by a cut in exports. This led to a spurt in the price of international crude oil.

As Israel refused to withdraw from the territories it had occupied, OPEC maintained its resolve on embargo and the price of crude oil increased in a few days by over 70 per cent from $2.9 a barrel. Egypt, Syria and Israel declared a truce on 25 October 1973, but OPEC allowed its embargo on crude oil supplies to continue till about March 1974. OPEC ministers met in Teheran in December 1973, but there was no relaxation in the controls they had imposed three months ago. Crude oil prices kept rising and by March 1974 they had reached a shockingly high level of $11.65 a barrel.

The gradual rise in international crude oil prices could be attributed to the manner of the OPEC response to the West Asian crisis. OPEC had initially decided in October 1973 that its exports would be reduced by 5 per cent every month till such time Israel evacuated the territories it had occupied during the 1967 Arab–Israeli War. Since there was no response from Israel, OPEC declared a full embargo in December against the US and several other countries.

This gave rise to an international energy crisis that saw in its wake shortages of fuel and even rationing of its distribution through consumer outlets in many markets dependent on foreign oil; such harsh measures were initiated even in the US. US Secretary of State Henry Kissinger's interventions in March 1974 led to the military disengagement between Syria and Israel. OPEC's embargo on supplies of oil to the US and other countries was lifted. But this could hardly soften international crude oil prices. Instead, they kept rising, thanks also to OPEC's periodic announcements and implementation of plans to cut oil output.

The impact of the OPEC embargo on supplies of oil to the US and a rise in crude oil prices on the US economy was not insubstantial. The recession in the US economy from 1973 to 1975 was largely caused by the wage-price controls imposed by Nixon, which compelled businesses to lay off workers to cut costs.

The Federal Reserve's monetary policy is also blamed for the economic slowdown in the US. The Federal Reserve raised and cut interest rates frequently and that led to uncertainty in the business environment. But no less responsible for the recession in the US was the increase in crude oil prices, caused by the embargo enforced by OPEC. Inflation in the US, which was already ruling at around 10 per cent for a few commodities, got worse with rising crude oil prices.

No respite came from domestic oil output from US companies as they were already operating at peak capacity. They could not raise their output any further to meet demand if the US government decided to cut imports of crude oil from OPEC countries. That route—a retaliatory move to impose curbs on imports of crude oil—was also closed. Higher crude oil prices also resulted in a demand compression as consumers, after paying for higher petroleum product prices, had less money at their disposal to buy other goods and services. A crisis of sorts had dawned on the US, dampening consumer confidence even as Americans were getting used to the idea of waiting in long queues to fill petrol in their cars.

Shortage of petroleum products too hit consumer confidence as petrol stations had to often display signs to indicate whether they had petrol in stock. Some states in the US introduced petrol rationing using an innovative odd–even formula—something that residents of Delhi, India, experienced many decades later in 2016 to reduce pollution in the city. Beijing too experienced it in 2008 just before it held the Olympic

Games. But those were measures to counter pollution. What happened in the US in the aftermath of the OPEC decision on raising oil prices was to keep a check on fuel consumption—cars with licence plates ending with odd numbers could buy petrol or diesel only on odd-numbered days and cars with even-numbered licence plates could do so on even-numbered days. That was also the time when the US decided to create a Strategic Petroleum Reserve, which would have adequate crude oil in it to meet domestic consumption for about ninety days. The idea was to ready the nation to meet any fresh challenge that could arise from another OPEC embargo on oil supplies to the US. The national vehicular speed limit was reduced to 55 miles per hour to help curtail consumption of fuel and Nixon introduced the idea of daylight saving time in 1974. The crisis had also prompted the US government to impose fuel economy standards and the creation of the International Energy Agency, an idea that came from none other than Henry Kissinger.[5]

CHAPTER 11

THE SEARCH FOR BLACK GOLD

The oil scene in India in the 1970s was relatively easy, stable and without any complications. Before the OPEC decision of October 1973 sent international crude oil prices soaring, India's dependence on crude oil imports was about 65 per cent of its total requirement in 1972–73. The country's domestic output of crude oil was 7 million tonnes, while imports were estimated at 13 million tonnes. Domestic refineries had the capacity to process and produce 19 million tonnes of petroleum products, but this was not enough to meet domestic consumption. Hence, India had to import 3 million tonnes of petroleum products. For the next two years, India's volume of imports of crude oil and petroleum products did not see any significant increases. Crude oil imports stayed at 14 million tonnes each in 1973–74 and 1974–75, while petroleum product imports for this period were 3 million tonnes and 2 million tonnes, respectively.

The impact of the global oil shock on India's trade balance, however, was substantial, thanks to the sharp rise in the price of international crude oil. Crude oil imports were valued at $266 million in 1972–73, before the OPEC decision on crude oil prices was effected. But in 1973–74, India's crude oil import bill almost trebled to $719 million. India, which enjoyed an overall trade surplus of $136 million in 1972–73, had run up a trade deficit of $554 million in 1973–74. The following year, which bore the brunt of even higher crude oil prices internationally, saw India's oil import bill double to $1.5 billion and the trade deficit too widened to $1.4 billion. India's external economy had faced perhaps its biggest disruption. And the key factor that contributed to this crisis was India's dependence on crude oil imports and the OPEC shock of 1973.

On 20 January 1974, the *New York Times* carried a long report[1] on the second page of its New York edition. The headline of the report said it all: India, Slow to Grasp Oil Crisis, Now Fears Severe Economic Loss. The report began with a dire forecast on the impact of a sharp increase in crude oil prices. This is how it read:

Economists and government officials are now convinced that the rising cost of oil imports places India in a bleak position as the nation is beset by inflation, political dissension, lagging growth, a spiralling population and unchecked poverty. In the aftermath of the decision by Persian Gulf nations to double the posted price of crude oil, the Indian government remains torn by uncertainty about 1974.

Indeed, India's food production took a hit in 1974, a delayed impact of the oil price hike. Indian agriculture had begun riding high on the back of a successful Green Revolution that helped the country's foodgrain output cross the magical mark of 100 million tonnes for the first time in its history. From 99.5 million tonnes in 1969, India's foodgrain output jumped to 108 million tonnes in 1970. In the following years, however, foodgrain output did not maintain steady growth and fell below the 100-million tonne mark during two years—in 1972–73 to 97 million tonnes and to 99.8 million tonnes in 1974–75. The decline in 1974–75 was largely attributed to the OPEC decision to increase crude oil prices. Prices of chemical fertilizers, which are influenced by crude oil prices, rose sharply after the OPEC embargo and supply cut. India's foodgrain output suffered as higher prices of fertilizers discouraged farmers to use them as abundantly as they would have liked. The effectiveness of the hybrid varieties of wheat, which helped usher in the Green Revolution, was crucially dependent on the adequate use of fertilizers, among other things.

The Fifth Five-Year Plan, which was due to be rolled out from 1974, also took a hit. The government decided to redefine its ambitious goals and development expenditure in light of the sudden burden the economy had to bear in the wake of the import burden on account of higher crude oil prices. In 1972–73, India's oil import bill at $266 million was only 10 per cent of its total dollar earnings through exports of about $2.6 billion. But in the next two years, that proportion would get worse at 22 per cent in 1973–74 and an alarmingly high 35 per cent in 1974–75.

Not surprisingly, the Fifth Five-Year Plan document made no secret of the enormity of the oil impact. Its review of the economic situation stated:

The draft Fifth Five-year Plan was formulated in terms of 1972–73 prices and in the context of the economic situation obtaining in the first half of the fiscal year 1973–74. Thereafter, two major developments took place. The inflationary pressures gathered momentum till September 1974 and the balance of payments position worsened due to the steep rise in the prices of imported oil and other materials.

Inflation, measured by the movement in the wholesale price index (WPI), rose from 5.6 per cent in 1971–72 to 10.1 per cent in 1972–73. If that was not alarming enough, the WPI-based inflation rate for the next two years must have been even more unsettling as it skyrocketed to unprecedented levels—20 per cent in 1973–74 and 25 per cent in 1974–75. Consumer price indices for industrial workers and agricultural labourers also showed a similar rise in these two years—20.8 per cent and 21.5 per cent, respectively in 1973–74 and 26.8 per cent and 34.4 per cent in 1974–75. Analysing the inflation data, the government concluded that food articles and industrial raw materials accounted for about two-thirds of the price increase. The pressure on the economy was also felt because of severe drought conditions of 1972–73, followed by shortages of various essential consumer goods and critical raw materials and inputs.

There was no respite for India's balance-of-payments situation either. The requirement of importing huge quantities of foodgrain and the increase in the cost of importing oil, fertilizers, non-ferrous metals and machinery caused stress for the country's meagre foreign-exchange reserves. The value of three main items of imports—food, fertilizers and petroleum—was more than half of the total import bill in 1974–75, compared to just 43 per cent in 1973–74 and 23 per cent in 1972–73. The merchandise goods trade gap—the difference between exports and imports—turned from a surplus of $136 million in 1972–73 to a deficit of $554 million in 1973–74 and $1.4 billion in 1974–75.

In its 1974 report, the IMF did not mince words to forecast the crisis that India could face in the wake of the global oil price increase. It said:

Among countries whose prospective increases in the cost of oil imports loom especially large in relation to reserves or total imports, a number are net importers of cereals. Most of these face adverse non-oil terms of trade shifts from 1973 to 1974, and only a few of them (e.g., Korea) have a recent history of buoyant exports. Although some of these countries may find access to international credit markets to cushion the initial impact of the combined increases in their oil and cereals import bills, it is within this group that some of the most severe problems of readjustment seem likely to arise in 1974. Such problems may be especially acute for countries (e.g., India, Bangladesh, and Sri Lanka) whose own export earnings include relatively substantial amounts from commodities that have not shared strongly in the recent primary commodity price upsurge.[2]

The government was left with no option other than to approach the IMF to meet its deficit on the external account. In 1974–75, India succeeded in obtaining about Rs 485 crore ($610 million) under a special oil facility of the IMF, which it had opened in the wake of the OPEC decision to increase oil prices. The IMF loan helped India prevent any further depletion of its foreign-exchange reserves, which stabilized at around $1325 million in 1973–74 and $1379 million in 1974–75. This was the second time in less than seven years that India had sought recourse to assistance from the IMF—it had got assistance under its compensatory financing facility in November 1967 in the wake of the food crisis.

The Fifth Five-Year Plan responded to the oil crisis through its renewed emphasis on developing the petroleum sector in the country. The government decided to step up the programme for oil exploration and production. The focus was on the most promising oil-bearing areas, so that the results in terms of higher domestic output of crude oil could be realized quickly. There was thus an attempt at channelling the available resources to the development and production of oil from offshore and selected onshore areas in the country.

Bombay High oilfields received special attention from the planners. A time-bound plan was drawn to develop and produce oil from Bombay High to achieve an annual output level of 10 million tonnes by 1980–81. At the time the plan was being framed, the total domestic output of crude oil was barely 7 million tonnes. The outlay for ONGC was also revised upwards, from the earlier Rs 420 crore to Rs 1056 crore. Necessary capacity augmentation for oil refineries also became a thrust area in the revised plan to reduce the country's dependence on imports of petroleum products.

While the OPEC decision of 1973 impacted the Indian economy at the macro level, the ordinary lives of people and activities of businesses also changed significantly. As retail petrol and diesel prices went up, there were fewer cars on the streets of India's major cities. The *New York Times* reported that 'many businessmen and civil servants are using buses for the first time'. Soon, rationing of kerosene supplies was introduced to ensure that the needy sections of society got their fuel. There were also reports that riots over the shortage of petroleum products forced a situation where these had to be distributed from police stations. Farmers were not only complaining about higher prices of fertilizers, which had become scarce, but also found that operating tractors became prohibitively expensive with the price of diesel shooting up. Finance Minister Yashwantrao Chavan was quoted as saying that the increase in oil prices would have 'profound implications' for the Indian economy, just as Agriculture Minister Fakhruddin Ali Ahmed ominously said that India's food production was upset by the energy crisis and this could become worse in the coming years.

The disruption caused by the OPEC decision on oil prices was limited not just to the domestic prices of petroleum products in the country, but had spread wide enough to result in a fall in India's food output, a runaway inflation rate and a fragile balance-of-payments situation. So severe was the impact that the size and focus of the Fifth Five-Year Plan also had to be reoriented in light of the oil shock.

The Nation Responds

Just about four months after the OPEC oil shock, the Oil and Natural Gas Corporation (ONGC), a state-controlled enterprise, had discovered the Bombay High oilfield, which turned out to be the biggest discovery in India. The OPEC decided to enforce its embargo on oil supplies to the US on 19 October 1973 and raise prices of crude oil. On 19 February 1974, oil was struck in Bombay High, about 160 kilometres from the shores of Mumbai and the depth of water at the drilling locations ranged between 75 and 90 metres. The Bombay High structure was delineated with the help of a Russian exploration ship *Academic Arkhangelsk,* while the first well was drilled by an acquired jack-up rig, Sagar Samrat.[3] The role of Bombay High in managing the disruption caused by the OPEC decision to jack up oil prices could hardly be overestimated. There is little doubt that the urgency of ONGC stepping up efforts to explore and produce more oil from domestic sources was triggered largely by the oil shock of October 1973. In the ten years after the Bombay High oil discovery in February 1974, India's total crude oil production rose from 7 million tonnes to 28 million tonnes in 1983–84.

The only companies producing crude oil in undivided India, before India's Independence in 1947, were the Assam Oil Company in the north-east and Attock Oil Company in the north-west. Many international experts had given India up as a region whose sedimentary basins could bear any oil or other mineral resources. But efforts were stepped up to develop hydrocarbon resources soon after India's Independence. The Industrial Policy Statement of 1948 had underlined the need for developing the hydrocarbons industry, but allowed private companies to operate in oil exploration and production. The Assam Oil Company continued to produce oil at Digboi in Assam and Oil India Limited, a joint venture between the Indian government and Burmah Oil Company, had opened two fields in Assam. Another joint venture between the Indian government and Standard Vacuum Oil Company of the US was engaged in exploration work in West Bengal.

In 1955, the government decided to develop oil and natural gas resources in different parts of the country as state-sector projects. This was a year before the Indian government unveiled its Industrial Policy Resolution that reserved many industries for the state sector, including oil exploration and production. Thus, the Oil and Natural Gas Directorate was set up in 1955, which kicked off India's indigenous efforts at developing a robust oil and gas sector. The focus was more on scientific research to discover oil and gas, and the directorate hired a good number of geoscientists from the Geological Survey of India. A delegation, led by the then minister of natural resources, K.D. Malviya, visited several countries to study and understand the oil industry there so that adequate training to Indian professionals be imparted to give the domestic industry a kick-start. Foreign experts from the US, West Germany (West and East Germany were two separate countries at the time), Romania and the erstwhile Union of Soviet Socialist Republics (USSR) visited India to discuss ways to help India's nascent oil industry.

At the end of those consultations, the Nehru government opted for the plan for geological surveys and drilling operations submitted by the Soviet Union and incorporated it in the Second Five-Year Plan, which began in 1956–57 and ended in 1960–61. The choice of the Soviet Union as partners in India's oil industry development was also indicative of the country's political tilt that had become evident by then. It was a tilt that was also a political necessity. The attempts of Malviya and Nehru to develop the oil and gas sector in India did not receive much support from Western countries; the only country that extended its helping hand was the Soviet Union, which agreed to train Indian scientists and engineers in addition to sending experts and equipment to India on soft rupee-payment terms. The USSR also helped India set up two state-of-the-art research and development institutes for petroleum exploration and drilling technology, which built indigenous capacity to undertake oil exploration and drilling. Indeed, ONGC's discoveries in Gujarat, Assam and Bombay High were largely possible because of the support India got from the Soviet Union.[4]

The irony of this association with the Soviet Union was that it came under stress as India grew its domestic crude oil production and embarked on new fields, including those in offshore blocks. Subsequent efforts by ONGC to explore oil and gas in other blocks in the Arabian Sea and also in the Krishna Godavari Basin in the Bay of Bengal were made with the help of technology provided by Western countries.

The Soviet Union was not thrilled with Western countries helping ONGC in India's offshore exploration efforts. It felt marginalized even as a few rounds of exploration contracts were awarded to companies from the West. This was largely because the Soviet Union did not have technology as advanced as the Western companies had for offshore exploration. To salvage the situation, an Indo-Soviet cooperation agreement in the oil exploration sector was signed and many onshore sites were handed over for exploration in collaboration with the USSR. Such efforts, though, did not bear much fruit, and in any case, the collaboration almost fell apart as the USSR disintegrated into many different countries and India embraced market-based reforms and also moved closer to the United States in the early 1990s.

The launch of the ambitious Second Five-Year Plan, on the other hand, laid the foundation in the country for a strong oil and gas sector, capable of reducing the dependence on crude oil imports and insulating the Indian economy against sharp fluctuations in international crude oil prices. Thus, the Nehru government quickly recognized that the structure of a directorate was not adequate for the kind of rapid development that was required in the oil sector. In August 1956, the Oil and Natural Gas Directorate was converted into a commission, with enhanced powers to access finance and technology. Renamed as the Oil and Natural Gas Commission, it was made into a statutory body with the enactment of a law by Parliament in October 1959. ONGC was now mandated by law to 'plan, promote, organise and implement programmes for development of petroleum resources and the production and sale of petroleum and petroleum products produced by it'. ONGC found new resources in Assam and established new oil exploration areas in the Cambay basin in Gujarat. And finally, its offshore explorations that began in the early 1970s gave quick results and oil was discovered in Bombay High in February 1974. The rapid rise in the importance of the ONGC is certainly one of the many outcomes of the OPEC decision to hike oil prices.

It is worth noting that Indian geologists working towards improving the domestic availability of crude oil played a crucial role. As Vijay L. Kelkar, an economist with a long stint with the government and a vast experience of having dealt with India's oil sector, points out, every drop of oil was discovered in India, thanks to the hard work put in by Indian geologists associated with different government departments and organizations.[5] Kelkar also believed that India's march towards developing domestic oil resources would have been rapid if only the country's politics surrounding Assam had not played a spoilsport. The problems around resource nationalism came in the way of faster development and commercial exploitation of oil and gas in that region.

An Enduring Disruption

The OPEC decision in October 1973 fundamentally changed the way India's macroeconomic policies were to be framed in the coming decades. This is one disruption whose impact continues to influence economic policies in India. Two factors are responsible for this.

One, the OPEC oil shock of 1973 was not an isolated or solitary event. It cut production many more times in the 1970s, and repeated as also carried out these threats on several occasions in subsequent decades. Apart from the 1973 decision, oil prices were raised again in 1979 in the wake of the Iranian revolution as Iran cut oil production drastically. Global oil production fell by about 10 per cent and oil prices jumped to $35 a barrel. Between 1980 and 1986, there was a lull in oil prices as the global economy slowed, depressing demand for petroleum products, and conservation efforts picked up reining in consumption levels across the developed world in particular.

The sense of relief from the fall in crude oil prices disappeared in 1990 and again by the turn of the century. In 1990, crude oil prices crossed the $23 mark in the wake of the Gulf War, with Iraq invading Kuwait. Once that crisis was over, oil prices settled down at lower levels and by 1998 they were down to about $12 a barrel. But they started rising again by the turn of the century and reached a high of $97 a barrel by 2008. The global financial crisis of 2008 saw the oil prices soften a bit, but again they rose to $111 a barrel by 2012.

The volatility in international crude oil prices continues unabated, though at a price range of $70–80 a barrel it seems to be at a point where OPEC sees the price stabilizing; any price higher than this makes the alternative development of shale oil (hydrocarbons extracted from types of sedimentary rock) look attractive and can pull down the prices. It is this volatility and the assessment that crude oil prices can shoot up any time that has made countries like India permanently vulnerable to disruptions and forced them to frame policies that could absorb such shocks.

The second issue that makes international crude oil prices such an important factor for India's economic policies is the country's continued dependence on imports. In spite of the progress made by ONGC in the 1970s by striking oil in Bombay High, and a few other discoveries by ONGC and other enterprises in different basins—both offshore and onshore—during the subsequent decades, India's domestic crude oil production is woefully short of its rapidly growing demand for domestic consumption.

Till 1990–91, India still managed to produce more crude oil at home than its total imports— crude oil production was estimated at 33 million tonnes, compared to imports of 22 million tonnes. Higher growth after the economic reforms of 1991–92 saw India's demand for crude oil rise at a rapid pace even as its domestic crude oil production plateaued. Crude oil production from Indian wells rose to a high of 38 million tonnes by 2010–11 before dipping to 36 million tonnes in 2017–18. In contrast, import of crude oil skyrocketed to 164 million tonnes in 2010–11, and further up to 220 million tonnes in 2017–18. It is ironical that while the OPEC price hike of 1973 was a positive trigger for a rise in domestic crude oil production in the 1970s and the 1980s, the same did not hold true for the subsequent decades. Policy failure on boosting exploration activities in subsequent decades has proved to be costly for India. Attempts were made to invite domestic as well as foreign players to undertake the exploration of oil as well as natural gas in Indian geological reserves. But success was limited with only a handful of private operators striking oil and gas. Even those few discoveries were mired in controversies, and subsequent policies, even though they were liberalized and made more attractive with higher incentives, failed to make much headway in promoting domestic oil and gas exploration and production. This only increased India's dependence on imports of crude oil and gas—a dependence that continues to worry the country's energy experts and planners.

India's trade policies, too, were impacted by the OPEC developments. Oil has remained the permanent spoilsport in India's foreign trade performance.

With the cost of oil imports going up, petroleum products, including crude oil, continued to account for the largest chunk in India's import basket. India's exports were never enough to take care of the country's oil imports. The problems of a widening trade deficit got worse after the crude oil price increased in 1973. Take out oil trade—both exports and imports of crude oil and petroleum products—and India's foreign trade performance for many years in the wake of the OPEC decision of 1973 showed that the overall trade deficit remained marginal in the first three decades after the oil shock. Indeed, in as many as eighteen years between 1970–71 and 2003–04, non-oil trade for India has seen a surplus. The oil factor, therefore, definitely cast its long shadow on India's trade policy, biasing it more towards imposing controls on overall imports to reduce the impact of the rising oil trade deficit on the balance of trade. If policies towards exports promotion did not have too many takers in the government of the 1970s and the 1980s, oil prices certainly were responsible to a great extent. A trade policy shift aimed at promoting exports did take place in the 1990s, but the Indian economy had been set back by at least two decades.

The government's finances too took a hit on account of the OPEC-led oil price disruption. Initially, after the increase in the price of imported crude oil and petroleum products, the Indian government decided to absorb a part of the additional burden on its finances and passed on only a part of the higher costs to the consumers. The government's pre-Budget Economic Survey for 1973–74, tabled in Parliament in February 1974, summed up its approach to retail pricing of petroleum products in the wake of the crude oil shock in these words:[6]

Mineral oils offer a prime example whereby higher import costs can upset the domestic price structure. Up to October 1973, the pricing policy for petroleum products was so designed as to raise prices to the extent warranted by changes in the price of crude, while at the same time, insulating, to the maximum extent possible, a mass consumption item like kerosene and important inputs like naphtha for fertilisers and diesel oil for transport (including agricultural tractors). Anticipating further increase in the price of crude oil and the need to moderate the growth of consumption of petroleum products, the excise duties on motor spirit and kerosene were raised in November 1973 so as to restrict consumption. However, no increase was effected in the price of naphtha and the price of HSD was brought down slightly to bring it into parity with that of kerosene.

Thus, there was no government attempt to soften the impact of higher crude oil prices on retail prices of petrol and other petroleum products. The government, however, did try to reduce the prices of kerosene, naphtha and diesel, but overall, the principle of pass-through of higher crude oil prices was followed. This fuelled inflation and contributed to popular resentment and unrest—developments that the opposition political parties used effectively to mount a united challenge against the Indira Gandhi government in 1975. What, therefore, cannot be ruled out is the causal connection between rising petroleum product prices contributing to higher inflation and Indira Gandhi's response to the opposition political parties' challenge to her government by declaring a state of internal emergency in 1975.

But as the crude oil prices began declining from 1980, the government decided to introduce an Oil Pool Account system. This account was maintained by the government. The surplus of the oil companies as a result of the falling crude oil prices was deposited in the Oil Pool Account. The objective was to use the Oil Pool Account resources to reimburse the oil companies when crude oil prices rose, putting pressure on their finances. This became necessary as the government had kept retail prices of petroleum products under an administered pricing mechanism (APM). With reforms underway, the APM for the oil sector was dismantled from 2002–03, and the government's subsidy provisions for the oil sector became even more explicit. With rising oil prices and the government's failure to pass on the entire increase in international crude oil prices to consumers, the burden of petroleum subsidies kept rising—from Rs 6265 crore in 2002–03 to Rs 38,371 crore in 2010–11. With the decision to link prices of petrol and diesel to the international market in phases from June 2010, the overall petroleum subsidy burden was kept under check and was estimated at only Rs 24,480 crore in 2017–18. It was clear that the pattern of international crude oil prices had continued to affect the government's finances even after almost three decades of economic reforms.

There was also an indirect positive fallout of the OPEC oil shock of 1973 for the Indian economy. With the West Asian economies benefitting from higher price realization from their oil, there was a spurt in construction activities in that region. Indians and Indian companies were quick to exploit this as an opportunity. Several Indian companies explored project exports as a way to earn foreign exchange from the oil-rich countries in West Asia. While this boosted the country's export earnings, there was an added benefit by way of rising remittances that Indians working in

West Asia began sending back home. From $430 million of remittances in 1975, India's remittance income rose to $642 million in 1976 and further to $2.7 billion by 1980. The remittances saw a bigger increase from 1991 onwards, when India relaxed its exchange control rules by which dollar remittances could realize higher rupee earnings. Economic reforms and more Indian companies and Indians spreading their networks across the world boosted remittances, which eventually made India the world's number one country, receiving close to $70 billion by 2017. But the OPEC oil price increase of 1973 was the first trigger for India's gains from dollar remittances.

The disrupter for India in its oil economy was not an Indian entity. It was a combination of factors, whose roots lay in foreign lands. US President Richard Nixon deciding to take his country's currency off the gold standard and supporting Israel in its defence against attack from Syria and Egypt were the key factors that led to the OPEC response by way of increased oil prices. For India, the impact of the disruption was a mixed bag. While it contributed to the country's resolve to undertake more rigorous and extensive oil exploration and production to reduce its dependence on imported oil, the higher oil prices also had an adverse impact on government finances and balance of payments. No other external disruption has had such a long-lasting influence on Indian economic policies, particularly with regard to public finance.

CHAPTER 12

TOPPLED IN COURT

For three separate reasons, not entirely unconnected with each other, 12 June 1975 was an important day for Prime Minister Indira Gandhi. Early in the morning, she received the news that D.P. Dhar, her adviser and trusted lieutenant for years, had died of a massive heart attack. Dhar at that time was India's ambassador to the Soviet Union. He had just been sent to Moscow for his second stint after he served the Gandhi government in different capacities including as a minister. He played a key role in India's war with Pakistan that led to the secession of East Pakistan, which eventually led to the creation of Bangladesh. He also played a crucial role in the formulation of India's friendship treaties with both Bangladesh and the Soviet Union.

By the evening, the same day, news about a Congress debacle began trickling in from Gujarat, where the Assembly elections had been held earlier and the results were due that day. The Janata Morcha, a coalition of political parties, led by Jayaprakash Narayan, an Opposition leader, and Morarji Desai, who was then the leader of the Congress (O), was ahead of the Indira Gandhi-led Congress. A defeat for her party in the state looked certain and that would be a big setback not only for the party but also for Indira Gandhi personally, as she had led the entire Congress campaign in the Gujarat Assembly elections.[1]

Between these two developments—one in the morning and other in the evening, another piece of news had broken around 10 a.m. The Allahabad High Court passed an order that unseated Indira Gandhi as a member of Parliament. The high court judge, Justice Jagmohan Lal Sinha, held her guilty of having used the services of a government servant and securing the help of some Uttar Pradesh government officers for campaigns during her Lok Sabha elections in 1971.

Even as Gandhi was scanning Justice Sinha's judgment that day, she could not have missed the deep irony behind the direct or indirect involvement of his close adviser for many years in developments that led to her conviction. Parmeshwar Narayan Haksar was a diplomat who worked with Gandhi for almost six years—first as secretary, then as her principal secretary, and then was hired by her to be the deputy chairman of the Planning Commission for almost two years. On 13 January 1971, Yashpal Kapoor met Haksar, who was then her principal secretary, with a request that he be relieved immediately so that he could work for Gandhi's election campaign. Haksar apparently accepted the resignation orally and Kapoor began campaigning for Gandhi, even though the official order accepting his resignation was issued only on 25 January 1971.

However, this version was contested by others, who believed that the resignation letter was backdated and there was a technical violation in the election code that a government servant cannot work for the election campaign of a candidate. Her joint secretary in the prime minister's secretariat then, Bishan Narain Tandon, wrote in his diary:

> The truth is that Kapoor had submitted his resignation only on 25 January but he had backdated it to 13 January. Action was taken on it on the 25th. The official noting makes it clear that there was nothing to suggest that its acceptance had been mooted before the 25th. The noting is followed by the signatures of two officials and then by Haksar's. He accepted the noting and if the resignation had been accepted on the 13–14th, he would have written so on the file. But he wrote no such thing and signed the file. Later Seshan (private secretary to Gandhi) conveyed the PM's approval. In the light of these notings and signatures, there can be no doubt left in anyone's mind that Kapoor's resignation had not been accepted before the 25th.[2]

Justice Sinha of the Allahabad High Court also believed that Gandhi was guilty of having obtained the services of a government servant for her election campaign work and cited that as one of the reasons for declaring her election in 1971 void. Haksar was also summoned by Justice Sinha and his answers in the court on 12 February 1975 could not change the judge's view on the matter. Jairam Ramesh cites this instance in his book *Intertwined Lives: P.N. Haksar and Indira Gandhi* and also notes a deeper irony behind the development. It was Haksar again who in February 1972 had advised Gandhi to clear the appointment of Justice Sinha as a permanent judge in Allahabad High Court. Three years later, the same judge would deliver a verdict that would nullify Gandhi's elections.

Four elements in the Allahabad High Court judgment stood out starkly: One, the election of Indira Gandhi had been declared void. Two,

Gandhi was disqualified from seeking re-election for a period of six years. Three, the high court order did not take immediate effect and had been stayed for twenty days. This was because immediately after the high court judgment, Gandhi's counsel had sought time for appeal and a twenty-day grace period was granted before the order could take effect so that she could file an appeal. Four, on the expiry of the twenty-day period or as soon as an appeal against the high court order was filed in the Supreme Court and admitted, the order on declaring Gandhi's election void would cease to be effective. Technically, therefore, Gandhi could have simply gone in for an appeal and stayed on as the prime minister and hoped that the apex court would rule in her favour, which is what broadly happened later. But not before Gandhi took the pre-emptive and unprecedented action of declaring an internal emergency in the country on the night of 25 June 1975.

A Fortnight of Intense Political Drama and Conspiracy

The fortnight that preceded the proclamation of the Emergency saw how Indira Gandhi and her close advisers set in motion a series of actions to create an impression that the prime minister had been wronged by the Allahabad High Court judgment and that she should not resign ignoring the demands that were made by the opposition parties and their leaders. Soon after the judgment, Delhi's Lieutenant Governor, Krishan Chand, got a call from the prime minister's house. Chand, an Indian Civil Service (ICS) officer, decided to send his secretary, Navin Chawla, to be present at the prime minister's residence.

Chawla, a young 1968-batch Indian Administrative Service (IAS) officer then, would later become a favourite bureaucrat of the Congress and be made, amidst controversy, the chief election commissioner by the Congress-led United Progressive Alliance (UPA) government in 2009 just before the general elections were due to be held. Chand, however, died under tragic circumstances soon after the submission of the report by the Shah Commission of Inquiry, which examined the circumstances under which the Emergency was imposed. The Indian Express carried the following news item on its front page on 11 July 1978:

> The body of Krishan Chand, former Lt-Governor of Delhi, was found in an abandoned well near Shahpur Jat village. The body bore no signs of injury. A note was found stuck to a brown shoe at the periphery of the

well. Another note was found in a personal file in Chand's bedroom. The note found at the well said: "I am fed up with life. I have decided to commit suicide by drowning myself. Jeena zillat se ho to marna accha hai (it is better to die than live a life of humiliation). The note from his bedroom addressed his wife Seeta and said he was depressed due to the pending investigation into his acts during the Emergency.[3]

But what Chand learnt from Chawla that day after the latter's meeting at the prime minister's house indicated the shape of things to come after the Allahabad High Court order. And this is what he learnt from Chawla: 'In order to cope up with the law and order situation that might develop from the threatened Opposition rallies, it was decided to organise rallies in support of the Prime minister; and for this purpose people had to be collected from various places.'[4] In his deposition before the Shah Commission, which examined the circumstances under which the Emergency was imposed, Chand stated that he was told that 'public utility services would also be mobilised for the purpose. These services included New Delhi Municipal Committee, Delhi Transport Corporation and Delhi Electric Supply Undertaking.'[5] He further stated that 'rallies and bringing of people to the House of the Prime Minister continued after the 12th of June in order to show support to the Prime minister'.[6]

Delhi Transport Corporation, or DTC, was at that time a Central government undertaking. Between 12 and 25 June 1975, there was a sharp rise in the number of DTC buses booked by private parties, mainly by the AICC and the Delhi Pradesh Congress Committee (DPCC). These buses were used by the Congress party to ferry its supporters from across the city and the adjoining towns to take part in rallies held in support of Indira Gandhi. The report of the Shah Commission of Inquiry noted that the instructions for booking these buses came from Navin Chawla, a government officer posted as secretary to Delhi's Lieutenant Governor. Even after two years of those bookings, the AICC and the DPCC did not clear their entire dues to the DTC—the outstanding amount was still as high as Rs 4 lakh.

The inconvenience caused to the ordinary citizens was immense and the misuse of public utilities for a political party's gains was brazen and unprecedented. On 13 June 1975, DTC had taken off its entire fleet of 983 buses and diverted them to the prime minister's residence, to help the Congress ferry its supporters to take part in the Congress rallies. Residents of Haryana, Punjab, Rajasthan and Uttar Pradesh were sent in vehicles 'commandeered by the state authorities' for this purpose. On the same day, about 800 to 900 employees of Delhi Electric Supply Undertaking were persuaded to join the rally outside Gandhi's residence. Another rally took place on 20 June, where as many as 497 DTC buses, over half its entire fleet, were requisitioned by the Congress to transport its supporters to the residence of the prime minister. DTC rules allowed only a maximum of ninety-five buses to be booked by private parties on any given day.

Even as the Congress was organizing rallies almost on a daily basis in support of its leader, the Opposition leaders, spearheaded by Jayaprakash Narayan, decided to hold a rally on 24 June to renew their demand for Gandhi to resign. This set off a chain reaction among the close advisers to Gandhi. Sometime around the evening of 23 June, Gandhi's personal assistant, R.K. Dhawan, indicated to Lieutenant Governor Krishan Chand that senior Opposition leaders might have to be taken into custody after the rally on 24 June. Even a list of the leaders who were to be arrested was prepared at the prime minister's house, in consultation with the superintendent of police in charge of the criminal investigation department (CID). These were the early signs of Gandhi's plans to take drastic measures to consolidate her control over the government.

However, the Opposition rally was delayed by a day and the new date was 25 June. But even before the rally was held, on 24 June, Justice Krishna Iyer in the Supreme Court passed his judgment on the petition that Gandhi had filed for a review of the Allahabad High Court order. Justice Iyer's judgment came as a relief for Gandhi, as it was effectively a conditional stay on the Allahabad High Court order. Her disqualification as a member of the Lok Sabha was stayed and she was also allowed to continue as prime minister. The only restriction imposed on her was that she could not exercise her vote in Parliament. Once Gandhi and her team of advisers understood the import of the judgment they decided that the plan of action on arrests of senior Opposition leaders should take place after the public rally on 25 June. It was clear that the decision on arresting the leaders was taken even before the rally and there was no merit in the claim that the arrests and the imposition of the Emergency were a reaction to the Opposition leader's call at the rally that the people should disobey orders that were illegal.

Indeed, it was on the morning of 25 June that West Bengal Chief Minister Siddhartha Shankar Ray met Gandhi at her residence. Gandhi suggested that in view of the all-round indiscipline and lawlessness there was need for some action. Ray reminded her that on two or three previous occasions he had suggested to her that 'some sort of emergent power or drastic power was necessary'. As Coomi Kapoor revealed in her book *The Emergency: A Personal History*, Ray had sent a note to Gandhi as early as 8 January 1975, where he suggested that she should consider imposing an internal emergency in view of 'the seriousness of the situation in the country'. On 25 June, however, Ray told her that he would come back later in the day with a proposal. Ray was back at the prime minister's house by 5 p.m. and suggested that Gandhi could use Article 352 of the Constitution to impose an internal emergency. Soon, thereafter, the two met the President, Fakhruddin Ali Ahmed, for about 20 minutes, where they explained the available legal provisions of imposing an internal emergency. Once apprised of the provisions in the Constitution for taking such a step, the President told Gandhi that she could make her recommendation.

The country was preparing for a long dark period in its democracy, which was still in its infancy—just twenty-eight years after it gained freedom from foreign rule. Perhaps in a bid to give this entire exercise the semblance of a democratically endorsed plan, Gandhi decided to consult other senior Congress leaders, but only after securing the President's consent for her Emergency decision. Congress President Dev Kant Barooah was briefed on the plan of action. Already in the morning, Gandhi had got in touch with several chief ministers of the Congress-ruled states and apprised them of her plan to take tough action like arresting senior Opposition leaders. No Congress leader Gandhi met that day opposed her plan of imposing an internal emergency. The only dissenting note came from Home Minister Brahmananda Reddy, who said that India was already under an emergency rule, as the one imposed in the wake of India's impending war with Pakistan in November 1971 was still in force and the provisions under that could be used to deal with the situation. Gandhi remained unconvinced. Reddy was summoned again to the prime minister's house and informed that his suggestion was examined and it was found that an internal emergency was necessary. The home minister then told the prime minister 'to do what she thought was best'.[7]

Subsequently, Barooah, Ray and Gandhi held another meeting and decided to write a letter to the President. The letter from the prime minister of India, marked 'Top Secret' and dated 25 June 1975, said it all:

Dear Rashtrapatiji,

As already explained to you, a little while ago, information has reached us which indicates that there is an imminent danger to the security of India being threatened by internal disturbance. The matter is extremely urgent.

I would have liked to have taken this to Cabinet but unfortunately this is not possible tonight. I am, therefore, condoning, or permitting a departure from the Government of India (Transaction of Business) Rule 1961, as amended up-to-date by virtue of my powers under Rule 12 thereof. I shall mention the matter to the Cabinet first thing tomorrow morning.

In the circumstances and in case you are so satisfied, a requisite Proclamation under Article 352 (1) has become necessary. I am enclosing a copy of the draft Proclamation for your consideration. As you are aware, under Article 352 (3) even when there is an imminent danger of such a threat, as mentioned by me, the necessary Proclamation under Article 352 (1) can be issued.

I recommend that such a Proclamation should be issued tonight, however, late it may be, and all arrangements will be made to make it public as early as possible thereafter.

With kind regards,
Yours sincerely,
Indira Gandhi.

Gandhi's letter[8] reached the President at around 10.30 p.m. Fakhruddin Ali Ahmed had some doubts about the sequence of events that should lead to his signing the Emergency order. After a brief conversation between Gandhi and the President, the former's personal secretary, R.K. Dhawan, walked into Rashtrapati Bhavan with a draft of the Emergency order. At around 11.45 p.m. on Friday, 25 June 1975, the President signed the order, which read:

In exercise of the powers conferred by Clause 1 of Article 352 of the Constitution, I, Fakhruddin Ali Ahmed, President of India, by this Proclamation declare that a grave emergency exists whereby the security of India is threatened by internal disturbances.

At around 8 a.m. on 26 June, Indira Gandhi walked into the studios of the All India Radio to deliver an address to the nation—to announce that she had declared an internal emergency. A Cabinet meeting had approved her proposal earlier at an emergency session convened at 6 a.m. And the President, Fakhruddin Ali Ahmed, had already signed the proclamation of the ordinance to declare the Emergency. The previous evening, power supplies to most newspapers' printing presses had been cut off so that newspapers could not be brought out in the morning. Opposition political leaders were already being rounded up to be either sent to jail or kept under house arrest. But what Gandhi broadcast that morning was chilling in effect and ominous for the prospect of democracy in India.

Without referring to any specific developments by name, she cited the political challenge that Opposition leaders had mounted against her to unseat her from power and referred to the public rallies these leaders, particularly Jayaprakash Narayan, addressed and called for a public disobedience movement. She also promised a new economic policy package for the people, but did not outline any of the draconian measures she had already taken or would take such as arresting Opposition leaders or throttling press freedom.

Indira Gandhi's address was brief and started with the most obvious point on the declaration of the Emergency:

The President has proclaimed the Emergency. This is nothing to panic about.

I am sure you are all conscious of the deep and widespread conspiracy, which has been brewing ever since I began to introduce certain progressive measures of benefit to the common man and woman of India. In the name of democracy, it has been sought to negate the very functioning of democracy. Duly elected governments have not been allowed to function and in some cases, force has been used to compel members to resign in order to dissolve lawfully elected assemblies. Agitations have surcharged the atmosphere, leading to violent incidents. The whole country was shocked at the brutal murder of my Cabinet colleague, Shri L.N. Mishra. We also deeply deplore the dastardly attack on the Chief Justice of India.

Certain persons have gone to the length of inciting our armed forces to mutiny and our police to rebel. The fact that our defence forces and the police are disciplined and deeply patriotic and, therefore, will not be taken in, does not mitigate the seriousness of the provocation.

The forces of disintegration are in full play and communal passions are being aroused, threatening our unity.

All manners of false allegations have been hurled at me. The Indian people have known me since my childhood. All my life has been in the service of our people. This is not a personal matter. It is not important whether I remain Prime Minister or not. However, the institution of the Prime Minister is important and the deliberate political attempts to denigrate it is not in the interest of democracy or of the nation.

We have watched these developments with utmost patience for long. Now we learn of a new programme challenging law and order throughout the country with a view to disrupting normal functioning. How can any Government worth the name stand by and allow the country's stability to be imperilled? The actions of a few are endangering the rights of the vast majority. Any situation, which weakens the capacity of the national Government to act decisively inside the country, is bound to encourage dangers from outside. It is our paramount duty to safeguard unity and stability. The nation's integrity demands firm action.

The threat to internal stability also affects production and prospects of economic improvement. In the last few months the determined action we have taken has succeeded in largely checking the price rise. We have been actively considering further measures to strengthen the economy and to relieve the hardship of various sections, particularly the poor and vulnerable and those with fixed incomes. I shall announce them soon.

I should like to assure you that the new Emergency proclamation will in no way affect the rights of law-abiding citizens. I am sure that internal conditions will speedily improve to enable us to dispense with this proclamation as soon as possible. I have been overwhelmed by the message of goodwill from all parts of India and all sections of the people. May I appeal for your continued cooperation and trust in the days ahead?

The speech was delivered by Indira Gandhi in less than five minutes. But its disruptive impact on India's politics would last for many decades to come. In her address, Gandhi made no reference to the Allahabad High Court judgment that had declared her election to the Lok Sabha void or to the Supreme Court order giving a conditional stay on it. Instead, she presented a different story—one where disruptive forces were targeting her and her colleagues and distracting the government from its resolve to bring about faster economic development. It was an appeal to the people to cooperate with her instead of joining those protestors who in her view were trying to destabilize the country.

The Son Also Rises

The influence of Sanjay Gandhi, the younger son of the prime minister, during this period was on the rise, though not as distinctly visible as it would become after the imposition of the Emergency. Ray would recount his brief encounter with Sanjay Gandhi on the night the Emergency was imposed. Ray was apparently upset that even before the rules had been framed under the Emergency, the government had ordered the shutdown of the high courts and disconnection of power supplies to newspaper offices. He was waiting at the prime minister's house to advise Gandhi against taking such steps before framing the rules. At this point,

> Sanjay Gandhi met him in a highly excited and infuriated state of mind and told him quite rudely and offensively that he [Ray] did not know how to rule the country. Ray stated in his evidence that he did not lose his temper, but made Sanjay understand that he should mind his own business and should not try to interfere with what was not his sphere.[9]

In his book, *PMO Diary-I: Prelude to the Emergency*, B.N. Tandon, joint secretary in the prime minister's secretariat, recounted three specific instances of the growing clout of Sanjay Gandhi during that fortnight. On 12 June, soon after the Allahabad High Court verdict was public, Gandhi began consultations with her colleagues including Law Minister H.R Gokhale and West Bengal Chief Minister Siddharth Shankar Ray. But a little later, Gandhi was seen having a whispering discussion with her son, Sanjay, and her personal assistant, R.K. Dhawan, after which the latter began calling 'people around Delhi to organise demonstrations in favour of the PM'.[10]

Another diary entry by Tandon shows Sanjay Gandhi's dramatic rise. Referring to a conversation that the Information and Broadcasting Minister, I.K. Gujral, had with N.K. Seshan, private secretary to the prime minister, where Tandon too was present, the diary entry for 21 June 1975 stated the following:

> I learnt from Gujral today that Sanjay had given him a severe dressing down because yesterday's rally had not been properly publicised. He was also annoyed that the campaign that is under way in support of the PM too is not getting proper publicity. Gujral was upset that Sanjay should upbraid him. He had been summoned to meet the PM but was asked

to meet Sanjay. His meeting today with the PM was also not pleasant. She expressed her dissatisfaction at the inadequacy of the publicity and wanted the proposed demonstration in front of Morarji's house to be properly highlighted. She said that she wanted to see the radio and TV scripts, not just of this but all news bulletins before they were broadcast. Gujral replied that he too didn't ordinarily see the scripts. The PM then angrily remarked that if he didn't see the scripts why was he the minister for information and broadcasting. She said that whether or not he saw the scripts, the prime minister wanted to see them.[11]

Within weeks of this incident, Gujral was sent off to Moscow as India's ambassador to the Soviet Union. V.C. Shukla was brought in as his successor and he played along with the directions that Gandhi and her son would issue on the question of media censorship.

On 23 June, Tandon recounts another incident that is ample proof to show how Sanjay Gandhi had become more powerful in even key appointments. Tandon was told by the prime minister's secretary, P.N. Dhar, that the chief secretary of Rajasthan, S.L. Khurana, would be replacing Nirmal Mukherji as the new home secretary. The sequence of events was as follows:

> The PM had summoned Khurana that day. He reached Delhi at night and met the PM yesterday. She met him just for five minutes. Seshan (her private secretary) said that after meeting him, she sent him (Khurana) to meet Sanjay and Dhawan, who interviewed him for about half an hour. Dhawan then went to the PM and said that Khurana was suitable for the job. After getting the green signal, the PM told Prof Dhar to inform the cabinet secretary to appoint Khurana as the home secretary and further that he should assume charge today itself.[12]

Dhar, according to Tandon, looked very upset by such a turn of events. The rise of Sanjay Gandhi as an unconstitutional authority appeared to have disturbed him hugely. The incumbent home secretary's next posting too had not been decided even though his successor had been named. The irony of the whole exercise was that even though Khurana's appointment was cleared by Sanjay Gandhi, the home secretary was completely dark on the night of 25 June, when the Emergency was imposed. He had phoned Tandon to check if any major arrests had to be conducted or if any major orders of the prime minister had to be carried out.

The rise of Sanjay Gandhi as an extraconstitutional power centre in New Delhi during those months was as big a political disruption as the very imposition of the Emergency in the entire country. Sanjay Gandhi derived his power from being the son of the prime minister. It also paved the way for the continuation of a dynastic rule. The Congress even till today has not been able to get rid of the stigma of being ruled and led by the Gandhi family. The growing clout of Sanjay Gandhi during the Emergency months was dangerous and disastrous for the country, but the continuation of the dynastic rule in the Congress also made the party considerably weaker and vulnerable to attacks from other political parties, particularly the Bharatiya Janata Party, where dynasty is yet to capture the organization.

Perspectives on the Political Shock

So much has been written about how Gandhi imposed the Emergency that it would be useful to recount how different people saw the sequence in which this decision was taken less than a fortnight after the Allahabad High Court order. What happened during that fortnight? Why did Gandhi not let the legal process take care of her prime ministership and control of her party? Why did she use a provision in the law that nobody before her had used and nobody after her has used so far?

The best account of what transpired before Gandhi decided to impose the Emergency is given by P.N. Dhar in his autobiographical book, *Indira Gandhi, the 'Emergency', and Indian Democracy*, where he recounted how the prime minister responded to the legal challenge she faced. Dhar had a ringside view of the goings-on during those days in the prime minister's secretariat, where he joined in 1973 as the principal secretary and remained in the job until 1977.

An early morning phone call on 12 June 1975 informed Dhar that his friend, D.P. Dhar, ambassador to the Soviet Union, had died at the Govind Ballabh Pant Hospital in New Delhi after a massive heart attack. The two had been good friends since their college days in Srinagar. In early 1975 Indira Gandhi had sent D.P. Dhar to Moscow on his second stint as India's ambassador. After he returned from his two-year tenure there in 1971, Gandhi had made him the deputy chairman of the Planning Commission, but she sent him back to Moscow again from 1 January 1975.

The previous evening, P.N. Dhar met his friend at the hospital and spent some time together as the next day he was to get a pacemaker, an electronic device that would help his heart beat regularly. He couldn't believe that the man whom he had met just a day before and who had expressed his concern about the political situation in the country was no more. He was just fifty-seven.

When P.N. Dhar reached the hospital, Gandhi was already there giving instructions on the funeral arrangements to be made by the government for his friend. He wanted to speak to his deceased friend's wife who was still in Moscow. He returned to his office to make that telephone call. But even before he could speak to her, the second piece of bad news of the day hit him.

H.Y. Sharada Prasad, information adviser to Indira Gandhi, walked into his room and told him without concealing the agitation in his mind: 'The Allahabad judgement has come and the prime minister has been unseated.' Dhar was already crestfallen by the news of his friend's death. And now came the shocking news about his boss. He went over to the prime minister's house and Congress President Dev Kant Barooah and other senior ministers were assembled in small groups discussing various options to respond to the court verdict. Gandhi was engaged in discussion with smaller groups by turn.

On the first day after the judgment, it was clear to Dhar that Gandhi wanted that the government's work should not suffer in any way. The prime minister also asked him to see her every morning in her house and not in her office, which she might not attend for the next few days. This was significant.

It is remarkable that during the first two days after the Allahabad High Court judgment the discussion between Dhar and Gandhi every morning was primarily focused on the routine official work and the political crisis that had engulfed her did not figure. Only on the third day did Dhar refer to the many letters of support he had received from many people during her meeting. Gandhi looked a little relieved after hearing that Fali S. Nariman, the additional solicitor general, believed that the Allahabad High Court judgment had many flaws, based as it was on weak arguments, and it would not pass muster at the Supreme Court. What pleased Gandhi more was that the British daily the *Guardian* had described the charges levelled against her as similar to the violation of traffic rules. The only discordant note Dhar discerned during those conversations was that she seemed to ignore his suggestions that she should not let the Congress launch a counter-agitation against the verdict and the best response to the Opposition political parties' demand for her resignation would be that she was waiting for the Supreme Court's verdict on her appeal against the high court judgment. On the contrary, Dhar noted how her trusted associates like Dev Kant Barooah, president of the Congress party, Siddhartha Shankar Ray, West Bengal chief minister, and Rajni Patel, veteran Congress leader, would be busy confabulating with her. And outside her residence, there would be Congress workers shouting slogans in her support. All this did not make Dhar very happy.

A few days later, Dhar felt slighted by Gandhi when the prime minister accused him of deliberately sitting on 'certain home ministry files relating to appointments'. A deeply hurt Dhar checked back if indeed any home ministry files were being delayed in his office. What transpired was an indication to Dhar that a new lobby of powerful people was growing its roots around Gandhi. The file that was the trigger for Gandhi's accusation against Dhar pertained to her direction that some appointments should be routed through Om Mehta, who was at that time the minister of state for home affairs. Dhar's experienced eyes immediately got wind of the underlying purpose of that direction. A minister of state is a junior minister and, unless he is given independent charge of a ministry, he doesn't even attend the meetings of the Union cabinet. Mehta did not have an independent charge of the home ministry as he had a senior cabinet minister for home affairs in Brahmananda Reddy. If some appointments were to be routed through Mehta, that would have amounted to bypassing his senior, Brahmananda Reddy. Dhar also realized that if his attention had been drawn to this procedural lapse, he would surely have apprised the prime minister what such routing of files could mean for the senior home minister. But Gandhi's accusation had already taken the matter to a different level.

Om Mehta belonged to the coterie of powerful officers and private secretaries in the prime minister's house which included R.K. Dhawan. Dhar sent to Gandhi a note wherein he desired to put in his papers. There was no communication between Dhar and Gandhi on this issue for a couple of days, till one morning Gandhi became emotional and with moistened eyes said she had full faith in Dhar. She also added that it was a terribly testing time for her and her friends. Dhar felt bad that he had hurt Gandhi in that manner and did not raise the issue of his resignation again.

On 24 June 1975, the Supreme Court passed an order that conditionally stayed the Allahabad High Court verdict that had declared Gandhi's 1971 Lok Sabha election void.[13] It looked as if Gandhi had won a major reprieve and she had succeeded in warding off the Opposition demand for her resignation and now, with the stay order, she gained the legitimacy of continuing to remain as prime minister. But a phone call at 11 p.m. the next evening asking Dhar to meet the prime minister at her residence proved all such calculations wrong.

Dhar writes in his book:

> The atmosphere in the house was tense. Ray and Barooah were there. Ray looked grim while Barooah wore a huge grin and was trying to look relaxed as usual. Mrs Gandhi told me tersely: 'The situation in the country is very bad. We have decided to declare internal emergency. There is going to be a Cabinet meeting early in the morning tomorrow after which I am going to broadcast the decision on AIR.'
>
> Having said this, she handed me the draft of the proposed speech. Just at that time Sharada Prasad, who had also been summoned, walked in. I went over the draft with Sharada and suggested the addition of the following line in the concluding paragraph of the draft: 'I am sure that internal conditions will speedily improve to enable us to dispense with this proclamation as soon as possible.'[14]

Dhar began wondering if he made the wrong decision by not pressing for his resignation a few days earlier. He did consult his predecessor Haksar, now deputy chairman of the Planning Commission, who felt that it was necessary for people like him to stay within the system to improve the situation.

Dhar stayed on in the job till Gandhi called for elections in early 1977. After she lost the elections, Dhar left the prime minister's secretariat at the end of March that year as Morarji Desai succeeded Gandhi to head the government.

A Civil Servant's Assessment

Bishan Narain Tandon, an IAS officer, joined the prime minister's secretariat as a joint secretary on 4 October 1969 and functioned in that capacity till 24 July 1976, when he was promoted as additional secretary and shifted to the ministry of education. Tandon, therefore, saw from close quarters how Indira Gandhi functioned as prime minister and how she changed over those years to eventually declare an internal emergency. His diary entries, captured in his book, *PMO Diary-I: Prelude to the Emergency*, shed additional light on the events during the days leading up to the night of 25 June 1975 when Gandhi declared the Emergency.

A day after the Allahabad High Court delivered its order unseating Gandhi, Tandon noted how a political campaign had been mooted to prove that a government official's resignation could be accepted orally. The court order had indicted Gandhi for having used the services of Yashpal Kapoor, before his resignation from service was formally accepted by the government. Uttar Pradesh Chief Minister Hemwati Nandan Bahuguna had left a note on this issue and the prime minister's secretariat was engaged in an internal discussion on whether that as a defence would pass muster. A day later, Tandon even received a call from the prime minister's house that inquired if Kapoor received his salaries after 13 January 1971. The suggestion seemed to be that if he had not, then it could be argued that Kapoor had ceased to be in government office after that date, when Gandhi's election campaigning had begun.

Gandhi's private secretary, N.K. Seshan, had already told Tandon that the prime minister's house had become a centre of activity for organizing public rallies in support of the prime minister. Haryana Chief Minister Bansi Lal and Delhi Lieutenant Governor Krishna Chand would convene there and plan the logistics of these rallies, and often commandeer the services of the official machinery from Delhi and Haryana. Tandon also began recording how various Congress chief ministers of states, including J. Vengala Rao of Andhra Pradesh and Devraj Urs of Karnataka, would visit Gandhi during this period. While they would tell Seshan privately that she should resign, none of them would have the courage to say so in her presence.

Signs of the growing clout of the coterie within the prime minister's house also became evident to Tandon, as he noted in his diary how the key appointments of senior officials were being vetted by Gandhi's personal assistant, R.K. Dhawan, and her son, Sanjay Gandhi. An indication of the impending declaration of an internal emergency was available on 25 June, when Krishan Chand requested Tandon that a RAX telephone line (a service that is accessible and provided to only top civil servants and ministers to provide quick connectivity among them) should be immediately installed at the residences of P.N. Behl, who had joined the prime minister's secretariat a couple of days ago, and Navin Chawla, secretary to the Lieutenant Governor.

The Account of a Trusted Insider

Pranab Mukherjee, who was a minister of state finance in the Indira Gandhi government in 1975, had an understandably charitable view of the Allahabad High Court judgment on 12 June. In *Dramatic Decade: The Indira Gandhi Years*, he wrote that the court found her guilty on two 'technical grounds—taking assistance of government officers to construct rostrums and supply power for loudspeakers at two election rallies and taking the assistance of Yashpal Kapoor, a government official, for furthering her election prospects'. But he also noted that she was acquitted of other charges like exceeding the ceiling on election expenses, bribery of voters with gifts etc., use of Air Force aircraft during electioneering and the use of the cow and the calf symbol to exploit the voters' religious sentiments.

Political rumblings after that judgment increased. Jayaprakash Narayan said that her 'failure to bow to the High Court verdict would not only be against the law as found by the Allahabad High Court, but also against all public decency and democratic practice'.[15] Opposition party leaders in New Delhi sat on a dharna outside Rashtrapati Bhavan and demanded Gandhi's resignation. The dharna by these leaders went on for about four days, till President V.V. Giri returned from his tour of Jammu and Kashmir on 16 June and gave them a hearing.[16]

Congress members of Parliament loyal to Gandhi did not take these protests lying down. The Congress Parliamentary Party (CPP) held a meeting on 18 June, where Gandhi said: 'My continuance does not depend on what the Opposition demands but on what my own party and the people want.' Having thus put the onus on the Congress party on her continuing as prime minister, Gandhi gave the entire issue a different dimension. A resolution was passed by the CPP, which reposed complete faith and confidence in Gandhi and resolved that her continued leadership as prime minister was 'indispensable for the nation'. It was at this point in time that the Congress president, Dev Kanta Barooah, made his famous statement that India was Indira and Indira was India. Barooah added that the Allahabad High Court judgment did not diminish her moral authority and observed that the party might have lost a battle, it must now win the war. Even Mukherjee felt that such statements reeked of sycophancy and reflected the desire of the Congress to fight back for sheer survival. They also held a public meeting at the Boat Club, near Raj Path, on 20 June, which was attended by a large number of Congress supporters. Gandhi addressed the rally and said quite ironically that democracy in India had been endangered and the Opposition parties had hatched a conspiracy in the name of rule of law, but essentially aimed at removing her from office.

Almost in response, the Opposition parties held a huge rally at the Ramlila grounds on 25 June, a day after the Supreme Court vacation judge, Justice V.R. Krishna Iyer, had given Gandhi a conditional stay against the Allahabad High Court order. Urging people to start a civil disobedience movement, JP also requested the Chief Justice of India, A.N. Ray, that he should not hear Gandhi's appeal as he was obliged to her for his appointment that took place after superseding other senior judges. The same evening Gandhi informed President Fakhruddin Ali Ahmed of her decision to proclaim an internal emergency. A few minutes before midnight on 25 June, the President promulgated an ordinance to announce a state of emergency under Article 352 of the Indian Constitution.

Ray had played a key role in helping Gandhi make up her mind on the need to proclaim an internal emergency in the country. Gandhi had called Ray to meet her on the morning of 25 June and told him how she had received reports of country-wide agitation, lawlessness and indiscipline, leading to a crisis and requiring strong corrective action. Ray's response was that there were adequate legal provisions within the existing administrative framework which she could use to quell such early signs of instability and violence. Gandhi shared with Ray the intelligence reports that suggested at the proposed public rally to be held at the Ramlila grounds on 25 June, Jayaprakash Narayan would call an all-India agitation, suggest the setting up of parallel administrative networks across the country and appeal to the army and police forces to disobey illegal orders.

Ray's understanding of Gandhi that evening was that the prime minister was clear in her mind that the country was heading towards instability and chaos. The West Bengal chief minister sought some time and promised to come back to her later in the evening. At a meeting that began at 5 p.m., the idea of proclaiming an internal emergency was mooted by Ray, citing provisions of Article 352 of the Constitution. Once that idea was accepted, Gandhi and Ray visited President Fakhruddin Ali Ahmed to convince him of the need to urgently declare the Emergency.

Mukherjee, however, was not with Gandhi that evening, when many of her other advisers were discussing with the prime minister what steps needed to be taken in response to the 25 June public rally to be addressed by JP and Desai. He was in Calcutta for his Rajya Sabha election scheduled for 26 June. He learnt of the decision on the Emergency only on the morning of 26 June as he got a call from Gandhi to return to Delhi as soon as possible. Mukherjee at that time was a minister of state for finance, in charge of the departments of revenue and banking. Siddhartha Shankar

Ray, who was then the chief minister of West Bengal, had returned to Calcutta on 26 June and he met Mukherjee and D.P. Chattopadhyaya, who was then the minister of state for commerce at the Centre.

Many years later, Gandhi would tell Mukherjee that until Ray gave her the idea of an internal emergency, she was unaware of such a provision in the Constitution, particularly when there was already an external emergency in the country after the 1971 India–Pakistan War. It was also ironical that when it came to taking the blame for who mooted the idea of proclaiming an internal emergency, many of those who had endorsed it had disowned it and disclaimed any responsibility.

Mukherjee's analysis of why Indira Gandhi responded to the 25 June meeting with the Emergency is interesting, as she went for that extreme step in spite of the opinion of several international leaders that she should resign instead and gain popularity like Gamal Abdel Nasser did in Egypt though under slightly different circumstances. The Opposition parties, according to Mukherjee, were desperate to challenge Gandhi's growing authority and charisma and the Allahabad High Court judgment seemed like a golden opportunity to them. There was no apparent unity among these political parties but with JP providing them moral leadership, they could come together and launch a united attack against Gandhi.

In the final analysis, Mukherjee felt that even though the Emergency brought about many 'positive changes—discipline in public life, a growing economy, controlled inflation, a reversed trade deficit for the first time, enhanced developmental expenditure and a crackdown on tax evasion and smuggling', it was an avoidable event as it led to the suspension of fundamental rights, large-scale arrests of political leaders, censorship of the media and an extension to the tenure of the Lok Sabha beyond the normal period of five years. Coming from a Congress leader who was a close associate of Gandhi during that period, Mukherjee's qualified assessment of the Emergency shows how disruptive Gandhi's decision was for the country.

A Student Activist's Take

Arun Jaitley's account of the days in the run-up to the declaration of the Emergency was equally telling. Jaitley then was a young student leader at the helm of the Akhil Bharatiya Vidyarthi Parishad (ABVP), the student wing of the Jana Sangh, which later became the Bharatiya Janata Party. In his foreword to Coomi Kapoor's book *The Emergency: A Personal History*, Jaitley recalls how soon after the verdict of the Allahabad High

Court the Opposition political parties were getting together under the overall leadership of Jayaprakash Narayan, popularly known as JP, who had already tasted considerable success while leading a students' agitation against the government. That the economy was not doing well only helped the movement launched by JP, which was now ably supported by other parties ranged against the Congress. Gandhi's appeal against the Allahabad High Court verdict was heard by the Supreme Court vacation judge, V. R. Krishna Iyer. According to Jaitley, Justice Krishna Iyer's verdict staying the Allahabad High Court order was qualified in many ways. He writes that the judge 'admitted an appeal and passed the usual interim order that she could attend the House but not vote, nor could she draw her salary as a member of Parliament. She could speak as the prime minister but not as an MP.'

It is possible that Justice Krishna Iyer's stay order did not fully satisfy Gandhi and she sensed that the Opposition demand for her resignation and the movement against her leadership would not see any respite or decline. On the evening of 25 June, JP, along with Morarji Desai, addressed a massive rally on the Ramlila Grounds in Delhi. His address that evening was explosive and he gave a clarion call to the people for an open rebellion against the authorities:

> Friends, the civil disobedience will be of varied types. A time may come when, if these people do not listen, it may be necessary to derecognise the government. They have no moral, legal or constitutional right to govern; therefore we would de-recognise them; we would not cooperate with them; not a paisa of tax shall be given to them.

Gandhi and her advisers who had kept track of the rally at the Ramlila grounds had reasons to believe that the Opposition parties were raising the pitch to a level where the government could be in serious trouble. In the same address, JP had asked the army, the police and government servants to disobey the orders which they felt were wrong. JP knew he was treading a risky path when he challenged the government to try him for treason for having made such a statement at a public rally. Morarji Desai added fuel to fire when he asked the audience for their approval of the programme of agitation outlined by JP.[17]

Jaitley recalls that he returned home late in the evening after attending JP's rally.[18] At around 2 a.m., the doorbell at his residence rang and the police were outside to arrest him. His father, a lawyer, engaged with the police officers demanding on what grounds they were seeking his son's arrest. Meanwhile, Jaitley slipped out of his home from the rear door and escaped arrest. But the next morning, he decided to go to the Delhi University and addressed a rally, which led to his arrest.[19] By the time he was arrested, Gandhi had announced over All India Radio her government's decision to declare the Emergency, press censorship was imposed, senior Opposition leaders including even those Congress leaders like Chandra Shekhar and Ram Dhan, who were close to JP, were arrested and the fundamental rights of people were suspended. To his horror, Jaitley found that he was served a detention order under the dreaded Maintenance of Internal Security Act (MISA), which gave the government powers to detain people for an indefinite period of time. Worse, blank detention orders were signed by an additional district magistrate and the names of the detainees were filled in at the time of the arrest. A bigger blow came when a petition filed in the Supreme Court to seek its intervention in upholding a detained citizen's right to move a court was defeated. It was a majority verdict of four judges in favour and only one opposing it. The Emergency and authoritarian rule over the nation had caused the most harmful political disruption in India.

A similar fate had befallen Lal Krishna Advani and Atal Bihari Vajpayee, both of whom at that time were the two tall leaders of the Jan Sangh. From 26 to 27 June, a Joint Parliamentary Committee to examine a law against defection was to hold its meeting in Bangalore (as Bengaluru was known then). Vajpayee had left New Delhi on 24 June and Advani took a flight out of Delhi a day later. At around 7.30 a.m. on 26 June, Advani received a call from Delhi informing him that senior leaders of the Jana Sangh and other Opposition leaders including Jayaprakash Narayan and Morarji Desai had been arrested at midnight and both Advani and Vajpayee, too, were likely to be arrested soon. Advani and Vajpayee had a quick chat and decided not to evade arrest. They heard Gandhi's radio address about her decision on declaring the Emergency, issued a statement condemning the move and by around 10 a.m., the local police knocked their doors to arrest them.

CHAPTER 13

WHY IT ALL HAPPENED

Without doubt, the imposition of the Emergency in June 1975 would be classified as India's most dangerous disruption. It was a shock to the political system that few could anticipate less than thirty years after India's Independence. Grave forecasts made earlier about the future of India's democracy came back in circulation. Democratic practices were suspended. Press freedom was curbed. Elections to the Lok Sabha were postponed. A small coterie of ministers, including Prime Minister Indira Gandhi, along with her son, Sanjay Gandhi, who enjoyed no constitutional authority, ran the government. Citizen's rights were abrogated so much so that even a habeas corpus appeal to challenge the legality of an imprisonment was not upheld by the Supreme Court. And all this largely because the Allahabad High Court had ruled that Indira Gandhi was found guilty of two corrupt practices while fighting her 1971 Lok Sabha elections.

The imposition of the Emergency on 25 June 1975 is often seen as a political response to a political challenge Indira Gandhi faced from a host of opposition parties. There can hardly be any disagreement with that proposition. But what is often not appreciated in the popular narrative about the causes of the Emergency is that Gandhi's response was also shaped by the economic plight India was going through in the early 1970s.

India's economic woes had ironically begun when Gandhi was at the peak of her political power, after India's successful intervention in East Pakistan. This had led to the birth of a new nation in Bangladesh in 1971. India's western neighbour was taught a lesson in a war where it was at the receiving end in every respect. But that war had also meant a huge economic burden on India in the form of an influx of over 10 million refugees who had crossed over from then East Pakistan and many of them did not go back after normalcy returned. The war with Pakistan also had an economic cost, which was aggravated by the US decision to suspend aid to India. Monsoons in the summer of 1972–73 failed and even the winter rains virtually disappeared that year. The resulting drought impacted

India's agriculture, largely dependent on rainfall, with a consequent drop in output by about 8 per cent.

If that was not enough, OPEC decided in October 1973 to raise crude oil prices by imposing a production cut and an embargo on supplies to the United States and a few of its allies. The cost of importing fertilizers went up as a consequence of the OPEC crude oil price hike. This, in turn, affected agricultural output also. Inflation soared and by 1973 it had crossed the 20-per-cent mark and reached about 30 per cent by the middle of 1974.

The Indira Gandhi government had to take a series of measures that were tough and even made her unpopular among her political supporters. India had to apply for a loan from the IMF. Licensing controls had to be relaxed and large business houses were allowed to expand production. In a bid to rein in the runaway inflation rate, the government had to curb demand in the economy. One such measure it adopted was to ban all increases in wages and half of the dearness allowance (meant for compensating employees for inflation) for salaried government employees was frozen and converted into compulsory deposits—a move that made Gandhi's government extremely unpopular. Even taxpayers in the higher income brackets were made to park an additional 4–8 per cent of their income into compulsory deposits.

In his book, P.N. Dhar analysed how Gandhi's old policies of state-led controls were becoming a liability for her in the new situation that obliged her to look at economic policy options that ran contrary to the spirit of her earlier policies.[1] 'The government thus became vulnerable to criticism for ideological retreat. Mrs Gandhi found herself in a difficult situation as she was now subjected to contrary pulls from her professional advisers and her party colleagues,' Dhar wrote.[2]

One instance that reflected this tension was Gandhi's decision to nationalize wholesale trade in wheat, a move she had to withdraw after it faced many implementation problems. While B.S. Minhas, an eminent economist and a member of the Planning Commission, had opposed the idea, the idea was supported by her party leadership. But when problems erupted over its execution, she had no option other than to withdraw her order.

Another major economic crisis that Gandhi faced just before the Emergency was the national strike by workers of the Indian Railways. In August 1973, militant trade unionism in the Indian Railways reared its ugly head when workers in the locomotives division went on an indefinite strike. The government made the mistake of succumbing to such pressure tactic and made the trade unions more bold and demanding. By November 1973, George Fernandes replaced Peter Alvares to lead the railway workers union. Alvares was a moderate, while Fernandes, who would later become the industry minister in the Janata Party government in 1977, upped the ante as soon as he took charge, demanding among other things, higher bonus and wage parity for railway workers with those prevailing in Central public-sector undertakings like BHEL and HMT.

In May 1974, Fernandes declared an indefinite strike in the Indian Railways, but Gandhi did not relent and forced the workers to resume work after twenty days of the strike. It was a victory for Gandhi, a failure for the railway workers, but it emboldened the Opposition political parties. Indeed, this was also the time the Opposition political parties, in spite of their ideological differences, came closer to each other to oppose Gandhi.

Just about five years earlier, Gandhi had unleashed a series of economic policy measures by which she had changed the way the Indian economy operated. Politically also, she had risen to the zenith of her political power and popularity by 1971. But the worsening economic situation in the country led to a series of policy decisions by the government that ironically strengthened the political unity among Opposition parties. This unity got a shot in its arm when the Allahabad High Court verdict declared Gandhi's 1971 election invalid and the Opposition demanded that she should step down. That cornered Gandhi and one of her options could have been to wait till her petition appealing the Allahabad High Court judgment was heard. She could have even considered stepping down, an option she clearly chose to ignore even though it could have made her more popular. Why she did not choose such a path, following the rule of law, will remain a mystery. But an attempt to analyse why she chose to go for an extreme step like the Emergency will be useful.

One possible explanation for Gandhi's aggressive stance on imposing the Emergency was the absence of saner voices among her advisers. For well over six years, P.N. Haksar was advising Gandhi, pointing out what was right and what was wrong with regard to her various decisions on government policy matters as well as Congress party issues. Gandhi would not always appreciate Haksar's frequent notes sent to her and, pointing out, for instance, the flaws he saw in the measures she took to address the turmoil in the Congress leadership team in Andhra Pradesh. Similarly, Haksar would not approve of many of Gandhi's decisions. He would write to her pointing out why she should not use a government-provided helicopter to travel to her own constituency in Uttar Pradesh. Once, he even wrote to her expressing his disapproval of how she addressed a Lions Club meeting at Calcutta even as she continued to decline requests to address meetings convened by national industry bodies like the Federation of Indian Chambers of Commerce and Industry.[3]

Haksar left the prime minister's secretariat in 1973. For about two years, he was not in the government; Gandhi occasionally requested his services as an envoy of the government to meet dignitaries coming to India from abroad or visit foreign countries. In 1975, Haksar was parked as deputy chairman of the Planning Commission and he was not as regular with his advice to Gandhi as he was when he was the principal secretary in the prime minister's secretariat.

In 1973, the same year as Haksar left the prime minister's secretariat, Gandhi lost another close adviser Mohan Kumaramangalam, who was also in her cabinet as a senior minister. Kumaramangalam died in a plane crash and this was a big blow to Gandhi as she now had one person less on whom she could count for advice on critical issues in the realm of both politics and economics. At around the same time eminent economist Pitambar Pant, who headed the perspective planning division in the Planning Commission, passed away. Another of her key advisers, D.P. Dhar had died just before she declared the Emergency.

In a short span of about two years, Gandhi no longer had the benefit of frank and forthright views of three of her trusted aides—two of them died and one of them decided to leave the prime minister's secretariat and was accommodated in the Planning Commission. The death of Pant did not affect Gandhi directly, but his absence was felt by others like Haksar, who depended a lot on the suave and mild-mannered economist.

It is not that Gandhi did not replace these advisers with their successors. P.N. Dhar joined the secretariat to succeed Haksar. But, clearly, Dhar did not have the kind of say or influence on Gandhi as Haksar did. This was particularly so when this period coincided with the rise in the influence and clout of Gandhi's younger son, Sanjay. There were views, though unconfirmed, that Haksar decided to leave the secretariat largely because he was uncomfortable with the way Sanjay Gandhi was interfering in governance matters and how he as an adviser would be ruled out by Gandhi as Sanjay's views gained precedence.[4] There was no love lost between Haksar and Sanjay—the former having objected to the latter's proposal for a licence to produce a small car in the country. Indeed, Haksar's close family was later harassed no end during the Emergency months, but

Haksar was too proud to raise the issue with Gandhi, although he knew full well that the excesses were being engineered at the behest of Sanjay Gandhi.[5] The sense of dignity and pride he had for himself perhaps did not allow him to take up this issue either with Indira Gandhi or her son.

There are also strong political factors that drove Indira Gandhi towards declaring the Emergency. She had notched up significant political gains as prime minister from 1969 to 1971, in particular. Bank nationalization in 1969 had isolated her critics within the Congress and her Pakistan policy, resulting in its break-up and the creation of Bangladesh, made her a popular leader in the country and even silenced her critics in the opposition parties. Even Jayaprakash Narayan, her sharpest critic, had begun to acknowledge her successes in ruling the country. That perhaps made her a little arrogant and she was unwilling to heed suggestions made in good faith by leaders within her own party and even by Narayan. Instead, she centralized the governance structure even more and the autonomy of the government as well as the party was a casualty. Her senior colleagues contributed to her decline as a democratic leader as they rarely stood up to her to tell the facts as they were. Instead, most of them were found concurring with whatever she proposed an easier and better option.

Around the same time, the growing political clout of Sanjay Gandhi made matters worse. A powerful coterie around her, led by her son and her personal assistant, Dhawan, was gaining in strength. Key appointments now had to be cleared by Sanjay Gandhi and even the prime minister's secretariat, in the process, got devalued. On the other hand, Jayaprakash Narayan stepped up his campaign against Gandhi and in particular the issue of rising corruption in government. The Navnirman Andolan in Gujarat gave a fresh impetus to this movement. Finally, Congress (O) leader Morarji Desai went on a fast in April 1975 against the manner in which Indira Gandhi was running her government. The Allahabad High Court judgment on 12 June 1975 was the proverbial straw that broke the camel's back.

Indira Gandhi will surely count as the key disrupter in enforcing internal emergency on the country. The consequences of what she did in 1975 have hugely influenced the nature of politics in the country in the subsequent decades. The political price she paid for having imposed the Emergency was so heavy that it is unlikely that any prime minister would ever consider using a provision in the Constitution to enforce something similar.

Gandhi lost her Lok Sabha seat in the elections that were held in March 1977 after the Emergency was lifted earlier in the year. The embarrassing loss of this seat was the price she paid for her political misadventure. Political leaders in the years to come would not consider the option of declaring an emergency not because they were averse to the idea, but because of the fear of its adverse impact they could face at the hustings. No Indian voter will forget what the Emergency did to their fundamental rights. In that sense, the Emergency as a disruptive force had a positive outcome in an indirect way.

The declaration of the Emergency was certainly the biggest jolt to India's nascent democracy and that is why perhaps this has so far turned out to be the strongest force for growing and nurturing deep democratic roots in the country by people and even political parties. Any trace of authoritarianism or dictatorship is frowned upon and can become a powerful issue on which leaders associated with such a stance would have to pay a heavy price in an election. This was a disruption that clearly had short-term negative outcomes, but with a long-term positive fallout by reminding the people what it could mean if anybody tried to undermine the country's democratic traditions and principles.

A comparison of Gandhi's style of leadership with that of Narendra Modi, who led a government with a single-party majority from 2014 to 2019 and was returned to power for another five-year term from May 2019 with an even greater majority, will be relevant and apt. Modi has often been compared with Gandhi and both introduced major disruptions in the policy space during their tenures. There is, however, a crucial difference between the two leaders. Gandhi used her powers to disrupt policies by not only nationalizing banks and other industries but also abridging the people's democratic rights through the imposition of the Emergency. Modi too used his powers to disrupt policies through demonetization and the launch of the GST. If Gandhi paid a huge political price by being voted out of power by the people, it was not because of her moves on nationalization, but because of the Emergency. For Modi, Gandhi's political career is a lesson in how to use or misuse power as a strong leader.

The Turning Point

A question that still remains unanswered is why did Indira Gandhi decide to end the Emergency in January 1977? The fact is, she was under no compulsion to call for the elections that were held two months later in March 1977. If she wanted to, she could have continued with the Emergency and perpetuated her authoritarian rule for a few more years. As veteran journalist Mark Tully wrote in his foreword to Kuldip Nayar's book, *On Leaders and Icons: From Jinnah to Modi*, 'When Kuldip asked

Sanjay why elections were called in 1977, Sanjay said he should ask his mother, adding that in his scheme of things there was to be no election for three or four decades. This implies that if Indira had won the 1977 election, Sanjay would have used his influence with his mother to retain the Emergency.'

This assessment is in tune with another widely held view that Gandhi might have taken the decision to call for elections in 1977 without even consulting her son. Indeed, Sanjay Gandhi got to know that elections had been called only from her radio broadcast on 18 January 1977, after which there was an altercation over this issue between the mother and the son.[6]

Another rather charitable explanation is that she might have been encouraged to call for the elections in the hope that she would make amends for the transgressions she had committed to India's democracy by declaring the Emergency. But it was clear that she was harbouring thoughts on holding elections in less than a year and a half after imposing the Emergency. In early November 1976, Gandhi told P.N. Dhar, her principal secretary, and H.Y. Sharada Prasad, her information adviser, her plans in confidence: 'I am going to call off the Emergency and hold elections. I know that I will lose, but this is something which I absolutely have to do. The intelligence agencies will tell me what they think I want to hear. But I know that I am going to lose, even though the IB is saying that I will win 330 seats.'[7]

This is contrary to the view held by many others that she actually believed in the intelligence reports that if elections were to be held in 1977, she had a good chance of returning to power.[8] Her aide during the Emergency years and after, R.K. Dhawan, said in a media interview that she called the Lok Sabha elections in 1977 after the Intelligence Bureau told her that she would win up to 340 seats in a Lok Sabha consisting of 540-odd seats. Kuldip Nayar, the journalist who had broken the news in January 1977 that Gandhi was expected to call for elections soon, wrote in *Emergency Retold*:

> Both the intelligence bureau and Research and Analysis Wing (RAW) had estimated that she would get more than 350 seats if she were to go to polls immediately. Only CBI Director D. Sen, whom she used to raid critics' houses, had struck a discordant note; he had emphasised that there should be a gap of six months between the release of detainees and elections so as to allow time for the halo around them to fade.[9]

There is, however, no authoritative corroboration of these versions. Either way, it was her desire to legitimize her rule through an electoral process that resulted in ending an unfortunate and dark chapter of India's democracy.

The Emergency was India's worst moment as far as political disruptions go, but its disastrous consequences also served as a warning to the nation and perhaps has so far prevented a repeat of that experiment by anybody else.

The Emergency's consequences for Gandhi were largely political in nature. She was trounced in the Lok Sabha elections in 1977 from Rae Bareli, which she had treated as her pocket borough—having won from there with huge margins in 1967 and 1971. The Emergency destroyed her image as a democratic leader and the Congress party faced an electoral rout in 1977 in almost all the north Indian states. In another way, Gandhi and her Emergency rule also galvanized the Opposition political parties to unite and form a coalition to defeat her in an election. That led to the formation of the first non-Congress government in New Delhi and the emergence of coalition politics in independent India. The defeat of the Congress and Gandhi in the 1977 elections, after the Emergency, also deepened democratic roots in India. The message went out loud and clear to political parties of all shades and opinion that voters are quick to retaliate with their ballots if any political party or its leaders make any attempts to abridge or curtail their democratic rights.

This was also a big lesson that Gandhi learnt from her Emergency experience. That she learnt it fast helped her recover politically and bounce back in less than a year or so, first in the Lok Sabha and then as the leader of a rejuvenated Congress to be the country's prime minister once again in 1980. Of course, the Janata Party, the coalition that had been formed after ousting Gandhi, was equally responsible for her return. It failed to operate as a cohesive coalition and its vindictive action against Gandhi (the Janata Party government sent her to jail on charges of corruption on 3 October 1977) swung the voter's sympathy back in her favour.[10]

What helped Gandhi recover from the Emergency setback was also the manner in which she responded to her election defeat, committing herself to the spirit of democracy. Immediately after she resigned in 1977, Gandhi acknowledged her defeat and said, 'The collective judgment of the electorate must be respected.' Shortly after resigning, Gandhi delivered an address over the All India Radio and said, 'Winning or losing of the election is less important than strengthening the country. My colleagues and I accept the people's verdict unreservedly and in a spirit of humility.'[11] And then before demitting office, Gandhi revoked her own Emergency rules, ending a sordid saga of India's politics.

CHAPTER 14

A POUND OF FLESH

Election months are usually quiet for civil servants in most economic ministries in the government. If officers are not assigned to election duty, they can actually take it easy during the few weeks that precede the elections. And if the elections are for the Lok Sabha, this is also the time for civil servants to engage in some useful gossiping among themselves over which political party has a greater chance to retain or regain power at the Centre.

In the summer of 1991, B.P. Verma, a joint secretary in the finance ministry, was hardly in that kind of a mood. His former colleague in the IAS, Yashwant Sinha, had become the finance minister a few months ago in November 1990, when Chandra Shekhar formed a minority government with outside support of Rajiv Gandhi's Congress. But Sinha could not present his Budget in February 1991 as Gandhi had withdrawn support to the government quite suddenly. And the government fell.[1] But the Chandra Shekhar government was asked to continue to function till a new government could be formed after the elections.

The Indian economy was going through one of its worst crises—an outcome of worsening balance of payments and growing fiscal indiscipline. A new and stable government was sorely needed to steer the economy and the country out of the perilous situation. The past two governments had lasted only a few months each—the government of Vishwanath Pratap Singh fell before completing even a year in office and Chandra Shekhar lasted for just four months before being asked by the President to run a caretaker government till the elections were completed. Just after the completion of the first phase of the elections, former prime minister Rajiv Gandhi, who was leading the Congress campaign to regain power at the Centre, was killed in a terrorist attack in Sriperumbudur in Tamil Nadu in the third week of May. The second phase of the general elections had to be postponed. This worsened India's economic situation, as it was running out of its foreign-exchange reserves and there were now doubts about its ability to honour its international payments obligations.

In such a grim and precarious situation, Verma received a phone call from the PMO. The message was brief: Verma had to go to Patna immediately with a confidential file, locate Sinha who was busy electioneering there, and get the file signed by the finance minister and return to New Delhi at the earliest. Soon, a file, marked confidential, arrived at Verma's office through a special messenger. Verma picked up the phone to contact Indian Airlines to book an air ticket to Patna.[2]

Those were the pre-liberalization days. Private-sector airlines were yet to start providing service in the domestic skies. The only air connection between Delhi and Patna was a daily service run by Indian Airlines. As a joint secretary, Verma had assumed that he would get a seat through a simple telephone call. But it was the peak election season and all the seats on the day's Indian Airlines flight from Delhi to Patna were booked and the state-owned airline expressed deep regret over its inability to provide him a seat. Verma was not to give up so easily. He was under instructions from the highest office in the country that he must reach Patna that day to get the file signed by Sinha.

Verma called up a senior official of the Indian Airlines and explained to him his predicament. The airline official gave him an idea: Would Verma mind standing in the cockpit of the plane and travelling to Patna? It was a bizarre question, Verma thought. Was the Indian Airline official joking with him? Could he possibly travel in an aircraft like he had travelled standing on a public bus many times in his life?

As it turned out, standing in the cockpit of the aircraft was the only option available for Verma to reach Patna the same day. Verma was helpfully told that the pilot of the aircraft would be aware of his emergency requirement and has been specifically instructed to allow him to stand in the cockpit.

Verma does not recall if he had been given a ticket for the travel and whether he got himself insured. But he did get an entry card, accompanied the pilots of the aircraft and entered the plane, with the confidential file held tightly and close to his chest. The flight was uneventful, though it was a little odd for him to complete a flight standing. Thankfully, there wasn't any turbulence, and Verma reached Patna, acutely conscious of the fact that as a law-abiding citizen and an IAS officer he had knowingly violated aviation rules of safety and security.

Locating Sinha in Patna was not a difficult task. The finance minister was busy campaigning for the SJP, which was hoping to win as many seats as possible in that election. On seeing Verma, Sinha looked a little puzzled. But the puzzled look disappeared soon when he opened the file and quickly signed the papers, and returned them to Verma with the instruction that they be taken back to the prime minister's office at the earliest.[3] Getting back to New Delhi by the next available flight was not a problem and the signed file was soon back in the PMO.

The file that Verma had carried on that flight, in the most dramatic and bizarre way, contained the government's proposal to sell 20 tonnes of confiscated gold kept with the SBI. Selling gold was the only way the government could have got some precious foreign exchange so that it could meet its international payment obligations. The government of Chandra Shekhar did its best to avoid a situation where India would have to default on its payments to global lenders and the sale of gold was one of those extreme steps taken. And Verma was one of the officials who played an important role of having carried a file in a plane, while standing, to reach Patna and get the finance minister's approval.

The Big Reform

On 2 July 1991, a minority government led by Prime Minister P.V. Narasimha Rao, assisted by Finance Minister Manmohan Singh, who had just made his ministerial debut and was yet to become a member of Parliament, took one of the boldest steps any government could take. Just ten days had passed by after the Rao government had been sworn in, but its finance minister in consultation with the RBI allowed the Indian rupee— long considered a symbol of India's economic pride—to depreciate by 9.5 per cent. That took the value of the Indian rupee per dollar down from Rs 21 to Rs 23 in one stroke. The next day, the Indian currency was depreciated by another 12 per cent. India was stunned. The last time such a sharp depreciation of the Indian currency happened was in 1966. Just like the 1966 devaluation was an outcome of a serious economic situation obtaining in the country, the downward adjustment in the value of the Indian rupee, too, resulted from an economic crisis of unprecedented proportions. But the difference in 1991 was that unlike what happened in the wake of the 1966 devaluation, the depreciation of the rupee twenty-five years later was followed by a series of path-breaking reforms. A series of bold measures followed in 1991 to bail the Indian economy out of its worst balance-of-payments crisis and introduce reforms in industrial, trade and fiscal policies. The disruptions these new policies unleashed in a short span of about two months had a long-lasting positive impact on India's politics and economic management. This was a disruption of a different kind—with an impact that was largely positive for the economy. Proof of that was the nearly irrevocable path of economic reforms rolled out after these measures, pursued by governments led by political parties of different beliefs and hues and resulting in a relatively high and stable growth experienced by the Indian economy in the succeeding years.

Just ten days before that shock decision on depreciating the Indian currency, Narasimha Rao had taken oath as the prime minister of the first Congress government that did not enjoy a majority in the Lok Sabha on its own. The formation of such a government in itself was a reflection of the kind of fraught politics and the crisis-ridden state of the economy that prevailed then. No opposition political party decided to contest the formation of a minority government. All of them realized that on their own they could not form a government and the Congress was indeed the single-largest party at that time in the Lok Sabha.

Another thought that influenced their decision not to create a hurdle in the Congress way was the delicate condition of the Indian economy, made worse by two short-lived governments and the killing of a former prime minister. The death of Rajiv Gandhi, while he was campaigning for the 1991 elections, delayed the process of concluding the poll process and the formation of a government that could take the necessary policy steps, on the basis of which the international multilateral bodies would extend assistance to India. Concerns over the nation's economic well-being obliged them to support a government that may be short on the requisite majority in the Lok Sabha, but was competent to take the tough measures necessary to rescue the economy out of that crisis. That was also perhaps one of the reasons not too many voices were raised when Narasimha Rao invited Manmohan Singh to be the finance minister of his government.

Before getting a phone call from Narasimha Rao to come for the swearing-in ceremony at Ashoka Hall in Rashtrapati Bhavan, Manmohan Singh had virtually retired at the end of what was certainly a long and successful career as a public servant. He had occupied almost every important position in the government's economic policy administration—from being a chief economic adviser, economic affairs secretary in the finance ministry and member-secretary of the Planning Commission to the governor of the RBI. Subsequently, he had been invited by the South Commission to be its secretary-general. Completing that assignment coincided with the looming crisis in the Indian economy. As he landed back in his country, Singh found that his services were required in the PMO. Prime Minister Chandra Shekhar invited him to be his economic adviser.

It seemed then that in 1990 Singh began a fresh innings of his life—one that would eventually launch him into a political career. Little did anyone anticipate then, let alone perhaps he himself, that his innings would take him further up—from being a finance minister for five years to the prime minister for ten long years. But during that summer of 1991, there was a short period of time when it seemed Singh's career in economic administration was coming to an end. As elections were called in 1990, the economic crisis got worse and Rajiv Gandhi was killed in a terrorist attack. At the time, Singh was working in a safe and apolitical position as the chairman of the University Grants Commission. When Singh got that call from Narasimha Rao, he was reconciled to leading a relatively quiet life and doing the work of guiding the fortunes of India's higher academic institutions.

Singh's meeting with Rao was short. By then Singh had already become famous for sporting a look that could be compared only to a *Sthitaprajna* or the Enlightened, as enunciated by Krishna in the Mahabharata. Singh sported a look of one who was unperturbed by sorrow or unmoved in joy. When Rao asked Singh if he would become the finance minister, three questions came in Singh's mind.[4] Why was Narasimha Rao taking him on board to tackle the economic crisis? Will the government agree to take the tough measures needed to bail the economy out of the crisis? And if there was political resistance to his moves, would he be made a political scapegoat? Narasimha Rao's replies were highly reassuring.

Narasimha Rao told Singh that having spent his entire life in politics, he thought that it was time now to do something fundamentally reformist and transformational for the country. Rao wanted to be in the history books with whatever can be done to rescue the country from that crisis. He also reiterated that the government was fully committed to backing the new finance minister in the steps that he planned to take. And if there was any political pushback or resistance, Singh would not be made the scapegoat. 'You take the steps needed, I will take the political flak, if necessary,' Rao was reported to have told Singh.[5]

At the end of that short meeting, Rao told Singh that after the swearing-in, he should start functioning from North Block, the headquarters of the finance ministry. It was only a couple of days after the swearing-in that the presidential communique allocating the finance ministry to Manmohan Singh had been issued. But Singh had already begun his damage repair work from North Block. One of the first letters Singh wrote after assuming charge as the finance minister of a government that could soon go bankrupt was to Michel Camdessus, the managing director of the IMF, seeking its financial help for India.

The seriousness of the Indian economy's crisis could be gauged from the key data on the government's own finances and the economy's performance. The Union government's fiscal deficit (not including those of the states) had widened to a record high of 8.4 per cent of the GDP. Worse, the balance-of-payments situation was sending alarm signals—the country's foreign-exchange reserves were ruling at around $1.3 billion to $1.5 billion, not adequate to meet its import needs for even three weeks. The total external debt was over $70 billion. Though only a small portion of this amount—an estimated $4 billion—could be classified as short-term debt, the risks arising out of such exposure could not be underestimated. The burden was huge for an economy whose size was just about $290 billion.

How It All Happened

The crisis for India did not erupt in one day. It had been brewing for quite some time. The formation of the National Front government, led by Vishwanath Pratap Singh as its prime minister, was a political victory for the Opposition parties in the country, but eventually turned out to be a recipe for economic disaster. Rajiv Gandhi had led the Congress party in the 1984 elections to an unprecedented victory, with 404 seats won out of the 514 that had gone to polls. However, by the time Gandhi was readying to face the electorate in 1989, his popularity among voters had taken a hit. His government's decision to purchase guns from Bofors, a Swedish arms manufacturer, became controversial as there were charges that the company had paid bribes to some Indian leaders to facilitate the deal. For buying 400 Bofors field guns at a price of Rs 1700 crore, the Rajiv Gandhi government faced its worst political crisis. A Joint Parliamentary Committee, set up by the government to probe the charges of bribery and the gun deal, submitted a report in May 1988 that concluded that there was no evidence that any Indian was involved in receiving the 'winding-up charges', which Bofors had paid to three companies based in England, Switzerland and Panama. A dissent note submitted by one of the members of the committee (Aladi Aruna, who was then with the AIADMK) revealed gaping holes in the clean chit issued by the JPC to the Bofors gun deal. Aruna said: 'The conclusions of the report conceal the facts of the deal and cover up the connivance of our government with Bofors and refuse to identify the recipients, who could be none other than Indians or Indian associates, or both.'[6]

In the run-up to the 1989 general elections, V.P. Singh had used to the hilt the sentiment that Aruna had expressed in his dissent note. Singh was one of Gandhi's favourite and trusted ministers when the Congress government was formed after the landslide victory in 1984. He was the finance minister in the Rajiv Gandhi government and presented two successive Budgets. But even as Singh was preparing to present his third successive Budget in 1987, differences between him and Gandhi had widened to reach a point where just about a month before the Budget (which used to be presented to Parliament on the last working day of February) was to be out, Gandhi divested Singh of his finance portfolio and transferred him to the defence ministry. This shift was attributed to Gandhi's increasing discomfort with Singh's crusade against many top business leaders by conducting raids at their residences and office premises as well as his keenness to launch an inquiry into charges of bribery levelled against the government's arms purchases, including Bofors field guns and HDW submarines.

Soon after his transfer to the defence ministry, Singh quit the government and even the Congress before the year came to an end. In the process, Singh had cemented his persona as an honest crusading political leader against corruption. And when he formed a party by the name of Janata Dal and built a nation-wide coalition of parties opposed to the Congress, in particular, it was clear that Singh had secured his victory in his political battle against Gandhi.

Singh's election campaign against Rajiv Gandhi on the question of Bofors corruption did yield handsome results for the Janata Dal leader. Gandhi tried to dismiss those charges, but the popular mood had turned in favour of Singh. Even Gandhi's attempts to woo the Hindu voter by launching his campaign from Ayodhya and blessing the foundation ceremony for building a Ram temple there failed to reap the kind of electoral benefits he had hoped to garner for his party. Instead, the nature of Gandhi's campaign led to the Congress losing the sympathy of the Muslim community, till then a safe constituency for the party. The election results did not give the Congress the requisite number of Lok Sabha seats to allow Gandhi to form a government at the Centre. Singh, on the other hand, managed to cobble together a coalition government with support from different political parties—some supported by being part of the coalition and others from outside.

Even as Singh took oath as prime minister on 2 December 1989, the precarious situation of the Indian economy started becoming clearer to him. His finance minister, Madhu Dandavate, announced at a crowded news conference soon after the formation of the National Front government, that the nation's coffers were empty. After such an alarming statement, the challenges for rescuing the economy from its perils became even more onerous. Madhu Dandavate's Budget presented in March 1990 outlined tough fiscal measures to mobilize more revenues to address the problem of growing fiscal indiscipline. But the state of the Indian economy was nowhere near a path of recovery. On top of that, the balance-of-payments situation was getting worse, even as the global situation got adverse with international crude oil prices seeing a spike, imposing greater foreign exchange burden on the Singh government. Having won a political battle against Gandhi, Singh was now facing a more difficult battle on the economic front.

In its attempts to rescue the economy, the National Front government decided to seek support from the IMF, even though ideologically it was opposed to the idea. In September 1990, the government borrowed about $550 million from the IMF under the gold tranche facility. It was a loan obtained without making any public disclosure at that time. It was a quiet operation, and only about a year after the loan was obtained that the P.V. Narasimha Rao government, formed in the second half of 1991, made this public. That secrecy perhaps also explained why the National Front government obtained the loan, but got away without taking any significant corrective steps to bolster the economy. Singh's woes got worse when he was faced with political uncertainty and a worsening economic situation. Rebellion within the Janata Dal surfaced all of a sudden. As many as sixty-four members of Parliament belonging to the Janata Dal broke away from Singh and joined the Samajwadi Janata Party (SJP), which Chandra Shekhar had set up in 1990. The defection of so many MPs also meant the fall of the V.P. Singh government and this paved the way for a minority government to be formed in November 1990, led by Chandra Shekhar, with the support of Rajiv Gandhi's Congress from outside. That government with Chandra Shekhar as the prime minister appointed Sinha as its finance minister.

The Chandra Shekhar government's tenure, however, was almost equally short-lived. It had, nevertheless, begun preparing a plan for reviving the economy in earnest. One of those key steps was to convince the IMF by January 1991 that it must sanction two loans to India—for an amount of $775 million under the first credit tranche facility and for $1.02 billion under the compensatory and contingency financing facility. The government had promised to the IMF that in return for those loans, needed to keep India's record of meeting international payments obligations intact, the government would introduce a series of economic policy reforms. The Budget that the government was expected to announce in February 1991 would contain a list of those measures. However, by the middle of February that year, Rajiv Gandhi's Congress withdrew its support to the Chandra Shekhar government on a specious issue and that left President R. Venkataraman with no other choice than calling for fresh elections and asking Chandra Shekhar to continue as the head of a caretaker government till a new government was elected. This also meant that the IMF loans that could have come to help the Indian economy could not be cleared till an elected government was in place and the country's economic crisis worsened.

After having short stints as cabinet secretary in 1989 and as a member of the Planning Commission in 1990, T.N. Seshan, a 1955-batch IAS officer, found himself in Nirvachan Sadan, headquarters of the Election Commission of India, as Chief Election Commissioner, a post he would hold for five years, conducting two general elections—one would see the formation of a minority government led by P.V. Narasimha Rao in 1991 and the other would see the defeat of the same government and the formation of a series of unstable coalition governments for the next two years. As soon as the Chandra Shekhar government fell, Seshan swung into action, putting in place a schedule for holding the general elections in the month of May so that a new government could be formed soon enough to prevent any further deterioration in the state of the economy.

On Raisina Hill, at the Cabinet Secretariat, there was at around the same time a new occupant of the post of cabinet secretary—Naresh Chandra, a 1956-batch IAS officer. He had succeeded Vinod C. Pande, another IAS officer, whose tenure ended just as V.P. Singh exited from the PMO. Pande was the revenue secretary in the finance ministry when

V.P. Singh was the finance minister and helped the latter carry out the many raids and investigations against allegedly corrupt business leaders and controversial government deals.

In many ways, Chandra Shekhar's appointment as prime minister was closely linked to the positioning of both Seshan and Chandra at these two crucial jobs. Seshan, who in 1989 was the cabinet secretary under the Rajiv Gandhi government, was sent to the Planning Commission by V. P. Singh to make way for Vinod Pande. Soon after Chandra Shekhar formed his government in November 1990, he brought in Chandra, who was then the home secretary, as the cabinet secretary and shifted Seshan from the Planning Commission to head the Election Commission. While Seshan was busy taking steps to hold the crucial elections in May, Chandra was busy providing guidance to a caretaker government on how important decisions could be taken to prevent the crisis from escalating but without violating the Constitutional niceties that would bar a caretaker government from taking any policy decision.

The visit of Finance Secretary Sriranga Purushottam Shukla to Washington in April 1991 was one such move that had been okayed by Chandra. Shukla had the RBI Governor S. Venkitaramanan as his company and both were in Washington on 28 April to attend the annual spring meeting of the IMF and World Bank. They had a tough time facing up to the officials of the two Bretton Woods institutions, who were extremely unhappy with India for its failure to honour the promise of reforms because of political uncertainties caused by the sudden fall of the government. Venkitaramanan and Shukla stomached those words of admonition and broached gingerly the idea of the Aid India Consortium, a group of developed donor countries, including the US, Japan, Germany, the UK, France and the Netherlands, the IMF and the World Bank, to consider extending temporary loans of about $700 million to help India meet its emerging international payments obligations. Finance Minister Yashwant Sinha also visited Tokyo to seek Japan's financial assistance. Foreign Secretary Muchkund Dubey was in Washington at around the same time to persuade the US to lean on Japan and Germany to accommodate India's request for financial help. Their efforts did not go entirely in vain. A few days later, Japan sanctioned to India a soft loan of $150 million and a further commitment of $350 million, Germany granted a loan of about $400 million and the Netherlands too agreed to offer India $30 million as a soft loan.[7]

These loan amounts were small compared to the overall need for the Indian economy to bail itself out of that balance-of-payments crisis.

But they were useful to prevent an escalation and, more importantly, showed the commitment of even a caretaker government to honour its international payments obligations, instead of seeking recourse to the option of a default, like some Latin American countries chose to do, and a course that was advocated in a section of the Indian political class.

The loans kept the country's foreign-exchange reserves above the critical level of about $1 billion and the caretaker government, led by Prime Minister Chandra Shekhar and Finance Minister Yashwant Sinha, with able assistance from Cabinet Secretary Naresh Chandra and RBI Governor S. Venkitaramanan, took a series of belt-tightening measures. Thus, a squeeze on imports was enforced, inconveniencing no end Indian traders and industrialists. In addition, the State Trading Corporation and MMTC, the government's two biggest trading arms, started cancelling import orders to prevent any fresh payment liability accumulating on them. This was also partly in response to many foreign suppliers refusing to honour letters of credit issued by Indian banks, unless they were guaranteed or confirmed by internationally reputed banks. This raised import costs and taken together with the measures taken by the RBI to tighten the money supply, it was a tough time to do business in India.

On 3 May, the RBI introduced a cash-reserve ratio for banks at 10 per cent of their net demand and time liabilities, which effectively meant a total CRR requirement of 25 per cent. CRR is that share of the commercial banks' total deposit that must be kept with the RBI in the form of liquid cash and this is done in a bid to regulate the total lendable resources that the banks have and to keep inflation under control. With the resultant tightening of the money market, call rates shot up to 30 to 40 per cent. A week later, the government came out with another round of measures to tighten money supply by imposing a 25 per cent surcharge on bank credit for import finance. Within weeks after these extremely tight measures to choke money supply and raise the cost of imports, the government realized that there was now no recourse left to it other than approaching the IMF for an emergency loan.

On 13 May, a two-member team left for Washington. Its members included Chief Economic Adviser Deepak Nayyar and RBI Deputy Governor Chakravarthi Rangarajan. On its agenda was a proposal for seeking a bridge loan of $700 million from the IMF to help India avert a payments default. It was one of the most serious situations the Indian economy had faced since it became an independent country. Almost all senior political leaders of different parties agreed that the country had little option other than seeking an IMF loan and the leaders who supported the Chandra Shekhar government's move then included Rajiv Gandhi, Lal Kishan Advani and Vishwanath Pratap Singh. This was also an early indication of the political mood that would envelop the country in the next few months, where all political parties irrespective of their political ideologies would either remain neutral or support the dramatic but path-breaking steps needed to rescue the economy from its crisis.

The crisis was aggravated with another tragedy—this time it was the dastardly manner in which Rajiv Gandhi was killed in a bomb attack at Sriperumbudur near Chennai. That was on 21 May. The election schedule was upset. This added to the uncertainty over an early conclusion of an economic rescue package. The election calendar for the remaining phase had to be rescheduled and it became clear that a new government to take the necessary decisions on the economy would not be in place before the third week of June. A big relief came in the form of statements from the World Bank and the IMF, reiterating their support to India. But these statements also made it clear that they would not sanction any fresh loans before a new government was in place.

By then, the country's foreign-exchange reserves had dipped below $1 billion, sending out alarm signals to the markets and the managers of the economy. It was at that point in time that the Chandra Shekhar government took perhaps the boldest step that any caretaker government can take—it decided to mortgage 20 tonnes of confiscated gold, kept with the SBI, to UBS in Zurich with the option of buying it back after six months.

All it got in return was a loan amount of $240 million. Something was better than nothing. The entire operation of shipping the gold was conducted in complete secrecy and the shipment was completed by 30 May. The news of the sale of the confiscated gold was out only about a week later. Of course, the political reaction was on expected lines. After Yashwant Sinha made it public, most political reaction was adverse and the narrative was that the government had sold its gold as it failed to manage the economy. Even Congress leader Pranab Mukherjee criticized the move.[8]

International markets, however, continued to punish India. Rating agencies like Standard & Poor's downgraded India's long-term rating to the speculative category. It had reasoned in its rating statement that the dangers of India defaulting on its international payments obligations had not receded. Indeed, such a statement actually halted the government's

fresh moves on sending another consignment of gold abroad for securing
fresh foreign exchange to repay its loan liabilities becoming due in the
next few weeks.[9] There was a view that any such move might downgrade
India's rating further. Cabinet Secretary Naresh Chandra convened a
meeting of secretaries on 6 June to review the economic situation and
the meeting pointed to yet another risk that the Indian economy was
exposed to. It was reckoned that non-resident Indians (NRI) had parked
an estimated Rs 20,000 crore by way of deposits in India and if another
round of gold sale was resorted to, there was a fear of a flight of such
NRI deposits out of the country. And this could have further worsened
the balance-of-payments situation. A day after that meeting, the finance
minister and RBI Deputy Governor Chakravarthi Rangarajan issued
a public statement assuring the nation that there would be no further
pledging or sale of gold. As subsequent events showed, that statement
was nothing but a balm to soothe the market sentiment; India did
dispatch a few more rounds of gold shipments abroad, but only after a
new government was in place.

* * *

On 21 June 1991, P.V. Narasimha Rao took oath as the prime minister
of a new minority government after the Congress won 232 out of the 521
seats in the lower house, for which elections were held then. No other
political party in that house was in a mood to challenge the formation of
the Congress government, given the state of the economy and the need
to have a government in place at the earliest opportunity. The Bharatiya
Janata Party had won the second largest number of seats at 120, but its
stance was no different.

Thus, the Rao government started its innings as a minority
government, putting an end to what turns out to be the longest rule by
a caretaker government in independent India's history. The Chandra
Shekhar government fell on 6 March, but President R. Venkataraman
asked it to function as a caretaker government till the elections were
completed and a new government was in place. In these three months and
a couple of weeks, the Chandra Shekhar government took some of the
most dramatic decisions to prevent the country's economic crisis from
getting worse. But more dramatic decisions were to follow in the next few
weeks as Rao took charge as prime minister and held his first Cabinet
meeting on the very same day he and his colleagues had been sworn in.

At that Cabinet meeting, Rao asked Manmohan Singh to take charge of the finance ministry and take the necessary steps to shore up the economy. Singh was the only minister that day who knew of his portfolio, as the full list of ministers with their portfolios came out only after a day.[10]

Singh realized at the very start of his innings as finance minister that the tasks for him were formidable. His team in the ministry, with S.P. Shukla and Deepak Nayyar, finance secretary and chief economic adviser respectively, had already helped the Chandra Shekhar government take a series of steps to prevent further deterioration in the economic situation. Singh did not enjoy a great equation with either Shukla or Nayyar, but he made no immediate changes in his team in North Block. Instead, he widened his consultation process to arrive at the package of measures that needed to be taken to tackle the imminent crisis. Apart from his officers in the finance ministry, he roped in senior secretaries and economic advisers in different ministries for consultation, including Montek Singh Ahluwalia, who was then the commerce secretary, and Rakesh Mohan, who was then in the industry ministry as its economic adviser. There was general concurrence on the need for taking urgent remedial steps that would reassure the international business community and institutions that India meant business and was keen on bailing itself out of its crisis. The prime minister played a stellar role by offering his full support to the finance minister for the steps he thought were necessary.

About a week later, Singh decided to go in for a steep correction in the value of the Indian rupee by depreciating it by more than 20 per cent. Barring a few voices of mild dissent, there was a general view that the proposed depreciation was a credible path to take. The only debate was on whether the correction should be brought in two phases or in a single round. The RBI was in favour of a single-stroke depreciation of 20 per cent. Clearly, that was a view of a technocrat, but the awareness of the political implications of such a sharp correction in the value of the currency influenced Singh and other bureaucrats in the government to go in for a two-stage depreciation. The logic was that a two-stage correction would allow businesses, trade and the people absorb the shock. The counter-argument was that a two-stage depreciation could build political pressure within the ruling party. After the first round of depreciation, there could be pressure on the finance minister to go soft and avoid the second round of depreciation. And that is exactly what happened. It is a different matter that Singh's deft handling of the situation saved the day.

On 2 July, a depreciation of 9.5 per cent in the value of the rupee against the US dollar was announced and the official explanation was that it was a routine adjustment in the currency value. To prevent any political mobilization against the next round, Singh even issued a public statement to quell rumours that the government might be buckling under the pressure of the IMF for securing loans. He said: 'We will not do anything under pressure and which is not consistent with our national interest.' Indian industry's response was unusually positive. The Confederation of Engineering Industry, as CII was known then and which by then had become the most influential industry voice in the country, welcomed the move, but Lalit Mohan Thapar, chairman of the Thapar group and an influential member of the Bombay Club that had serious doubts on the efficacy and need for opening up the economy, issued a guarded statement: 'More steps should follow towards liberalization and other long overdue measures.' Backchannel communication from the government was also in full swing. Commerce Minister Palaniappan Chidambaram held a meeting with senior media representatives to put the entire depreciation move in the context of the prevailing economic and political situation. Chidambaram had also taken the media leaders into confidence on the contours of the big structural economic policy changes the government wished to initiate in the coming days.

While this helped the government to get media on its side, political forces against depreciation were not adequately reined in. On 3 July, the RBI had prepared to go in for the second round of depreciation— by about 12 per cent. This would have meant the Indian rupee's value against the US dollar would go down from about Rs 21.09 to Rs 25.95 in just about two days—a fall of over 23 per cent. Just when the second round was going to be announced, Singh got a call from his prime minister, P.V. Narasimha Rao, who had by now been approached by several senior politicians. These leaders wanted the prime minister to rein in Singh on effecting these changes so rapidly and with such sharp consequences. Rao asked Singh if the second round of depreciation could be held back. Singh paused and told him what was not entirely accurate, yet he could not be faulted for telling a lie. He explained to the prime minister that the depreciation process had already been effected, and it would be difficult to roll it back at that stage. It was after all a two-stage depreciation and the process, Singh referred to in his reply to Rao, had begun on 2 July. Rao had no option. In the meanwhile, Singh allowed the deputy governor of the RBI, Chakravarthi Rangarajan, to go ahead with the depreciation.

The same evening Commerce Minister Chidambaram announced a series of trade policy changes. He abolished the system of export subsidies in the form of providing cash compensatory support, removed supplementary licences, aimed at helping exporters with import facilities, and decanalized the import of a host of goods. Decanalization removed the monopoly of the state-owned companies in sourcing these goods from foreign countries and allowed any Indian company, be it in the private or the public sector, to import them freely through their own channels of trade. He also announced a plan for transitioning to a new system of offering import benefits to exporters. In the system prevailing then, exporters used to get replenishment licences against their shipments. These licences gave exporters the benefit of duty-free imports. Abandoning that system, Chidambaram introduced exim scrips to be issued to exporters and these could be traded in the markets. Within a few weeks, there was a new trade policy and a time table was outlined for making the rupee convertible on the current account. By March 1992, the government announced the Liberalized Exchange Rate Management System or LERMS, which essentially introduced a dual exchange-rate system. Exporters could convert 60 per cent of the dollars they earned at a market rate and the remaining at the official exchange rate. By March 1993, a unified exchange rate, linked to the markets, was in place and exporters could convert their entire dollar earnings at that market-linked exchange rate. This paved the way for the country's biggest exchange rate policy reform in the country and ended the incentive for sustaining what was till then a thriving illegal market for converting dollars into rupees or hawala.

The crisis that Singh was dealing with on the macroeconomic front in July, however, was far from over. The foreign-exchange reserves had dipped just below $1 billion and Singh went in for three more rounds of pledging of gold kept with the RBI. The pledging was done with the Bank of England and required the physical movement of a part of the RBI's gold reserves. On 6 July, 25 tonnes of gold was air-freighted to London, to be kept with the Bank of England as security against which the government obtained a loan of $200 million. Two more such gold shipments—of 9.8 tonnes a week later and 12 tonnes on 18 July—took place as a result of which India could borrow up to a total amount of $400 million. A week later, on 24 July, Singh presented his first Budget that outlined a road map for the economic reforms that would be needed in the coming years. More important than the Budget was the laying on the table of Parliament the government's decision to liberalize industrial policy, changes that would unshackle Indian industry from licensing controls of the previous forty years and help, in the words of Singh, release the 'animal spirits' of Indian business leaders.

Each of the industrial policy changes announced on 24 July would fundamentally alter the way Indian business would operate in the coming years and indeed decades. The asset limit for companies governed by the MRTP Act was scrapped in one stroke. This meant virtually unlimited freedom for Indian industries to grow without worrying about breaching the ceiling on their assets, initially set at Rs 20 crore in 1969. It had been relaxed twice in the past—to Rs 50 crore in 1980 and to Rs 100 crore in 1985, but now it was scrapped. Even bolder was the decision to abolish industrial licensing for all sectors except eighteen specified groups. Giving a big boost to the private sector's freedom to operate in new areas, Singh allowed private enterprises to enter as many as ten new areas, which till then were reserved exclusively for the public sector. A few of the sectors, which were reserved for the public sector and now thrown open to the private sector, were iron and steel, heavy electrical plants, aircraft manufacturing, air transportation, ship-building, telephones, telephone cables and power generation as well as distribution. Automatic approval for foreign equity participation up to 51 per cent in thirty-four selected industries was permitted and companies entering into foreign technology agreements were freed from the requirement of obtaining the government's permission. Such approvals for a host of technology agreements, often a bone of contention and a cause for delay, were made automatic. In a big relief to the private sector, Singh also scrapped the clause that allowed conversion of loans into equity for new projects. This clause would earlier result in financial institutions being saddled with equity shares of many companies just because they had given loans to them. In another major move, Singh also allowed the process of state-owned enterprises to shed their stake in the market with the twin intention of raising revenues for the government through the sale of stakes in the PSUs and consequently subjecting these enterprises to greater market discipline.

That was just the beginning. The changes brought about by the industrial policy liberalization on that day would set off a series of policy changes in other sectors of the Indian economy. Their impact would be felt for several decades later.

CHAPTER 15

AN ANATOMY OF THE CRISIS

What led to the first set of disruptions that caused India's fiscal indiscipline to reach an unsustainably high level and the balance of payments deteriorate to a precarious situation? The root cause of the problems was the pace of growth that was pursued by the Rajiv Gandhi government between 1985 and 1989. Gandhi had finalized an ambitious plan for investments to boost growth. Aiming at an annual growth target of 5 per cent, the Seventh Five-Year Plan (1985–90) had hugely relied on borrowing to fund the requisite investments. While the five years of the plan indeed saw the growth rate at 6 per cent per annum, exceeding the target by a clear margin of one percentage point, pressures on the government's fiscal situation and on the balance of payments were becoming too obvious to be ignored. By 1988–89, the Union government's fiscal deficit had deteriorated to over 7 per cent of the GDP. The current account deficit, too, widened to 2.7 per cent of GDP. With no recourse to any support from the capital account (foreign investment flows those days were almost negligible, and foreign institutional investors were not allowed to invest in India's stock markets), even that level of current account gap became difficult to meet without drawing down foreign-exchange reserves. Not surprisingly, the economy had hit a major roadblock as it faced difficulty in meeting its import needs and honouring its past international payment obligations.

Three factors could be identified as the cause of this disruption. One was a borrowing-led pursuit of growth. Two, political uncertainty that got deeper with the V.P. Singh government falling less than a year after its formation and then the Chandra Shekhar government falling in just four months. And three, the emergency measures that were needed to prevent further deterioration of the economy. If Rajiv Gandhi was responsible for the first two disruptions, then Chandra Shekhar was the key force behind the third disruption. Qualitatively, these three disruptions are of different types, although there are strong causal connections between them.

Gandhi, of course, has been accused of having led an economic policy in the 1980s which relied on borrowings to boost growth and contributed to the economic crisis in 1991. The World Bank in a report in 1991 observed: 'In this environment, the shift in the stance of macro-policy from the conservative management of aggregate demand in the 1960s and 1970s to the fiscal expansionism of 1980s resulted in large and potentially unsustainable accumulations of domestic and foreign debt.'[1] Imagine a situation where Gandhi had been less ambitious about his growth projections and had ensured adequate availability of resources for investment without relying excessively on borrowing, or had preceded that investment-led growth drive with basic reforms by at least partially opening up the economy to foreign investment and by liberalizing trade and industrial policies! The consequences for the economy would certainly have been far less severe. Indeed, that phase of policymaking has left an indelible impact on all governments that followed it.

The idea of a fiscal deficit had not yet made its debut in media discussions or even in a national debate. It was only after the economic reforms of 1991 that the concept of a fiscal deficit came into vogue. Till then, what constituted Budget deficit was broadly equivalent to net credit from the RBI. By its very nature, there was no check on such deficit financing as the government was not made adequately responsible for its borrowing excesses. After the concept of the fiscal deficit was introduced, the next big reform in this area was when over a period of three years starting from 1994 and ending in 1997, the government's recourse to the issuance of ad hoc treasury bills to finance its deficit was completely stopped. These bills were issued by the government to raise resources to meet its budget deficit. An agreement between the RBI and the government was signed on 9 September 1994 that stipulated that ad hoc treasury bills would be discontinued from 1 April 1997. In order to help the government meet its temporary mismatches in its receipts and payments, the RBI introduced a scheme of Ways and Means Advances (WMA). The new scheme of WMA helped the government obtain necessary cash at a mutually agreed interest rate to meet its temporary payment needs. Any cash withdrawal by the government from the RBI in excess of the WMA limit was allowed only for ten consecutive days. The day the government used up 75 per cent of this limit, the RBI would start floatation of a fresh round of government securities. With the discontinuation of ad hoc treasury bills and the introduction of WMA, the idea of the government's budget deficit became irrelevant and the practice of gross fiscal deficit, capturing the government's total borrowing requirements in a year, became the key indicator of the deficit or the gap between the government's total revenues and expenditure.[2]

The excesses committed by the Gandhi government between 1985 and 1989 proved to be so costly that they led to a new awakening in the minds of India's economic administrators to introduce durable fiscal reforms for the Union government enforcing, thereby, curbs on the government's borrowings. It is quite ironical that Finance Minister S.B. Chavan said with unconcealed pride in his 1989–90 Budget speech that the Seventh Five-Year Plan would be spending an amount that was 150 per cent more than what was envisaged. The outlay target was exceeded, but at the cost of the government's financial discipline. Finance Minister Madhu Dandavate, who presented the next Budget—for 1990–91—did not mince his words when he described the state of the economy as his government had inherited from Gandhi in these words:

> Let me, at the outset, deal with the economic situation that we inherited from the previous Government. I do so not in a spirit of acrimony, but with a view to revealing to the House the ground realities. The Central government's Budgetary deficit was Rs 13,790 crore as on 1st December 1989, a level nearly double the deficit projected for the whole year in the 1989–90 Budget. Wholesale prices had risen by 6.6 per cent since the beginning of the financial year. The balance of payment was under strain and the foreign-exchange reserves (excluding gold and Special Drawing Rights) were down to around Rs 5,000 crore. Stocks of food grains had fallen to 11 million tonnes.

There was yet another consequence of the disruption caused by the political uncertainty in the years before India's economic crisis blew up in 1991. Both the fall of the National Front government, led by Vishwanath Pratap Singh, in November 1990 and the collapse of the Chandra Shekhar government just four months later in March 1991 were caused largely due to political adventurism of a few leaders. The sixty-nine Lok Sabha members of the Janata Dal who defected to form a new party, brought about the fall of the Singh government and formed a new government with the outside support of the Congress were as guilty of such adventurism for political gains as Rajiv Gandhi, who decided to withdraw his party's support to Chandra Shekhar, once again in the hope of securing some political gains.

The collateral damage of such political adventurism for the Indian economy was huge. The disruption that those two incidents caused has taught such a long-term and enduring lesson for India's political class for the next few decades that such narrow, opportunistic political adventurism has never been used so brazenly by any political party after the 1990s, particularly when it is perceived that such actions would entail heavy damage for the economy. Thus, no elections were forced on the nation at the end of the thirteen-day government of Atal Bihari Vajpayee in 1996, and instead, regional opposition parties got together and formed a coalition government that ran for about two years. And when elections had to be called after the sudden fall of the BJP government in 1998, all opposition political parties got together and agreed to first pass the Budget before the Lok Sabha could be dissolved. Similarly, governments that did not enjoy full majority were not usually disallowed from passing economic laws that by common consensus would benefit the economy. While there would be opposition to laws such as opening up foreign direct investment in insurance sector or retail outlets, eventually they would receive the green signal of Parliament with some modifications in the original proposal, after some political give and take. But economic laws would not always be a casualty of political gamesmanship. This certainly is one of the big consequences of the disruption that Rajiv Gandhi's decision had caused in 1991.

Chandra Shekhar, too, qualifies as a disrupter in 1991. He assumed charge as prime minister in November 1990 knowing full well the grim economic situation facing the country. The nature of the policy prescription that his government, under advice from his finance minister, Yashwant Sinha, had outlined, was not very different from what was eventually adopted by the P.V. Narasimha Rao government a few months later after the general elections. Sinha was ready to present his Budget that would outline a series of economic reforms to help the country bail itself out of that crisis on a sustainable basis. However, with Rajiv Gandhi withdrawing support to the government, all that Sinha could do was to present an interim Budget without any of the taxation proposals that he wanted to introduce. The decision to sell 20 tonnes of confiscated gold to UBS, impose curbs on the easy availability of credit for imports and initiate discussions with the IMF for loans were among the many steps that contributed in the long run to the disruption in the Indian economy. It was, of course, a disruption that had a positive intent of preventing further disorder and even chaos in the economy. More importantly, it was a disruption aimed at conveying a larger message to the international community—that India as a nation would not consider default as a credible option to get out of the crisis and instead submit itself to the rigours of hard policy reforms to be recognized as a responsible nation in the world. That intent of the disruptive measures taken by Chandra Shekhar was no less important.

Rebuilding the Economy

The duo of P.V. Narasimha Rao and Manmohan Singh would perhaps stand out as the most effective disrupter in this phase of the Indian economy. Rao's disruption was to bring in an economic administrator like Manmohan Singh to be the finance minister in his minority government. Rao could have easily followed the trodden path of giving the usually coveted job of the finance minister to a veteran politician, who would have then been a little more cautious with his steps, mindful of the political implications and consequences. If Rao had chosen a politician to be his finance minister, the story of India's economic reforms would have been substantially different. But Rao decided to embark on a completely new path— no prime minister ever chose a finance minister who was not a politician. Initially, Rao had thought of offering the finance minister's portfolio to former RBI Governor I.G. Patel, who was not interested in the job. But later Manmohan Singh's name cropped up as an alternative. Rao's preference for a technocrat, instead of a politician, to be the finance minister only shows how serious and complicated the economic challenges before the country were in 1991.

That is also why Rao treated his finance minister like few other prime ministers did or would do after him. As prime minister, he gave his finance minister the freedom to devise the measures to rescue the economy out of a crisis. And when it required some political management to ensure the acceptance of the tough measures that the finance minister was proposing, Rao would step in to find a way out. Singh's decision to hike fertilizer prices by a steep margin of 40 per cent in his first Budget of July 1991 came under intense attack from all quarters including even the CPP, which targeted Singh so viciously that the finance minister offered his resignation to the prime minister. Rao was reported to have asked Singh: 'Are you going to desert me at this lonely hour?'[3] Singh did not press for his resignation and the next day went back to Parliament and announced a rollback of the fertilizer price increase by 10 percentage points. In other words, deft political management of the fertilizer price hike issue allowed the Rao–Singh duo to effect a 30 per cent increase—which was the highest increase in such a politically sensitive input for farmers in many years. That was the other face of the modus operandi of the disruption caused by the Rao–Singh duo.

Similarly, the process followed by Rao and Singh while framing the new industrial policy showed how conscious they were of the need to effectively manage the political fallout of their proposal. The new industrial policy statement made generous references to Nehru and the government's commitment to upholding the values espoused by India's first prime minister. And when the proposed changes, which would actually rewrite almost every aspect of Nehru's Industrial Policy Resolution of 1956, came up for debate in the Cabinet and expectedly met with stiff resistance, Rao chose the noisiest among the opponents of the change, Makhan Lal Fotedar, a long-time Nehru–Gandhi family loyalist, to chair a committee to review the policy before it could be considered again by the Cabinet. The policy was reviewed by the committee. Marginal changes were introduced, while keeping the overall thrust of the policy intact. Rao made sure that the industrial policy changes got the endorsement from Fotedar, who was the sharpest critic of the proposed liberalization. A revised document was presented to the Cabinet a day before the Budget was to be presented on 24 July.

It is important to remember that at the Cabinet level, Rao had kept with himself the portfolio of the industry ministry. This was yet another move of Rao to take charge of the reforms that he wanted to implement. The reforms of 1991 were largely seen in the areas of fiscal policy, trade policy and industrial policy. For trade policy, he had P. Chidambaram, a committed reformer, and he delivered on trade policy changes as the commerce minister. For fiscal policy, he had Manmohan Singh. And for industrial policy, he kept the portfolio with himself at the Cabinet level, a point that is not often recognized. But on the day of the Budget, he decided that instead of reading out the new industrial policy, the document should be simply tabled. And the task of tabling that document in Parliament was, ironically, given to the minister of state for industry, P.J. Kurien, who was not really convinced of the need to bring about such radical changes in industrial policy, doing away controls, removing public-sector monopoly in many areas and allowing a liberalized automatic foreign investment rules in several sectors of the economy.

The disruption that the Rao–Singh duo caused to the Indian economy is also a lesson on how to sequence those disruptive steps. Both of them were aware that the industrial policy changes would hit the vested interests in domestic industry and the political class opposed to such deregulation. In retrospect, thus, the tabling of the industrial policy document in Parliament on the same day as the Budget was a carefully planned strategy. The first Budget of a new government was always expected to elicit special attention from all quarters—trade, industry, political parties and the people in general. In that excitement, the industrial policy statement, which had a greater disruptive impact on economic policymaking, received relatively far less attention. Indeed, the media and the newspapers the next morning, with notable exceptions, talked more about the Budget and less about the liberalized industrial policy.

If the industrial policy deregulated the economy, the Budget struck the right notes as far as politics was concerned. The Budget could be seen as one that soaked the rich. It raised duties on all items that were consumed by the upper-middle-class Indians. The income-tax rates at the lowest income slabs remained unchanged. Barring customs duty cuts in certain goods, Manmohan Singh's first Budget raised taxes on cigarettes and the consumerist India. Was that a political act? Presenting a Budget that was largely popular to bolster the government's revenues and drawing all attention there, so much so that the industrial policy statement deregulating India Inc. remained below the radar? The execution of what caused the biggest disruption to India Inc. was carefully planned to minimize its political consequences.

The durability of the disruptive moves initiated through the reforms of 1991 in fiscal policy, trade policy and industrial policy has been the most robust. If the policy shift from 1950, the Industrial Policy Resolution of 1956 and the Second Five-Year Plan started a new phase in India's economic policies, the policies of 1991 gave those policies a different direction and the changes they brought about have been enduring. The continuation of the policies introduced in 1950 lasted for forty years and that was largely possible because the Congress ruled at the Centre for much of this period. But almost three decades have passed after the reforms of 1991 and there have been different political parties with commitment to different ideologies, but the overall direction of the economic policies have remained the same. There may be differences in minor details of the economic policies framed and followed by the United Front government in 1996–97, the BJP-led coalitions from 1998 to 2004, the Congress for ten years between 2004 and 2014 and the BJP-led government from 2014. But the trend and direction of economic policymaking in these years since

1991 have remained unchanged even though its pace and quality may have undergone some variation.

This is perhaps the biggest tribute to the kind of disruptions that the Rao–Singh duo introduced to India's governance. Not surprisingly, therefore, Rao stood by Singh when the latter faced political attacks because of his economic reforms, and Singh recognized the role Rao played and the support he gave him. In spite of Rao becoming a virtual persona non grata for the Gandhi family, Singh continued to pay Rao the respect that he deserved. Singh was among the very few senior Congress leaders who attended Rao's funeral in Hyderabad and he recognizes the role Rao played in bringing about the most durable disruptions in the Indian economy, for which the history books will never forget either Rao or Singh.

Turning Points

What were the key turning points in the run-up to the Indian economy's fiscal and balance-of-payments crisis of 1991 and the reform policies introduced in its wake? The bribery controversy over the purchase of the Bofors guns by the Rajiv Gandhi government was certainly one of them. The allegations of bribery against a prime minister, who till then was considered Mr Clean, stalled Gandhi's own efforts at reforming the economy and cleansing his own political party and the political processes. The government had signed an agreement in March 1986 to purchase 400 155 mm Howitzer guns from AB Bofors, a Swedish arms manufacturer, at a total price of Rs 1700 crore. About a year later in April 1987, the Swedish Radio had broadcast a report claiming that Bofors had paid bribes to top Indian politicians and defence personnel to secure the deal in its favour. It was a controversy that diverted Gandhi's attention away from governance so much that for the remaining period of his tenure, his primary concern was to defend his reputation as an honest prime minister of a clean government. Gandhi spent more time and energy on defending himself against those bribery charges and his focus on reforms was considerably diluted. Instead, he decided to follow a safe and well-trodden path of reviving growth through investments, even though that meant increased borrowing, adversely affecting the fiscal health of his government. But with no reforms preceding those investments, the Indian economy began hurtling towards a crisis that erupted finally in 1991.

At the same time, the Bofors controversy strengthened the opposition political forces, which were galvanized by none else than Gandhi's former finance minister, V.P. Singh. Gandhi had secured a landslide win for the Congress in the 1984 general elections, with 404 seats out of the 514 Lok Sabha seats for which the polls were held, and a vote share of 49 per cent. Five years later, Gandhi could win only 197 seats (out of 529), with a vote share that shrank to 39.5 per cent. He decided not to stake claim to form a government, even though his was the single-largest party. This paved the way for the formation of an unstable minority government, led by V.P. Singh, whose Janata Dal had won only 143 seats, but had the support of forty-five Left members of the Lok Sabha and the support of eighty-five members of the Bharatiya Janata Party from outside. If the Bofors controversy had not rocked Gandhi and his government about two years after he was sworn in with a record majority, it is possible that Gandhi would have embarked on a different path and the Indian economy and its polity would have taken a different direction.

The second turning point in this phase was the assassination of Rajiv Gandhi on 21 May 1991, while he was campaigning for his party at Sriperumbudur, near Chennai, during the ongoing general elections. Gandhi's death at this point led to a series of developments leading to the formation of a minority government headed by Congress leader P.V. Narasimha Rao. The first phase of the general elections had been completed when Gandhi was killed. As the election results were declared in June 1991, it became clear that the Congress performance was boosted significantly by the assassination. If Gandhi had not been killed, the Congress would have won over forty seats fewer than their actual tally of 232 Lok Sabha seats.[4] That performance would have been worse than the 197 seats it had won in 1989. Without Gandhi's death, therefore, a Congress government was unlikely in 1991. Instead, there could have been another coalition government, which could well have been as unstable and short-lived as the previous ones led by V.P. Singh and Chandra Shekhar. Serious questions would have also arisen over whether the coalition government would have been able to introduce the much-needed economic reforms and tough steps to bail the Indian economy out of that serious crisis.

On the other hand, the death of Gandhi created a sympathy wave in favour of the Congress, which emerged as the single-largest party in the Lok Sabha. Even though it was a minority government, the economic crisis became an opportunity for the Congress leadership to introduce economic reforms by liberalizing the economy. As prime minister of a minority government, Narasimha Rao understood that he had a short window of opportunity to rush through the necessary policy changes.

All the major policy relaxations were introduced within the first 100 days, when the political opposition to those changes were relatively muted. No opposition political party wanted to pull down another government, having already experienced the uncertainty and plight arising out of two successive short-lived unstable governments between 1989 and 1991. Indeed, even as the Rao government acquired the necessary strength in the Lok Sabha to cement its majority, the pace of economic reforms too slowed considerably. Political developments also were responsible from 1992 onwards for slowing down the pace of economic reforms in the remaining period of the Rao government, which completed its full term of five years.

The third and final turning point was Rao's surprising choice of a technocrat as the finance minister of his government in 1991. Traditionally, finance ministers of any government have always been a political heavyweight. Rao, too, must have been under pressure to appoint a political person as the finance minister. But he decided to break away from tradition and chose Manmohan Singh, an economist who had spent almost his entire career in the government system occupying virtually all the top jobs in economic administration. Singh took to his new job as the finance minister like a duck takes to water. Of course, Rao gave him full political support so that Singh could initiate the steps needed for the Indian economy. But Singh not only used his vast experience of having worked in different departments of the government to ensure effective policy implementation, but also built a strong team of bureaucrats and technocrats around him to steer the Indian economy out of that crisis. In retrospect, it is difficult to imagine the reforms of 1991 without Rao's masterstroke in identifying Singh to be the finance minister and Singh's astute shepherding of the Indian economy from his corner office in North Block, the headquarters of the finance ministry in New Delhi.

CHAPTER 16

THE GAME OF LIFE AND DEATH

As his wife and the baby boy, who was born a few days ago, were being discharged from the nursing home in a West Delhi locality, Ranjit Sarkar was both excited and a little tense. Excited, because his life had taken a significant turn with the arrival of a new member in his family. And a little tense, because he knew he was responsible for ushering someone into a world that was getting more complicated as a result of divisive politics not just at home, but also in the entire world.

When he broke the news of the birth of his first child, a son, to his colleagues, one of them had joked and suggested that he should name his baby Saddam. Ranjit did not take too long to understand why that odd suggestion was made to him. Just about a month and a half before his child was born, Saddam Hussein, the dictator ruling Iraq, had stormed Kuwait on 2 August 1990, ignoring global advice that he should restrain himself.[1] Saddam Hussein had soon become an icon of defiance and rebellion—he could take on the might of the United States, the global cop and a super power at that time which had gained in power immensely as the world was turning unipolar with the disintegration of the Soviet Union.

Saddam's invasion of Kuwait had raised the international price of crude oil and its impact on India was severe. With growing concerns over depleting foreign-exchange reserves not being adequate for imports of oil, whose price had skyrocketed, the government had imposed a surcharge of 25 per cent on the prices of petrol and diesel. It had also imposed rationing of sorts by placing curbs on the quantity of sale of petrol or diesel to each vehicle at retail outlets. In addition, orders were issued to all dealers of petroleum products asking them to cut short the number of hours for which they could keep their retail outlets open for the sale of products. Long queues of vehicles outside petrol pumps became a regular spectacle and Ranjit, who had just acquired a car, was wondering if he should go back to using public transport for travel.

But that day when he reached the nursing home with his car to pick up his wife and son, he was a little worried not because of the fuel shortage. He was worried about being able to drive on Delhi's roads without any interruptions to reach about 30-odd kilometres to drop his wife and the newborn baby at his in-laws' home. Streets in Delhi had turned into an open field for staging demonstrations in protest against the then government's decision to extend the scope of reservations in jobs and educational institutions to cover backward classes as well, in addition to members belonging to scheduled castes and scheduled tribes. While the move was justified by the then prime minister V.P. Singh as his attempt at ensuring social reform and justice for the backward classes, large sections of middle-class India were apprehensive that their scope for getting admissions in educational institutions and securing government jobs was increasingly getting narrower. Students of many colleges affiliated to Delhi University came out on the streets of the Capital and indulged in a novel kind of protest. They would build a human wall on busy cross-sections of major roads and block the passage of vehicles. The most remarkable aspect of such protests was that they enjoyed tacit support from even travellers in their personal vehicles or public transport as the larger message of the protests struck a sympathetic chord in many of them.

For an economy that was not doing well and with oil prices as well as inflation on the rise, the attempt to reserve more seats in educational institutions and jobs in government departments came as yet another blow to the aspirations of all those who did not belong to either scheduled castes and tribes or to the backward classes. And the appeal had made an impact on the upper castes, irrespective of their economic status. The poor Brahmin, for instance, joined hands with the middle-class Brahmin or Kshatriya (another category of upper caste in India) in lodging their protests against the V.P. Singh government's proposal on reservations.

The movement reached a crescendo after a twenty-year-old student of Deshbandhu College, affiliated to Delhi University, Rajeev Goswami, tried to immolate himself on a busy cross-section outside New Delhi's premier state-owned hospital All India Institute of Medical Sciences (AIIMS) on 19 September.[2] Goswami did not succeed in immolating himself, but sustained almost 85 per cent burn injuries and after hospitalization survived to live for another thirteen years before succumbing to a liver-related disease in a missionary hospital. But the immolation attempt in 1990 had not only made Goswami a national celebrity but also raised the movement to a pitch where the government faced difficulty in restoring law and order.

In September 1990, Ranjit Sarkar was worrying about whether he would be able to drive his wife and his newborn baby to R.K. Puram, a sprawling residential colony of government flats in south Delhi, without any traffic disruptions and delays. Ranjit was stressed throughout his journey. He was worried that a mob would intercept his car.

The Mandal Commission and its recommendations for extending the scope of reservations to backward classes, and which the V.P. Singh government had agreed to implement, had made their impact on Ranjit Sarkar in a way that he would never forget.

The Mandir and the Mosque

6 December 1992 was a Sunday. Even senior government officials spend their Sundays in a relaxed way. Most of them spend Sundays at home. But for Ram Mohan Rao, the principal information officer for the Indian government, this was an unusual Sunday. A huge congregation of Kar Sevaks (an army of people wearing saffron bandanas on their head and claiming to be followers of the Vishwa Hindu Parishad or the Bharatiya Janata Party) at the site of the disputed Babri Masjid in Ayodhya had made the P.V. Narasimha Rao government a little tense and restive.

The Supreme Court had ordered that even if Hindu devotees committed to the idea of building a Ram temple there were allowed to congregate at the site, the state government of Uttar Pradesh would have to tender an undertaking that the law and order would be its topmost priority.[3] UP was ruled by the BJP then and Chief Minister Kalyan Singh gave an undertaking as required by the country's apex court. BJP's central leaders like Lal Krishna Advani were present at Ayodhya. From initial reports trickling in from UP, it seemed that the security forces deployed there were not enough to manage the huge crowd that had gathered near the mosque. Ram Mohan Rao could not take that Sunday lightly and from fairly early during the day was monitoring the situation in Ayodhya.

By early afternoon on Sunday, Rao had received information that not all was well. The Kar Sevaks had outnumbered the police forces by a huge margin. The top leaders of the BJP were present at the site and their exhortation to a mob of Hindu zealots that the Supreme Court's order must be respected fell on deaf ears. By 4.30 p.m. there was confirmation that the mosque had been pulled down and the demolition was complete. The whole nation learnt in utter shock and disbelief that the sixteenth-century mosque that the first Muslim ruler of India had built in this country had been destroyed by a mob of about 2 lakh people, many of whom claimed to owe allegiance to VHP and the BJP. Advani expressed his disappointment that a kar seva had turned into an exercise to demolish a mosque. Kalyan Singh had promised to the Supreme Court as also to the National Integration Council that he would not let the mosque be damaged or destroyed. Seeing that the mosque had been demolished, Singh lost no time in tendering his resignation.[4]

There was complete silence from the office of Prime Minister P.V. Narasimha Rao. One of his Cabinet colleagues would complain that while the Kar Sevaks were on a rampage in Ayodhya, his frantic calls to the prime minister and senior intelligence as well as police officials, went unanswered. On the other hand, Principal Information Officer Rao held an informal briefing with the assembled media representatives. An eerie silence pervaded the air. Breaking his silence, Ram Mohan Rao said: 'Now the only course available to the government is to see how the mosque can be rebuilt.'[5] It looked like a statement that held out a reassuring promise from a government that was trying to do some damage control. Rao also argued that maintenance of law and order was the responsibility of the state government and the Centre could not have been expected to intervene in Ayodhya when there was a popularly elected government in Lucknow, the state capital.

Questions were being raised about whether Narasimha Rao should have reacted well in time, after seeing the huge mass mobilization at Ayodhya, and dismissed the UP government. There were counter-questions as well. Narasimha Rao was still running a minority government at the Centre and upsetting the BJP by dismissing its state government in Uttar Pradesh could have been politically risky for the survival of his government.

By 6.30 p.m. that Sunday, the Union government convened a meeting of its Cabinet. It was a meeting that saw some exchange of cold stares among senior ministers and the prime minister. The meeting almost bordered on mutual recrimination, with each holding the other responsible for inaction against a politically motivated mob with religious zeal, destroying a mosque of historical importance. The Cabinet decided to recommend to the President the dismissal of the Uttar Pradesh government and the dissolution of the Assembly. But by that time, the Kalyan Singh government had tendered its resignation and President's rule was imposed immediately and the UP Assembly was dissolved. It seemed that Kalyan Singh and the BJP leaders had acted swiftly by offering the resignation perhaps in a bid to salvage their reputation and establish that they took the moral responsibility for not having honoured their word to the Supreme Court that the mosque would not be allowed to be demolished.

The demolition of the disputed Babri mosque in Ayodhya was also a cause for concern on the economic front. After being rescued from the brink of an economic disaster, the Indian economy had just begun to stabilize, with inflation coming under control. Early signs of green shoots of recovery were becoming visible, the foreign-exchange reserves were showing a healthy pace of increase and international financial institutions were beginning to repose their faith in the Indian economy once again. But the demolition of an ancient mosque and the consequent political turmoil could have seriously dampened the prospects of revival of the Indian economy that has just come back from the brink of a collapse about two years ago. Worse, there were now fears of retaliation from the minority Muslim community. As it turned out, within months of the demolition of the mosque, Mumbai saw bomb blasts in busy localities killing innocent people. The blasts were followed by violent riots in which Muslims and Hindus clashed, leading to many deaths and destruction of properties.

If Ram Mohan Rao that Sunday talked about the need for rebuilding the Babri mosque as the only option before the government, he had good reasons to make such a statement. It was clear that he did not make that statement unprompted. Perhaps he understood that after the demolition of the mosque, applying balm on the hurt sentiments of the Muslim community was of utmost importance to avoid communal tension from flaring up.

Rao's suggestion or the thinking of a section of the government on the need to shift the agenda from building a temple for Ram to rebuilding the mosque was discarded soon after the initial shock of that event. This was a reflection of how India's political debates and politics were taking different directions. Ram Mohan Rao may well have expressed a view that was shared by very few in a government that recognized the rise of Hindu mobilization as an inevitable process. Perhaps the government felt that the need to pander to demands of the majority was more optimum, even though that meant further marginalization of the minority Muslim community. That process, unfortunately, would speed up in the coming decades.

Rao's suggestion on that fateful Sunday indeed appeared to be the expression of a lonely voice.

Mandal as the Trigger for the Mandir

The two events—expanding the coverage of reservation of government jobs and seats in government-run educational institutions to include backward classes and the movement for building a Ram temple in Ayodhya in place of the Babri mosque—took place under two different governments, separated by more than two years. The decision on accepting the Mandal Commission's recommendation to extend reservations for backward classes was taken in August 1990 by the V.P. Singh government. And the Babri mosque was demolished in December 1992 when P.V. Narasimha Rao was ruling at the Centre, albeit at the head of a minority government. The composition of the Lok Sabha then was such that it would not have posed a real threat to the survival of the Rao government. Against the 232 members of the Congress, the BJP had 120 members, followed by Janata Dal with fifty-nine and the two Left parties with forty-nine members. It was unlikely that the different groups of opposition parties would ever get together to pull down the Rao government. But the Congress leadership realized that a comfortable relationship with the BJP in such a situation was a safety net for the government and a politically useful instrument for keeping other opposition political parties at bay.

But there is little doubt, and less scope for any debate, that they are closely interconnected events and indeed one led to the other. Remember that the BJP had supported the V.P. Singh government from the outside. If the Left had not opposed, the BJP may well have been part of the National Front government. V.P. Singh had to make a compromise of sorts by not including the BJP as an alliance partner since taking that path would have deprived his government the support of the Left.[6]

It was under these circumstances that V.P. Singh decided to implement the Mandal Commission's recommendations on reservation. This hurt the BJP the most, and in response, they had to intensify the mobilization of the Hindu vote bank through the movement for building a Ram temple in Ayodhya. Both were disruptions. The reservation politics, even as it upheld the principles of according social justice, impacted economic opportunities for large sections of Indians. The Mandir movement, on the other hand, was aimed at consolidating as well as exploiting a specific type of vote-bank politics. At one level, they were an outcome of the past four decades of policies; at another, they would leave an enduring impact on the way the economy would fare and politics would be practised in the decades to come.

The Mandal Commission was set up on 1 January 1979 by the Janata Party government. Its prime minister, Morarji Desai, was acutely conscious of the need for ensuring social justice for those who needed affirmative action from the State to help them realize their potential for growth and development. Headed by Bindhweshari Prasad Mandal, it was called the Socially and Educationally Backward Classes Commission. At the time Mandal was asked to head the Commission, he was a member of the Lok Sabha representing Madhepura in Bihar. Earlier, Mandal had led a short-lived government in Bihar as its chief minister—just for forty-seven days. He belonged to a backward shudra family and had suffered the ignominy of public humiliation when he was a schoolboy. Mandal took just about two years to submit the Commission's recommendations, but by that time the Janata Party government had fallen and a Congress government with Indira Gandhi as prime minister was in place at New Delhi. On 31 December 1980, Mandal submitted his report to the then President Neelam Sanjiva Reddy, recommending among other things reservation of 27 per cent of jobs under the Union government and public-sector undertakings for backward classes. This in effect would have raised the job reservation level in government undertakings to 49.5 per cent, as already people belonging to scheduled castes and scheduled tribes were given reservation of about 22.5 per cent of the available jobs.[7]

For almost about a decade after the Commission's submission of the report, there was no response from the government. Indira Gandhi from 1980 to 1984 and Rajiv Gandhi from 1985 to 1989 kept the Mandal Commission's recommendations on hold. Even V.P. Singh showed no signs of looking at this report in the early part of his short tenure that began in November 1989.

On 7 August 1990, Singh decided to accept the recommendations of the Mandal Commission. It, of course, could be implemented from 1993 after the Supreme Court had given its go-ahead, but the ball was set rolling in 1990. Singh's decision in 1990 was one of the major disruptive steps that any government had taken in the sphere of social reforms aimed at ensuring social justice for people from underprivileged and backward classes. More than a quarter century later, the movement for expanding the scope for job reservation has seen no respite, let alone the raising of any questions on diluting the existing job quotas for people belonging to scheduled castes, scheduled tribes and specified backward classes. Indeed, in 2018, the Narendra Modi government passed a bill to amend the

Constitution to provide constitutional status to the National Commission for Backward Classes.

If in August 1990, V.P. Singh turned to the Mandal Commission's report, which had been gathering dust in government cupboards for about ten years, there were many reasons. One, Singh as a politician has always believed in wearing his integrity and honesty on his sleeve. As commerce minister in Indira Gandhi's government, he believed in holding open-house sessions with industry and trade representatives to resolve their problems related to exports or imports. This was a durbar style of governance. Perhaps knowing it full well that dismantling the highly deleterious and discretionary controls on trade and industry would take a longer time, he tried to liberalize the clearance process through such open consultations, which were held not only in New Delhi but also in important state capitals. Such interventions were largely discretionary, but they certainly improved the ease of doing trade and business at that time. And Singh acquired the halo of one who was open about addressing industry's problems. It was in the same spirit that Singh would take a tough stance on tax evasion, corruption and fraud, when he became the finance minister in the Rajiv Gandhi-led government. He would launch raids at industrialists' houses on suspicion of tax evasion and if Singh targeted any industry, it was left with no option other than making peace with the minister or coming clean.

It was in a similar spirit that Singh wanted to display to all his commitment to social reform and delivering social justice to those who had remained backward for ages and had been denied the basic privileges and equal opportunities because they were born as backwards. And once he decided on extending reservation to backward classes, there was no going back for him, nor any scope for making some concessions here or making some minor adjustments there. In a newspaper interview, months after he had accepted the Mandal Commission's recommendations leading to social and economic upheaval in the country, Singh stated: 'Transformational forces are not the same as transactional forces. You cannot do good politics, you cannot transform the country through transaction. Transformation has its own dynamics. It is uncompromising. There is no quid pro quo.'

Two, Singh soon realized that the political equations that he had worked out for running a coalition government was not sustainable for long. Within the Janata Dal, he had to keep in mind that his deputy prime minister, Devi Lal, remained highly ambitious and had not yet forgotten the pain of having come so close to becoming the prime minister but settling for the number two slot in the government. On the other hand, Chandra Shekhar, who had merged his Janata Party with Singh's newly launched Janata Dal in 1988, was getting increasingly restive as he felt he and his followers were not getting their due under the new dispensation.

After the 1989 election results were out, it had become clear that V.P. Singh would be the undisputed choice to lead the next government. However, there were other claimants too— Devi Lal of the Bharatiya Lok Dal, who was then the chief minister of Haryana, and Chandra Shekhar. In a secret alliance between Lal and Shekhar, it was agreed that the latter would propose the former's name as the leader of the National Front to head the new government. However, Lal proved to be even wilier and he entered into an arrangement with Singh that he would be happy with a deputy prime minister's post provided his name as the prime minister was proposed at the Central Hall, where the National Front was holding its meeting to select the leader of the group. A crestfallen Shekhar was a mute witness to how he was robbed of an opportunity to become the kingmaker and instead, Singh proposed Lal's name as the prime minister and immediately thereafter Lal declined to lead the Front and requested Singh to take up the job instead.[8] At the swearing-in ceremony in Rashtrapati Bhavan, so keen Devi Lal was to declare himself as the deputy prime minister that he took his oath as deputy prime minister. It was a violation of Constitutional propriety as apart from the person who takes oath as the prime minister, all other members of the council of ministers, irrespective of whether they enjoy the Cabinet rank or are simply a minister of state, take oath as a minister for the Union. President R. Venkataraman's direction that Devi Lal should not insist on taking the oath as deputy prime minister was ignored. The beginning of the National Front was thus fraught with such devious politics and it did not take long for Singh to realize that the coalition could not last for long.

Indeed, Singh had thought of a snap election within months of taking charge in New Delhi, in the hope that he would be able to garner more seats for his party and could run the government without any reliance on the fractious members of his own party like Devi Lal and Chandra Shekhar or even the BJP, which were not part of his government but had given it support in Parliament. This support was crucial and helped Singh enjoy a majority in the Lok Sabha and form the government. Lal too had little trust in Singh or his politics. Not surprisingly, on 9 August 1990, Lal had planned a massive farmers' rally in New Delhi to flex his political muscle and remind Singh how dependent he was on his grassroots support.

Three, Singh appeared to be getting increasingly uncomfortable with the kind of Hindu mobilization the BJP had embarked on.[9] Aware of the Rajiv Gandhi-led Congress's attempt to woo Hindus in the run-up to the 1989 general elections (Gandhi had allowed the Shilanyas at the Ram Janambhoomi complex near the Babri Masjid and had even launched his party's poll campaign from Faizabad), the BJP had stepped up efforts to mobilize the temple movement. Singh too appeared to be conscious that he must have a political answer to the BJP's attempts at wooing a monolithic Hindu vote bank.[10] The Hindu vote must be split, without which the BJP can become a bigger and bigger electoral force. The Congress had already sensed the power of the Hindu vote bank and had begun to tap into it. But without a proper strategy, the Congress, with its soft Hindutva campaign and its involvement in Shilanyas, succeeded in upsetting the Muslims, without making any substantial gains from the Hindu vote bank. The Hindus did not come on board because of the lack of an unambiguous approach to this issue. Singh did not want to commit the same mistake.

On 7 August, just two days before Devi Lal was to hold a massive rally of farmers in New Delhi, Singh announced in Parliament that his government had decided to accept the recommendations of the Mandal Commission. Opponents of Singh within the Janata Dal were taken by surprise and the BJP saw trouble on the horizon. Streets of north Indian cities, particularly in Delhi, were witness to a series of protests and rallies against accepting 27 per cent reservation for backward classes in government jobs and admissions in educational institutions. It was not just the ordinary lives of people in cities that were disrupted, but India's politics and economics too were disrupted in a fundamental way.

Genesis of Reservation

The Mandal Commission, set up by the Morarji Desai government on 20 December 1978, was not the first body to look into the question of steps to ameliorate the social and economic conditions of backward classes in the country. A presidential order issued on 29 January 1953, had set up the First Backward Classes Commission, headed by Dattatreya Balkrushna Kalelkar, also known as Kaka Kalelkar, a member of the Rajya Sabha at that time. Its terms of reference were to determine the criteria for considering if any sections of the people in India, in addition to the scheduled castes and scheduled tribes, should be classified as socially and educationally backward, prepare such a list, investigate the conditions of such socially and educationally backward classes and make recommendations. The Kalelkar Commission submitted its report on 30 March 1955. It had finalized a list of 2399 backward castes or communities, of which it opined 837 were the most backward. Its recommendations were quite controversial, and indeed Kalelkar as the chairman had recorded his differences with some of the Commission's views in his letter, while submitting the report to the President. The Commission had suggested that a caste-wise enumeration of the population should be undertaken in the 1961 Census, all women be treated as backward, 70 per cent of seats in all technical and professional institutions be reserved for qualified students of backward classes and minimum graded reservation of vacancies be kept in all government services and local bodies for other backward classes. Graded reservation implied that the quotas would not be the same for all kinds of jobs—lower the category of service, the higher would be the reservation quota. For instance, the Commission said backward classes should have a reservation of 25 per cent in Class I jobs, 33 per cent in Class II jobs and 40 per cent in Class III and IV jobs. The Nehru government at the time found those too problematic to handle. It decided not to accept the recommendations of the Kalelkar Commission, but advised the states that they could go ahead and prepare their own lists of other backward classes and outline measures to ensure their social and educational advancement.

It was crystal clear to Nehru that extending reservations for other backward classes, beyond the 22.5 per cent reservations already done for scheduled castes and scheduled tribes, was a political hot potato. That was the Congress view. With the first non-Congress government at the Centre in 1977, its prime minister, Morarji Desai, decided to set up the second commission that could make recommendations for improving the social and economic conditions of backward classes. Chaired by B.P. Mandal, the second commission also submitted its recommendations in just about two years. But by then the Congress was back at the Centre, with Indira Gandhi starting her second stint as India's prime minister.

The Mandal Commission had recognized that there were already 22.5 per cent of all government jobs and seats in educational institutions were reserved for scheduled castes and scheduled tribes and the responsibility of identifying the more numerous backward classes was even more complex and onerous. It noted that as much as 52 per cent of India's population belonged to backward classes, but recommended that an additional 27 per cent of the government jobs and seats in educational institutions should be reserved for the identified backward classes. The Mandal Commission was more pragmatic as it sought to keep the overall reservation below the 50-per-cent-mark, so that it did not fall foul of the Supreme Court directive that such affirmative action could not be enforced on more than half of the available jobs and seats in educational institutions.

Two Congress governments sat on the recommendations of the Mandal Commission for ten years. This was a telling comment on how disruptive the Congress must have found the recommendations if they were to be implemented. It could also be said that it was not just a question of its concern over administrative difficulties in implementing a highly disruptive move, but also a reflection of their political beliefs where social justice for the backward classes did not enjoy a very high priority in their thinking or political equations. It was V.P. Singh's National Front, a non-Congress government at the Centre, which decided to implement it. In its election manifesto, the National Front had talked about the Mandal Commission and even the President's address after the formation of Singh's government (the President's address before the start of a new government is the statement of the political executive and is endorsed by the Cabinet) had referred to the need for ensuring social justice through the Mandal Commission. But the manner in which the decision on its implementation was taken raises deeper questions about its political motives.

The Modus Operandi

On 6 August 1990, V.P. Singh surprised many of his top secretaries and even a few ministers, when at the usual Cabinet meeting he proposed a discussion on the implementation of the recommendations made by the Mandal Commission. Both his principal secretary, B.G. Deshmukh, and his cabinet secretary, Vinod C. Pande, were taken aback and sought more time before the implications of the Mandal Commission could be studied and a note could be prepared on the basis of which the Cabinet could discuss the issue. Singh shot down that suggestion. Instead, he asked the Social Welfare Minister Ram Vilas Paswan, who himself was born in a Dalit family, to start the discussion. Paswan, who was the minister for labour and employment, argued for the acceptance of the recommendations and he was supported by Sharad Yadav, the minister for textiles, and Ajit Singh, minister for industries, who even suggested that the reservations should be extended to cover Jats as well. Only a few of the ministers seemed to be not very enthusiastic about the idea of implementing the Mandal Commission recommendations in such a hurry. Finance Minister Madhu Dandavate was asked why he was being equivocal. Home Minister Mufti Mohammed Sayeed had some reservations and pleaded for time. The home minister feared that there could be a law and order problem after the announcement and the country should be prepared to ensure peace and harmony in such a situation. There was also a suggestion by some that apart from social and educational backwardness as criteria for determining reservation quotas, economic backwardness too should be one of the criteria to decide on reservation. But Singh was determined to get the Cabinet to approve his proposal. A day earlier, on 5 August, he had mooted the idea of removing a recalcitrant Devi Lal, the deputy prime minister, from the party and the government. However, a large gathering of backward leaders did not approve of Singh's proposed action against Lal and instead asked him to implement the National Front's poll promise of giving effect to the Mandal Commission's recommendations on reservations. Time was of the essence. Singh immediately convened an informal meeting of the Political Affairs Committee of the Cabinet, where it was decided that the recommendations of the Mandal Commission should be adopted. That explained the full Cabinet meeting on 6 August. The next day, he made an announcement to this effect in Parliament.

Even as protests and rallies disrupted normal life in the capital and in many other cities of India, many questions arose. Did the decision on implementing the Mandal Commission disregard the importance of merit and capability in government jobs and educational institutions? By implementing the Mandal Commission's recommendations, the government was seen to have ushered in social reform and secured social justice for the backward classes. But at what cost this was achieved continued to be debated.

A related question pertained to the necessity of introducing a sunset clause along with the decision to expand the quotas. A sunset clause would have helped governments in the future to automatically phase out the reservation quotas once the goals of social justice were secured. The question that agitated people was whether introducing reservations without that sunset clause was a long-term disruption for governance. There were more disturbing questions. Were economic criteria for extending the reservations ignored? Was it a blow to India's syncretic and secular fabric where minorities like Muslims and Christians were left out of the reservation policy for backward classes? Even as the demand for more reservation of government jobs and seats in educational institutions continues to be made more than two decades after that abrupt decision, no government has so far found an answer to most of these questions.

CHAPTER 17

THE POLITICS OF THE MANDIR

The demolition of the Babri Masjid happened on 6 December 1992, under the watch of the P.V. Narasimha Rao government at the Centre. In Uttar Pradesh, the chief minister was Kalyan Singh of the BJP. But the clock had begun ticking in an ominous way from 1989. In spite of the Allahabad High Court order on 14 August 1989 that directed that status quo of the disputed mosque should be maintained, political parties, including the Congress, the VHP and the BJP, had started making efforts towards a Shilanyas ceremony, which essentially meant laying the foundation of the temple with the help of sanctified stones. The role of the BJP and the VHP is quite well-publicized, but that the Congress too had an equally significant role is what makes the entire disruption of the temple demolition more problematic.

The Rajiv Gandhi-led Congress government did not hesitate to play a soft communalism card as it came close to facing the electorate at the end of its five-year-long tenure. This was largely due to its realization that it could hardly make any inroads into the Hindu vote bank that the BJP had so solidly built and nurtured over the previous few years and nor could it hope to gain anything substantial from the Muslim because of its flip-flop over the famous Shah Bano case. This was because after having first taken a bold step in supporting the apex court's verdict in 1985 that in effect enforced a common personal law for all Indians irrespective of their religion, Gandhi succumbed to pressure from orthodox Muslim clergy and the All India Muslim Personal Law Board, which argued that the apex court's verdict was against the spirit of sharia, the Islamic personal laws for Muslims, mandated by the Quran. After about a debate for over one year on this issue, Gandhi developed cold feet and brought in a new law, the Muslim Women (Protection of Rights on Divorce) Act, 1986, to set aside the judgment of the Supreme Court on the Shah Bano case. At the same time, Gandhi in early 1986 paved the way for the opening of the locks of the Babri Masjid in Ayodhya, thereby allowing the worship of Hindu gods kept inside the precincts of the mosque. Such moves from

Gandhi presented the Congress to the voters as a party that was either prevaricating or ambiguous about what it stood for.

Not that Gandhi had not been advised to desist from following a soft communal approach on the question of Babri Masjid. UP chief minister at that time Narayan Datt Tiwari met Gandhi and advised that the Babri Masjid issue should be treated as a local issue and left to the state government. There were reports that the influential local Shia community might agree to relocating the mosque to a different site and allow the construction of a Ram temple at Ayodhya in return for an amicable settlement of the dispute. However, such suggestions fell by the wayside. Going by the account given by B.G. Deshmukh (*A Cabinet Secretary Looks Back: From Poona to the Prime Minister's Office*), it would appear that major political parties, including the Congress and the BJP, saw electoral dividends from such an issue. Thus, no serious attempts were made to defuse the crisis or find an amicable solution to the problem. Tiwari made yet another suggestion to Gandhi, which too was turned down—let the Shilanyas ceremony at the mosque site be held as early as possible, perhaps in April or May of 1989 so that it could be sufficiently distanced from the holding of the general elections to prevent any adverse impact on the Congress's Muslim vote bank. But Gandhi was keen on pursuing a soft Hindu line to retain his government at the Centre. The calculation was that by permitting the Shilanyas the Congress would woo away the Hindu vote bank that the BJP was relying on. The chief secretary of UP was asked specifically to earmark a plot of land in the undisputed portion of the Babri Masjid site, where the Shilanyas could take place on 9 November 1989.[1]

Simultaneously, the Congress government under Gandhi went ahead with its plans to hold the general elections on 22, 24 and 26 November 1989.[2] The election schedule was decided at a Cabinet meeting held on 16 October. The electoral calculations behind the advancement of the elections were too obvious to be ignored. The Chief Election Commissioner, Peri Shastri, was clearly upset. Deciding the election schedule is a prerogative of the Election Commission, and here was a government that had taken a decision on the days when elections could be held. Cabinet Secretary B.G. Deshmukh was sent to the Election Commission to discuss the dates with Shastri and explain why the government had decided on those dates after keeping in mind the administrative exigencies. Soon, the Commission announced the election schedule as the government under Gandhi had desired. That was an era before T.N. Seshan took charge of the Election Commission about a year later and gave the organization the power and authority that it by and large continues to enjoy even about three decades later.

On 9 November, when the Shilanyas took place adjacent to the mosque in Ayodhya, Gandhi was not present there, but an impression was created that the entire event had the blessings of the top Congress leadership. Not surprisingly, the Congress campaign for the general elections was kicked off from Faizabad, the district headquarters of Ayodhya. Gandhi was present at that time and he made the grand announcement that only the Congress could re-establish 'Ram Rajya' in the country, a hint at the construction of the Ram temple. During the election campaign, Gandhi was advised by a few of his bureaucrats that he should at least make a statement clarifying that the Babri Masjid would never be demolished, since the Congress manifesto had stated that the party was for the 'construction of a temple without dismantling the mosque'. A combination of factors—the charges of Bofors bribery and Muslim disenchantment with the Congress for its soft Hindutva agenda—led to Gandhi's party fetching only 197 Lok Sabha seats, about seventy seats short of what would have given the party an absolute majority to form a government on its own. This was more than what V.P. Singh's Janata Dal could win—143. But Gandhi was of the view that the popular verdict was against his party and decided not to stake any claim to form the government with the help of some other regional parties, leaving the field open for Singh to forge a coalition with the outside support of the BJP with eighty-five seats and Leftist parties with forty-five seats.

In retrospect, Gandhi paid a price for adopting a soft Hindutva stance. He ignored the writing on the wall. On the other hand, Singh reaped the dividends for filling in the void created by Congress's exit from the Muslim vote bank. Delivering his only Independence Day address in 1991, Singh announced that there would be a Central government holiday on the birthday of Prophet Muhammad.

If Gandhi laid the grounds for Hindu mobilization through the Ayodhya movement, the role of the state media could not be ignored either in contributing to an environment that reignited religious fervour among the Hindus. Doordarshan, which had a complete sway and indeed monopoly over the electronic media in the 1980s, got two religious series based on Hindu epics Ramayana and Mahabharata aired for several years. The *Ramayana* serial made its debut on Doordarshan in early 1987 and the *Mahabharata* a year later. Two of the Mumbai film world's popular and successful directors were roped in to produce the serials—Ramanand Sagar for *Ramayana* and B.R. Chopra for *Mahabharata*. Every Sunday morning during that period, the streets in large parts of India would virtually become empty as people would remain glued to their television sets devouring the exploits of their religious and epic heroes like Ram and Yudhishthir. These serials were defended on the ground that these were popular epics, but there was no gainsaying that the telecast of those two serials on Doordarshan did help promote a Hindu sentiment among people. For the political parties, be it the Congress or the BJP, the Hindu voter's mind had become a fertile ground for exploiting it for electoral gains.

The trigger for the BJP's resolve to speed up its Ram temple agenda seems to have come also from the V.P. Singh government's decision to implement the Mandal Commission's recommendations. The BJP view was that such reservations would hurt its Hindu vote bank by splintering it into castes. While the BJP would gain by consolidating the Hindu community as a vote bank, reservations for jobs on the basis of caste had the potential of fragmenting the same vote bank and encashing that would become more difficult for a party like the BJP.

Less than a month after the National Front government's decision to implement the Mandal Commission, Lal Krishna Advani decided to undertake his famous Rath Yatra in September–October 1990, whose sole goal was to mobilize support among Hindus across the country for building the Ram temple in Ayodhya. The Rath Yatra was expected to culminate in a Kar Seva at the Babri mosque site by the end of October.

In less than a month of Advani beginning his tour of the nation on 25 September 1990, the V.P. Singh government made a serious attempt at finding a solution to the question of the VHP demand for a temple in that complex and protecting the monument. Indeed, on 19 October 1990 the government came out with an ordinance that seemed to suggest that a solution had been found, with the Babri mosque and the land around it to be kept as government land and the area surrounding it to be handed over to those who wish to build a memorial for Ram. However, distrust and refusal of some forces within the BJP and the VHP to agree to that arrangement led to the revocation of the ordinance just four days later on 23 October 1990. That was also the day when Advani's Rath Yatra came to a premature end as he was arrested in Samastipur by the state government of Bihar, which was then headed by Chief Minister Lalu Prasad. That arrest, however, did not end the kar seva (self-less service rendered physically by believers with their hands) and UP Chief Minister Mulayam Singh Yadav had to use force to defuse the crisis on

30 October 1990, as the devotees climbed the domes of the mosque and hoisted saffron flags on them.

The BJP leadership took serious exception to the way the V.P. Singh government and the Mulayam Singh government in UP dealt with its Ayodhya movement. The BJP withdrew its support to the Janata Dal government at the Centre. As Chandra Shekhar, too, had left the Janata Dal with sixty-four MPs, the Singh government fell on 10 November 1990. Even as Chandra Shekhar formed a minority government with support from the Congress, the country's political situation got even more fragile. According to one estimate,[3] the frequency of incidents of violence increased and there were about 750 deaths and 1400 injuries resulting from communal riots relating to the Ramjanambhoomi-Babri Masjid issue between September 1989 and November 1990.

Advani's Rath Yatra began in Somnath in Gujarat on 25 September 1990. The next couple of months saw a series of dramatic developments that further complicated the political situation. The ordinance that had seemingly found a solution to the dispute was withdrawn. Advani was arrested in Bihar. Violence erupted in Ayodhya and in particular around the Babri mosque site with kar sevaks marching there in a procession. The Uttar Pradesh government under Mulayam Singh Yadav as the chief minister cracked down on the kar sevaks. The BJP in retaliation withdrew its support to the government, which led to the fall of the V.P. Singh government in November 1990.

The Demolition

In June 1991, the political situation changed with P.V. Narasimha Rao of the Congress becoming prime minister at New Delhi and Kalyan Singh of the BJP forming his government in Uttar Pradesh. Within months of Kalyan Singh taking charge of UP, the state government issued notifications for land acquisition around the mosque, and even the high court passed orders allowing the UP government to take possession of the acquired land, but prohibiting permanent construction.

A worried Rao convened a meeting of the National Integration Council in New Delhi and secured the assurance from Kalyan Singh that nothing unlawful would be allowed to take place. However, the UP government continued with the steps that were needed to further the VHP–BJP agenda on the Ram temple at the disputed site. In February 1992, the boundary wall around the mosque was constructed and a month later the government handed over the 42 acres of land acquired in 1989 to the Ram Janmabhoomi Nyas for building the Ram Katha Park around that area. Between March and July 1992, all other structures on the acquired land were demolished, digging and levelling operations were undertaken and the construction of concrete platforms started. It was only on 15 July that the high court issued orders prohibiting any further construction work on that site. By the end of July, thanks also to the Supreme Court's intervention, all construction activities at the site came to a halt. On 30 and 31 October 1992, the date for the next kar seva was announced and that happened to be 6 December 1992. A worried Rao government convened a meeting of the National Integration Council—which was boycotted by the BJP—and passed a unanimous resolution: 'The NIC meeting after considering all aspects of the Babri Masjid-Ram Janambhoomi dispute and the report of the Government extended its whole-hearted support and cooperation in whatever steps the Prime Minister considered essential in upholding the Constitution and the rule of law and in implementing the Court orders.' The ball was in Rao's court.

Within a day of the resolution, passed by the National Integration Council, Rao ordered the stationing of central paramilitary forces near Ayodhya. After holding a series of hearings in the last week of November, the Supreme Court observed that it had been assured by the state government that no construction activity would be allowed to take place at the disputed site and the kar seva to be performed would be only of a symbolic nature. The Court also appointed an observer, who would monitor the developments on 6 December that eventually turned out to be one of the biggest political disruptions to have hit India.

On that fateful day of 6 December 1992, the mobs that had assembled as kar sevaks around the Babri mosque from the morning became large and uncontrollable by early afternoon. With exhortation from senior leaders of the BJP and other Hindutva parties, the kar sevaks soon climbed on to the domes of the Babri mosque. The demolition exercise began soon thereafter. By 4.30 p.m. that day, the Babri Masjid was demolished.

Why weren't the Central paramilitary forces called in to control the mob? One explanation was that the local law enforcement agencies feared a breakout of widespread violence if the paramilitary forces, which had been stationed near Ayodhya, were to be summoned. The forces would have had to open fire, resulting in the killing of thousands of people assembled near the mosque and the fallout of that would have been more unmanageable.

But the account of then Prime Minister P.V. Narasimha Rao points the finger at the state administration in Uttar Pradesh. As many as fifteen companies of paramilitary forces (between 1200 and 2250 men) were ready to move to Ayodhya from Faizabad, where they had been stationed since the morning of 6 December. The distance between Faizabad and Ayodhya was less than seven kilometres. It would have taken about half an hour for the forces to move in. The Union home secretary in Delhi had been impressing upon the state administration from the morning to summon the paramilitary forces. But the law required that such paramilitary forces could move in only after a local magistrate had given permission and accompanied the Central forces to the site. This permission was neither refused nor given.

Rao writes:

Even at the very last moment when the force had actually moved hallway towards the structure, at 2.20 p.m. – by which time the demolition was going on, but could have stopped even then – the deliberate act of the magistrate in not allowing the Central force to proceed further and thus officially aborting the very last possibly successful attempt to save the structure, became transparently visible, and will always be cited as a wanton and mala fide step to stop the saving of the structure.[4]

It was a dangerous combination of a state government that was reluctant to give permission to a central force to prevent the demolition of the structure and a Centre that failed to read the intentions of the state government, perhaps guided by its political agenda.

A Tale of Two Disruptions

The acceptance of the Mandal Commission and the demolition of the Babri Masjid were both disruptions and both interconnected. One led to the other. It is debatable whether V.P. Singh would have shown the same urgency in rolling out the plan for reservation of government jobs and seats in educational institutions for other backward classes if he had not sensed the BJP's grand plan to ramp up its Hindutva consolidation efforts through the movement for building a Ram temple at Ayodhya. Conversely, it is also arguable that if the BJP leadership had not sensed that V.P. Singh was feeling uncomfortable with the durability of his government and coalition and could plan some disruptive move to consolidate his voters' base, it would have likely gone a bit slow in ratcheting up its temple movement.

There was a third element in this equation—P.V. Narasimha Rao of the Congress and the party's relatively newfound love for nurturing the Hindu vote bank. It is not just Rajiv Gandhi, who had allowed the Shilanyas at the Babri Masjid site and launched his 1989 election campaign from Faizabad, but even Rao was not politically averse to bringing the Congress closer to espousing Hindu sentiments.

In many ways, the rollout of the reservation plan for other backward classes and the demolition of the Babri Masjid had been triggered by many forces and Singh, Advani and Rao played important roles in all these developments. Nor were these disruptions sudden. These were the outcome of a series of developments that preceded what happened in August 1990 and in December 1992.

Reservation as a disruption did not end in itself. It led to more disruptions with more people demanding reservations —the Jats and now the Patels.[5] The acceptance of the Mandal Commission by V.P. Singh showed to the political leadership that it was possible to widen the scope of reservation for backward classes. Till then, successive governments may have endorsed the idea of using jobs reservation as a tool for ameliorating the social, educational and economic conditions of those who remained backward in the country even after Independence. But none of them agreed to expand the scope of reservation.

The Nehru government, for instance, did not accept the recommendations of the Kalelkar Commission that had submitted its report on extending reservations for jobs in government services in 1955. Similarly, the Mandal Commission submitted its recommendations in 1980, when Indira Gandhi had just returned to power. But she took no action on the report's recommendations till she was killed by her bodyguards in October 1984.

Ironically, Mandal had great hopes that Indira Gandhi would be very receptive to his recommendations. While submitting the report to President Neelam Sanjiva Reddy, Mandal had said:

> It may be mentioned that although this Commission was appointed by the previous Janata government, Smt. Indira Gandhi's government not only gave two extensions but extended all support and cooperation in the discharge of our work. This clearly shows her devotion and commitment to the cause of the suppressed, depressed and the oppressed.[6]

The Mandal Commission's report was ignored even by Rajiv Gandhi, who took no view on its recommendations from November 1984 to November

1989. It was the V.P. Singh government at last that mustered the courage to accept it in 1990. And he took that decision, arguably, to counter his political opponents within the National Front and outside. In the nearly three decades since then, the clamour for more reservations for more backward castes has only increased. Not only backward castes, but also members of some minority communities have suggested that reservations as a policy tool for their social, educational and economic emancipation should be used for them as well.

V.P. Singh's highly adventurous move on reservations, whatever be its motives, has shown that many castes and economically underprivileged sections of society want to be covered by reservations. In a highly unequal society like India's, there is certainly strong logic behind reservations from the point of view of securing social justice and compensating the backward classes for the social exploitation, suppression and injustice perpetrated on them for many generations. But at the same time, the implications of the reservation policy for a merit-based system are serious. And the fact that the reservations policy pursued till recently does not give any weight to the economic conditions of people is a pointer to the deeper problems and resentment that this approach has created for the government.

Not surprisingly, therefore, the Narendra Modi government, almost at the end of its first five-year tenure of the government, got the Constitution amended to provide for an additional 10 per cent reservation of government jobs and seats for economically weaker sections in the general category. The new law has defined economically weaker sections and one of the conditions is that the annual household income would be less than Rs 8.5 lakh. Parliament passed the Constitution amendment bill on 9 January 2019. The politics of reservation that V.P. Singh had started in 1990 continues to stay relevant even after almost three decades, triggering reactions and counter-reactions from different political parties.

The temple movement, on the other hand, has been an equally powerful disruption for the secular fabric of the nation. It certainly gave a push to the political movement for a Hindu rashtra, an idea propagated by the BJP for obvious political gains. There is no doubt that the BJP managed to use the idea of building a Ram temple at Ayodhya as a tool for political mobilization and gaining power at the Centre. And the demolition of Babri Masjid in 1992 was seen as a move to realize that goal. The BJP's rise has been truly remarkable—from 1984, when it had just two Lok Sabha seats, to its emergence as a single-largest party with 182 Lok Sabha seats in 1998 and forming a coalition government, and then becoming the first political party in three decades to secure a single-party majority in the Lok Sabha in 2014 after winning 282 seats and completing its tenure of five years without any political hiccup. And in 2019, the BJP improved its majority in the Lok Sabha by winning over 300 seats in the general elections.

At another level, the demolition of Babri Masjid caused probably the biggest disruption to the social fabric of the nation. It deepened the communal divide in the country. Not just Muslims, but other minority communities have also, after the demolition of Babri Masjid, become apprehensive about their status and position in India. It has also raised questions over India's claims that the rule of law prevails in the country under all circumstances. To that extent, this disruption has also had an impact on India's reputation as a diverse and democratic country in the international community of nations.

Turning Points

There are three clear turning points in this disruptive phase of India's politics and they could have influenced the course of the developments in many different and as yet unanticipated directions. The first turning point is V.P. Singh's decision to accept the Mandal Commission's recommendations for extending reservation to backward castes. It was perceived to have given Singh two advantages. One, it was aimed at reining in the followers of Devi Lal, his deputy prime minister, who had decided to flex their political muscles through a public rally. Two, it was aimed at countering the BJP's political ploy to mobilize and consolidate the Hindu vote bank around its movement for a Ram temple at Ayodhya. As it turned out, neither of Singh's objectives was actually fulfilled. Even after announcing the acceptance of Mandal Commission's recommendations, the V.P. Singh government fell as the dissidents moved away along with Chandra Shekhar to form a new government with the latter as prime minister. Devi Lal continued to remain the deputy prime minister even under the new dispensation. Singh was the eventual loser. Even the BJP's Hindu vote bank mobilization drive saw no respite after Singh used the Mandal card. On the contrary, the temple movement got a fresh impetus as the threat of the Hindu vote bank getting fragmented in smaller caste groups became real. What would have happened, if Singh had not made that abrupt announcement of accepting the recommendations of the Mandal Commission? It is likely that Singh would have got a few more months to rule from New Delhi, after making some concessions to the Devi Lal camp. It is possible that the steady decline of the Indian economy could have been averted or at least delayed as Singh certainly had a better and saner sense of running the economy as prime minister. And certainly, the demand for more reservation from different caste groups could have been averted, as the acceptance of the Mandal Commission encouraged many other groups to make similar claims for reservation. The genie of reservation and clamour for more reservation was out of the bottle and all prime ministers after V.P. Singh have unsuccessfully tried to put the genie back inside the bottle.

The second turning point is the arrest of Lal Krishna Advani in Samastipur in Bihar in October 1990. The arrest of Advani, ordered by the Bihar government, which was then led by Chief Minister Lalu Prasad, helped both the Mulayam Singh government in Uttar Pradesh and the V.P. Singh government at the Centre in getting the political satisfaction of foiling the BJP's attempts at mass mobilization near the disputed Babri mosque in Ayodhya. But it also intensified the BJP agitation for a Ram temple and converted that demand into an emotive issue with a wider appeal among large sections of the Hindu population in north India, in particular. It is debatable what would have happened if Advani's Rath Yatra had been allowed to complete its journey unchallenged. Did Lalu Prasad's decision to arrest Advani make him a Hindu Hriday Samrat (darling of the Hindus) and help the BJP widen its appeal among the Hindu electorate? Or would it have been better to strengthen the law and order enforcement in Ayodhya and prevent any mass mobilization around the mosque, instead of arresting Advani in Samastipur? These are the imponderables of the Mandir–Masjid politics of that time.

The third and final turning point is P.V. Narasimha Rao's response to the December 1992 congregation planned by the BJP in Ayodhya. Should Rao have taken pre-emptive action against the Uttar Pradesh government, then led by Kalyan Singh of the BJP? It had reports from all sources, official and unofficial, that a large mob would be mobilized to gather outside the mosque area on 6 December 1992. Rao has argued that he went by the rule book and the commitment the UP government had given to the Supreme Court on maintaining law and order on that day. But as prime minister, should Rao have acted in advance and possibly removed the UP chief minister and imposed the President's rule on the state? If he had followed such an action plan, the history of the BJP movement on building a Ram temple in Ayodhya would have taken a new course. Whether it would have helped the BJP or not is, of course, a moot point.

Economic and Political Consequences

Both the disruptions—reservations of jobs and the demolition of the mosque—have had huge economic consequences. Since reservation of government jobs and seats in educational institutions has been extended to people only on the basis of their birth into a backward or scheduled caste, the benefits have largely been enjoyed by those who were slightly better off and relatively less underprivileged. In other words, the same family has continued to enjoy the reservation benefits, instead of these being spread over a larger group of deprived sections of society. The concept of a creamy layer for excluding the economically and socially well-off among the backward castes has so far been applied only to the other backward castes (OBC) and not to scheduled castes and tribes. The creamy layer concept, introduced in 1993, implied that OBC members enjoying constitutional positions or employed with the rank of Class I officers and those whose parents have a gross annual income of over Rs 8 lakh would not be eligible for reservation benefits.

In spite of a September 2018 order by the Supreme Court that suggested that the creamy layer concept could be extended to scheduled castes and tribes, the government is yet to act on it.[7] The lack of an economic criterion for deciding on extending reservation benefits to SC and STs has thus harmed the policy's effectiveness to a great extent. The Modi government's decision in early 2019 to amend the Constitution to grant 10 per cent reservation for everyone belonging to economically weaker sections of society was aimed at addressing that weakness. But its impact is yet to be felt on the ground.

On the other hand, the demolition of Babri Masjid had initially dealt a blow to India's attractiveness as an investment destination. With bomb blasts, violence on the streets of Mumbai and riots in other parts of the country, India was seen as an unstable place for doing business by both domestic businesses as well as international investors. The demolition also coincided with a particularly delicate state of India's economy, when it had just begun to revive international confidence in its markets. Fortunately, the adverse fallout of the demolition of the mosque was contained after a few months. But the risks the disruption posed to India's economic stability cannot be underestimated.

It is ironical that the short-lived National Front government led by Vishwanath Pratap Singh would be known less for its campaign against corruption, for which it was largely voted to power, and more for its decision to extend the scope of affirmative action or reservation of seats in educational institutions to backward castes. Both economically and politically, the acceptance of the Mandal Commission to extend the scope of reservation caused a massive disruption. India's politics changed in fundamental ways from 1990 and its impact on the economy was no less significant.

Politically, it was a big blow against the Bharatiya Janata Party, which relied on Hindus, which till then was a largely monolithic vote bank, to expand its footprint in the country. Reservation for backward communities splintered the Hindu vote in many smaller divisions—a bigger challenge for the BJP to use its community card. The agitation for demolishing the disputed structure at Ayodhya and the demand for building a temple there got a fillip. In less than a year, the Babri mosque was demolished and the movement for building a Ram temple continues unabated.

The rise of the BJP was one of the offshoots of the disruption caused by V.P. Singh's reservation policy. The fault lines in India's polity had become wide open. The politics over reservation and the Ram temple is still being played out in India.

CHAPTER 18

IN SEARCH OF A LANDLINE

The tardy pace in the growth of India's telecommunication services and their poor quality in the pre-reform era have spawned many stories—some of them may well be apocryphal. But recounting at least one of them would help underline at least the perception of the deep mess the telecommunications sector was in during the 1980s and how sorely it was neglected by the authorities.

In 1981, the number of telephone connections in India was estimated at 2.15 million. But the number of applicants waiting for a telephone connection, at 0.45 million, was more than a fifth of that. Two years later, in 1983, the situation got worse. The number of landlines went up by merely 15 per cent, to 2.47 million, reflecting the relatively slow rise in capacity to set up new telephone exchanges. This was an annual average growth rate of merely 7.5 per cent. The demand for telephones, however, was growing at a much faster pace, with the growth in the number of applicants waiting for a phone connection increasing by 47 per cent in two years to 0.66 million.[1] Worse, the quality of telephone services was pathetic. Mere possession of a telephone connection was not good enough for talking to people on the phone. Frequently and often for long durations, telephone lines would remain dead and telephonic communication was virtually impossible.

C.M. Stephen, the minister for communications in Indira Gandhi's government from 1980 to 1982, was one of the founders of the Indian National Trade Union Congress, the trade union wing of the Congress. He was steeped in socialist values and was reported to have once made a statement in Parliament that a telephone was a luxury, not a necessity.[2] That statement was made before reforms were initiated in the communications sector and reflected how the absence of investment and policy focus had played havoc with the quality of telephone service that was a severe handicap for Indian businesses. The level of dissatisfaction over the quality of telephone services reached such a high that a joke doing the rounds then was that Indira Gandhi once became so exasperated with

Stephen that she wanted to convey to him on the phone her disapproval of the way he was supervising the telecommunications department, but she was not able to connect with him since the phones were either dead or the line was so poor that no conversation was possible.

Even after Rajiv Gandhi succeeded his mother as prime minister in 1984–85, the state of India's telecommunications saw no distinct improvement even though the young prime minister was relatively more focused on the need for developing new technology. He wanted to expand capacity for the manufacture of telephone exchanges to meet the rising demand for telecommunications. But Gandhi promoted domestic development of telecommunication technologies to such an extent that it delayed the government's programme to meet the growing demand for telephones by allowing the state-owned company, Indian Telephone Industries, or ITI, to tie up with foreign companies and set up new exchange manufacturing capacity. Already, the Centre for Development of Telematics (C-DoT) had been set up in 1984 with the mandate to develop digital telephone exchanges for the country. The presence of C-DoT and the support it got from Rajiv Gandhi meant that the proposed tie-up between Alcatel of France and ITI was further delayed. It was ironical that Gandhi, who had succeeded in pushing the country towards computerization with a sharp focus on the need for using technology to improve productivity and ensure modernization, had stood in the way of India's technological upgrade in the telecommunications space. The net result of an unhealthy contest between building technology indigenously and importing technology was that the pace of providing new telephone connections lagged far behind that of demand. The government policy of reserving the manufacture of equipment for telephone exchanges in the public sector contributed to the long waiting period for Indians to get telephone lines.

Even as the number of telephone connections went up from 2.9 million in 1985 to 4.17 million in 1989, the waiting list increased from 0.84 million to 1.42 million in the same period. The gap between demand and availability was widening at an alarming pace. In spite of the economic reforms of 1991, when the new industrial policy removed the monopoly of the public sector in the telecommunications sector, the problems did not go away. Indeed, there was no policy instrument or licensing provisions to allow any new player to enter the telecommunications sector. By 1993, the number of telephone lines had risen to 6.8 million, but the waiting list had also gone up to 2.84 million. A reduction in the waiting period for a telephone line from four years and two months in 1990 to two years and eleven months in 1993 did appear to be a significant reduction in the waiting time, but clearly, this was not enough. And the situation was ripe for a big push to telecommunications in India.

The Shock of 1994

What followed in May 1994 was nothing short of a disruption—but a positive one that fundamentally changed the contours of India's telecommunications system. This development ushered in technology without restrictions, allowed capacity to grow unhindered and offered more choices to consumers at lower costs.

The background of the developments in May 1994 was no less dramatic. The government was making preparations for a high-profile visit of its prime minister, P.V. Narasimha Rao, to the United States. The dates of Rao's visit were fixed—he was to be in the US from 15 to 20 May and during this period he would be visiting New York, Houston, Boston and of course Washington, DC to address a joint session of the Congress. The economic reforms of 1991 had opened up many sectors of the economy for foreign investment, but there was no visible impact of that liberalization on the telecommunications sector. The US was getting more interested in the Indian economy and its large market. Telecommunications was one sector with huge potential and one that US giants like AT&T and Motorola were eyeing intently. It was made clear to the Department of Telecommunications (DoT) that Prime Minister Rao would like a new telecom policy to be readied just before he was to leave for the US. The objective was to enable him to share the details of the policy with the US industry so that it could review the new framework under which Indian as well as foreign companies could invest and operate without the restrictions that had bedevilled the Indian markets in the past.

Rao was travelling to the US along with his finance minister, Manmohan Singh, and a delegation consisting of top Indian industrialists. Those were the days when India was basking in the glory of its brave and bold reforms initiated in the background of an unprecedented economic crisis that had engulfed its economy in 1990–91. The Indian economy was of course out of that deep trouble and on its way to recovery, but there was also the urgent need to tell the world that the reforms that were used to rescue the country from a crisis were not one-off events. There was no better place than the US, the Mecca of free enterprise, from where such a message could be spread across the world. With Manmohan Singh by his side, Rao told American policymakers and investors that India's economic reforms were irrevocable and then he quipped, pointing a finger at Singh: 'He rescues me when I am in economic trouble, and I rescue him when he is in political trouble.' That left nobody in doubt about how Rao allowed Singh to implement reforms to rescue the economy and when Singh's proposals met with a political hurdle, Rao stepped in to bail his finance minister out.

The context of the National Telecom Policy of 1994 was thus set before global investors. The objective of the exercise was set in the backdrop of the government's 1991 economic reforms that were aimed at improving India's competitiveness in the global market and ensuring the rapid growth of exports, on the one hand, and attracting foreign direct investment and stimulating domestic investment, on the other. The highest priority to the development of telecom services was considered optimum so that their quality could be raised to levels prevailing in the developed world. Not without reason did the National Telecom Policy refer to the need to raise India's telecom service standards. At that time, the telephone density in India was about 0.8 per hundred persons, well below the world average of ten telephones per hundred persons. Worse, it was lower than even countries like China, with 1.7; Malaysia with thirteen; and even Pakistan, with two telephones per one hundred persons. The challenge of India's telecom policy got even more complicated as in spite of having eight million telephone lines, there was a waiting list of about 2.5 million applicants for a telephone connection. Rural India had a bigger challenge, with only 1.4 lakh out of 5.76 lakh villages covered by telephone services. The policy also made no compromise on the need to take care of the interest of consumers, recognizing that they were the victim of slow growth and poor quality of telecom services in the past many decades. It, therefore, laid down that a suitable arrangement must be made to protect and promote the interests of the consumers and ensure fair competition.

Thus, the National Telecom Policy set five broad objectives:

- The focus of the Telecom Policy shall be telecommunication for all and telecommunication within the reach of all. This means ensuring the availability of telephone on demand as early as possible.
- Another objective will be to achieve universal service covering all villages as early as possible. What is meant by the expression 'universal service' is the provision of access to all people for certain basic telecom services at affordable and reasonable prices.

- The quality of telecom services should be of world standard. Removal of consumer complaints, dispute resolution and public interface will receive special attention. The objective will also be to provide the widest permissible range of services to meet the customer's demand at reasonable prices.
- Taking into account India's size and development, it is necessary to ensure that India emerges as a major manufacturing base and a major exporter of telecom equipment.
- The defence and security interests of the country will be protected.

The policy also set ambitious targets. It wanted that telephone service should be made available on demand by 1997—in just three years. By the same target year, all villages had to be covered by telephone service. In urban areas, it was expected that a public call office (PCO) should be provided for every 500 persons by 1997. And all value-added services available internationally should be introduced in India to raise the telecom services in India to international standards within the Eighth Five-Year Plan period that would end in 1997.

To be sure, even before the framing of the 1994 policy, the Rao government had decided to liberalize the sector. Telecommunications was one of the sectors thrown open in 1991 for investment by the private sector and foreign investment too was allowed with some caps in a few areas. Thus, in July 1992, the private sector was allowed to enter the following eight areas of telecommunication services: electronic mail, voice mail, data services, audio text services, video text services, video conferencing, radio paging and cellular mobile services. Barring radio paging and cellular mobile services, operation of all other services was allowed on a non-exclusive basis and subject to the grant of a licence. A non-exclusive licence implied that operators under such an arrangement would not enjoy any monopoly in that area and other operators too would be allowed to obtain similar licences and provide those services. The 1994 policy mandated that the same policy would be continued. For radio paging and cellular mobile services, the new policy outlined that licences would be issued based on a set of criteria and through a system of tendering. A tendering system was favoured because it would allow applicants to bid for these licences and competition among bidders would help the government not only earn more fees, but also facilitate the offer of more efficient and cost-effective services to customers.

The conditions that applicants would have to fulfil before taking part in the tendering process included the track record of the company in question, compatibility of the technology, usefulness of the technology being offered for future development, protection of national security interests, ability to provide the best quality of service to consumers at the most competitive rates, and attractiveness of the commercial terms offered by the private parties. For basic services also, the 1994 policy allowed the entry of private players. It argued that companies registered in India will be allowed to set up and expand the telecom network to provide basic telephone services so that they could add to the efforts of the DoT in this area. The social obligation of maintaining a balance in the coverage between urban and rural areas was imposed on new players who wished to provide basic telephone services. Agreed tariff and other terms applicable to providers of value-added services were also enforced for entrants in this area. Revenue-sharing arrangements too were introduced, but not immediately. That happened much later in 1999.

Some crucial elements in the National Telecom Policy 1994 distinguished it. The policy projected that achieving the target of giving telephones on demand by 1997 would require releasing about 10 million connections during the Eighth Plan period compared to the earlier goal of only 7.5 million. The policy recognized that releasing the extra 2.5 million connections would require an additional investment of Rs 11,750 crore, assuming the unit cost is estimated at Rs 47,000 per line. The policy also projected an additional requirement of Rs 4000 crore for helping the telecom industry meet its target of providing additional rural connections. This raised the total additional investment requirement to Rs 15,750 crore.

An impending shortage of resources loomed large, and that is what prompted the policy to move for the next big change. It was estimated that the Eighth Plan was already suffering from a resources deficit to the tune of about Rs 7500 crore. The total additional requirement of investments was thus estimated at over Rs 23,000 crore. Finding additional resources of this order was beyond the government's capacity. Where would the government get these resources from? With the government's Budget constraints being what they were, the policy underlined the need for private investments to fill the gap. This meant the policy must allow the association of the private sector in the telecommunications sector in a big way. A new policy recommending the entry of the private sector to help the government overcome its resources gap was unheard of in India till then. The Telecom Policy 1994 in that sense marked a new phase in India's economic reforms.

The second aspect of the policy was its emphasis on technology. Recognizing that telecommunications is a vital infrastructure, the policy also noted that the sector was highly technology-intensive and, therefore, required close monitoring and administration from that perspective. The policy also recommended that its administration should be such that the 'inflow of technology is made easy and India does not lag behind in getting the full advantage of the emerging new technologies'.[3] While there was emphasis also on developing indigenous technology, the policy noted that since telecommunications had a strategic aspect, affecting national and public interests, a suitable funding mechanism should be developed that encouraged indigenous research and development so that Indian telecom companies could use indigenous technology to meet domestic demand and at the same time compete globally.

CHAPTER 19

THE FALLOUT AFTER 1994

How disruptive was the National Telecom Policy of 1994? In one stroke, it had broken the government monopoly in providing telecom services and even in manufacturing of telecom equipment. There was also progressive deregulation of the sector. It heralded the entry of the private sector in telecommunications, an area that was long considered an exclusive preserve of the public sector. And the DoT, which used to be the policymaker, operator and even regulator, had to gradually cede its regulatory functions to a newly set-up regulator under a new piece of legislation. Its role as an operator was also extinguished by 2000 as a newly created public-sector undertaking under its administrative control was set to take complete charge of its functions as an operator. There were, however, frequent allegations that the DoT continued to favour the state-owned telephone service providers in many ways. But, for all practical purposes, it was reduced to being just a policymaker.

The government had been seeking private-sector participation in the telecommunications sector even before the National Telecom Policy of 1994 was finalized. Initially, it sought applications from the private sector value-added services such as paging and cellular mobile telephone services. Later, after the policy, it invited private-sector participation for fixed telephone services as well. A competitive bidding process in 1992 resulted in the award of cellular mobile service operators' licences to eight players in four metropolitan cities. In the same process, fourteen more players in eighteen state circles were awarded mobile service operators' licences by 1995–96. In addition, licences were granted also to six fixed telephone service operators in six state circles and to paging operators in twenty-seven cities and eighteen state circles.

The response from the private sector to the opening up of the telecom sector was encouraging and it looked like the government had introduced a major reform in a sector that touched the people and the economy to bring about a qualitative improvement in the people's ease of living and in the industry's ease of doing business. The ultimate goal of reforms, after all, was to improve the quality of living and doing business.

But the reforms in the telecom sector were hugely disruptive as well in a variety of ways. The positive disruption was evident in the rapid increase in the availability of telephone services, following the release of the National Telecom Policy 1994 and its implementation. Of course, the rise in the number of telephone subscribers was rapid only after seven-eight years after the release of the policy, but that causal connection cannot be ignored. There were good reasons why the private sector's initiative took off after some years. While the private sector came in aggressively post 1992, the pace of activity in the DoT and the state-owned Mahanagar Telephone Nigam Limited (MTNL) also saw a sudden pickup.

The number of telephone lines, as a result of the rollout of new lines by the DoT and MTNL, went up by 11 per cent to 5.1 million in 1991 and jumped by another 15 per cent to 5.8 million in 1992. In 1993, the increase was even more at 17 per cent, with a total number of lines estimated at 6.6 million. The rapid rise was maintained in 1994, when the Telecom Policy was announced, and the total number of telephone lines then went up by 18 per cent to 8 million. The following two years saw an annual addition to these lines by 22 per cent each and the total capacity was estimated at 9.8 million in 1995 and 11.98 million in 1996. The waiting list kept rising till 1993, when the number of applicants increased to 2.8 million, compared to 1.9 million in 1991. But, thanks to the public-sector initiative, the waiting list started coming down from 1994, when it fell to 2.5 million and it further declined to 2.1 million in 1995.

Thus, when the cellular mobile service operators launched their services in four metros of India in August 1995, they faced a substantially different market reality from what they had estimated when the bidding process for licences began just three years previously. The number of customers that could be easily tapped (approximately those who were waiting for a phone) declined dramatically from 2.8 million in 1993 to 2.1 million in 1995 and a more crucial change was witnessed in the wait period for getting a connection—it was down from thirty-five months in 1993 to fifteen months in 1995. The throwing open of the telecom market had thus caused different kinds of disruption. For consumers, it was a gala time as their long wait for telephone lines was coming to an end. For public-sector operators of telephone services, it was an opportunity to ramp up their capacity to corner as large a share of the market as possible. And for the cellular mobile service operators, the latest kid on the block, the market suddenly did not look as attractive and waiting to be grabbed as it appeared when they bid for the licences.

The disruption for the new cellular mobile service operators had an even more serious implication. As argued by Ashok V. Desai,[1] Chief Consultant with the Union ministry of finance from 1991 to 1993, cellular operators at that time had bid a total licence fee of about Rs 20,000 crore for a period of about ten years, which amounted to Rs 2000 crore a year. Assuming that the operators were hoping to acquire the entire number of waiting telephone customers, estimated at over 2.5 million, the annual licence fee would be Rs 8000 a year per customer. As it turned out, this estimate was way out of line as they were paying much more than what they had budgeted for. Even as late as by 31 March 1999, the total customer base of these cellular mobile service operators did not cross 1.187 million. In other words, the licence fee per customer actually was as high as Rs 16,849. Their finances came under increased pressure as the government imposed a rental ceiling of Rs 1872 a year on the new mobile service providers. This was discriminatory as the DoT was charging an annual rental fee of Rs 3600 from its urban fixed-line subscribers. The calculations may look simplistic and may not include many other costs or revenues. But the financial pressure the new regime imposed on cellular mobile service operators was too obvious to be missed.

This led to yet another disruptive effect on the telecommunications market in India. With rental revenues capped well below the costs they incurred on obtaining the licences, the cellular mobile service operators realized that the only way they could become viable and remain profitable was to fix the tariff at the highest level permitted by the government. Thus, in the initial days, the tariffs for mobile calls used to be as high as Rs 16.80 a minute in peak hours, in addition to monthly rentals, an activation fee and a security deposit. These tariffs came down a little over the next couple of years. The cellular mobile phone tariffs were such that the caller as well as the receiver would have to pay for either making or receiving a call. This triggered a response from customers that was uniquely Indian. The idea of a 'missed call' arose from the cellular mobile phone operator's inordinately high tariffs compared to those prevailing for fixed telephone lines, which used to range between 80 paise and one rupee a minute. The 'missed call' was a ploy by which a customer avoided incurring any costs on making a call and yet a missed call was a signal to a mobile subscriber that either he or she should call back, or use a fixed-telephone line to connect. With gradually falling tariffs over the years, the relevance of the missed call went down but many old-timers continue to use this facility to communicate through signals instead of just talking.

Problems for cellular mobile service operators got more complicated with the one-sided norms the government introduced for interconnection charges. Instead of enforcing a uniform practice for levying charges for different service providers to connect calls with each other, the DoT imposed a regime that hurt the financial interest of cellular mobile service providers. The department had begun consultations with the service providers in 1995 but failed to make any progress.

By September 1996, the department introduced a highly inequitable interconnection regime. Cellular mobile companies had to pay for connecting to subscribers of the existing telephone service providers in the state sector like the MTNL or the DoT. However, MTNL or DoT did not have to pay interconnect charges to private cellular mobile companies, when the former's subscribers had to connect with the latter's network. This created an anomalous situation, disadvantaging the cellular mobile service operator once again. It encouraged subscribers to make more calls within the DoT/MTNL networks and avoid making calls from a mobile phone to a fixed telephone. Revenues of the cellular mobile companies, already struggling with a cap on rental fees and high tariffs, took a hit.

But the telecommunications market continued to enjoy its glamour even after such setbacks to the private-sector providers. The government had by then decided to divide the Indian telecommunication market under four broad market categories, depending on their market potential. The first category was for the four metros—Delhi, Mumbai, Kolkata and Chennai. This was followed by three circles: A Circle included the states of Gujarat, Karnataka, Tamil Nadu, Andhra Pradesh and Maharashtra; B Circle covered Haryana, Punjab, Kerala, Rajasthan, West Bengal, Uttar Pradesh (West), Madhya Pradesh and Uttar Pradesh (East); and C Circle included Bihar, the Northeast, Assam, Odisha, Himachal Pradesh and Jammu and Kashmir.

When in January 1995, DoT invited companies to apply for licences to operate fixed-line or wire-line telephone services, the waiting list of subscribers had declined considerably and mobile phone companies would launch their services in about seven months. Yet, as many as sixteen companies submitted as many as eighteen bids for twenty circles in the country. There was no bidder for Jammu and Kashmir and only in

2002 the newly set up state-owned Bharat Sanchar Nigam Limited (BSNL) launched a cellular service in India's northern-most state. BSNL was set up in 2000 as a wholly owned government enterprise and it had taken over all the services that DoT was running till then.

The bidding process soon became controversial over the government's right to cap the number of licences. Two companies, Himachal Futuristic Communications Limited (HFCL) and Reliance Infocomm, had submitted the highest number of bids—as many as fourteen out of the twenty circles. One of the winners in these auctions was HFCL, which had partnered with Bezeq, an Israeli government-owned company. The HFCL–Bezeq combine won nine licences for its bids valued at a whopping Rs 85,000 crore. Even before the winning companies could celebrate, the government decided to invoke a provision in the tender documents that allowed it to cap the number of licences for each player.

Accordingly, not more than three licences could be retained for A Circle markets by a single bidder. A major political controversy ensued over the government's attempt at changing the conditions after the bid results were out. HFCL's dreams were shattered, as even though it had won as many as nine licences, it could retain up to only three licences as per the policy. There was, however, an escape clause for HFCL to exit from the entire process. The policy allowed a combined entity like the HFCL–Bezeq to move out under such circumstances, but that would mean a revenue loss for the government. The issue was raised in Parliament as well in December 1995, with members of the Opposition political parties demanding the resignation of the communications minister who was responsible for the loss of revenue to the exchequer. The government's decision not to accept bids lower than the reserve price, like the ones from Reliance, for many C Circle markets, kicked up another row. All these issues not only became controversial but also reached the courts. Much to the sector's relief, the Supreme Court ruled that the government was within its rights to change the criteria for such bidding processes. But that marked the first big controversy to have hit the Indian telecommunications sector after it was liberalized and thrown open to the private sector and foreign investment. A few more controversies would engulf this sector in the decades that followed.

What contributed to the telecom disruption in the 1990s was the way the government dealt with the policy framework for telecom service delivery by state-sector entities. The government had decided that even as there would be auctions for the award of telecom licences, state-owned operators or entities (which would have included MTNL and the DoT's service delivery division) would not be permitted to take part in the auction for licences. One of the reasons for taking what appeared to be a strange decision was that the government did not want to use up its own resources to build additional telecom capacity. After all, the logic of the National Telecom Policy of 1994 in opening up the sector to private players was to overcome the resources gap it had faced. This meant that MTNL or the DoT was not able to launch mobile services. But just about a year after the new private players had launched their mobile operations, MTNL decided in October 1997 to start its mobile phone service. This represented a volte-face in the government's thinking. MTNL, after all, was a wholly owned government company. But the government's defence, parroted by MTNL subsequently, was that the licence documents had earlier indicated clearly that the government had retained its rights to enter the mobile telephone services segment.

By then the regulator for the telecom industry was already in place. Parliament had passed a law—the Telecom Regulatory Authority of India Act or TRAI—to regulate telecom services, including the fixation and revision of tariffs for telecom services. These were powers earlier vested with the government and from 20 February 1997, TRAI became operational. The government decision to allow MTNL to launch mobile services was contested by the existing mobile service operators. Under the auspices of the Cellular Operators Association of India, the industry moved TRAI to question the government decision. Its argument was that licensing conditions had promised a duopoly regime in each circle, which meant only up to two operators could provide mobile phone services. Allowing MTNL would herald the entry of a third player in a circle and violate the duopoly rights.

TRAI issued a nuanced order—it opined that while the government had the right to give licences, the sequence and need for issuing a new licence had to be cleared and recommended by the regulator. Since MTNL refused to provide any details on why it needed the licence, the regulator was prompted to deny the state-owned fixed-line telecom operator the right to enter the mobile telephony space. The government retaliated and moved the Delhi High Court and by 1998 obtained a favourable order. That was perhaps the first lesson that TRAI learnt. The government was the sovereign authority in laying down the policy, and TRAI as the regulator was empowered to ensure that adequate regulations were in place for a smooth and successful implementation of the policy. If at all there was a perception of a conflict between TRAI and the government in which the former appeared humbled by the latter, it was because of the flawed notion that policymaking could be equated with regulation. Nevertheless, India's private-sector telecom players could not be blamed for believing that the rules of the game were being changed after laying down the guidelines. This too was a disruption with a significant impact on the industry's morale and spirit of enterprise.

At another level, the disruption in the telecommunications sector had acquired a new dimension. Financial woes of the private telecom players were getting worse. On the one hand, their finances were adversely impacted as the mismatch between the costs they incurred on payment of licence fees and the revenues they earned were becoming a cause for concern. Soon, many telecom companies began defaulting on the payment of their licence fees to the government. It was a problem that engulfed the entire industry within months and the government was being approached for a more lenient approach while demanding fulfilment of their financial liabilities.

The advent of technology, in the succeeding couple of decades, would play a bigger role in complicating the disruptions for the telecom sector. With Internet service provision gaining in popularity, the government had already decided to throw this sector open to private players. In the next few years, even as private companies began operating Internet services, the challenge for the cellular mobile service operators became more formidable. Technology would later allow the use of Internet services as an alternative to mobile telephone, initially for data and later even for voice transmission. For the present, however, the operators were upset by the licence conditions set by the government for Internet service providers. For a fee of one rupee, an Internet service provider could set up the infrastructure and provide last-mile access to the subscribers. Telephone service providers protested that this violated the understanding they had with the government when they entered the space. Their demand: Let the government protect their exclusive right to set up fixed infrastructure for provision of Internet services. Legal recourse as also a plea for financial relief from the government were among options that the basic telephone service providers explored. The adverse impact of technology and its rapid pace were being felt by the telecom players. Over time, the disruption caused by technology had to be absorbed by the telecom companies. Those who took advance action by preparing for the advent and spread of the new technology survived the disruption, and indeed prospered, instead of being swamped by the rapid stride of technological disruption.

The battle in the courtroom got intense as the operators not only demanded compensation and financial accommodation, but also a migration from the current system of paying annual licence fees to a new regime of revenue share with the government. The government won the case, though it recognized the need for a new policy package to address the growing weaknesses in the telecom sector. ICICI, which was till then a development financial institution, was asked to examine the performance of the industry and the need for extending licences for cellular mobile services. The Bureau of Industrial Costs and Prices too was entrusted with the task of assessing the viability of the mobile telephone industry. In its report, ICICI suggested that instead of a ten-year period, the licences for telecom service providers should have a validity of fifteen years, which was promptly accepted.[2]

A fraught relationship between the telecom players from the private sector and the government made the going tough and added to the complexity of the disruption that had already taken a heavy toll on the industry's financials. In December 1998, Jagmohan, a retired IAS officer who joined the BJP after having served as Governor in Jammu and Kashmir, took charge of the Ministry of Communications and soon became vocal about his disenchantment with the industry over its failure to pay up the licence fees and requests for either a deferred payment window or migration to a new revenue-sharing system. Less than a month later, Jagmohan caused yet another disruption: He asked the telecom players to pay up 20 per cent of their outstanding dues on account of licence fees. The remaining 80 per cent of the dues could be securitized by the end of February 1999. And if they did not follow the new guideline, the industry would face punitive action, Jagmohan warned.

Even as the industry was weighing its various options, the effectiveness of the telecom regulator came under dispute—a sorry spectacle whose impact on the industry was no less disruptive. In 1999, TRAI ordered that mobile service rentals (the fixed charge that subscribers must pay every month to the telephone company) must increase by 200 per cent and tariffs should be brought down to less than half of the prevailing rate of about Rs 16 per minute. TRAI also introduced the 'Calling Party Pays' regime, replacing the earlier system in which all mobile service users were being charged for both their incoming and outgoing calls. Cellular mobile operators were in favour of this move, but it was challenged by other sections of the industry and even by some consumer protection bodies. They questioned TRAI's authority to deal in a matter that had been decided and determined under the licensing policy. It was a major setback for TRAI and it created greater uncertainty in the telecom market.

Preparing for a New Policy

In just about five years, the telecom industry had raised high hopes for consumers and operators seemed to have got bogged down in a variety of problems. Its market was not growing as fast as it thought it would, given the huge unmet demand for telephone services that existed. The operators were under huge financial pressure on account of the annual payment of licence fees. A regulator had been set up, but its effectiveness was in serious doubt. Complicating the situation further was the government that was treating the private-sector telecom players like the hen that lays golden eggs. But at the same time, the government was influencing policy in a way that benefitted only the state-owned entities in the business of telephony. Fortunately, the Atal Bihari Vajpayee government recognized the need for fixing these problems and set up a committee under the chairmanship of Jaswant Singh, who was then the deputy chairman of the Planning Commission, to examine the need for a new telecom policy that would be able to address the industry's problems. The committee prepared a draft telecom policy and sought feedback from stakeholders to ensure that there was acceptance of the provisions in the policy that would be finally enforced.

By April 1999, a new National Telecom Policy was announced and addressed many of the concerns that the industry had been voicing for long. More freedom was given to the cellular mobile service providers, allowing them to enter into new areas like carrying their own long-distance traffic within their service areas, direct interconnectivity among different service operators and sharing of infrastructure. The licence period was raised to twenty years, extendable by another ten years. The 1999 policy announced the graduation to a revenue-sharing regime, along with a one-time entry fee. It also legitimized the entry of the third operator in a circle. It said that based on available frequency spectrum band, MTNL or DoT would be licensed to become the third operator in a circle, apart from the already licensed two private operators.

The policy also imposed the obligation of licence fees on the state-sector service providers, but the government was expected to reimburse DoT the cost it would incur for paying the licence fees. The consideration here was that DoT had to incur a lot of social costs for providing services in uneconomic rural or hilly areas. Similarly, the policy package for migrating the mobile service providers from a licence fee model to a revenue-sharing arrangement was subject to their paying an entry fee, locking in their existing shareholdings for five years and withdrawing all legal cases on the matter in the courts. The remarkable success of the National Telecom Policy of 1999 was that all operators signed up for the migration package.

The 1999 National Telecom Policy also beefed up the legal framework for TRAI so that it could function like an effective regulator. The policy had reiterated the government's commitment to a 'strong and independent regulator with comprehensive powers and clear authority to effectively perform its functions'. It, therefore, suggested that the regulator's jurisdiction now covered the private as well as the government-owned operators. It could also adjudicate all disputes arising between the government as a service provider and any other service provider.

The government issued an ordinance in 2000 to amend the TRAI Act, 1997, which was later passed by Parliament. The amended law made two important interventions as far as regulation was concerned and was an indication that the government did not want to give up all its levers of control. The power to adjudicate disputes among service providers and those between the government and service providers was entrusted with an appellate body, the Telecom Dispute and Settlement and Appellate Tribunal. Equally important, the government retained its power to remove any member of TRAI, without referring the case to the Chief Justice of the Supreme Court, as long as the member concerned was given an opportunity to be heard. The amended Act also cut short the tenure of TRAI members from five years to three years.

Another major move of the Telecom Policy of 1999 was with respect to the restructuring of the state-sector entities operating telecom services. The policy recalled that licensing, policymaking and service-provision functions were vested in a single government authority, i.e. DoT. This needed to change as there was not just a conflict of interest, but the system was such that the government was often influenced to frame policies that were one-sided and favoured only the state-sector players.

Thus, the Policy of 1999 brought about a significant shift in the governance structure for telecommunications. The Department of

Telecommunications (DoT) till then was responsible for both providing telephone services and framing policies that would govern the business of telephony. The 1999 policy split these two functions, stipulating that DoT would be responsible only for framing policy and its functions of running a telephone or related services would be hived off to a different entity. This paved the way for setting up a new state-owned corporation that would take over the functions of running telecom services across the country. The target date for completing the governance structure shift was 2001. To make it abundantly clear that the corporatization move was aimed at ushering in commercial principles in the way these entities functioned, the Policy stated: 'All the future relationship (competition, resource raising, etc.) of MTNL/Videsh Sanchar Nigam Limited with the corporatized DoT would be based on best commercial principles. The synergy of MTNL, VSNL and the corporatized DoT would be utilised to open up new vistas for operations in other countries.'[3]

The corporatization and restructuring plan was implemented without much delay or any policy hiccup. By 2000, the Department of Telecommunications Services (DoTS), that used to operate fixed-line and mobile services, was corporatized and it was known as BSNL. The policy functions were performed by the Telecom Commission and DoT. If the restructuring faced no delays or hurdles, it was because all the engineers and employees were allowed to remain part of the Indian Telecom Service cadre and hence their pension claims were protected. This was a tactical bargain that later would hurt the government in its attempts at privatizing BSNL.

Policies as Disruptions

India's telecom scene changed fundamentally in the five years from 1994 to 1999. The disruptions caused during this period were many, but each of them eventually had a positive impact for sustaining the long-term growth of the telecommunications sector in India. Not all the targets set by the 1994 policy were achieved within the specified timelines. Telephones were neither available on demand by 1997 nor were all villages covered by then.

However, most value-added services available internationally were introduced in India and the density of PCOs in urban areas had exceeded the target of one such centre for 500 persons. Phone capacity in the country went up from 8 million lines in 1994 to over 21 million lines in 1999. Just about 1 million cellular mobile connections were provided in this period.

The developments in the telecom sector during the 1990s significantly changed the business environment for Indian companies and brought about a perceptible improvement in the way Indians communicated with each other on the phone. It created new business opportunities for growth and expansion for companies. It offered consumers more choices. The overall quality of telecom service improved. Regulation was strengthened. Yes, private telecom players were financially bleeding as they had overbid without recognizing the rapidly changing market situation. The government-owned telecom service providers had speeded up capacity addition in this period and that was one of the factors that contributed to the changes in market dynamics. The government too kept the policy framework largely biased in favour of the state-sector players and that harmed the private players. But even those distortions got corrected to a great extent by the National Telecom Policy of 1999.

This is one sector that saw many changes through disruptions at many stages, but there weren't too many individual protagonists who drove those changes. Yes, Narasimha Rao's desire to open up the telecom sector and finalize a telecom policy before he left for the US so that he could attract investments from there was certainly a factor responsible for the push that the telecom sector got. Similarly, Atal Bihari Vajpayee, by taking charge of the communications ministry at crucial stages and forcing the rollout of a revised policy in 1999 could also be identified as a disrupter. Contrary to popular belief, Rajiv Gandhi, who had ushered in computerization and a technology-led focus in governance, made little contribution to the telecommunications sector and instead encouraged an indigenous thrust, which only delayed the onset of the telecom boom in the country.

Without the push from Rao and Vajpayee, the telecom sector might not have seen the pace of policy changes that were witnessed in just five years. But towering above them all, there were two agents of disruption—technology and growing demand from consumers. The pressure of technology and the demand from consumers for more and better telecom services were huge forces that drove the change. It was a confluence of factors, including the momentum of economic reforms, which pushed the telecom sector on the fast track.

Beyond 1999

It is largely for this reason that the story of disruptions in the telecom sector did not end with the policy of 1999. The forces of change continued

to exert their pressure on the sector, irrespective of the political party at
the helm of affairs in New Delhi. Three major developments defined the
telecommunications sector in the decades after the roll-out of the Telecom
Policy in 1999. Telephone subscribers' growth reached dizzying heights in
the first decade of the twenty-first century, thanks to more competition
and falling tariffs. The telecommunications sector also became the
centre stage of a major scam over the allotment of spectrum to telecom
companies, with huge economic implications for the companies and even
bigger political consequences for the fortunes of the UPA government,
under whose watch the scandal had broken. And finally, the entry of a new
corporate behemoth in the telecommunications sector made competition
more intense and the battle for gaining market share even more fierce.
The financial health of the telecom companies worsened. The rapid pace
of technological change made any recovery from that situation even more
challenging.

Understandably, there was a lag effect of the new telecom policies
of 1994 and 1999 on the telephone subscription numbers in India. The
first six years of the telecom policy liberalization actually did not see
any significant jump in the number of subscribers, although the growth
even in this period—between 1994 and 2000—was quite substantial. At
the end of March 1993, the total direct exchange lines India had was 6.8
million. By March 1999, this more than trebled to 21.59 million. But the
growth in the following decade was truly exponential. By March 2010,
the total subscriber base crossed 621 million. The compounded annual
growth in the subscribers' base between 1993 and 1999 was 21 per cent.
But this annual rate of growth shot up to 36 per cent in the eleven-year
period between 1999 and 2010.

The sharp acceleration in the pace of subscribers' growth in the
Noughties in itself had a disruptive effect on the health of the Indian
telecommunications sector. Even as more Indians began acquiring
telephone connections, the quality of service did not keep pace with that
growth. Necessary investments in creating adequate infrastructure to
maintain quality of service were lacking and the problems arising out of
spectrum shortage was made worse by the controversy over its allocation.
Nobody expected the telephone subscribers' base to continue growing in
the second decade of the twenty-first century, as the telephone density
had reached a healthy level of 52.74 per cent by March 2010, compared to
less than 3 per cent in 2000. By February 2019, the subscribers' base rose
to over 1205 million—a cumulative annual growth rate of 7.6 per cent.

The telephone density, too, had reached almost 92 per cent. Few countries have achieved this level of telecom density in so short a time.

The post-1999 phase saw even bigger disruptions than the acceleration in the growth of telephone subscriptions. One of these pertained to the manner in which the policy of spectrum allocation was handled. Spectrum is a key raw material for the mobile phone industry—offering a range of frequencies through which electromagnetic waves travel, carrying with them voice or data. Spectrum is a resource that is owned by sovereign countries and much of it is reserved for the defence forces of a country. India is no exception. What is available for non-defence use, therefore, is scarce and mobile telephone companies have always tried hard to corner as much spectrum as possible to run their services and gain market share with better quality and larger coverage.

The first big controversy over spectrum arose out of the manner in which the UPA government had tinkered with the process of awarding spectrum to the telecom players in 2008. That decision gave rise to a major controversy. In November 2010, the Comptroller and Auditor General of India (CAG) came out with a damning report on how the Communications Minister, A. Raja, under the UPA government, followed incorrect, opaque and improper processes for the award of spectrum to various companies in an arbitrary and inequitable manner. The highlights[4] of the CAG report were: Spectrum, in spite of being a scarce national resource, was allocated to new players at throwaway prices; the DoT had kept spectrum pricing issues out of the purview of a group of ministers set up for this very purpose and it did not follow its own policy of 'first-come first-served' in letter and spirit; Raja had ignored the advice of the prime minister, the finance minister and even the law minister; based on the revenues collected from the 3G spectrum auctions held earlier in 2010, the CAG report had estimated the notional revenue loss as a result of Raja's decisions to be up to Rs 1.76 lakh crore. Soon after the CAG report became public, the Central Bureau of Investigation had registered cases against DoT officials, officials of some telecom companies who had benefited from the spectrum allocation and Raja, who belonged to the Dravida Munnetra Kazhagham, a political party of Tamil Nadu that was a partner of the UPA.

Two years later, the Supreme Court got into the act after taking cognizance of the CAG report highlighting the irregularities in spectrum allocation. Its verdict was even more damning for the UPA government. The apex court held that the procedures followed by the government in 2008 were flawed and it directed the government to allocate natural resources like spectrum only through auctions. The court also cancelled as many as 122 licences and the spectrum allocated to as many as eight companies through that process. The irony of that verdict, however, was that five years later, in 2017 a special CBI court acquitted all the accused in the 2G spectrum allocation case. The judgment said:

> There is no evidence on the record produced before the Court indicating any criminality in the acts allegedly committed by the accused persons relating to fixation of cut-off date, manipulation of first-come first-served policy, allocation of spectrum to dual technology applicants, ignoring ineligibility of STPL and Unitech group companies, non-revision of entry fee and transfer of Rs 200 crore to Kalaignar TV (P) Limited as illegal gratification . . . The charge sheet . . . is based mainly on misreading, selective reading, non-reading and out of context reading of the official record.[5]

It must be noted that even though the accused in the 2G spectrum allocation case were acquitted, the special CBI court had taken to task the CBI for its sloppy investigation and the judge, O.P. Saini, even stated that the prosecution had failed to prove any charge made against the accused in its 'well-choreographed charge sheet'. While criminal misconduct in the allocation of spectrum could not be established in the special CBI court, the earlier Supreme Court order cancelling the licences and spectrum allocations was a big blow to the industry. As a long-term consequence, the system of allotting spectrum was strengthened and a transparent auction process put in place. But not before the Manmohan Singh government had to pay a political price for allowing the spectrum allocation irregularities to snowball into a major controversy that cast aspersions on the UPA's ability to run an honest administration. Opposition political parties, led by the Bharatiya Janata Party, used the 2G spectrum allocation controversy as a major election issue and cited it as an example of how the UPA allowed corruption to grow under its watch. The 2G spectrum allocation irregularities had a significant role to play in the UPA losing to the BJP in the 2014 general elections. In a unique way, the controversy had caused a major political disruption in the country, contributing to a change of guard in New Delhi.

The entry of Reliance Jio in 2016 was the third big disruption that shook the telecommunications sector in the last two decades. In less than three years, Reliance Jio, backed by the financial muscle of Mukesh Ambani, who controls Reliance Industries Limited, India's largest company, has already become the third largest player by subscriptions. At 297 million subscribers by the end of February 2019, Reliance Jio is not very far behind the number two player, Bharti Airtel, at 340 million, and the number one player, Vodafone Idea, at 409 million. Equipped with its latest 4G technology, Reliance Jio has triggered another war among the incumbents to retain and grab a larger share in the market with lower tariff and better data service. This too has been no less disruptive than how the 2G controversy changed the government's approach to spectrum allotment.

The drop in data tariff plans has led to a spike in data traffic to 1.5 billion gigabytes a month in 2017, making India a country that consumes more data than even the US and China put together.[6] Consumers have benefited from the drop in tariffs. The market shares have changed dramatically. Before the entry of Reliance Jio in 2016, there were about ten telecom service providers, with Bharti as the leader accounting for 25 per cent of the total market and the remaining nine accounting for the rest. By February 2019, the industry has consolidated with the three largest players accounting for 88 per cent of the market—led by Vodafone Idea at 34 per cent, Bharti Airtel at 29 per cent and Reliance Jio at 25 per cent. The name of the game has also changed during this period. The focus is now less on voice and increasingly more on data. This shift is driven by the 4G technology. The leadership of the industry is likely to be determined more by who accounts for a larger share of the data market. Not surprisingly, Reliance Jio had finalized by 2018 plans to increase its 4G coverage to 99 per cent, compared to Bharti Airtel's 4G coverage of 90 per cent and Vodafone Idea's 4G coverage of just 50 per cent. With the emergence of data as a key driver of the telecom industry, the market leadership race too will be largely determined by who corners more data in the next decade.

The worrying feature of the new direction in India's telecom growth is the financial condition of the industry. All the top telecom companies have had to incur huge debts to finance their expansion plans. With the pressure on tariffs, the prospects of profitability for these telecom players do not look too rosy. Only two of the top three telecom companies made profits in 2018. At the end of 2018, Reliance Jio had made huge investments totalling Rs 2.5 lakh crore, but had also run up a debt of Rs 80,000 crore. The debt profile of Vodafone Idea and Bharti Airtel is worse—at Rs 1.2 lakh crore and Rs 1.13 lakh crore, respectively.

Which direction the telecom industry takes in the coming decades in view of its financial burden is difficult to gauge. What is clear is that India's telecom story that got a kickstart in 1994 is not yet over. Given how technology-sensitive the sector is and how major telecom players are not showing any sign of relaxing or letting up in their efforts at expanding their market share and consolidating gains, there will be no early end to the story of telecom disruptions either.

CHAPTER 20

THE GENESIS AND RISE OF NPAS

A rise in the non-performing assets (NPAs) of banks or their bad loans can be hugely disruptive. They constrain the banks' ability to make further lending and at the same time put pressure on promoters of the banks to find more capital for them if they want to stay in business. It is a double whammy—the banks don't earn interest on their bad loans and on top of that, they are required to set aside money to provide for any losses they may incur on those bad loans. Since almost 70 per cent of the Indian banking system in terms of assets is controlled by the government,[1] the pressure on the Central government's finances rises if the volume of stressed loans rises rapidly. At the same time, for a financial system where banks meet close to half of its commercial credit requirement, poorly capitalized weak banks, overburdened by bad loans, can be a big hurdle in reviving investments and growth in the economy.

That was the nature of the challenge the Indian economy faced from rising bank NPAs in the first decade and a half of the twenty-first century. The annual report of the RBI for 2017–18 revealed that the gross NPAs plus restructured loans of Indian banks had reached 12 per cent of their gross advances by the end of March 2018. The higher the share of NPAs in the banks' gross advances, the lower is their ability to sanction fresh loans to the productive sectors of the economy. A higher NPA ratio also requires banks to pump in more capital to make them financially sound. Within the banking sector in India, the NPAs of private-sector banks were much lower—in single digits—than the NPAs of the public-sector banks, which were over 15 per cent (a few of the PSU banks had run up NPAs of more than 25 per cent), reflecting how the state-owned banks were in a deeper financial mess than their private-sector counterparts.

The rise in bank NPAs is directly attributable to the enforcement of more transparent and stringent norms for recognizing bad loans, a practice that was not followed as diligently in the past as was in the three years that ended in March 2018. Thus, the aggregate gross NPAs of scheduled commercial banks increased from Rs 3.23 lakh crore as on 31 March 2015 to Rs 10.35 lakh crore as on 31 March 2018.

What went wrong? The root of the problem can be traced back to the pursuit of a borrowing-led investment and growth strategy between 2005 and 2010.

The Economic Survey for 2016–17 explains the phenomenon succinctly:

> The origins of the NPA problem lie not in the events of the past few years, but much further back in time, in decisions taken during the mid-2000s. During that period, economies all over the world were booming, almost no country more than India, where GDP growth had surged to 9-10 per cent per annum. For the first time in the country's history, everything was going right: corporate profitability was amongst the highest in the world, encouraging firms to hire labour aggressively, which in turn sent wages soaring. It seemed that India had finally 'arrived', earning the long-awaited reward for the efforts made since 1991 to establish a modern, competitive economy. And the next step seemed clear: the country was going to join the path blazed by China, in which double-digit growth would persist for several decades.

This mood was infectious. Indian companies began dreaming big and launched new projects worth lakhs of crores, particularly in infrastructure-related areas, like power generation, steel and telecommunications, where there was a perceived capacity gap. Large Indian companies also went on a global acquisition spree, helped of course by lending from banks. The Tata Group acquired European firms like Corus, the global steel giant, and JLR, the internationally famous luxury and high-end passenger vehicle manufacturer. The Aditya Vikram Birla Group acquired Novelis, the US aluminium maker. In a short period of just four years, the country's investment–GDP ratio rose to 39 per cent by the end of 2007–08, compared to 35 per cent in 2004–05. This was a measure of how rapidly investments in the country were growing in relation to the overall size of the economy. Make no mistake about the source of the funds that fuelled the investment growth. The bulk of these investments were financed by a bank credit surge. The flow of non-food bank credit had more than doubled in just four years—from 2004–05 to 2008–09. Those were the days of relatively high growth and moderate inflation. Annual credit growth during this period ranged between 17 per cent and 36 per cent, much higher than the nominal GDP growth in this period that ranged between 12 and 17 per cent per annum. Wholesale price-based inflation, on the other hand, stayed moderate, ranging between 5 and 8 per cent.

Making this slightly risky was the fact that the domestic rise in bank credit was supplemented by a sharp rise in foreign capital flows, which rose to about 9 per cent of GDP in 2007–08. A rise in the share of foreign capital flows made the economy and its growth vulnerable to exchange rate fluctuations and external uncertainties. The cost of such capital carried the extra burden of any depreciation the Indian rupee suffered, which in turn jacked up the cost of the projects undertaken with that money.

The mood was also buoyant. Every other company was planning to invest big, and borrowing merrily. This led to a rise in the debt of companies, which were seemingly attracted by the prospects of higher growth in spite of the fact that they had given up caution, settled for a debt–equity ratio that was a little unsafe and they were becoming even more indebted. The situation got even riskier as the external environment became adverse. Apart from rising inflation jacking up costs, these projects also became victims of bureaucratic lethargy and the red tape. Securing environment clearances and acquiring land posed difficulties, delaying the rollout of the projects. Another external factor that took them by surprise was the global financial crisis of 2008, which upset the growth assumptions based on which most companies had planned their expansion of capacity and investment in new projects. The Lehman crisis that led to the collapse of many financial giants led to bailout measures from the US Federal Reserve. These resulted in a loose monetary policy to boost consumption. The consequence was the inflation rates shot up and the banks had little option other than recasting loans to protect their assets. The Indian economy too was not spared from the impact of these developments.

A double whammy hit the Indian companies when domestically their cost of borrowing rose with the RBI jacking up interest rates in a bid to rein in inflation. Higher interest rates also meant that the companies' cost of servicing the loans increased, which put pressure on their profit margins as well. And for companies that had borrowed in the international markets, their costs went haywire with the rupee depreciation. From around Rs 40 a dollar in January 2008, the value of the Indian rupee against the US dollar fell to around Rs 65 by September 2013. With the Indian companies' exposure to external commercial borrowing having already risen significantly, the impact on their projects and financials was adverse as their repayment liability in rupee terms rose. Several Indian companies, with significant exposure to foreign currency convertible bonds (FCCB) or external commercial borrowing, ran the risk of default. They included Subex, Moser Baer, Aksh Optifibre and GTL Infrastructure.[2]

The situation got so bad that higher costs, lower revenues and increased financing costs gave rise to a debt-servicing problem for many of these companies. The government's Economic Survey for 2016–17 estimated that by 2013 the interest–coverage ratio deteriorated to an alarmingly low level. Interest–coverage ratio is an indicator of a company's earning ability to pay off its dues or clear its debt and interest liabilities. It, therefore, shows the ease or difficulty with which a company can pay for its interest costs on the debts it has incurred. Since this ratio is arrived at by dividing a company's earnings before interest and taxes by its interest expenses, any figure lower than 1.5 raises serious questions about the company's ability to meet its interest costs. Companies with an interest–coverage ratio of less than 1 accounted for about a third of the total corporate debt. In other words, repayments on almost 33 per cent of India's corporate debt had become doubtful by 2013.

It was a recipe for disaster—both for the companies that had become hugely indebted and the banks that were now staring at the prospects of one-third of their corporate loans turning sick or non-performing.

Worryingly, many of these companies were from the infrastructure sector having invested in projects in power generation and metals, many of them in steel. Yet another external development hit some of these companies badly. China began experiencing slowing growth and that triggered a fall in international steel prices. Steel prices fell globally as also in India, adversely affecting the earnings of Indian steel companies, which had premised their new projects and expansions on steady growth in their price realization.

By 2015, almost 40 per cent of corporate debt was accounted for by companies with an interest–coverage ratio of less than 1. The government stepped in by imposing a minimum import price, to prevent Chinese steel companies from dumping their products in the Indian market. The move helped the Indian steel companies, but they along with other companies in different sectors continued to remain under stress as the overall market situation was yet to improve. Even by 2016, the share of companies with an interest–coverage ratio of less than 1 in total corporate debt of Indian banks remained high at 40 per cent.

What happened in India during those years was a classic replay of events that have taken place in many other countries and are globally characterized as a twin balance sheet problem. There was a sudden spike in borrowing. The corporate sector was overleveraged and faced debt-servicing problems. At the same time, financial companies, or primarily the banks, were weighed down by rising volumes of non-performing or bad loans, which eroded their capital. As there was some reluctance or delay in the government recapitalizing the banks as their majority shareholder, fresh lending for projects suffered, which in turn raised a question mark on growth and the much-needed investments in key infrastructure areas.

Yet, India's twin balance sheet problem was different in quality and its outcomes. For one, its impact on economic growth was not very significant compared to what happened to many other developed countries in Europe and the US, where there was economic slowdown after the global financial crisis of 2008. Ironically, the predominance of public-sector banks in India's financial sector ensured that the adverse impact of the twin balance sheet problem on the economy's growth prospects was significantly minimized. Even though the public-sector banks saw the volume of their sticky loans rising, there was no way the government, as the majority shareholder, reined them in for fear of any adverse impact on investments. A government keen on an early removal of the infrastructure gap in the economy was using its lever of control on the banks it owned to keep the loan flow unimpeded. Even the RBI, led by a former finance secretary, agreed to indulge in regulatory forbearance and allowed the banks to restructure their stressed assets so that their loan programmes remained unaffected.

The absence of an effective law on bankruptcy to wind up companies that failed to honour their loan repayment obligations also helped in prolonging the twin balance sheet problem. Instead of even enforcing the available legal provisions like the Securitization and Reconstruction of Financial Assets and Enforcement of Security Interest Act, 2002, which could have been used for recovery of bad loans, the government, the banks and the central bank maintained an accommodative stance towards defaulting debtors. This was done in the hope that the economy would perhaps turn for the better, like it did from 2004 onwards, and the troubled projects would turn the corner, resolving the twin deficit problems in the process.

Then and Now

By 2014–15, the banking sector allowed troubled enterprises to defer their loan repayment schedule and forbearance accounted for as much as 6.4 per cent of their outstanding loans. In addition, fresh loans too were extended to them so that these enterprises could regain strength to overcome the financial headwinds till demand recovered. Ironically, this only led to an increase in the overall burden of stressed assets as the financial system now had to bear the burden of not only actual bad loans but also those that were restructured or ever-greened.

The Economic Survey for 2016–17 quoted market analysts to state that the unrecognized debts were 'around 4 per cent of gross loans, and perhaps 5 per cent at public-sector banks'. The total stressed assets for the banking sector by the end of 2016–17 thus had been estimated at 16.6 per cent, of which 9 per cent loans were gross NPAs and another 3.6 per cent were restructured. For the public-sector banks, the situation was worse at a total stressed assets estimated at 20 per cent—of which 11 per cent of loans were gross NPAs and 4 per cent loans were restructured. In this respect, the Survey had argued that India was following the model made famous by China, which too had followed a path of allowing a credit surge, irrespective of the magnitude of stress, to keep the growth engine revving. However, there are serious doubts and questions on the sustainability of that model as subsequent years, at least in India, began to show.

This was also not the first time that Indian banks ran up huge amounts of sticky loans or Indian companies became unsustainably leveraged. The banking sector's NPAs had risen as sharply between 1997 and 2002, when they were estimated at 11 per cent of gross advances. The problem was more acute for public-sector banks at 12 per cent of NPAs, as the private banks performed better and their numbers brought down the NPA level by a percentage point. Of course, the total size of NPAs was lower at Rs 71,000 crore in 2002, compared to the total gross advances estimated at Rs 6.81 lakh crore.

Like the 2013–16 NPA crisis, the banking mess in 1997–2000 was also caused by a combination of domestic and international factors. The Asian meltdown of 1997 had its own impact on Indian exports and companies in particular. The nuclear tests conducted by the Indian government in May 1998 evoked a strong response from the global community and financial flows to India were impacted as the US, Japan and other countries imposed sanctions on India. These sanctions were lifted only after a few years. Making things worse for the financial sector were the economic slowdown—the annual growth rate declined from 7 per cent in 1994–97 to 5 per cent in 1997–2002—and the downturn in the information technology industry as the high expectations of business growth in the wake of the

Y2K phenomenon turned out to be exaggerated and remained largely unfulfilled. The turn of the century had given hopes to the information technology industry that likely disruptions in view of the advent of the new century and the resultant technological need for adjustments would keep their business growing at a rapid pace. However, such hopes were simply exaggerated and eventually dampened the Indian economy's prospects.

There were similarities as well as differences between what happened to the financial sector in 2013–16 and in 1997–2002. They were similar because both external and domestic factors were at play. Also, the sectors that showed exuberance in using debt to finance growth belonged, by and large, to the same sectors—steel, power, textiles and commodities. But the reasons that led to the NPA crisis in the two periods were different.

The first difference lay in the fact that the NPA woes that hit the financial sector at the turn of the century were of a smaller size, while what happened in 2013–16 was much bigger in impact. Bank credit in 1997 was just 18 per cent of the GDP and was growing at the rate of 12 per cent per annum. But bank credit was about 32 per cent of the GDP in 2012, just before the NPA crisis of 2013–16, and was growing at over 24 per cent. The second difference, and a crucial one, was that the earlier NPA crisis solved itself without any major policy intervention. Commodity prices, which had remained depressed for several years and adversely affected the financial performance of many companies, had begun to rise again, indicating an upturn in the commodities cycle. This boosted overall demand, the pace of economic activities picked up and businesses got back in the black. Eventually, the NPA crisis had begun to get resolved virtually on its own and as a result of the upturn in commodity prices.

Thus, there was no need for any preventive or remedial action either from the government or the RBI, even though there were many such demands. The NPA crisis of 2013–16, however, was bigger and more serious in nature. There was an early attempt to follow the steps that the government had adopted the previous time such a crisis had erupted: Wait out the crisis in the hope that the economy would recover, demand would pick up and the international economic environment would get better. This is perhaps one of the reasons for the delayed remedial action from the RBI and the government debating over what action it should take with regard to the public-sector banks.

The question that will be debated for long is whether the RBI acted quickly enough to resolve the NPA crisis for banks. There were many warning signals for the RBI and the government to act more promptly and decisively to tackle the banking crisis. As early as in June 2014, the

RBI's Financial Stability Report had painted a rather grim scenario for the banking sector. It had noted the following:

> The banking sector is facing some major challenges, mainly relating to public-sector banks. Although there has been some improvement in the asset quality of scheduled commercial banks since September 2013, the level of gross non-performing advances as a percentage of total gross advances of public-sector banks was significantly higher as compared to the other bank groups. While the ownership pattern and recapitalization of public-sector banks are contingent upon government policy and the fiscal situation, there is a case for reviewing the governance structures of the public-sector banks, with a greater emphasis on market discipline.

Even earlier on 4 September 2013, when Raghuram Rajan assumed office as the new governor of the RBI, the NPA concerns received due attention in his first statement. He said, 'Finance is not just about lending, it is about recovery loans also. We have to improve the efficiency of the recovery system . . . I have asked Deputy Governor Dr Chakrabarty to take a close look at the rising non-performing assets and the restructuring/ recovery process, and we too will be taking next steps shortly.'

In spite of such concerns, the RBI and the government took several more months before any credible and effective action plan could be initiated to strengthen the public-sector banks and address the growing NPA problems of the banking sector. It was only in the middle of 2016 that the Insolvency and Bankruptcy Code got enacted to give powers to the banks to enforce early resolution of bad assets. And the government announced its public-sector bank recapitalization plan only in October 2017. As events would later show, this delay would cost the Indian economy and the financial sector dearly.

The Rajan Era

Raghuram G. Rajan, who was the governor of the RBI for three of the years when India's banking crisis went from bad to worse, has an interesting anecdote to explain why Indian promoters and Indian bankers have a mindset that is largely responsible for bringing down the financial sector to its knees. Early in his tenure as the RBI governor (he moved from North Block as chief economic adviser in the finance ministry to head the central bank in Mint Road in Mumbai in September 2013), Rajan happened to be seated next to the CEO of a public-sector bank during a plane ride. The conversation Rajan had with the bank honcho revealed a lot about how bankers looked at credit discipline.[3]

The bank CEO told Rajan about a well-known promoter of a company, who was gaming the banking system by paying off the loans taken from one bank with the money obtained from drawing a loan from another bank. This was his way of financing his enterprise, even though it was clear to both the banker and the promoter that it was a failing business. On one occasion, the promoter had promised the banker that the loan would be repaid with the money he was getting. But what he did instead was to divert that money to one of his other enterprises. A promise was broken. The banker was angry. When a curious Rajan asked the banker about his action in response to the non-payment of his loan, the reply showed how accommodating the banking system had become. 'I cut his credit line by 20 per cent,' the banker had said. 'In most countries with a strong financial system, broken promises by an incompetent borrower would be met with a complete cut-off of credit and the initiation of recovery measures,' Rajan observed in one of his commentaries on the problem of stressed assets in his book, *I Do What I Do*. In India, all that the banker could think of was to cut the lending by only a fifth of the borrower's credit line.

Rajan found two other reasons responsible for the banking system's failure to resolve its stressed assets. One, even though there were quite a few laws on the statute book that could be used to recover secured debt, the effectiveness of such legal recourse was fairly limited. Indeed, there were at that time at least two laws aimed at helping banks and financial companies recover their debts and facilitate the securitization and reconstruction of loans—the Recovery of Debts Due to Banks and Financial Institutions Act, 1993, and the Securitization and Reconstruction of Financial Assets and Enforcement of Security Interest Act, 2002. While the former operated through debt recovery tribunals (DRTs), the latter facilitated the creation of asset reconstruction firms and allowed securitization of loans.

In spite of that, however, these laws were mostly used against small promoters, who presumably could not use the services of professional lawyers to defend themselves under these laws. In contrast, affluent promoters with political connections would get away by using the best lawyers, who could use the judicial system to the advantage of the borrowers. Not surprisingly, the amount recovered through the DRTs under the Recovery of Debts Due to Banks and Financial Institutions Act, 1993, was meagre at just Rs 30,590 crore in 2013–14, compared to

Rs 2.36 lakh crore of outstanding debt that was waiting to be recovered. While the recovery rate was pretty low, more worrying was the delay—an average wait of four years, against the mandated six months. This also meant that the backlog of cases with DRTs kept rising.

The second reason cited by Rajan was that bankers were generally averse to taking a patently commercial decision like writing down debt for fear of investigative agencies. There were many cases where a commercially sound decision taken by a bank on restructuring or settling the loan was a subject of inquiry by investigation agencies and the bankers involved in taking such decisions had been asked to defend their decision. This was also a factor for an excruciatingly slow pace of resolution of stressed assets in India.

The third reason, which Rajan did not specifically cite as a factor contributing to NPAs in the banking sector but nevertheless had a significant role, was the growing nexus between bankers and India Inc. Rajan did talk about how bankers were reluctant to get tough on promoters of companies for violating a loan contract or were averse to taking stringent steps for the recovery of their loans. But behind this reluctance and aversion was the existence of a cosy relationship between some bankers and India Inc.'s leaders. A working paper on frauds in the Indian banking industry,[4] brought out by the Indian Institute of Management, Bangalore, estimated that, between 2013 and 2016, 'public sector banks in India had lost a total of Rs 22,743 crore on account of various banking frauds'. It attributed such frauds to the 'lack of adequate supervision of top management; faulty incentive mechanism in place for employees; collusion between the staff, corporate borrowers and third party agencies; weak regulatory system; lack of appropriate tools and technologies in place to detect early warning signals of a fraud; lack of awareness of bank employees and customers; and lack of coordination among different banks across India and abroad'.

What, however, is more significant is the working paper's conclusion that the 'delays in legal procedures for reporting, and various loopholes in the system have been considered some of the major reasons of frauds and NPAs'. The government did respond to frauds through a series of actions against some bank officials, Between January 2017 and April 2018, at least half a dozen senior public-sector bankers were booked under various cases of fraud and corruption. It had a negative impact on the morale of public-sector bankers and made other bankers even more reluctant to take decisions on lending. Frauds and corruption in banking may not be the root cause of growing NPAs, but certainly one of the factors that needed better and more mature handling, particularly in public-sector banks.

The stage, thus, was set for one of the biggest disruptions in India's financial sector. The bank NPAs had risen to an unsustainable level that the collateral damage of such a crisis would be huge for the Indian economy. The government as also the RBI got down to the task of addressing the NPA problem. Just as the RBI was expected to play its role as a regulator, the government too had to step in as it was the majority shareholder in public-sector banks, which accounted for about 80 per cent of India's banking system.

From June 2014 to February 2018, the RBI took a series of steps to attack the NPA problem. It changed the way the banks could do business and altered the behaviour pattern of borrowers.

The 5/25 Refinancing of Infrastructure Scheme

Under this facility, a larger window for the revival of stressed assets in the infrastructure sectors and eight core-industry sectors was offered. This allowed lenders to extend amortization periods to twenty-five years with interest rates adjusted every five years. Extended amortization allowed the projects to write off or recover the cost of their assets over a more reasonable and longer period of time. This was aimed at matching the funding period with the long gestation and productive life of the projects. Longer amortization helped improve the credit profile and liquidity position of borrowers. At the same time, the scheme allowed the banks to treat these loans as standard in their balance sheets, which in turn helped them reduce their provisioning costs. An adverse consequence of the scheme was that with amortization spread out over a longer period, it imposed higher interest costs on borrowers, who faced difficulty in repaying their loans. Banks were thus forced to give more loans to the same borrowers. Such evergreening actually aggravated the earlier problem.

Private Asset Reconstruction Companies or ARCs

Even though the formation of asset reconstruction companies was allowed under the Securitization and Reconstruction of Financial Assets and Enforcement of Security Interest Act, 2002 (better known as the Sarfaesi Act), not too many of them were set up and even fewer were operational. ARCs are set up with the object of buying the debts of banks at a mutually agreed upon value and recovering those debts. In the process, banks are freed up of their bad loans and ARCs can make money by buying off the debt at a value lower than the amount they get by recovering the loan. ARCs have professionals on their boards, who undertake the tasks of resolving sticky loans and relieve their burden on the banks.

However, as the ARCs were prepared to take over the stressed loans at a very low price, banks were unwilling to transfer their loans to these companies. In August 2014, the fee structure of the ARCs under the law was modified, obliging them to pay upfront in cash a higher share of the purchase price of the stressed loan. ARC-led resolution did not make any progress after the modification and only about 5 per cent of the total NPAs at book value were sold in 2014–15 and 2015–16, according to the Economic Survey for 2016–17.

Strategic Debt Restructuring (SDR)

In June 2015, the RBI introduced the SDR scheme, which allowed banks to convert the debt of companies to 51 per cent equity and sell them to the highest bidders. Two conditions had to be fulfilled before any bank could use this scheme. One, loans of only companies whose stressed assets had been restructured earlier but could not eventually fulfil the conditions attached to the restructuring would qualify for the scheme. Two, the sale of equity to the highest bidders would be subject to the authorization of existing shareholders of the companies. The scheme had stipulated a period of eighteen months by when these transactions would have to be completed and the loans after that could be classified as performing. The response to this scheme too was lukewarm and by the end of December 2016, only two sales under the scheme had materialized.

Asset Quality Review (AQR)

In October 2015, the RBI enforced a new set of norms under which banks were forced to recognize the bad loans that had earlier been either ignored or had enjoyed some sort of regulatory forbearance. The principle of AQR was that resolution of the problem of bad assets required a robust system of recognizing them. The RBI advised the banks that they must undertake a thorough review of the quality of their loans as per the norms in force and any deviation from those rules must be rectified by March 2016—a window of just five months. This was an ongoing scheme and banks have been regularly monitoring their assets under AQR since then.

Sustainable Structuring of Stressed Assets (S4A)

This was introduced in June 2016. Under this arrangement, an independent body hired by the banks would decide on how much of the stressed debt of a company could become sustainable. The portions of the debt not defined as sustainable would be converted into equity and preference shares. The difference between S4A and SDR was that while in the latter scheme ownership could change after the sale of equity, there was no provision for any change in the ownership of the company under the former.

Prompt Corrective Action (PCA)

On 12 February 2018, the RBI took a big step in its efforts at early recognition and resolution of stressed assets. Under the revised framework, lenders were required to identify incipient stress in loan accounts immediately on default by classifying stressed assets under three broad special mention account (SMA) categories: SMA-0, where principal or interest payment or any other amount is wholly or partly overdue for between one and thirty days; SMA-1 for accounts with overdue amounts for thirty-one to sixty days; and SMA-2 for accounts with overdue amounts for sixty-one to ninety days.

Once they were identified as a stressed asset, they would have to be mandatorily referred to the national company law tribunal for processing under the Insolvency and Bankruptcy Code. A bank could not make fresh lending once it was placed under PCA. Not surprisingly, the revised guidelines under PCA were seen as the most stringent. Industry protested and complained that in its zeal to insist on early recognition of bad assets, the RBI was destroying whatever chances of recovery there were for some sticky loans. Industry complained that RBI's earlier PCA guidelines in May 2014 and April 2017 were not as stringent. Even sections within the government were not too happy with the strict enforcement of PCA. Nobody could have quarrelled with the intention of the RBI though.

The government's statement in Parliament in 2018 explained that the PCA framework was aimed at helping the banking sector maintain sound financial health and take corrective steps in a time-bound manner if its loans had gone bad and unrecoverable. The government also assured Parliament that its objective was not to constrain the banks' normal performance but to encourage them to avoid undertaking risky activities, focus on conserving capital and improve operational efficiency. Eleven public-sector banks were brought under the PCA framework; these were Dena Bank, Central Bank of India, Bank of Maharashtra, UCO Bank, IDBI Bank, Oriental Bank of Commerce, Indian Overseas Bank, Corporation Bank, Bank of India, Allahabad Bank and United Bank of India.

These eleven banks accounted for quite a significant portion of banking activities in the country. With over 30,000 branches spread across the country, these banks held public deposits worth close to Rs 25 lakh crore. Denying them the right to take up any fresh lending activities was one of the toughest measures against NPAs and hugely impacted their customer base and their banking activities. The disruption it caused to the economy can hardly be overestimated. Many of these banks over time came out of the PCA framework by recovering their sticky loans and maintaining prudence. But a big setback was when in 2019 the Supreme Court, on an appeal from a clutch of affected companies, struck down the PCA framework on the ground that it was not consistent with the law. Consequently, the RBI had to reissue the same PCA circular after amending certain provisions that were frowned upon by the apex court. The revised circular was far less stringent, but its overall approach remained unchanged.

A question that is still being debated is whether the banks were saddled with the non-performing loans as a result of a decision that was taken in the early days of economic reforms. By the turn of the century, the government and the RBI had decided that developmental financial institutions would be given the option of turning themselves into commercial banks. Most of India's developmental financial institutions including the ICICI and IDBI had soon turned into commercial banks. This also heralded the demise of developmental financial institutions in this country. However, many experts are of the view that most of these universal banks did not have the requisite skills of evaluating the risks of project financing. In many cases, this led to an asset-liability mismatch for the universal banks. The euphoria of the high-growth phase in the first half of the Noughties led to indiscriminate financing of projects, which had not been subjected to thorough scrutiny. The banks' loans began turning sticky after the global financial crisis of 2007–08. But few attempts were made to recognize the growing NPAs and take corrective steps. Thus, the demise of the developmental financial institutions, arguably, could have played an indirect role in the NPA crisis of India's banking sector.

CHAPTER 21

RECOGNITION, RECAPITALIZATION, RESOLUTION AND REFORM

Even as the banking sector was trying to come to terms with the various schemes introduced by the RBI to force them to recognize bad loans before they became a bigger problem, the government on its own introduced a set of measures for ensuring early Recognition, Recapitalization of public-sector banks, Resolution of bad assets and Reforms of banks (the four Rs). The implementation of each of these Rs posed new challenges for the financial sector and saw different types of disruption in the economy.

With respect to the first R—recognition of bad loans—a lot of action had already been initiated by the RBI in spite of resistance from banks, promoters who borrowed money from the banks and even from the government. It all started with the introduction of the AQR process and it was soon supplemented by the PCA. In between, there were many other initiatives like the 5/25 Refinancing of Infrastructure Scheme, SDR, Asset Reconstruction Corporations and S4A, and many of them posed their own implementation challenges. But what really worked were two initiatives—AQR and PCA. And resistance was the most in respect of these two initiatives.

The government also appeared to be not too happy about the RBI's strict approach to enforcing its PCA guidelines. There was increasing clamour from industry that a large number of banks were out of business as a result of those strict recognition norms and that this was stifling funds flow to them, needed for making productive investments, which in turn would help the economy achieve higher growth. The case of a clutch of power companies that were in deep financial distress and needed a bank bailout became a bone of contention. The government wanted the RBI to allow some of the public-sector banks to resume lending to the stressed power companies so that they could rescue themselves from a financially tight situation. But the RBI was in no mood to listen to such entreaties.[1]

The matter went to the Allahabad High Court, which opined that the RBI could not be expected to change its guidelines and the government had the powers under the RBI Act to issue if necessary a direction to the central bank for making exceptions to the power sector firms for lending purposes. The government did issue a letter to the RBI governor to seek consultations with him under Section 7 of the RBI Act. However, there was not much progress on those consultations, particularly with regard to the enforcement or relaxation in the PCA framework for banks. While the relations between the RBI and the government had become tense for some time, there was truce later on after both the government and the RBI recognized that they must not air their differences through public forums and instead talk to each other to resolve their differences. But the problems that the enforcement of the PCA norms threw up showed how difficult as also disruptive these challenges could be for the country's framework for governing and regulating the financial sector.

Reform

The second R was about reforms in the financial sector. The government was quite proactive on this front. In just about six months after the Narendra Modi government was sworn in, a bankers' retreat called Gyan Sangam was convened in Pune on 3 January 2015. Prime Minister Modi was present at the meeting himself along with his Finance Minister and the top officials in the finance ministry. All top bankers were present at the meeting. While Modi talked about how the government had no desire to interfere in the functioning of the public-sector banks, the meeting resulted in the adoption of a programme or a plan of action that was called Indra Dhanush.

The Indra Dhanush package had four broad components. The first of these was to set up the Banks Board Bureau, which would be entrusted with the task of overseeing the governance of public-sector banks and seeking to distance their running from the political leadership in the government.

The second component was about the infusion of fresh equity into the public-sector banks to improve their capital adequacy. This was linked to the NPA problem these banks were suffering from and more capital was to have helped them attain the desired capital adequacy norms and continue to remain in the lending business.

The third component envisaged induction of private-sector talent to head the PSU banks, and the fourth component of Indra Dhanush underlined the need to set up a new institutional mechanism to repair the balance sheets of the stressed banks.

Some progress had certainly been achieved in many of these areas outlined in Indra Dhanush. For instance, the Banks Board Bureau was soon established and it set the ball rolling for appointing a few private-sector managers to head PSU banks. But that exercise slowed a bit after a while and the experiment of inducting private-sector talent into the public-sector banks did not yield the kind of positive results that were anticipated. The distancing of the bank managements from the political masters in North Block or South Block was a critical imperative, but the government did not make any progress in this area. No clear structure, as recommended by many expert committees in the past, was put in place to distance the management from the political executive as far as running the banks was concerned.

Recapitalization

The Indra Dhanush goal of recapitalization also made significant headway. There was some delay, of course. The promise of an Indra Dhanush package was announced in January 2015. But it took more than two years and nine months for the government to finalize its bank recapitalization plan. On 24 October 2017, the government announced a recapitalization package of about Rs 2.11 lakh crore, after consultation with the RBI. The package had three components: Rs 18,000 crore of capital to be issued to the banks from the Budget, Rs 58,000 crore of capital to be raised by the banks from the market over the next two years and Rs 1.35 lakh crore of capital for the banks after the government issued 'Recapitalization Bonds' in two instalments—one in 2017–18 and another in 2018–19. The government fulfilled its promise of issuing recapitalization bonds and providing capital to public-sector banks from the Budget without any further delay.

On 24 January 2018, Finance Minister Arun Jaitley announced that an estimated Rs 88,000 crore of capital would be infused into public-sector banks so that they could improve their capital adequacy and resume commercial lending and, in the process, help revive the economy's investment cycle. The minister also referred to a set of performance yardsticks based on which the proposed capital infusion would take place. The government was also encouraged by the fact that in the wake of its announcement of the Indra Dhanush package, a few public-sector banks had already raised about Rs 10,000 crore from the capital market. This took the total recapitalization effort during the year close to Rs 1 lakh crore.

Issuing the recapitalization bonds was a smart move from the fiscal management perspective. The bonds had a tenure of ten to fifteen years. However, when it came to allocating the recapitalization bonds, the list of the banks that benefitted from such capital infusion raised disturbing questions on whether any performance criteria were indeed used to provide such capital assistance. Weaker banks got more bonds than those which had shown better performance. The government could certainly justify this approach as it felt that weaker banks needed the capital more than those that were relatively better off. But the principle of merit-based capital infusion was honoured more in its breach. The eleven public-sector banks that were under the RBI's PCA plan got as much as 57 per cent of the total recapitalization bonds on offer and the remaining amount—about Rs 34,550 crore—was offered to non-PCA banks like the SBI, Punjab National Bank, Bank of Baroda, Canara Bank, Union Bank of India, Syndicate Bank, Andhra Bank and Punjab & Sind Bank.

Thus, the government opted for expediency instead of taking the hard step. Yes, disruption with respect to fiscal management was averted, but an easy option also meant that the government doled out the recapitalization bonds just to keep the banks running. Perhaps the risks of a disruption in the financial sector, which the closure of unviable banks would have surely caused, made the government more discreet and choosy about the banks that should get the capital. The total amount of capital available might have been less. But since this was capital provided at considerable cost, the government could have ensured that the banks that got recapitalization bonds performed as per expectations and the banks which did not get them wound down their businesses or even got merged with stronger entities. Avoiding a financial sector disruption had sown the seeds of a bigger disruption for the banking space perhaps after a few years. Conversely, embracing disruption at this stage could have paved the way for a stronger public-sector banking system, less vulnerable to the disruption and accumulation of more stressed assets.

Restructuring

The government stuck to its word on the question of restructuring of public-sector banks as one of the ways to rescue them from their financial stress. Jaitley had stated in his press conference, while announcing the bank recapitalization package, that the need for banking reforms was independent of the government's objective of encouraging consolidation in the banking sector. The first big move on bank mergers was initiated on 1 April 2017. The Bharatiya Mahila Bank was merged with the SBI, India's largest commercial bank. On the same day, five associate banks of the SBI were merged with it. The State Bank of Bikaner and Jaipur, the State Bank of Mysore, the State Bank of Travancore, the State Bank of Hyderabad and the State Bank of Patiala became part of the SBI, making it an even bigger behemoth. The process of mergers did not end here. On 17 September 2018, Jaitley announced the government's plan to merge three public-sector banks—Bank of Baroda, Vijaya Bank and Dena Bank. While recapitalization bonds would help strengthen the balance sheet of as many as nineteen banks, the move to merge the three banks—one of them was a PCA bank—showed that the government was following up on its banking reform package. Even this move caused a major disruption in the public-sector banking space, like any merger does, raising serious questions on synergies and complementarities, but the government went ahead in the hope that the merged entity would be stronger and more capitalized to take on the challenges of staying healthy and meeting the investment needs of the economy through sustained lending. The merger of Vijaya Bank and Dena Bank with Bank of Baroda was completed on 1 April 2019. In a short span of just two years, the number of public-sector banks in India came down from twenty-six to nineteen. With no resistance or hurdles coming in the way, the government has now moved to implement yet another round of public-sector bank mergers. The proposed round could see the Union Bank and the Bank of India merge with the Punjab National Bank. When that happens, the number of public-sector banks would be seventeen—a reduction of more than a third of government-controlled banks in the country.

Resolution

The fourth R for addressing the twin balance sheet problem of the Indian economy was potentially the most disruptive of all the measures mooted by the government. This pertained to the resolution of stressed assets. Parliament passed the Insolvency and Bankruptcy Code in May 2016, which was a comprehensive insolvency legislation covering all companies, partnerships and individuals, excluding of course financial companies. The Code addressed the knotty problems of a multiplicity of different bankruptcy laws in a decisive way. It replaced all such laws like the Sick Industrial Companies Act, the Recovery of Debt Due to Banks and Financial Institutions Act, and the Securitisation and Reconstruction of Financial Assets and Enforcement of Security Interest Act.

It provided a speedy process for early identification of financial stress and the resolution of entities if their underlying business was viable. Either a restructuring, if the entity was found to be viable, or liquidation was mandated under the Code within a timeframe—180 days after the process was initiated plus a ninety-day extension for resolving insolvency cases. A regulator—the Insolvency and Bankruptcy Board of India—was set up. The Code ensured that there was an adequate number of resolution professionals who could assist in the process of resolution or liquidation of an entity that had become insolvent under the law. Operational or financial creditors could approach the National Company Law Tribunals seeking redressal of their unsettled dues. Once an entity was admitted as insolvent, its management was entrusted with a committee of creditors, a body of professionals, who took charge of the company and ran it till a resolution was arrived at.

In a short span of time, the Insolvency and Bankruptcy Code made a considerable impact on insolvent companies and the problem of banks' stressed loans, but not before the government stepped in with a crucial amendment in the Banking Regulation Act to expedite the NPA resolution. The law, amended in 2017, provided that the Central government could now authorize the RBI to issue directions to banks for initiating proceedings in loan repayment default cases under the provisions of the Insolvency and Bankruptcy Code, 2016. Accordingly, the RBI could periodically issue directions to banks for resolution of stressed loans and specify committees to advise banks on the resolution of stressed assets. The amended law was made applicable to the SBI and the regional rural banks. Thus, the government empowered itself to issue directions to the RBI for initiating the resolution of stressed assets under the Insolvency and Bankruptcy Code. The objective was that the government authorization would allow the RBI to move on such resolution quickly without any delay. Soon, the RBI did receive an authorization letter from the government under the amended law to move ahead with the resolution of stressed assets.

As at the end of 31 March 2019, a total of 1858 companies had been admitted under the Code. Of these, 152 cases, or 8 per cent, were closed on appeal or review. As many as ninety-one cases were withdrawn by those who applied before the courts under the Code. This was an indication of how the behaviour of borrowers changed as they were now becoming more compliant once the insolvency cases were taken up before the courts under the Code and they knew that they ran the risk of losing their company if they did not repay the dues. Ninety-four, or about 5 per cent, of the insolvency cases were successfully resolved and 378 companies, or about 20 per cent of the total cases, had to be liquidated. Importantly, almost three-fourths of the cases that had to be liquidated are about companies that were either defunct or languishing at the Board for Industrial and Financial Reconstruction, set up under the Sick Industrial Companies (Special Provisions) Act of 1985. This was also an indication of how the Code had worked much more effectively than the earlier law which had failed to bring about a quick resolution. The remaining 1143 cases were under different stages of the insolvency resolution process. A worrying aspect was that in spite of a stipulated timeframe of 270 days, as many as 362 of such cases or about 32 per cent had still not been settled in spite of their being admitted for more than 270 days. There were 186 cases (about 16 per cent) which were reported for the resolution process between 180 and 270 days and another 247 cases were reported between ninety and 180 days. And 348 cases were registered for less than ninety days. In other words, almost 48 per cent of the cases under different stages of the corporate insolvency resolution process had crossed the deadline of 180 days within which they were to be completed under the Code.

A big disruption the Code caused was in the area of promoters' ownership of stressed companies. This was the first time that India Inc. and borrowers, in general, realized that not paying back the loans could lead to dispossession of their companies or their assets. The Code was applicable to all types of companies, except the banks. As the finance minister said, this was the first time that instead of the banks chasing the borrowers for recovering the loans, the borrowers were chasing the banks for ensuring that they first paid up and were not dragged to the courts under the Code.[2] Of course, the government had to step in and push the process by suitably amending the Banking Regulation Act.

The borrowers' behaviour and their repayment discipline improved after the government issued a broad directive to the RBI under the Banking Regulation Act to initiate action against companies which had defaulted on loan repayments under the Insolvency and Bankruptcy Code. This paved the way for the RBI putting out periodic lists of companies that had become insolvent due to defaults on their loan repayment obligations. And many big promoters of India Inc. lost their companies through the process initiated under the Code and more were set to join that list. In a bid to make the process less vulnerable to misuse, the government also amended the Code to prevent promoters of all insolvent companies, except micro, small and medium enterprises (MSME), from bidding for their companies under the Code. Promoters of insolvent MSMEs were also debarred from the bidding process under the Code if they were declared wilful defaulters. The fear of losing a company was the biggest fallout of the Insolvency and Bankruptcy Code, even though its effectiveness would have been far greater, if the government had also simultaneously strengthened the capacity of the National Company Law Tribunals by setting up more benches to expedite the hearing of the insolvency cases. Nevertheless, its disruptive impact on India Inc. was huge.

Battle between RBI and the Government

Expectedly, there was a political backlash of such stringent measures against enterprises that failed to repay their loans. Enforcing tough measures against companies that defaulted on loan repayment, leading to their dispossession of companies that they helped set up, further strengthened the Narendra Modi government's image that it was not too friendly to big business.

But there was pushback as well. Within months of the Insolvency and Bankruptcy Code swiftly deciding on liquidation of insolvent companies or their takeover by other business entities, the government began exploring alternative means to soften the blow. It began engaging with the RBI for extending preferential treatment for companies in some sectors that suffered from specific developments forcing them to default on their loan repayment obligation. When the RBI declined to make any concessions on enforcing its stressed assets recognition norms for any sectors, the matter went to court and the government supported the industry's petition.

But the court asked the government to use provisions under the law to issue a direction to the RBI for making such a concession. That in many ways was the starting point of the RBI-government tiff over what approach should be adopted for resolving the economy's twin balance-sheet problem. Separately, the government framed an alternative stressed asset resolution package for the power sector companies. The alternative scheme was to be implemented outside the purview of the Insolvency and Bankruptcy Code. Fortunately, that scheme did not make much headway.

The pushback to the RBI's initiatives on the resolution of stressed assets came also from the Supreme Court. Borrowers aggrieved by the 12 February

2018 circular of the RBI moved the courts. They were unhappy with the RBI circular that laid down a strict time-bound recognition of stressed assets and their resolution plan. Less than a year later, in April 2019, the Supreme Court ruled that the 12 February circular of the RBI was unconstitutional, even though it stood by the insolvency resolution process under the Insolvency and Bankruptcy Code. It was a setback for the RBI's initiatives on stressed assets resolution. The RBI had no option other than reframing its guideline to address the concerns raised by the apex court of the country.

What complicated the relationship between the RBI and the government was a Rs 11,400-crore credit scam that hit the state-controlled Punjab National Bank, where diamantaires, Nirav Modi and Mehul Choksi, had used the bank's credit facilities to finance their projects without any collaterals or guarantees. Even as the Bank was engaged in its own efforts to recover dues from Nirav Modi and Mehul Choksi, the government put the blame on lax regulation of banks by the RBI and also introduced a new piece of legislation to facilitate criminal proceedings against economic offenders who became fugitives refusing to return to India and submit themselves to the arms of the law.[3] RBI Governor Urjit Patel responded in defence of the central bank and argued that the extant law had not sufficiently empowered him to deal with the management of public-sector banks in the same way as the law allowed him to do for private-sector bank managements. In as many as seven areas, the regulation for public-sector banks under the Banking Regulation Act was different from that for other banks. For instance, he argued that the RBI could not remove directors and managements at the public-sector banks. It could not supersede their boards. It could not remove chairmen and managing directors of public-sector banks. It could not force a merger of a public-sector bank. It could not even revoke the licence for public-sector banks, since they do not actually need a licence from the central bank, quite unlike the private-sector banks. Nor could the central bank trigger the liquidation of public-sector banks.

Finally, the RBI governor said that the top managements of public-sector banks came under dual supervision—as they had the sovereign as their shareholder and had to keep their interests in mind and at the same time had to come under the supervision of the regulator.

What was the RBI governor's prescription to remedy the situation? He asked for suitable amendments in the Banking Regulation Act. And all these suggestions were made by him in a public speech he delivered in Gandhinagar, Gujarat, on 14 March 2018. Patel had hit the nail on its head. Even the effectiveness of the Insolvency and Bankruptcy Code was likely to be impaired if the government failed to pay heed to the need for improving the governance standards in public-sector banks. Even after the Code helped these banks reclaim a part of their stressed loans, the questions of reforming the public-sector banks' management structure, giving them functional autonomy and bringing them under a stricter regulatory regime, would continue to arise with alarming frequency.

The government did not come out with any response to the governor's detailed critique on the weaknesses in the regulatory laws for public-sector banks. But it became clear that the relations between the RBI and the government were under stress. What started out as a stressed assets problem, largely for the public-sector banks, had aggravated to become a tussle between the regulator and the government. While the RBI showed determination in ensuring the enforcement of norms for recognition of bad assets for banks and their resolution, the government responded with a plan for recapitalization and reforms. But the surfacing of scams in public-sector banks and the government's discomfort over the RBI's refusal to show preferential treatment to some of the beleaguered sectors created fissures in the relationship between the two entities. The government had argued that a selective relaxation was necessary to boost investment, which had slowed down the economy, but the RBI was concerned over the long-term damage such relaxation would cause to the financial system. Differences between the government and the RBI were coming to the fore.

Even earlier, when Rajan was the RBI governor, the government's relations with the central bank had become strained. On the one hand, Rajan would make public speeches that would criticize the government's policies on manufacturing or even its performance. Rajan defended those speeches, but critics found that as the RBI governor, he should have refrained from making such comments that either criticized the government's Make In India policy or compared the Indian economy's growth performance to a one-eyed man becoming the king in the land of the blind. The government was not pleased with such statements and their relationship soured even as Rajan left the RBI on the completion of his three-year tenure in September 2016. Even while Rajan was in charge of the central bank, the government would gradually nibble away at the RBI's powers and autonomy. The setting up of the Monetary Policy Committee was hailed as a bold reform, entrusting the task of formulating the monetary policy with a committee consisting of the RBI governor, representatives of the central bank and a few independent experts. But the task of appointing the independent experts for the committee was left to a government committee, headed by the cabinet secretary with the RBI governor as one of the members. Similarly, the earlier freedom RBI governors would enjoy in appointing their deputy governors was gradually curtailed and brought under the discipline of an official appointments committee.

Strains in the relationship between the government and the RBI began surfacing in other areas as well. Larger questions of the central bank's autonomy were raised and the government's approach to the entire issue also came under attack, just as the central bank was criticized for bringing its differences with the sovereign out in the open, without trying to resolve them within the board room or through bilateral consultation with the finance minister. Deputy Governor Viral Acharya delivered a public speech in October 2018, where he forecast a grim scenario for any economy that did not heed the importance of preserving the autonomy of the central bank. Acharya's speech was interpreted as a direct attack against the government, which had earlier cut short the tenure of one of the directors and appointed one who was politically sympathetic to the government.

The government chose to use Section 7 under the RBI Act to seek consultation with the RBI governor for some of these issues. While truce was called after a few rounds of meetings and no directions were required to be issued under the provision of the law, the relationship between the RBI and the government got strained and the resultant stress was a deeply worrying development. Eventually, on 10 December 2018, RBI Governor Urjit Patel decided to resign, citing personal reasons. The government took just a day to identify Patel's successor—a retired IAS officer, Shaktikanta Das.

Looking back, it does appear that the growing stress in the banking system and the methods that should have been adopted to resolve the economy's twin balance sheet problem resulted in a ruptured relationship between the central bank and the government. The delicate balance in the equation between the RBI and the government was disturbed. Differences of opinion surfaced between the RBI governor and the government over the manner in which the banks' NPA problem should be resolved and how the public-sector banks' governance structure should be revamped. Questions over the RBI's autonomy also were raised over whether the government could tap into the central bank's capital reserves. In the end, it was a huge disruption for the delicate balance in the relationship between the central bank and the government. This will no doubt have a long-term impact on the relationship between governments and the central bank governors of the future.

Who were the key disrupters in the financial sector? Clearly, RBI Governor Raghuram Rajan was the primary disrupter. He put in place a series of actions to impose greater financial discipline on banks and forced them to recognize stressed assets as well as undertake corrective steps to resolve them. He may be accused of not taking those steps as quickly as possible, but the disruption he caused to the financial sector is irrefutable. Urjit Patel and Finance Minister Arun Jaitley would also rank among the other prominent disrupters. They changed the way banking stress was tackled, increasing the pressure on the banks and the overall financial system. But in that process they allowed their different approaches and strategies to resolve stressed assets to become a cause for a strained relationship between the regulator and the government. The long-term consequences of such a disruption are not yet known. It will take a lot of effort for future finance ministers and governors of the central bank to amend the relationship, repair the damage inflicted on the perception of a regulator's independence and ameliorate the impact of the disruption that the economy experienced as a result.

CHAPTER 22

SHOCK THERAPY OR A BOOMERANG?

Nine days after Diwali was celebrated on 30 October 2016, Prime Minister Narendra Modi decided to address the nation on the evening of 8 November. Diwali is a festival of lights, celebrated in almost all corners of the country and it also marks the start of a new year for most traditional Indian businesses. But this year Diwali was spent amidst the spectre of a war looming large on India's western borders. Just about a month earlier, on 29 September, India had undertaken what it called a 'surgical strike' on two sites located in the Pakistan-occupied Kashmir.[1] The Pakistani Army played down the intensity of the attack. A BBC report[2] claimed that there were no air-dropping of Indian soldiers into those two sites, two kilometres inside the Line of Control that separates India from Pakistan. But the Indian side maintained that considerable damage was inflicted on two camps in Pakistan-occupied Kashmir, from where Pakistani terrorists used to plan terror attacks in Indian cities.

The Indian counterattack came within weeks of a Pakistani terrorist attack on an Indian Army base in Kashmir's Uri, killing nineteen Indian soldiers. The retaliation from the Pakistani side to the 29 September 'surgical strike' by Indian forces was swift. Between 29 September and the first week of November 2016, there were more than sixty ceasefire violations by Pakistani forces along the Line of Control and the international border. According to another report, there were over 120 ceasefire violations during the same period. As many as 175 schools in the nearby areas on the Indian side were shut down in order to avoid civilian casualties due to shelling or firing from across the border. Also, Indian villages near the border with Pakistan were evacuated to minimize the number of civilian deaths on account of attacks from across the border. Already, about fifteen Indians were killed and forty more injured in this period.

Hours before the prime minister's scheduled address to the nation on 8 November 2016, a high-level meeting took place at the prime minister's office. It was a routine meeting, but the context of the heightened tension on India's western border and the firing incidents leading to many deaths was unusual. Military chiefs briefed Modi on the situation along India's border with Pakistan and apprised him of the preparedness of the armed forces to tackle the situation on the border. National Security Adviser Ajit Doval was present at this meeting, which significantly took place on a day when one Indian soldier had been killed hours earlier due to Pakistani shelling in Jammu and Kashmir.

So, when the government put out an advisory at around 7 p.m. the same day that the prime minister would address the nation around 8 p.m., speculation was rife about whether India was planning a second surgical strike or something similar had already been undertaken, or the prime minister would be making a bigger announcement concerning Pakistan. Such speculation was further fuelled by the news that a Cabinet meeting had been called just before the scheduled address by the prime minister.

When the nation heard the prime minister for about thirty-seven minutes, it was stunned. Yes, a surgical strike had been undertaken, but not against any terrorist camps in Pakistan, but against high-denomination currency notes in circulation in the country. Notes of Rs 500 and Rs 1000 denomination, which accounted for about 86 per cent of the total currency in circulation, were to be denotified or annulled by midnight and a detailed action plan was outlined on how the demands for cash would be met over the next few months and how individuals could exchange their old annulled notes with the new ones in the next fifty-odd days. The prime minister spoke in a sombre mood, as though a grave threat was looming large over the economy. Viewers initially feared that a serious external security threat had engulfed the nation and only after about fifteen minutes into his speech did they realize that the grave threat was not from across the border, but economic and within the country—a threat of black money, fake currencies and counterfeit notes financing terror acts in the country. Two and a half years into his tenure, Modi had delivered his government's most disruptive blow to the Indian economy, which will define to a great extent his governance record as India's thirteenth prime minister.

The Road to Demonetization

The decision to demonetize 86 per cent of the country's currency in circulation has been widely understood to be a sudden decision by Modi and took everyone by surprise. Few people even within the government knew of the decision before it was announced by Prime Minister Modi.

The jury may be still out on whether it was a decision made suddenly or the seeds of the move had been sown many months before that fateful evening of 8 November 2016. But a few developments that took place during a period of about eight months before demonetization do suggest that the government may have planned the move much earlier, and why the decision appeared to have been taken suddenly is because utmost secrecy was maintained by the few officials that were responsible for executing the demonetization plan.

At least eight months ago, on 29 February 2016, Finance Minister Arun Jaitley had risen in the Lok Sabha, the lower house of the Indian Parliament, to present what would be the Narendra Modi government's third Budget—to outline the taxation and economic policy plan for 2016–17. Jaitley claimed credit for how the Indian economy had been rescued from the decelerating growth of the last few years of the Manmohan Singh government and announced how the Modi government had accelerated the growth. The government's own data, however, showed a slightly different story. Economic growth had indeed begun slowing down and GDP growth had dropped to 5.5 per cent in 2012–13. But the recovery had started in 2013–14, when GDP growth rose to 6.4 per cent. The finance minister's intention was to convey that the new government had taken quite a few bold initiatives to bolster the economy and boost its growth. True to form, Jaitley doled out some tax incentives for individuals and companies and made an attempt to settle the vexatious issue of retrospective taxation for foreign companies, in particular.

The Manmohan Singh government had changed a taxation law with retrospective effect through its Budget for 2012–13. The Income-tax Act, 1961, was amended retrospectively to force companies like Vodafone to pay capital gains tax on its purchase of controlling shares of an overseas company, whose assets and businesses were located in India. Vodafone had argued that since its acquisition of shares in the telecom company, then owned by Hutchinson Whampoa of Hong Kong, was an international transaction, it was not obliged to pay any tax in India. The government had argued that since the business underlying those shares was located in India, the Indian government had the right to levy a capital gains tax. But the government's tax demand on Vodafone for Rs 11,000 crore was quashed by the Supreme Court in January 2012. The Manmohan Singh government retaliated in the Budget it presented in February 2012. Since there was a lack of clarity in the law, a loophole that the apex court used to strike down the government's tax notice on Vodafone, Finance Minister Pranab Mukherjee, in his Budget for 2012–13, changed the Income-tax Act retrospectively, raising a storm of protest in international circles and even within India. Described as the Vodafone tax, this turned industry against the Manmohan Singh government and the succeeding government led by Narendra Modi was expected to provide legal clarity. But all that the Modi government did was to retain the Vodafone tax, but assured industry and foreign investors that such retrospective amendments to taxation laws would not be introduced again.

Other efforts by the Modi government to bring about factor market reforms, however, made little headway. The government faced a major political setback on account of its failure to relax the land acquisition norms and introduce labour reforms in the first year and a half, and was preparing to undertake some big reforms—by introducing a law that would resolve stressed assets of banks by forcing time-bound liquidation or resolution of indebted companies and replacing a plethora of indirect taxes at the Central and state levels with a uniform indirect tax. The former would be later known as the Insolvency and Bankruptcy Code, which would be passed by Parliament by May 2016. And the latter would usher in India's biggest indirect tax reform and would be known as the GST, which would be launched from July 2017.

Little could anyone tracking the finance minister's speech that day sense that the government was readying for a much more dramatic and disruptive change about eight months later. Demonetization was announced by Prime Minister Modi on 8 November 2016. Yet, there were perhaps some hints of the government's thinking even at that time. They became a little too obvious, of course in hindsight. For instance, Jaitley announced a big push to the Pradhan Mantri Mudra Yojana (PMMY) for the benefit of entrepreneurs at the bottom of the pyramid. The amount sanctioned under PMMY, essentially loans on easy terms to entrepreneurs in the informal sector, had already reached about Rs 1 lakh crore by the end of January 2016 and the number of beneficiaries crossed 25 million. The target for 2016–17 was raised to Rs 1.8 lakh crore. The push for Mudra Yojana was aimed at providing financial support and incentives to small and medium enterprises, a sector that would be hit hard by demonetization. The idea was to provide them adequate financial support so that they could withstand the shock of demonetization. This became evident in retrospect when it was argued in BJP circles that if demonetization adversely hit small businesses it was because the planned Mudra Yojana failed to take off as per the government's expectations. The RBI had indeed expressed some doubts that the loans granted under Mudra Yojana could result in more non-performing loans for banks. S. Gurumurthy, an adviser to the BJP and who later became a director on the board of the RBI, had tweeted soon after demonetization: 'Only micro businesses suffered for finance as the full Mudra scheme to alleviate them was blocked.'[3]

In another Budget announcement, Jaitley proposed to expand the reach of the automated teller machines (ATMs), particularly in rural areas. A nation-wide rollout of ATMs was planned to provide better access to financial services. Once again, the government seemed to be quietly planning for strengthening the ATM network. Post-demonetization, the use of ATMs would have become more critical for the limited cash individuals would be allowed to draw. Not only would there be a requirement of expanding the ATM network, but it would also have to be recalibrated for the new currency notes. As in the case of Mudra Yojana, the advance action on ATMs too was found to be wanting.

The most significant announcement from the perspective of what happened to the nation eight months later was Jaitley's enunciation of the government's taxation philosophy and the fight against black money. 'We are moving towards a lower tax regime with a non-litigious approach. Thus, while compliant taxpayers can expect a supportive interface with the department, tax evasion will be countered strongly. The capability of the tax department to detect tax evasion has improved because of enhanced access to information and availability of technology-driven analytical tools to process such information. I want to give an opportunity to the earlier non-compliant to move to the category of compliant,' Jaitley announced.

It is in this background that the finance minister announced a compliance window for a limited period for domestic taxpayers to come clean and declare their undisclosed income or income represented in the form of any assets. This was called the Income Declaration Scheme, 2016. The compliance window would essentially allow such taxpayers to clean up their past tax violations by paying tax on such undisclosed income at the rate of 30 per cent and a surcharge at 7.5 per cent and a penalty at 7.5 per cent. Thus, a penal income tax rate of 45 per cent was proposed for domestic taxpayers to wash their past sins of tax evasion. Describing it a compliance window was perhaps a euphemism. It was nothing else but a tax immunity scheme by another name. The only difference was a penal rate of tax. Thus, there would be no scrutiny or inquiry regarding income declared in these cases either under the Income-tax Act or the Wealth Tax Act. Those taking advantage of the 'compliance window' would enjoy immunity from prosecution as also from the provisions of the Benami Transaction (Prohibition) Act of 1988.

The four-month window under the scheme—from 1 June to 30 September 2016—helped the government secure declaration of undisclosed income amounting to Rs 65,250 crore. This was a preliminary estimate, but helped the government mobilize a tax revenue of Rs 29,362 crore, which amounted to just 8 per cent of the total individual income taxes collected in 2016–17. The response was not overwhelming by any yardstick, perhaps because the scheme required the declarants to pay penalty, taking the overall tax incidence to 45 per cent. In contrast, the Voluntary Disclosure of Income Scheme (VDIS), 1997, required the declarants to pay an effective rate of taxation that could be in single digits and thus helped the government rake in additional tax revenues of Rs 9760 crore, which amounted to 34 per cent of the total income tax collected in 1997–98. VDIS 1997 was probably the most successful of all the eleven such tax amnesty schemes that have been rolled out by various governments from 1951 to 2016. The Supreme Court had directed the Centre after VDIS 1997 that it should desist from announcing any more tax amnesty schemes. But the government had defended the Income Disclosure Scheme, 2016, on the ground that since it had imposed a penalty on the declarant, it was not similar to the previous schemes.

A justification for the Income Disclosure Scheme, 2016, from the social expenditure point of view was provided when the finance minister announced that the surcharge of 7.5 per cent would be called Krishi Kalyan surcharge and used for agriculture and rural economy. What Jaitley did not disclose in his Budget speech in Parliament was that the collection of the Krishi Kalyan levy would help him collect the entire amount by way of surcharge and keep it for Central expenditure without sharing that with the states under any devolution formula. While a specified share of taxes collected by the Centre is distributed among the states and Union territories in accordance with a formula devised periodically by the Finance Commissions, there is no such sharing of what the Centre levies by way of surcharges and cess. Indeed, many finance ministers in the past have sought recourse to the levy of surcharges and cess on commodities or even on direct taxes in order to mobilize more revenues for the Centre and without sharing those special levies with the states. This is a practice that has been frowned upon by fiscal experts who believe that this dilutes the principle enshrined in the Indian Constitution on how the Centre should share its revenues with the states. The Krishi Kalyan surcharge was such a levy that the Centre was not obliged to share with the states.

But two features of the tax compliance window scheme are worth noting. One, Jaitley concluded his announcement on the scheme by reiterating the government's objective behind it. He said: 'Our government is fully committed to remove black money from the economy. Having given one opportunity for evaded income to be declared once, we would then like to focus all our resources for bringing people with black money to books.' Two, the scheme was to start from 1 June and end by 30 September, with the option to those taking advantage of the scheme to pay the due tax amount within two months of the declaration. Did the warning that the government would crack down on black money with greater force after having given taxpayers an opportunity to come clean have a signal hidden in that of what was to come on 8 November 2016? And why was the last day of the scheme kept on 30 September? There is enough in Jaitley's Budget speech that debunks the speculation that Modi's demonetization was a sudden unplanned move.

It may be sheer coincidence, but it must be remarkable that even while Jaitley was announcing the drive against black money and a tax compliance window in the morning, his ministry was busy issuing an Office Memorandum detailing what the government was planning on the promotion of payments through cards and digital means across the country. It was a detailed note emanating from the Currency and Coin Division of the Department of Economic Affairs in the Finance Ministry. On 29 February 2016, it was sent to all secretaries of the central ministries, the RBI governor, the chairman of Telecom Regulatory Authority of India, the CEO of NITI Aayog and of course to the cabinet secretary. With a six-point objective in view, the grand plan was aimed at improving the ease of conducting card or digital transactions for an individual, reducing the risks and costs of handling cash, reducing the costs of managing cash in the economy, building a transactions history to enable improved credit access and financial inclusion, reducing tax avoidance and reducing the impact of counterfeit money. In particular, the emphasis on greater use of digital transactions, reduction in the use of cash and crackdown on counterfeit money was an idea that had already gripped the minds of government policymakers by then.

The scope of the scheme was equally significant and should have given adequate hints about the government's thinking on what it wanted to do a few months later. It had outlined plans to provide access to financial payment services to every citizen along with the ability to conduct card or digital transactions, digitize government collections by equipping each collection point with a method to accept card or digital payments and migrate payment transactions currently dominated by cash to non-cash modes. The government wanted to incentivize people to use card or digital transactions and disincentivize the use of cash-based transactions. Steps were taken to strengthen the infrastructure for acceptance of cards or digital transactions and encourage companies, institutions and merchant establishments to facilitate card or digital payments. Different departments of the Union government were given specific responsibilities to achieve both the short-term and medium-term goals—the short-term goals were to be realized in one year and the medium-term goals in two years.

For instance, the Ministry of Road Transport and Highways and the Ministry of Urban Development were asked to facilitate the use of existing open-loop systems issued by a bank for multipurpose use, including for making transit payments with a dedicated application like toll fees, metro rail ride or bus services. This was essentially aimed at facilitating the payment of toll fees through cashless instruments. The Department of Financial Services in conjunction with the RBI was expected to ensure that each eligible account holder under the PMJDY should be provided access to the digital financial services in addition to the RuPay card. The Department of Electronics and Information Technology was entrusted with the task of formulating an action plan wherein all government departments and organizations introduced infrastructure for acceptance and collection of all revenues, fees and penalties through card or digital means, beyond a specified threshold, through electronic platforms or 'PayGov India', which it must develop as a single unified portal across Central and state governments as well as their public-sector undertakings for collection purposes.[4]

Similarly, the Department of Financial Services and RBI were expected to take steps to rationalize merchant discount rates (MDR) on card transactions and formulate a differentiated MDR framework for key transaction segments such as utility payments and railway ticketing by examining the matter holistically in consultation with the stakeholders. A detailed plan for creating infrastructure for accepting such digital payments was outlined. This included the introduction of adequate numbers of point-of-sale or POS terminals or mobile POS terminals for card payments and a review of the requirements under the Prevention of Money Laundering Act and rules to bring uniform know-your-customer norms based on an authorized identity for all payment systems.

The message from the government was unmistakably clear. There was an attempt to reduce the preponderance of cash in all transactions in the economy, although cash in itself did not always represent black money. There was also an attempt at greater formalization of the economy, bringing more people under banking coverage. The presence of credit card companies and their desire to expand their business also helped in this push towards non-cash transactions. In retrospect, it seems the government had made up its mind on the massive attack it would launch on high-denomination currencies in circulation a few months later. It is clear that the government was building the infrastructure where transactions could be made in non-cash modes once the crackdown on cash was announced.

Taken together with Finance Minister Arun Jaitley's Budget announcement on a crackdown on black money and a tax compliance window, which gave taxpayers a final chance to declare their undisclosed income after paying a penal rate of tax at 45 per cent, the finance ministry's office memorandum on the same day completes a full circle. The government had by then made up its mind on a crackdown on cash. It is also possible that because the government was not sure how successful its drive would be against black money in terms of declaration of undisclosed income, it had begun exploring alternative methods to reduce the preponderance of cash. How and when that would happen was perhaps left to a smaller group of people in the government, including, of course, the prime minister. But it would be wrong to assume that demonetization was a disruption that the government caused without much thinking or prior planning. It was kept a well-guarded secret till its announcement on 8 November 2016. But it would not be incorrect to assume that the government had been toying with the idea of demonetization from as early as February 2016.

What Went On behind the Scene

Sometime in February 2016, the government of Narendra Modi had initiated a highly secret conversation with the then RBI governor, Raghuram G. Rajan.[5] His views on demonetization were sought and Rajan told the government that although there might be long-term benefits, the 'likely short-term economic costs would outweigh them'. More importantly, Rajan told the government that there were potentially better alternatives to achieve the main goals that it sought to achieve. The government did not stop there and asked the RBI governor to prepare a note on demonetization.

According to Rajan, the RBI prepared a note and submitted that to the government. What did the note contain? Rajan writes in his book, *I Do What I Do*, that the note 'outlined the potential costs and benefits of demonetization as well as alternatives that could achieve similar aims'. And if the government, after weighing the pros and cons of the move, decided to go ahead with demonetization, Rajan's note explained in detail what kind of advance preparations the government needed and how much time such preparation would require. The note also pointed out the consequences of inadequate preparation before the rollout of demonetization.

It is after receiving that note from Rajan that the government set up a committee to consider the issues that would arise out of demonetization if such a decision were to be taken. Rama Subramaniam Gandhi, the deputy governor in the RBI, in charge of currency, attended the meetings held by the government. While it is true that the government did not ask the RBI to take a decision on demonetization while Rajan was in charge of the RBI till 3 September 2016, the issue of demonetization did come up in a media interaction with the governor earlier in 2014. Rajan said at the annual Lalit Doshi memorial lecture in August 2014: 'I am not quite sure if what you meant is demonetize the old notes and introduce new notes instead. In the past, demonetization has been thought of as a way of getting black money out of circulation. Because people then have to come and say how do I have this 10 crore in cash sitting in my safe and explain where they got the money from. It is often cited as a solution. Unfortunately, my sense is, the clever find ways around it.'[6]

In a detailed report in the *Hindustan Times*, Rajan was quoted further to say the following:

> Black money hoarders find ways to divide their hoard into many smaller pieces. You find that people who haven't thought of a way to convert black to white, throw it into the hundi in some temples. I think there are ways around demonetisation. It is not that easy to flush out the black money.[7]

Elaborating further, the report added, Rajan said that a fair amount of unaccounted cash is typically in the form of gold and, therefore, even harder to catch. Rajan explained that his approach would be to crack down on incentives that led to generation and the retention of black money. Black money expert Arun Kumar, however, disagreed with Rajan's views on black money hoarders. According to him, neither do most of them keep black money in gold nor do they throw their unaccounted wealth in the *hundi* in temples.[8]

Nevertheless, what the above indicated was that Rajan had to deal with the demonetization issue even during his public speeches almost one and a half years before the matter was even broached with him by the government in February 2016. For the government and the RBI, also, demonetization as an idea was not something that just sprang up one fine morning. There were discussions, meetings and debates within a small group of officers, which were, of course, kept secret and confidential. Within the government, a handful of officers in the PMO and the finance ministry were aware of the government's plan to demonetize eighty-six of the currencies in circulations. And within the RBI, except the RBI governor, Rajan, his deputy governor in charge of currency management, R. Gandhi, and a few of their trusted lieutenants, nobody had any inkling of the disruption that was awaiting the nation.

Urjit Patel was at that time the deputy governor in charge of monetary policy and one whose reports on a new monetary policy framework and an inflation-targeting mechanism mandated by law were receiving serious attention within the RBI and the government. This would eventually pave the way for a new regime from September 2016. The new monetary policy framework meant a departure from the existing practice in which the RBI governor would decide on the monetary policy review, after consultation with his senior team and a clutch of technical advisers, whose advice, however, was not binding on the head of the central bank. In the new system, the monetary policy review exercise would be undertaken periodically by a committee to be chaired by the RBI governor. But the monetary policy committee will have two other members from the RBI and three members from outside the central bank. And the appointment of these three members would be made through an official search committee, to be headed by the cabinet secretary and the RBI governor would only be a member.

Similarly, a law was being framed to set an inflation target of 4 per cent, based on the movements in the consumer price index, with a range of 2 per cent either way. If the RBI failed to adhere to that inflation target, the governor would be obliged to explain to the government why such deviation took place.

This was going to be a new regime, where the RBI governor was made more accountable to a committee system of reviewing the monetary policy and a legally mandated inflation target. Urjit Patel as the deputy governor was a key player in framing the contours of this new regime.

Little did he know then that he would be the next governor, succeeding Rajan from 4 September 2016, implementing the new system from the very first monetary policy review exercise that he undertook as the new governor. He was also completely unaware of the other big move that was being initiated by the government and the RBI. Patel had no idea then that more than the new monetary policy regime, he would have to handle the biggest disruptive event that any RBI governor had done in the past.

In 1946, before India became independent, currency notes of Rs 1000 and Rs 10,000 were removed from circulation. This had little impact on the people as their circulation was very low. But later in 1954, both these were reintroduced along with Rs 5000 currency notes. Twenty-four years later, the first demonetization took place in independent India. That was in 1978. Prime Minister Morarji Desai wanted to crack down on black money and decided to demonetize currency notes of Rs 1000, Rs 5000 and Rs 10,000. However, the governor of the RBI at that time, I.G. Patel, disagreed with that strategy. That left Desai with no option other than getting an ordinance on demonetizing these notes promulgated. Subsequently, he followed that up with the passage of the High Denomination Bank Notes (Demonetization) Act in Parliament. But the impact of that demonetization on ordinary people was relatively small as the share of these high-denomination currency notes in the total currency in circulation was less than 1 per cent. In 2016, Prime Minister Modi opted for a new route for demonetization. He sought recourse to Section 26 (2) of the RBI Act, 1934, under which the government, on the basis of recommendations from the RBI, could declare that bank notes of any denomination would cease to be legal tender. Thus, unlike Desai, Modi did not need an ordinance for demonetization. An RBI board meeting recommending demonetization to the government was good enough.

Coincidentally, both in 1978 and 2016, when demonetization took place, a Patel was at the helm of the RBI—I.G. Patel in 1978 and Urjit Patel in 2016. Also, both the prime ministers behind the two demonetization plans hailed from Gujarat. Demonetization in independent India has a strong Gujarat factor!

Where the 2016 demonetization stood out in contrast was the manner in which the decision was implemented. The question that arose was if a good number of people in the RBI and the government knew of the demonetization plan, certainly the preparations that should have been undertaken before implementing it were inadequate. It is possible to argue that the exigencies of keeping the move a secret did not allow larger dissemination of the information and necessary action to be undertaken for a glitch-free implementation. The disruption may have been sudden and the decision process was kept secret. But a few people in the government and the RBI knew of the steps that were being planned. They were also presumably aware of the consequences of those steps and what preventive measures and safeguards needed to be taken or put in place to manage the disruption and minimize its impact. Yet, the adverse consequences to the economy in the wake of demonetization, as outlined in a later section, brings out another stark failure of those who planned this massive disruption. Even after being involved with the planning before demonetization, these important players in the government system underestimated its actual impact. The failure to manage the disruption, clearly, accentuated its adverse impact on the economy and society.

CHAPTER 23

THE HAND OF THE RBI AND MODI

Rama Subramaniam Gandhi, a postgraduate in economics, joined the RBI in 1980 and rose pretty fast in the hierarchy to become its executive director in 2011. Barring a short stint at the Securities and Exchange Board of India (SEBI), the mild-mannered Gandhi spent the bulk of his working life at the central bank. So, when on 3 April 2014, Gandhi became the deputy governor, it was hailed as the rise of an in-house officer of the RBI to occupy a board-level position in that august organization. In the three years that he occupied that post, Gandhi handled a wide range of portfolios—regulations of banks, non-banking entities and cooperative banks, financial and operational risk management, financial stability, management of foreign-exchange and external reserves, payment systems, information technology, financial market regulation and currency management. Gandhi retired from the RBI in April 2017. But of all the various portfolios he handled as deputy governor, the one pertaining to currency management will remain deeply etched in his mind.

Not without reason. In February 2016, Gandhi was summoned by RBI Governor Raghuram G. Rajan and asked to assist the government in examining the pros and cons of a move to demonetize high-denomination currencies in the system. It was a top-secret assignment. Nobody in the RBI system apart from Gandhi and RBI Governor Rajan knew of the plan. Even within the government, there were not too many who had any information on why the government was seeking information on what steps needed to be taken if a large number of currencies were to be replaced with new ones. A note had also been prepared by Rajan on what the short-term and medium-term consequences would be if all high-denomination currencies were to be declared invalid and what preparations needed to be made if the government still went ahead with the proposed demonetization. Like Rajan, Gandhi too was not comfortable with the idea of such a disruptive measure, even though the problem of counterfeit currency was getting worse, though its incidence was a very tiny proportion of all the high-denomination currency notes in circulation at that time. But the solution for that was not demonetization, but a more concerted attack on fake currencies and bringing in new currency notes with better designs and more robust security features.

Work on bringing out new currency notes and changing their designs started as early as in February. The PMO and the RBI were in close consultation over the design and new features of the new currency notes to be circulated. Gandhi was in charge of the entire operations from the RBI's side. The procedures were elaborate and followed while maintaining utmost secrecy. As many as eighteen designers worked on the new currency notes at the Mysuru currency printing press of the RBI and they took about forty-five days to complete the design work. An official at the RBI printing press at Mysuru would travel to the PMO in New Delhi and get the designs approved. In a digital age, no emails or postal correspondence was undertaken. Instead, all the processes followed a physical drill, in a bid to ensure secrecy. By May 2016, the matter was referred to the RBI board, which then cleared the introduction of currency notes with a value of Rs 2000.

In June, the printing presses at Mysuru and Salboni in West Bengal were told to undertake no more fresh printing of currency notes of Rs 1000 and Rs 500 value. This was probably the most significant pointer that the government had by then decided about its demonetization plan. Raghuram Rajan was at the helm of the RBI at that point in time. While Gandhi implemented that decision and got a clear sense of the government plan, Rajan too must have realized by then that demonetization was in the offing. On 18 June 2016, Rajan announced his decision to return to the academia and not continue as the RBI governor beyond the completion of his three-year tenure on 4 September 2016. This was almost two and a half months before his tenure was due to end and discussion was on with the government on the nature of his next term. Rajan made public his letter to his colleagues in the RBI on that Saturday morning. Recounting his achievements as the governor, Rajan also noted the fresh challenges that he would have liked to tackle in the coming days. These challenges included the operation of the new monetary policy framework, the tasks of completing the clean-up of bank balance sheets by resolving their stressed assets and a few potentially risky international developments.

Rajan noted in his letter to his colleagues:

While I was open to seeing these developments through, on due reflection, and after consultation with the government, I want to share with you that I will be returning to academia when my term as Governor ends on September 4, 2016. I will, of course, always be available to serve my country when needed.[1]

For Gandhi, however, the resignation announcement made little impact on his work schedule in the next few months. By mid-September, 2016, Gandhi made sure that the printing of the new Rs 2000 notes had begun. Simultaneously, the printing of the new Rs 500 notes too had begun in other printing presses in Dewas in Madhya Pradesh and Nashik in Maharashtra. Urjit Patel had become the governor of the RBI on 4 September 2016. And the new notes thus bore the signature of Patel.

The challenge of maintaining secrecy over the currency note exercise was proving to be formidable. A report in a Hindi publication, *Dainik Jagran*, on 28 October,[2] seemed to have revealed it all about a fortnight before the decision on demonetization was made public. Brijesh Dubey, a business journalist based in Kanpur, wrote that the government was likely to soon issue new currency notes of Rs 2000 value with high-security features to curb black money. The report also said that in a bid to curb fake currencies, a serious view was being taken on the existing currency notes of Rs 500 and Rs 1000 value. It was significant that the board of the RBI under its new Governor, Urjit Patel, held its meeting at Kanpur on 20 October. Within days of Dubey's report in *Dainik Jagran*, a WhatsApp picture of the new Rs 2000 note became popular, raising questions on what the government was planning to do with a new currency.

On 30 October, a Sunday, Diwali was celebrated across the country. The government weighed the pros and cons of advancing the decision on demonetization to pre-empt further leakage of information. Eventually, it opted for 8 November 2016 to be the big day. The schedule for advance preparations for managing the consequences of demonetization certainly suffered. But the embarrassment of further leaks was avoided.

Gandhi told Gopika Gopakumar of the *Mint* about a year after demonetization that the government went in for Rs 2000 notes to keep a check on the circulation of high-value currency notes. 'We had to ensure that a minimum value of new notes was available before the government went ahead with demonetization. Hence we decided to introduce Rs 2000 notes,' Gandhi said. As early as in 2014, the RBI had mooted the idea of printing currency notes of higher denomination, but the finance ministry agreed to the idea of printing only Rs 2000 notes. An area of concern was over the pace of the printing of these new currency notes, which later became a major headache for the government and the RBI as demonetization was rolled out.

But the government's concern over fake and counterfeit currency was real in many ways. A sharp surge in the detection of counterfeit notes had been noticed since 2008. They more than trebled from 1,95,000 pieces in 2007–08 to 6,32,000 in 2015–16 and most of these notes came from across the border in Pakistan. The sophistication in the way these counterfeit notes were produced in printing presses in Pakistan was a major worry and this put more pressure on the RBI to come out with a new series of currency notes, particularly with higher denominations.[3] Since then the government and the RBI kept consulting each other on the new currency series that needed to be issued to counter the menace of counterfeit currency notes. This also raised the awareness level among banks and people about the menace of fake and counterfeit currency notes. Also, thanks to the rapidly spreading technology of currency note counting and sorting machines, the rate of detecting counterfeit notes improved dramatically increasing the reported incidence of the menace.

A few more steps were explored by the RBI to address the problem of counterfeit currency. In 2013, the central bank explored the idea of switching over to printing of plastic currency notes as these were difficult and also expensive to counterfeit. Another big move was taken in 2014, when the RBI issued a circular saying that all currency notes printed before 2005 would have to be phased out and a three-month window was given during which such old notes could be exchanged with the new ones. This created uncertainty and even fear among the people if this was a veiled demonetization being introduced by a different name. The RBI quickly issued clarifications to quell such fears and the window of exchanging such notes was extended till 31 December 2016.

Gandhi also made sure that necessary steps were taken to build the capacity of the Indian government to print sufficient numbers of currency notes within the country. In 2013, the Bank Note Paper Mill India Private Limited was set up in Mysuru as a subsidiary of Security Printing and Minting Corporation of India Limited and Bharatiya Reserve Bank Note Mudran Private Limited. The objective of this move was to reduce the country's dependence on imported paper for printing currency notes. According to reports, an estimated 18,000 tonnes of paper was produced by the Bank Note Paper Mill between April and December 2016—a period of just eight months. This is much higher than its estimated capacity of producing 15,000 tonnes of paper for currency notes. In addition, another

30,000 tonnes of paper for printing currency notes was imported by the end of December 2016. All this to help the RBI to manage the consequences of demonetization and meet the demand for new currency notes after 8 November 2016.

For Gandhi, 8 November 2018 was not an ordinary working day. He had come to Delhi by the morning flight to attend a meeting of the RBI Board to be held the same afternoon. It was the 561st meeting of the Central Board of Directors of the RBI. No specific reasons were cited why the Board met at New Delhi. One of the Mumbai-based directors of the Board, Natarajan Chandrasekaran, who at that time was the CEO and managing director of Tata Consultancy Services and later became the Chairman of Tata Sons, could not attend the meeting. The board granted leave of absence to Chandrasekaran. After the customary signing of the minutes of the previous meeting of the RBI's Central Board (the 560th held in Kanpur less than a month ago on 20 October), Gandhi placed before the Board a memorandum from the RBI's Department of Currency Management.

The speculation and suspense over why a Board meeting had been convened got over. Gandhi's memorandum recommended the 'withdrawal of the legal-tender status of bank notes in the denomination of Rs 500 and Rs 1000 of existing and any older series in circulation'.[4] Along with the memorandum, Gandhi also presented a copy of a finance ministry letter of 7 November 2016 along with a draft scheme for implementing the withdrawal of the legal-tender character of existing Rs 500 and Rs 1000 bank notes. These were submitted before the RBI Central Board for its consideration and commending to the Central Government under Section 26 (2) of the RBI Act, 1934. Section 26 of the RBI Act pertains to the legal-tender character of currency notes in circulation. And Clause 2 of Section 26 says that on the recommendation of the RBI Central Board, 'the Central Government may by notification in the Gazette of India, declare that with effect from such date as may be specified in the notification, any series of bank notes of any denomination shall cease to be legal tender'.[5] The RBI Central Board was now required to recommend to the government to annul the high-denomination currency notes.

The RBI Board was also informed about the sharp rise in the circulation of bank notes in the denomination of Rs 500 and Rs 1000 in the five-year period between 2011–12 and 2015–16. The Board was informed that while the Indian economy in these five years grew by 30 per cent, the bank notes in the denomination of Rs 500 and Rs 1000 grew by over 76 per cent and

109 per cent, respectively, in the same period. This was an instance of a flawed use of statistics and, therefore, a weak and poor argument to justify demonetization. The 30 per cent economic growth figure was measured at constant prices, without adjusting for inflation during this period. The nominal economic growth (including the impact of inflation) in these five years would be about 57 per cent and the gap between the nominal economic growth and the increase in the high-denomination currency notes would have, therefore, shrunk considerably.

The government's argument presented before the Board touched upon a few other issues. It cited the Finance Ministry's White paper on Black Money to note the following:

> Cash has always been a facilitator of black money since transactions made in cash do not leave any audit trail. The White Paper also quotes the estimate made by the World Bank in July 2010 wherein the size of the shadow economy for India has been estimated at 20.7 per cent of GDP in 1999 and rising to 23.2 per cent in 2007. Incidence of counterfeiting is also on the rise in these two denominations. The total counterfeit currency in the country is estimated to be around Rs 400 crore.[6]

Present at that meeting of the Board were RBI Governor Urjit Patel, his two deputy governors—R. Gandhi and S.S. Mundra, and five other directors—Nachiket Mor, a former executive director of ICICI Bank whose second tenure as director was cut short a little after one year in September 2018, Bharat Doshi, a senior finance professional who worked in various capacities in the Mahindra group, Sudhir Mankad, a retired IAS officer and a former chief secretary in the Gujarat government, Anjuly Chib Duggal, an IAS officer who was then secretary in the department of financial services in the finance ministry, and Shaktikanta Das, an IAS officer who was then secretary in the department of economic affairs in the finance ministry and later in December 2018 was appointed the RBI governor. There is no documentary evidence on who all among the RBI Directors responded to the memorandum that was put up for the Board's recommendation. But some of those observations suggested that the memorandum did not have an easy passage at the Board meeting.

Three critical observations, which were recorded in the Board meeting's minutes, deserve to be recounted here:

> The growth rate of the economy mentioned is the real rate while the growth in currency in circulation is nominal. Adjusted for inflation, the

difference may not be so stark. Hence, this argument does not adequately support the recommendation.

While any incidence of counterfeiting is a concern, Rs 400 crore as a percentage of the total quantum of currency in circulation in the country is not very significant.

Most of the black money is held not in the form of cash but in the form of real-sector assets such as gold or real-estate and that this move would not have a material impact on those assets.

There were also comments that supported the demonetization move, though these too had struck a note of caution and sought an assurance that the concerns over the adverse impact on the economy would be addressed. These comments ran as follows:

It is a commendable measure but will have short-term negative effect on the GDP for the current year.

Exemption provided to medical stores can be extended to private medical stores as well.

Arriving domestic long-distance travellers, who may be only carrying high-denomination notes will be taken by surprise at railway stations/ airports for payment to taxi drivers and porter charges and hence put to hardship. It would also have an adverse effect on tourists.

The Board was assured that the matter has been under discussion between the Central Government and the RBI over the last six months during which most of these issues have been considered. Apart from the stated objectives, the proposed step also presents a big opportunity to take the process of financial inclusion and incentivizing the use of electronic modes of payment forward as people see the benefits of bank accounts and electronic means of payment over the use of cash.

The Board was assured that the Government will take mitigating measures to contain the use of cash.

The RBI management was extremely reluctant to make public the minutes of the 561st meeting of its Central Board. For months together, requests for releasing these minutes made under the Right to Information Act were turned down. It was only under the directives of the Chief Information Commissioner under the RTI Act that the RBI released those minutes in March 2019. What these minutes clearly show is that the decision on recommending demonetization was not an easy and smooth affair. Serious concerns were expressed over the impact and hardships that demonetization would create. The directors seemed to have recognized the inevitability of the decision on demonetization, but spared no efforts in seeking as much assurance as possible to help mitigate the adverse impact of annulling 86 per cent of the country's total currency in circulation. The minutes also established that the government and the RBI were in consultation with each other on the plan for demonetization for about six months. A puzzling development during the Board meeting was the presentation of a finance ministry letter dated 7 November 2016. It is not clear what the contents of this letter were. The RBI Act clearly mentions that the government can annul currency notes of any denomination on the recommendation of the RBI's Central Board of Directors.

What was the finance ministry letter doing in that Board meeting? Under what sections of the RBI Act was that letter written and sent? There is no clarity on this as yet. Was the RBI Board being guided by the finance ministry to recommend the declaration of high-denomination currency notes invalid? Such questions must have troubled many of the Board members on that day. But in the end,

> [the] Board considered the memorandum and after detailed deliberations concluded that in larger public interest, the balance of advantage would lie in the withdrawal of legal-tender status of Rs 500 and Rs 1,000 currency notes currently in circulation and passed the following resolution: Resolved that the proposal of the Deputy Governor recommending withdrawal of legal tender of bank notes in the denomination of Rs 500 and Rs 1,000 of existing and any older series in circulation, is hereby considered and commended by the Central Board of Directors for forwarding the same to the Central Government.

The 561st meeting of the Central Board of the RBI began at 5.30 p.m. on 8 November 2016. Going by the minutes of the meeting, the meeting could not have lasted very long. But it was not an easy meeting for the RBI Board to hold. The Board had been advised by the government to consider a proposal that some of its directors were not comfortable with. The resolution that was adopted and used to convey the RBI's recommendation for demonetization put the ball in the court of the RBI. Official records would show that it was after all a proposal of the RBI deputy governor that recommended demonetization. The consent of the RBI board was communicated back to the government. Having received the RBI recommendation, Prime Minister Modi held a Cabinet meeting to announce his plans and secure its approval before he started his address to the nation at about 8 p.m.

Even as Prime Minister Modi began his address, Gandhi kept his fingers crossed, busy checking if all the preparations were in order. 'I was busy going through my checklist over and over again to be sure that the RBI was ready with the action plan to stem the blow of the announcement,' Gandhi told Gopika Gopakumar in late 2017 while recalling the developments more than a year earlier.[7]

The Miscalculated Surgical Strike

The first five-odd minutes of Modi's address to the nation on 8 November 2016 were spent on how the government had improved the country's economic situation, reviving growth in spite of two years of severe drought—an economic performance that was hailed not just domestically but also by institutions such as the World Bank and the IMF. The prime minister also reiterated his government's commitment to development for all—*Sab Ka Saath, Sab Ka Vikaas*—and listed out the major schemes to uplift the poor and spread fruits of economic growth among larger sections of people, which included a drive to open bank accounts for the poor and increase financial reach and inclusion (Pradhan Mantri Jan Dhan Yojana, PMJDY); a scheme to widen the coverage of insurance for the poor (Jan Suraksha Yojana); a programme that provides loans to small entrepreneurs (PMMY); a scheme providing financial assistance and guidance to the Dalits, tribals and women (Stand-Up India); and a scheme providing cooking gas connection on easy terms to homes of people from economically weaker sections (Pradhan Mantri Ujjwala Scheme) among others.

After outlining these developments, the prime minister drew attention to the growing menace of black money and corruption, in spite of the many attempts his government had made to eliminate both the economic ills. Was it then a clear admission by the prime minister that because the earlier schemes to unearth black money had failed to secure the desired results, the government decided on demonetization?

A third ill that the prime minister added to the list of economic challenges was that of terrorism, which he said was holding the country back in its development march. He even mentioned how many terrorists were apprehended with fake currency notes of Rs 500 and Rs 1000, which were seized from them. Modi now reminded the nation how his government had launched a frontal attack on black money, corruption and terrorism. He listed some of them as well: Setting up the Special Investigation Team, headed by a retired Supreme Court judge, passing a law in 2015 for disclosure of foreign black money, signing of agreements with many countries, including the US, that compelled the signatories to share banking information among themselves, a strict law to curb *benami* transactions used to deploy black money earned through corruption and a scheme allowing the declaration of black money after paying a penal rate of tax.

At this stage of his speech, it became quite clear that the prime minister's announcement was not going to be about any external threat but about measures against black money, corruption and terrorism. Giving credence to such expectations were Modi's statement that the government had till then succeeded in bringing into the open about Rs 1.25 lakh crore of black money. He posited the fight against black money as a fight on behalf of honest citizens and poor people, who were harmed the most when black money prospered and corruption remained unchecked. He also noted how high circulation of cash boosted the hawala trade, which was connected to black money and illegal trade in weapons. No less worrying for him was the role of black money in elections.

Almost fifteen minutes of the speech were over. It was at that point in time that Modi dropped the bombshell:

To break the grip of corruption and black money, we have decided that the five hundred rupee and thousand rupee currency notes presently in use will no longer be legal tender from midnight tonight, that is the 8th November, 2016. This means that these notes will not be acceptable for transactions from midnight onwards. The five hundred and thousand rupee notes hoarded by anti-national and anti-social elements will become just worthless pieces of paper. The rights and the interests of honest, hard-working people will be fully protected. Let me assure you that notes of one hundred, fifty, twenty, ten, five, two and one rupee and all coins will remain legal tender and will not be affected.

Modi justified his announcement on the ground that it would strengthen the hands of the common man in the fight against corruption, black money and fake currency. And then he listed out twenty-one major steps to help enforce demonetization. These steps included guidelines to people on how they can deposit the annulled currency with banks and what kinds of purchases they could still make with the old currency notes. It was an attempt to assure the people that those who were not dishonest had nothing to fear from the big announcement he had just made. (Please see the Appendix for the entire list of guidelines.)

The twenty-second step he announced pertained to the release of new currency notes of Rs 2000 and redesigned currency notes of Rs 500. In other words, currency notes of Rs 1000 were completely eliminated from circulation. He added that the RBI would make arrangements to limit the share of high-denomination notes in the total currency in circulation.

Many of these steps had to be revised in the next fifty days. The RBI issued more than twenty such notifications to amend the various norms for issuance of cash and the purposes for which old currency notes could be used in legitimate transactions. Modi was conscious that the move to annul the high-denomination currency notes would cause hardships to people and urged the ordinary citizens to make sacrifices and face difficulties for the benefit of the nation in its fight against corruption, black money, fake notes and terrorism. He tried to confer on demonetization the status of a *Mahayagna* (an offering before the fire god) to rid the country of corruption and black money. 'My dear countrymen, after the festivity of Diwali, now join the nation and extend your hand in this *Imandaari Ka Utsav* (a festival to celebrate honesty), this *Pramanikata Ka Parv*, this celebration of integrity, this festival of credibility,' he said.

Modi had begun his address with a reference to Diwali and ended it also with a reference to Diwali with a clarion call to every Indian to contribute to 'this grand sacrifice for cleansing our country, just as you cleaned up your surroundings during Diwali'.

The Aftermath

Modi's speech was telecast at 8 p.m. that evening. But it had been recorded earlier in the day before the Cabinet meeting began. It was a short meeting. There was hardly any discussion. The ministers, who attended the meeting, had to deposit their mobile phones with security before entering the conference room. For most ministers, the move was like a bolt from the blue. Soon after the Cabinet meeting, the prime minister's address began. Ministers who attended the Cabinet meeting were made to sit at the same room till the prime minister's address to the nation ended. At one point in his speech, Modi explained the logic of the secrecy maintained by the government. 'Secrecy was essential for this action. It is only now, as I speak to you, that various agencies like banks, post offices, railways, hospitals and others are being informed,' he said. Indeed, the decision-making process was shrouded in complete secrecy. Only a handful of people knew of the decision in advance and they included the prime minister, the finance minister, the RBI governor and the RBI deputy governor in charge of currency management. Few government officials knew of the move in advance. Chief Economic Adviser Arvind Subramanian, for instance, was in the dark about it.[8] As he recalled, he saw the prime minister delivering the address on his television screen while he was still in office that evening.

That day, many departmental stores in the country did brisk cash business as late as till midnight, when they could accept the currency notes of Rs 1000 and Rs 500, whose legal validity was yet to be annulled. Several other desperate and adventurous shops, selling high-value items like jewellery, kept their counters open as there was a long queue of customers waiting to use the currency notes of Rs 500 and Rs 1000 for making purchases. Consumers came in large numbers, bought as much as they could. The nation was gearing up for facing one of its most devastating economic disruptions.

The enormity of the challenge could hardly have been overestimated. Demonetization, as announced by Modi that evening, would have flushed out about 86 per cent of the currency in circulation and its impact would have been huge for an economy like India, where the prevalence of cash was estimated at 12 per cent of gross domestic product or GDP and it accounted for almost 90 per cent of all its commercial transactions. As many as 250 million new bank accounts had been opened in the previous two years in an attempt to improve the banking sector's reach and financial inclusion. However, the overall penetration of banking services were still very low at the end of 2016—at nine branches per 1,00,000 persons and less than forty branches per 1000 square kilometres. The numbers for rural India were even more alarmingly low. Worse, just about 2,00,000 ATMs were operational across the country and most of them were located in urban centres. What complicated the situation was that within days of demonetization the government and the RBI realized that their efforts at remonetizing the economy had hit an unexpected roadblock. The new currency notes, with new specifications, size and security features, required the ATMs to be recalibrated—a cumbersome exercise that took about a couple of weeks at least. Thus, the intensity of disruption got worse.

The task of remonetization at hand was not easy. With about 17 billion pieces of currency notes of Rs 500 value and another 6 billion pieces of currency notes of Rs 1000 value to be replaced in quick time, the capacity constraints at the currency printing presses in the country proved a big hurdle. Already, the four currency note printing presses were overstretched and importing currency notes was considered risky and not feasible at short notice. In the wake of long queues of customers outside banks, waiting to withdraw a specified amount of new currency notes or deposit their old currency notes, serious questions over the wisdom of the move were being raised.

One such question pertained to the size of the fake currencies, which was one of the targets of demonetization. The government had estimated that the size of fake currency notes in circulation was about Rs 400 crore. But as K.C. Chakraborty, former deputy governor of the RBI, said, the attempt to reject an entire bag of rice, which may have some stones or other contaminated foreign products, is an exaggerated response, where the consequences would be far worse than the benefits. A bigger question was that if data showed that only a small part of India's black money (estimated only 23 per cent of India's GDP) resided in cash and the bulk of it was in the form of gold, land and real estate, was demonetization's drive against black money misdirected?

Half-way into the fifty-day period when the annulled currency notes could be exchanged, the government changed its narrative on the purpose of demonetization. In addition to fighting black money, corruption and fake currency used in terrorist activities, the government argued that demonetization was a tool for pushing India into a cashless economy. Digitization of payments was a new focus area and new electronic payment companies were encouraged to launch digital wallets and incentives were rolled out to encourage more transactions to take place through the electronic mode without using cash. Digital India—a government-run scheme to promote the use of information technology for delivery of services to citizens—was being used as an instrument for popularizing digital transactions.

Admittedly, the government and the RBI were a bit slow in responding to the disruptive impact of demonetization on the availability of cash in the economy and the pace of economic activity. After about a fortnight or so, the government machinery swung into action to reduce the adverse impact of demonetization on people. Queues began getting shorter outside banks and ATMs after the third week of demonetization. More ATMs got recalibrated and they could now dispense new currency notes. The restrictions on withdrawal of money from bank accounts were also considerably eased after some time. Guidelines for use of the annulled currency notes in many public utilities like petrol pumps, government hospitals, chemist shops, milk suppliers and mobile phone recharging outlets were relaxed to relieve the pain of demonetization.

But the relief announced for farmers, traders and small business establishments was inadequate. Thanks to the continuing shortage of cash, farmers experienced great difficulty in buying seeds and fertilizers. The government's response was partial as farmers were allowed to use the annulled notes only for purchasing seeds from state-owned companies. Many farmers who relied on buying seeds from private companies suffered in a big way and acres of their fields went uncultivated in the coming rabi season. Small businesses and traders, too, decided to down shutters as there was no cash in the system and the currency replacement pace was too tardy to compensate for their loss.

Demonetization was later justified by the government as a drive towards digitization, but ironically its actual impact was that the move deepened the digital divide in the economy. This was because achieving digitization through a sudden decision like demonetization meant that there was no proper and advance planning. One of the sectors that gained from demonetization was mobile banking and electronic payments. With access to cash getting severely limited, the only recourse for people to buy and sell goods and services of necessity was payments through digital wallet companies which saw a spurt in their usage and popularity.

For the next couple of days, major national newspapers carried full-page advertisements of Paytm, India's largest payment wallet company, to congratulate Modi on taking the boldest decision in the financial history of independent India. The advertisements carried the picture of Modi and the message in the advertisement was: 'Pay with Paytm to more than 15 crore people and businesses. Join the revolution. Ab ATM nahin, #PaytmKaro.'

Did Paytm have an inkling of the Modi government's demonetization move, which would give it a big business opportunity? Opposition political leaders suspected such a nexus. Delhi Chief Minister and Aam Aadmi Party convener, Arvind Kejriwal tweeted: 'Paytm biggest beneficiary of PM's announcement. Next day PM appears in its ads. What's the deal, Mr PM?' While these were only tweets and could not establish any nexus, the numbers told their own story. Paytm conceded that within hours of the announcement of demonetization, its wallet business grew by 25 per cent, though its growth slowed down over the next few months when cash returned to the system with remonetization.

Given the long queues and the disruption caused to the pace of economic activity, demonetization raised many other questions. Was the government aware of the state of its banking infrastructure and capacity in currency note printing presses? Was there advance planning to ensure that the ATMs were recalibrated well in time before the announcement of demonetization? Did anybody in the government point out that demonetization would target only the stock of black money held in cash and would not prevent the generation of black money or unaccounted income?

A more disturbing question was whether there was a political motive behind demonetization. With his task of fulfilling the promise of development and jobs becoming more difficult, Modi may have opted for a move that would have greater immediate salience and recognition as a seemingly bold action against black money.

Politically, therefore, demonetization might have worked in favour of Modi and his party, the BJP. As many as five state Assemblies were due to go to the polls in 2017, one of them being Uttar Pradesh, a state that the BJP was very keen to wrest from the incumbent party, the Samajwadi Party of Mulayam Singh Yadav. For Modi's political opponents, demonetization was a big setback. The bulk of India's electoral funding by political parties has mostly been in cash and demonetization flushed out cash from the coffers of many Opposition political parties. Did it help the BJP and did the party apparatus know of demonetization in advance to take advantage of that knowledge? There are no easy answers to such questions. But the election results in Uttar Pradesh held in early 2017 showed a thumping victory for the BJP.

The Shock to the Economy

The disruption that demonetization caused to the Indian economy is unquestionable. Economic growth slowed in the subsequent quarters. From 5.5 per cent and 6.4 per cent GDP growth in the last two years of the Manmohan Singh government (2012–13 and 2013–14), the Indian economy had revived with growth numbers at 7.4 per cent in 2014–15 and 8 per cent in 2015–16. The economy seemed set for take-off. Indeed, provisional GDP had grown by 8.1 per cent in the April–June period of 2016 and stayed at 7.6 per cent for the July–September period of the same year. And then demonetization of 8 November 2016 took the toll of the economy.

Provisional estimates on national income, released on 31 May 2018,[9] showed that GDP growth for the three quarters after demonetization had decelerated—from 6.8 per cent in October–December 2016 to 6.1 per cent in the January–March period of 2017 to and further down to 5.6 per cent in the April–June period of 2017. It was only from the second quarter (July–September) of 2017–18 that economic growth began recovering. But the adverse impact of demonetization on growth was unmistakable. And going by the same set of May 2018 data, the annual GDP growth in 2016–17 had dropped to 7.1 per cent, compared to 8.1 per cent in 2015–16. In 2017–18, the growth further dropped to 6.7 per cent. Former chief economic adviser Arvind Subramanian expressed his surprise, after quitting the job he held for about four years, that the actual impact of demonetization was less than what he had originally feared. He admitted that it was a draconian measure, but it was a puzzle as to why the impact on growth was less than anticipated.

The Economic Survey for 2016–17, written by Subramanian and presented to Parliament in February 2017, also noted that 'growth slowed as demonetization reduced demand (cash, private wealth), supply (reduced liquidity and working capital, and disrupted supply chains) and increased uncertainty'. The Survey also concluded that cash-intensive sectors like agriculture, real estate and jewellery were affected the most. But on the long-term effect of demonetization, the Survey forecast a scenario that was broadly how the growth scenario panned out. It said that demonetization could be beneficial for growth in the long run if formalization increased and corruption fell. Many economists like Prof. Arun Kumar of Jawaharlal Nehru University were of the view that such an analysis was erroneous as in the succeeding years the investment rate declined, the employment rate fell and even output growth decelerated, creating conditions that were similar to an economic slowdown. Demonetization, in his view, could not be a panacea for growth since the unorganized sector, a large chunk of the economy, had taken a big hit.

Irrespective of such analysis, however, the government's assessment of demonetization acquired a completely new narrative when it released the first revised national income data for 2017–18 on 31 January 2019.[10] The Central Statistics Office, entrusted with the task of releasing national income data, revised its growth estimates for 2015–16, 2016–17 and 2017–18. Against the earlier estimates of 8.1 per cent, 7.1 per cent and 6.7 per cent, respectively, for these three years, the revised estimates showed them at 8 per cent for

2015–16, 8.2 per cent for 2016–17 and 7.2 per cent for 2017–18. In other words, the revised GDP numbers showed that demonetization did not have any adverse impact on growth. Quite to the contrary, growth increased in the year demonetization took place. Economic growth for 2017–18, a year after demonetization, however, dipped to 7.2 per cent, according to these revised numbers. And for 2018–19, two years after demonetization, the growth in GDP slowed down further to 6.8 per cent.

The revised numbers may have changed the official narrative on the impact of demonetization on growth, but the entire exercise raised many questions on the authenticity of the revised data and the basis on which the increased growth numbers have been calculated. Arvind Subramanian, who was earlier surprised over why growth did not suffer as much as the disruption that was caused by demonetization, would have been even more surprised with the higher growth numbers. It is possible that the official GDP numbers, even after accounting for some overestimation, did not adequately capture the impact of demonetization on the unorganized sector and agriculture. And the output data on agriculture may not have fully captured the extent of farming distress as a result of demonetization. In June 2019, a research paper, published by Arvind Subramanian at the Center for International Development at Harvard University, raised more doubts on India's GDP data by claiming that the country's annual economic growth in the 2011–17 period was 2.5 percentage points lower than the official estimate of 7 per cent. According to the study by Subramanian, who quit the Indian government in June 2018, economic growth in the demonetization year of 2016–17 was actually 5.7 per cent, compared to the official estimate of 8.2 per cent.

Popular narrative, anecdotal evidence and even some surveys, however, continue to indicate that demonetization did indeed have an adverse impact on growth and jobs. Mahesh Vyas of the Centre for Monitoring Indian Economy (CMIE) released in July 2017 the findings of his survey that showed that 1.5 million jobs were lost in the four months of January–April 2017, compared to the previous four months, which included the demonetization period.[11] This claim was challenged by Chief Statistician T.C.A. Anant by pointing out statistical flaws in the comparisons made by Vyas.[12] Vyas returned to this subject a year later in September 2018 to claim that the impact of demonetization on job losses was even more at 3.5 million, adversely affecting the job participation rate for youths.[13] In December 2018, the All India Manufacturers' Organization or AIMO released the report of a survey, based on a sample of responses from 34,700 traders and small/medium enterprises. It claimed that over 3.5 million jobs were lost in the previous four and a half years

largely on account of demonetization and the GST.[14] The PHD Chamber of
Commerce and Industry released a report in 2017 that admitted to an adverse
impact of demonetization on economic growth.[15] Analysis by researchers at
the Bengaluru-based Azim Premji University, made available in its report
'State of Working India, 2019' concluded that five million workers had lost
their jobs between 2016 and 2018, a period coinciding with demonetization.[16]

Giving further credence to it was a report of the National Sample
Survey Office's Periodic Labour Force Survey, which showed that the
unemployment rate in India had stood at 6.1 per cent in 2017–18, the highest
level in the last forty-five years. Initially, the report was not made public and
the government clarified later that its findings were not final. But the report
became controversial as two members of the National Statistical Commission
(NSC) had resigned alleging that the government had withheld the release of
the report in spite of NSC's approval.[17] However, the report and its findings
were confirmed to be final in May 2019, soon after the new government was
formed after the general elections. Similarly, the Sixth Annual Employment-
Unemployment Survey, conducted by the Labour Bureau showed that
the unemployment rate (defined as the share of the labour force available
for work, but unable to secure a job) had risen to 3.9 per cent in 2016–17,
compared to 3.7 per cent in 2015–16, 3.4 per cent in 2013–14 and 4 per cent
in 2012–13.[18] In other words, the unemployment rate had risen to a four-year
high. Even this report was withheld by the government and its release would
be subject to further review within the government.

The RBI's own finances too took a hit as a result of demonetization. Its
cost of printing new currency notes went up to Rs 13,000 crore in two years
after demonetization—in 2016–17 and 2017–18. Its cost of printing currency
notes in 2015–16 was much lower at Rs 3421 crore. The additional costs led to
RBI's lower profits and reduced dividends to the government. Against Rs 65,876
crore in 2015–16, the RBI transferred only Rs 30,659 crore of dividend to the
government in 2016–17. The following year saw an increase to Rs 50,000 crore.
But the lower dividends, largely due to demonetization, strained the relationship
between the Centre and the RBI over the quantum of dividends the central bank
should transfer to the government—an issue that had to be adjudicated on by an
official committee headed by former RBI governor Bimal Jalan.

Did demonetization impact the way Indians used cash in their
dealings? And did it help the government in tracking black money? About
a year after demonetization, the value of currency notes in circulation
had indeed seen a drop. The data with the RBI showed that the notes in
circulation at the end of 28 October 2016 (the last reporting fortnight

before demonetization took place on 8 November) were estimated at Rs 17.54 lakh crore. This was about 13 per cent of India's GDP for 2015–16.

By the end of March 2017, the total value of currency notes in circulation dropped to Rs 13.1 lakh crore and its share in GDP for 2016–17 was down to just 9 per cent, although critics pointed out that this drop did not signify much as the velocity of circulation increased even though the currency in circulation as per cent of GDP may have come down. Currency notes in circulation, however, started growing again after March 2017. At the end of 18 August 2017, notes in circulation rose to Rs 15.46 lakh crore, but at 12 per cent of GDP this was still lower than the 2016 end-October level and therefore represented a drop in one year.

But the situation changed somewhat by the end of March 2018, when the value of total currency notes in circulation rose to Rs 18.04 lakh crore. It was a sharp increase of about 38 per cent over the level that prevailed a year ago. A part of this increase was understandable. This was the period when the RBI had pumped in huge amounts of currency into circulation to relieve the shortage of notes in the economy. Economists described this as the impact of a massive remonetization exercise undertaken by the RBI in the wake of the November 2016 decision. But when compared to the GDP for 2017–18, the share of currency notes was still lower at about 11 per cent. India's cash-to-GDP ratio was yet to cross the 13-per-cent-mark reached by November 2016.

Look at it another way, the annual increase in currency notes in circulation in the Indian economy in the five years before demonetization ranged between 10 and 17 per cent. If demonetization had not taken place in November 2016, the notes in circulation would have increased by another 10 per cent to Rs 19.3 lakh crore during a year after November 2016. Demonetization had clearly reduced the use of cash in the economy. The pace of growth in currency in circulation was checked, but given their steady rise in the months after demonetization, it would be only a matter of time before cash would make a comeback.

On the other hand, non-cash transactions saw a healthy jump in this period. On an annual basis, transactions under real-time gross settlements (RTGS) through banks rose by 21 per cent in 2016–17, compared to an increase of just 15 per cent in 2015–16. RTGS like the National Electronic Funds Transfer or NEFT is an electronic payment system which allows individuals or companies to transfer funds between banks into each other's accounts, but within the country. Both the systems are run and maintained by the RBI. Such retail electronic payments saw a 45 per cent jump in 2016–17, up from 40 per cent in the previous year. A similar trend was noticeable in the use of credit and debit cards on point-of-sale machines, whose transactions in 2016–17 grew by 65 per cent, compared to 28 per cent in 2015–16. Pre-paid instruments too saw a 71 per cent increase in transactions, compared to a 128 per cent rise in the previous year.

The trend changed somewhat in the second year after demonetization. RTGS transactions growth in 2017–18 stabilized at the same level of 19 per cent. Retail electronic clearing, too, grew at a marginally higher rate of 46 per cent in 2017–18. But credit and debit card transactions value grew at a slower pace of 40 per cent and pre-paid instruments also saw a marginally lower growth rate of 69 per cent.

How well did demonetization do with respect to tracking black money? After one year of demonetization, the government pointed out that it had already used data analytics to identify about 1.77 million suspicious cases of deposits of cash with banks. The value of such deposits was estimated at Rs 3.68 lakh crore, deposited in 2.32 million bank accounts. Further analysis of such cases helped the government identify about 1,00,000 'high-risk' cases for action. Tax compliance also improved in this period. The share of direct taxes, for instance, in total tax collections by the government had declined from 56 per cent in 2014–15 to 51 per cent in 2015–16 and further down to 49 per cent in 2016–17. But in the 2017–18, which captured the full impact of demonetization, the share of direct taxes recovered to 52 per cent. Direct tax collections too grew by over 14 per cent in 2016–17 and by 18 per cent in 2017–18. The direct tax buoyancy, a measure of efficiency and responsiveness of revenue collections in relation to growth in GDP, also grew at a healthy rate from 0.8 in 2015–16 to 1.81 in 2017–18.

The sharp rise in tax collections could be attributable not only to demonetization-triggered increase in tax compliance but also to the after-effects of the tax amnesty scheme announced in 2016 and the higher salary pay-out to government employees following the implementation of the Seventh Central Pay Commission. The 2016 tax amnesty scheme led to the declaration of undisclosed income worth Rs 65,250 crore in 2016–17 and a tax collection of Rs 29,362 crore inclusive of penalty. As seen in past years after an amnesty scheme's launch, tax collections saw a natural rise. Similarly, the Central government's salary bill for 2016–17 shot up by about 16 per cent to Rs 1.16 lakh crore and by another 10 per cent to Rs 1.28 lakh crore. Both the amnesty scheme and the higher salaries on account of the Seventh Central Pay Commission were also responsible for a jump in tax collections and an improvement in tax buoyancy.

Another indication of the rise in tax compliance was available from the sharp rise in the number of Permanent Account Numbers (PAN) issued by the government. PAN is a unique ten-digit alphanumeric identity, issued by the income-tax department to each taxpayer. At the end of March 2018, the total number of PAN issued to ten categories of taxpayers was 379 million, of which individuals accounted for 97.5 per cent of the allotted PAN or about 369 million. This represented a 28 per cent increase in PAN in just one year. In other words, between April 2017 and March 2018, a total of 85 million new PAN holders were added to the taxpayers' community.

The number of tax returns filed in 2017–18 also increased to 68.4 million, 18 per cent higher than 54.3 million returns filed in 2016–17. Did demonetization help in the sharp increase in the number of PAN holders? There was no significant increase in PAN holders immediately after demonetization on 8 November 2016. The number of PAN holders in March 2016 was estimated at 246 million at the end of March 2016 and rose by just 16 per cent to 285 million by March 2017. But the increase in the twelve months after March 2017 was significantly higher at 29 per cent with the figure reaching 369 million by March 2018. It seems there was a delayed impact of demonetization in driving up the number of PAN.

Yet, demonetization disappointed hugely as almost 99 per cent of the currency notes that were annulled on 8 November 2016 finally made their way back to the banking system through deposits by individuals and enterprises. Of the Rs 15.44 lakh crore worth demonetized high-denomination currency notes in circulation as on 8 November 2016, an estimated Rs 15.33 lakh crore was returned to the RBI. This meant only about Rs 10,720 crore did not surface after demonetization. The Supreme Court had been earlier told that almost Rs 4–5 lakh crore of demonetized currency notes would not surface, suggesting thereby that this was the amount of black money which would be targeted or unearthed by demonetization. Even if that was only an opinion before the court, it clearly showed that the government had misread the effect of demonetization and Indians showed great ingenuity in gaming the system to deposit as much as 99 per cent of the high-value currency notes. Also, such a reading suffered from a flawed thinking that all cash is equivalent to black money. The government of course claimed that after the return of these notes it could now identify and check how much of this was illicit. Some action followed, though its pace and results were not very reassuring. In the wake of demonetization and the cash deposits made in November and December of 2016, the income-tax department had zeroed in on 23.5 lakh PANs. These accounts had shown post-demonetization cash deposits to be inconsistent with their income profiles. Statutory notices to only three lakh of these accounts were sent. Over 70 per cent or 2.1 lakh of all those who got such notices filed fresh returns and deposited additional tax of about Rs 6560 crore. The income-tax department later began following up the remaining cases, where no responses were received.[19]

But the question that is yet to be answered satisfactorily by anyone in the Modi government is whether all these gains in terms of widening the tax net increased digital transactions and detection of fake currency notes could not have been achieved without the huge disruption and output loss that demonetization caused to the Indian economy. Was a more sustained and steady campaign to achieve these goals better than the shock of demonetization, which as an *India Today* report[20] noted had led to the death of at least 105 people in the 'rush for cash across the country'? Was the pain from demonetization more than the gains from the exercise?

Dramatis Personae of This Tragedy

Who were the chief protagonists of the Modi government's biggest disruption? Of course, Prime Minister Modi was the chief architect of the government's demonetization plan. Modi may have been inspired by many presentations made to him in 2016. For instance, one such presentation from a Pune-based organization Arthakranti Sansthan suggested that high-value currency notes needed to be recalled and scrapped. The Sansthan, a non-governmental organization, claimed that one of its key members, Anil Bokil, shared his thoughts on demonetization with the prime minister at a meeting that lasted for about two hours. Bokil had been meeting Modi with his economic policy ideas quite regularly beginning in 2013, following it up with more presentations in 2014, 2015 and in 2016. One of the many suggestions Bokil had made was to recall and scrap currency notes of Rs 1000, Rs 500 and Rs 100.[21]

The name of Swaminathan Gurumurthy, a chartered accountant by profession and an ideologue of the RSS, has also figured among those who may have advised the government on demonetization. Just four days after Rajan announced his decision not to continue as the RBI governor beyond the end of his term on 4 September 2016, Gurumurthy came out with an article in the *New Indian Express* on 22 June 2016. Titled 'Rajan: The Exit That Was Inevitable', the article argued why Rajan did not have an adequate working knowledge of the Indian economy and, hence, was not suitable to run the central bank. He blamed Rajan for creating hurdles in the rollout of the Mudra scheme that would have facilitated the flow of loans to small businesses. One of Gurumurthy's observations indicated that he was aware of the government's plans on demonetization. He wrote:

> The new finance is sourced in an unprecedented rise in cash holdings which have risen to Rs 15 lakh crore in 2015–16 with the share of high denomination notes in the total currency in circulation rising from 33 per cent to 85 per cent in 2015–16. These distortions were occurring under the very nose of Rajan. But he overlooked them, because he had never handled economies where banks do not control the entire monetary system.[22]

Once demonetization was announced, Gurumurthy defended the move, but criticized the manner in which it was implemented.

But the final onus of this highly disruptive action will rest on Modi. His address to the nation on 8 November 2016 highlighted the need to tackle black money, stop the funding of terrorists and attack counterfeit currency as the key reasons for demonetization. Later, he defended the move on grounds of digitization of transactions and improvement in tax compliance as also tax coverage. Politically also, Modi was under pressure to deliver on the black money front. His promise of repatriating the black money stashed away abroad by Indians for the benefit of the common man was not yet fulfilled as only a small portion of the black money kept in overseas accounts had been recovered. Accusations against him for running a government that favoured the big business might have made him uncomfortable. The crucial Uttar Pradesh Assembly elections were just a few months away. There was a need for a new political narrative. Demonetization made an initial impact on the people as a strong attack against black money—a move that would hurt the rich even though it might inconvenience the common man. Modi was also successful in propagating among the underprivileged classes that their economic sacrifice due to demonetization helped him deal a body blow to the rich and the black money hoarders. Politically, that narrative sounded very attractive and was perhaps responsible for the ordinary people ignoring all other adverse implications of demonetization.

Finance Minister Arun Jaitley and RBI Governor Raghuram G. Rajan were aware of the demonetization move. Both the finance ministry and the

RBI were involved in the preparations for carrying out demonetization.[23] But Modi was so determined to carry out demonetization that he must have ignored at least the advice he got from Rajan, who had indicated that the short-term impact of demonetization would be harmful.[24] Modi was determined to spend his political capital on a move that he believed would position him as the biggest crusader against black money. Less than a week after the demonetization announcement, Modi appealed to the people to support his drive against black money and bear the pain for fifty days. He said on 14 November 2016: 'I have only asked for 50 days. Give me time till December 30. After that, if any fault is found in my intentions or my actions, I am willing to suffer any punishment given by the country.'[25] His political commitment to the idea was so complete that even after many months of its execution and the disruption it caused to the economy, ministers and officials in the government were wary of criticizing demonetization. Indeed, the government's sensitivity to any criticism of its move to demonetize 86 per cent of the currency in circulation did not go down even after two years of the event. A report in *The Hindu* noted how in an unusual move the Union agriculture ministry withdrew a submission it had made to a Parliamentary Committee on finance earlier. The report that was withdrawn had noted how demonetization had affected millions of farmers.[26] The agriculture secretary also talked about the stern action he had initiated against the officers who had allegedly sent in wrong inputs to the committee. A joint secretary and two directors in the ministry were served with a show-cause notice to explain their conduct.

In a certain way, demonetization became the yardstick for government officers and ministers on their stance towards the government. Those who made critical comments were considered opponents of the government, and those who supported the idea were not just favoured but even rewarded with decent postings. K. Subramanian, who became the chief economic adviser in December 2018, was a competent economist, but he had endorsed demonetization even before he had joined the government. Shaktikanta Das, who had to defend demonetization and oversee its implementation in 2016 when he was the economic affairs secretary in the finance ministry, was first made a member of the Fifteenth Finance Commission and a Sherpa for the Indian government at G-20 meetings. Later, Das became the governor of the RBI.

Politically, however, demonetization became a little risky for Modi. In his last Independence Day address as prime minister during his 2014–19 tenure, on 15 August 2018, Modi listed out all the major achievements of his government, but did not mention demonetization as one among them. Was that a slip or a deliberate omission? More significantly, the forty-five-page-long BJP manifesto for the 2019 elections, Sankalp Patra (released in April 2019), listed in great detail all the major achievements of the Modi government in the five-year period from 2014 to 2019. But demonetization as a word figured only once in the entire document, which listed the government's achievements and the BJP's promises along with short messages from Modi, BJP President Amit Shah and Rajnath Singh in his capacity as chairperson of the BJP Manifesto Committee. That word did not appear either in Modi's message or in Rajnath Singh's Sankalp Patra note. It was Shah who mentioned demonetization as one of the historic decisions that 'ushered in a comprehensive and fundamental transformation'.[27] The absence of emphasis on demonetization could be an outcome of the BJP's realization that the experiment with annulling high-denomination currency notes could become a political liability. Many political pundits believe that one of the reasons for the defeat of the BJP in three heartland states of Chhattisgarh, Madhya Pradesh and Rajasthan in December 2018 was the adverse impact of demonetization on small businesses and farmers. It was argued that voters felt the impact of demonetization, not immediately, but after about a year or so. Hence, the Assembly elections in UP in early 2017 were won by the BJP under the aura of demonetization, but as time wore on, winning elections became difficult for the BJP, with the spectre of demonetization hanging over its head. Gujarat was a narrow victory for the BJP and Karnataka could not be won. And by December 2018, the BJP faced its biggest electoral setback. There were many other reasons for the BJP's poor showing at the hustings in 2018, but the impact of demonetization on the economy with a time lag was certainly one of them.

The lessons of demonetization have been so stark that it is unlikely that it would ever be repeated by any other leader in India. Arguably, demonetization changed the course of the Modi government's track record. Till demonetization happened, the Modi government was having a smooth run, reviving the economy and the Modi juggernaut looked unstoppable in the political sphere. But after demonetization, the economic as well as political narrative of the Modi government changed and the challenges became more formidable and worrying. This is one decision of the Modi government, whose consequences for the economy and politics were so disruptive, that there is virtually no possibility of such an experiment being repeated for any government in the near future.

CHAPTER 24

ONE COUNTRY, ONE TAX

It took almost a decade of planning before India could introduce what is arguably its biggest and also the most disruptive tax reform in the country—the GST. The goal of a 'one country, one tax' must have been tempting for all finance ministers.

The realization of that goal required work and preparatory steps from governments ruled by different political parties. It was yet another example of key economic reform issues in the country seeing broad consensus cutting across political party lines. The first time the GST entered the government's official agenda was in the Budget speech for 2006–07, presented by the then finance minister, P. Chidambaram. On 28 February 2006, he said:

> It is my sense that there is a large consensus that the country should move towards a national level Goods and Services Tax (GST) that should be shared between the Centre and the States. I propose that we set April 1, 2010 as the date for introducing GST. World over, goods and services attract the same rate of tax. That is the foundation of a GST. People must get used to the idea of a GST. Hence, we must progressively converge the services tax rate and the CENVAT rate. I propose to take one step this year and increase the service tax rate from 10 per cent to 12 per cent. Let me hasten to add that since service tax paid can be credited against service tax payable or excise duty payable, the net impact will be very small.

That bold statement also reflected the flawed political understanding of the idea of the GST. The world over, the GST rates for essential goods are often different from those for services. A classic example is food items, which are often zero-rated, but restaurant services are taxed at a different rate.

But the more pertinent question that statement triggered was why Chidambaram was so confident that he would be able to launch the GST in about four years? Even the launch of the state-level value-added tax (VAT) system took more than a decade before it could be launched in April 2005. The state VAT system was far less complicated than the GST, which would have required an amendment to the Indian Constitution. Perhaps the fact that the state VAT system was launched just about a year ago and that it had been accepted by most states might have enthused Chidambaram to ride on it and launch the GST in the next four years. To be fair, while announcing the 2010 deadline for the launch of the GST, Chidambaram had already set the ball rolling as far as converging the duty rates on goods and services was concerned. His Budget for 2006–07 had raised the service tax rate from 10 to 12 per cent, so that reaching a desirable mean rate of 16 per cent (which was also the standard rate for goods excise at that time) would be feasible over a period of four years.

The idea of a state-level VAT was discussed at the official level for the first time when Manmohan Singh was the Union finance minister. He convened a meeting of all state chief ministers in 1995 and discussed the need for a VAT to replace the sales tax regime followed by different states. The Indian Constitution mandated that while the Centre could levy excise on manufacturing, the states had the exclusive right to impose sales tax—a levy at the point of sale. Such a sales tax regime, however, suffered from the problem of cascading of taxes. In other words, taxes would be paid at all points of sales and every sale would mean that the sales tax is paid over and above the various sales taxes paid at the earlier stages of the value chain or production. Such cascading of taxes was sought to be avoided through the introduction of a state VAT system by replacing the sales tax regime. In the state VAT system, the taxes paid during the various intermediate stages of production would be adjusted against the final tax paid at the last point of sale, resulting in either a set-off or a refund of excess taxes paid.

The advantages of a state-level VAT in lieu of sales tax were many. The state VAT would have far fewer tax rates and the taxes paid at the intermediate stages of production would be set off in the form of input tax credits. In subsequent years, follow-up meetings with state finance ministers on the advisability of introducing state VAT were held under different governments and a decisive stage was reached in 1999 when Finance Minister Yashwant Sinha under the Atal Bihari Vajpayee-led government held a meeting of state chief ministers.

Two broad decisions were taken by Sinha. One, the states had committed themselves to not engaging in a rate war among themselves and ensuring uniform rates for different commodities. This was a major concession granted by the states, which have historically tried to attract investments by offering lower taxes or specific tax exemptions. States like Maharashtra, Tamil Nadu, Karnataka and Gujarat have benefitted by offering these tax incentives. With the states giving such commitment now, they denied themselves the option of wooing investment through tax incentives. All that they could do to attract industries would be to promise better infrastructure and easier procedures to improve the ease of doing business. Two, there was a general agreement among all the states that they would have to discontinue the various sales tax incentive schemes that essentially offered exemptions and concessions under various circumstances. At that meeting, the expectation was that the state VAT regime could be launched from 2001.

However, delays began dogging the process as the Vajpayee government set up an Empowered Committee of State Finance Ministers to prepare the format for the new tax regime. Headed by West Bengal Finance Minister Asim Kumar Dasgupta, the Committee took its own time but eventually agreed on having a VAT framework which should have common features across all the states. At the meeting of the Empowered Committee of State Finance Ministers held in January 2002, it was decided that the new regime could be launched from 1 April 2003. But this deadline too was missed, except for Haryana which went ahead with the agreed VAT regime on the agreed date. Other states joined Haryana two years later only after the general elections were held in 2004 and a new government at the Centre was in place, with Manmohan Singh as the prime minister and Chidambaram as the finance minister. That seemed to have augured well for the state VAT regime, as it could be finally launched from 1 April 2005. The Union government had guaranteed all the states that if there was a revenue loss for them as a result of the introduction of the state VAT regime, the Centre would compensate them for a specified period of three years. Over the years, the compensation demands were relatively small and the states' revenues actually increased significantly in the subsequent years.

Did the state VAT regime get implemented as was planned? Not really. Taxation expert Satya Poddar vividly recalls that the key agreement among the states on not competing through tax incentives was violated at least in spirit, if not in letter. The form of tax incentives changed as they resurfaced in the guise of deferred tax payments. A deferral of tax payment essentially meant that the industries could collect the VAT, but need not deposit it with the state governments and keep it with themselves for a specified period of time. This amounted to be an interest-free loan to the industries—a tax incentive, but in a disguised form. Economist and fiscal policy expert Raja J. Chelliah had moaned many years ago that tax incentives were a race to the bottom. That race continued somewhat even after the launch of the state VAT system.

The idea of a VAT was quite old as it emanated from a committee that was set up in July 1976 under the chairmanship of Lakshmi Kant Jha, former governor of the RBI and a well-known economic administrator who had advised both Lal Bahadur Shastri and Indira Gandhi. Jha had recommended that in order to widen the tax base and improve tax mobilization it was necessary to move to an ad valorem tax system, where the tax rate was not a specific amount linked to the physical quantity of the product but would be levied as a percentage of its value. Thus, a product like the passenger car would attract an ad valorem rate of say 30 per cent. Every time the pre-tax price of the car would go up, the tax amount would also increase since that is levied as a per cent of the price of the car. But crude oil or petrol would attract a specific rate of duty, where the duty would be expressed as a specific amount to be levied per litre of oil. In the specific tax regime, even when the basic pre-tax price of the product goes up, the incidence of taxation does not go up automatically. Thus, an ad valorem taxation system has a built-in revenue buoyancy due to inflation and any increase in product prices. This concept was further refined and a modified VAT (Modvat) system was introduced by the then finance minister, Vishwanath Pratap Singh, in 1986. The coverage of Modvat initially was very limited, but the system allowed manufacturers to recover the taxes they paid on specified raw materials and components. Thus, under the Modvat system, a manufacturer of a product would pay the excise at the factory gate at a specified rate, but its incidence would be less as he would be availing the set-off benefits by way of credits against the taxes he may have paid on the inputs used by him in producing the final goods.

This process was expedited as the tax reforms committee, headed by eminent economist and fiscal policy expert Raja J. Chelliah, had also endorsed the idea of a VAT system in its reports in the early 1990s. Successive governments heeded these recommendations and expanded the scope and coverage of Modvat. Even in respect of the GST, it was Chelliah who led the critical thinking behind the idea of such a VAT system. The Tax Reforms Committee, headed by Chelliah, had recommended the levy of a service tax to broaden the indirect tax base. In his Budget for 1994–95, Finance Minister Manmohan Singh noted that even though services accounted for about 40 per cent of the country's GDP, they did not attract any taxes. He made a beginning by levying a 5 per cent service tax on the amount of telephone bills, the net premium charged by insurance companies and the commission charged by stockbrokers. Over the years, the number of services covered under the service tax rose to 119 by 2012, when a negative list was introduced. This meant all services barring the seventeen in the negative list attracted service tax. The introduction of service tax was significant as it created a base for healthy revenue source and paved the way for further reforms in the indirect taxation system, eventually leading to the introduction of the GST. First came the Cenvat and then its combination with the service tax resulted in the GST. What remained to be done was to frame the modalities.

Around the time the service tax was introduced, another big push towards the GST came from a 1994 report from the National Institute of Public Finance and Policy (NIPFP)—'Reform of Domestic Trade Taxes in India: Issues and Options'.[1] The task was undertaken at the instance of the finance ministry at the Centre, which wanted a design of 'possible system of Value Added Tax for India on which there could be a broad agreement among the Centre and the States'. The study team that worked on the report was led by NIPFP director Amaresh Bagchi, with assistance from four experts from the NIPFP, an IAS official from the government of Maharashtra and two international taxation experts—Satya N. Poddar, who was with Ernst & Young, Toronto, and Sibren Cnossen from Erasmus University, Rotterdam. The NIPFP report eventually would become the blueprint for both the state VAT system and the GST in India. One of the key recommendations of the report was that 'in exploring the possibilities of introducing VAT in India, one has to think of a dual system in which both the Centre and the States share the consumption tax base in a mutually acceptable arrangement'.[2] The GST that was launched in India from 1 July 2017 followed the dual model, thus becoming only the second country after Canada to adopt a similar system.

While discussion on a VAT system continued within the government on the basis of the NIPFP report of 1994, the government of Atal Bihari Vajpayee introduced the Central Value Added Tax (Cenvat) in 2002 to replace Modvat. The then finance minister, Yashwant Sinha, made sure that there were only three rates under Cenvat—a merit rate of 8 per cent for items of necessity for the common man, a demerit rate of 24 per cent for luxury or sin goods, like high-end vehicles, tobacco or alcohol and a mean rate of 16 per cent for the remaining items. At that time, the goods under 16 per cent, or the standard rate, accounted for almost 90 per cent of the government's total indirect tax revenues. The ultimate and ideal goal was to bring together all the rates to a single Cenvat rate.

Even before the launch of Cenvat, Vajpayee had taken a decision in 2000 that will have a far-reaching impact on the future of the GST. This led to the setting up of a committee, whose brief was to design a framework for a GST to be introduced in the entire country. Significantly, Vajpayee invited West Bengal Finance Minister Asim Kumar Dasgupta to head this committee. Seeds of a country-wide political consensus on the need for a GST were sown at that stage. Dasgupta was a member of the council of ministers of a state that was ruled by the Left Front, no ally or friend of the BJP or Vajpayee. Not only did Vajpayee realize that getting a finance minister of a Left Front-ruled state would help achieve political consensus, but even the West Bengal government's Left leaders allowed its finance minister to launch this initiative in the larger interest of the country.

Three years later, Vajpayee decided to set up a task force under the leadership of Vijay L. Kelkar, an economist who served the government in various capacities including as finance secretary in the Vajpayee government, to recommend tax reforms. A year later, after the Manmohan Singh government was formed and Chidambaram was at the helm in North Block, Kelkar, who continued to function as an adviser to the finance minister, recommended that the time was ripe for replacing the existing indirect tax regime with the GST. Kelkar largely adhered to the Bagchi model outlined in the 1994 NIPFP report and suggested that the new regime should have a dual GST structure, with a central GST of 12 per cent and a state GST of 8 per cent.

In a dual GST structure, there are two components of the overall duty rate. Any commodity or service will have these two rates combined into one. Ideally, the state rate is the same as the central rate. The state rate is levied in lieu of the various state-level taxes and the central rate is levied in lieu of the central excise and different types of cess. The overall GST rate is levied and collected through a centralized system and then shared between the Centre and the state where those goods or the services have been consumed. The GST is a destination-based tax and is levied at the point of consumption or use. But the duties collected are shared in accordance with a pre-determined formula between the Centre and the

states. The central GST rate would replace the Cenvat rate levied by the
Centre and the state GST would come in lieu of the VAT imposed by the
states.

Two years later, Chidambaram made his now-famous statement in
his February 2006 Budget speech that set the first official deadline for the
launch of the GST by April 2010, a deadline that would be shifted on two
more occasions before the new tax regime would be finally rolled out after
eleven years.

The Failure of the UPA

There was no dearth of political turns and twists impacting the GST
during this period starting from 28 February 2006 to the midnight of
30 June 2017. Work for rolling out the GST began at a good pace.[3] An
empowered committee of state finance ministers was constituted and
by November 2006 it discussed a report submitted by a working group
it had set up. Even as this Committee under the chairmanship of the
West Bengal Finance Minister Asim Kumar Dasgupta started meeting
regularly, the terrorist attack in Mumbai on 26 November 2008 cast
an indirect impact on the pace of progress on the GST front. In order
to beef up the home ministry in the wake of the terrorist attack in
Mumbai, Prime Minister Manmohan Singh shifted Chidambaram to
the home ministry. The finance ministry was looked after by the prime
minister himself as an additional charge till 24 January 2009, when
Pranab Mukherjee was asked to take charge of North Block. By then,
however, the government was preparing for the general elections to be
held in May 2009 and GST ceased to be a priority even for the finance
minister at least in the first half of that year. After the elections, the UPA
was back at the helm and Mukherjee retained his finance portfolio to
resume work on the GST. But a sense of unrealism was now noticeable
as in spite of less than a year left for the deadline of April 2010, the
newly elected government was still hopeful of meeting it. Only in the
last week of February 2010, did it realize that the deadline would have
to be deferred by a year.

A fresh political hurdle came up by the end of 2010 when the
Bharatiya Janata Party decided to oppose the launch of the GST. Leading
the Opposition charge was none else than then Gujarat Chief Minister
Narendra Modi. By March 2011, Mukherjee had readied a Constitution
Amendment Bill to bring in the GST. But the bill had to be referred to

the Parliamentary Standing Committee on Finance, which was headed by former finance minister Yashwant Sinha of the BJP. Two BJP-ruled states were opposed to the GST—Gujarat and Madhya Pradesh. In an attempt to bring Narendra Modi round to accepting the GST, Mukherjee visited Gandhinagar, the capital of Gujarat, and tried to convince Modi, but in vain. Gujarat Finance Minister Saurabh Patel made it clear to all that the manner in which the GST had been conceived would be a technical nightmare as traders and small businesses were simply not prepared. Madhya Pradesh Finance Minister Raghavji also was a staunch opponent of the GST as he feared that states, as a result, would be reduced to begging for central resources as they would lose the right to determine their taxes for meeting their revenue requirements.

The GST process received a minor blow when the Left Front lost the Assembly elections in West Bengal in 2011. A collateral damage was the resignation of Asim Dasgupta, who as the finance minister of West Bengal had been chairing the Empowered Committee on the GST with sagacity and foresight. Kerala Finance Minister K.M. Mani succeeded Dasgupta, but the GST movement lost one of its biggest and avid champions. Help for the GST process, however, came from the most unexpected quarters. Yashwant Sinha, a BJP member and the chairman of the Parliamentary Standing Committee, believed in the idea of the GST. As finance minister in the Vajpayee government, he had already brought the Cenvat rates closer to a point where the introduction of the GST would become easier. When the 115th Constitution Amendment Bill, introduced in the Lok Sabha to launch the GST, was referred to his committee, Sinha was eager to complete the examination without losing much time. However, there was some reluctance on the part of the finance ministry team to expedite the clearance of the GST Bill by his committee. Instead of looking at the GST law, Sinha was asked if he could expedite clearing two other pending laws—the Companies Bill, 2011 and the Benami Transactions (Prohibitions) Bill, 2011.[4] Thus, the consideration of the Constitution Amendment Bill on the GST had to wait for about a year. And when Sinha was ready with his colleagues to examine it after the Budget session of Parliament in 2012, Mukherjee had already begun his preparations for his election as the next President of the Indian Republic.

The return of Chidambaram to North Block helped expedite matters with regard to the GST. He held a meeting with all the state finance ministers in November 2012 and promised to them that all the pending issues would be resolved by the end of December that year. Indeed, in his Budget for 2013–14, Chidambaram made a provision for Rs 9000 crore to compensate the states for the revenue losses they might incur after rolling out the GST. True, this amount was quite inadequate and did not satisfy the states, but it nevertheless showed Chidambaram's resolve to move ahead with the GST. A decision that indicated the seriousness of the government pertained to the incorporation of the GST Network as a non-profit private limited company on 28 March 2013. The GST Network's ownership pattern would be changed later, but its constitution as a separate outfit soon became a source of confidence among the states as well as trade and industry about the new taxation system.

Yashwant Sinha, in spite of being a leader of the BJP and in the Opposition, responded positively and with sympathy to such government initiatives on the GST. His committee did its best to persuade the reluctant finance ministers of states like Gujarat and Madhya Pradesh and got Vijay Kelkar to make presentations to the state finance ministers to have their concerns addressed. The committee made many suggestions for improvements in the structure of the 115th Constitution Amendment Bill and returned it to the Lok Sabha for its consideration in August 2013. In these few months, Sinha emerged as the most articulate supporter of the GST reform. Earlier, as finance minister, his efforts at rationalizing the Cenvat rates were fully consistent with the idea and principles of the GST. And now in spite of his party not lending its full support, Sinha as the leader of the Parliamentary Committee examining the GST Bill produced a report that favoured a virtually flawless GST.

Quite ironically, just two months later, Modi, who was still the chief minister of Gujarat, issued a statement saying that his government was opposed to the GST as it would lead to a revenue loss of Rs 14,000 crore every year. By that time, the Manmohan Singh government had lost all hope of getting the Constitution Amendment Bill passed by Parliament in the remaining months of its tenure before the general elections were due in May 2014.

The general elections of May 2014 paved the way for a new government, headed by Narendra Modi. The Fifteenth Lok Sabha was dissolved by the President, Pranab Mukherjee, on 18 May 2014 as he constituted the Sixteenth Lok Sabha. And since the Fifteenth Lok Sabha got dissolved, the life of all the bills pending with it came to an end.

The 115th Constitution Amendment Bill for the launch of the GST was one of those bills which got extinguished. The irony was not lost on anyone. Mukherjee as the finance minister had introduced the Constitution

Amendment Bill for the GST, which he was effectively extinguishing as the President three years later. And a bigger irony would be that the man, who as chief minister of Gujarat had opposed the GST in 2013, would become one of its biggest proponents and usher in the GST at a midnight function in the Central Hall of Parliament about four years later.

CHAPTER 25

FROM CRITIC TO SUPPORTER

The three-year journey the Narendra Modi government traversed before launching the GST on 1 July 2017 was marked by many exciting phases of development. As the newly elected Narendra Modi government took on the mantle of economic reforms and governance in May 2014, it lost little time in pushing for the launch of the GST even though its prime minister had opposed it as the chief minister earlier. In just about seven months, the Union Cabinet on 18 December 2014 approved a proposal to amend the Constitution to introduce the GST. A day later, during the winter session of Parliament, Finance Minister Arun Jaitley introduced in the Lok Sabha the 122nd Constitution Amendment Bill and set a deadline for rolling out the GST from 1 April 2016.

The bill provided for a levy of the GST on supply of all goods and services except potable alcohol. What was proposed in the bill was a dual GST, but both the Centre and the states would be levying the taxes, to be known as the Central GST and the state GST. Parliament was also empowered to levy an integrated GST on interstate trade or on imports of goods and services. The bill also empowered the Union government to levy excise duty in addition to the GST on tobacco and tobacco products. For five categories of petroleum products— crude oil, petrol, diesel, aviation turbine fuel and natural gas—the bill had proposed that the decision to include them under the GST would be taken by the GST Council, which would take all decisions on tax rates under the chairmanship of the Union finance minister. All other state finance ministers would be its members.

The decision of the GST Council would be taken through the support of at least 75 per cent of the votes, although it was indicated that as far as possible decisions at the Council would be taken by consensus. The Centre would have voting strength of 33.3 per cent, while the thirty-one states with legislative assemblies would have voting strength of 2.15 per cent each. In other words, the Centre would have the veto power in shooting down any decision if it is not in agreement with a proposal. Also, it would need at least twenty states to side with it before it could get its decision ratified by the Council. On the other hand, if twelve states got together they could use their combined voting strength to veto any proposal. The functioning of the GST Council was thus governed such that neither the Centre could take a decision overruling the majority of states nor could the states get together and take a decision ignoring the Centre. Since both the Centre and the states were giving up their respective powers to fix tax rates, they needed to be assured that the Council would reflect their voices. Of course, the Centre had slightly more power in terms of its freedom to levy excise duty on tobacco products and it could exercise its veto on its own, while the states could exercise the same power only if twelve states got together. It was a delicate power-sharing formula that the GST amendment bill had proposed.

The Congress, with just about forty-four members in the Lok Sabha but enjoying good enough strength to stall the bill's passage in the Rajya Sabha, realized that it could return the compliments to the BJP by raising objections to the bill and creating political hurdles. The principal demand of the Congress was that the GST rate should be capped at 18 per cent, while the proposed rate structure, which was still not finalized, had envisaged multiple rates and the top rate was much higher than what the Congress was demanding. The government rejected these demands outright as it was supremely confident of getting it passed by the Lok Sabha and was hopeful that it would be able to bring the Congress round to agreeing to support the amendment bill. The BJP leadership was not entirely correct in its assessment.

At the end of the Budget session of 2015, the Lok Sabha passed the 122nd Constitution Amendment Bill on 6 May. The government's joy over this passage, however, was short-lived. Six days later it was sent to the Rajya Sabha, where the Congress demanded that the bill should be sent to a Select Committee of the upper house of Parliament. It was finally agreed on 14 May that the bill should be sent to a joint committee of the Rajya Sabha and the Lok Sabha. The Congress in the meanwhile upped the ante and demanded that in addition to placing a cap of 18 per cent on the GST rate, the government should abolish the 1 per cent duty to be levied on interstate supplies and set up an independent dispute settlement body. The government realized that it was nowhere near convincing the Congress to support the bill in its current form. By August 2015, the BJP gave up its plans for putting the bill to vote in the Rajya Sabha. Almost a year later, on 3 August 2016, the Rajya Sabha passed the bill after the government moved three amendments.

The spoilsport in the BJP government's GST design was the 1 per cent duty that was almost quietly introduced in an apparent attempt to please the manufacturing states like Gujarat and Maharashtra. Nobody had any inkling of such a tax, which distorted the GST concept, till this was suddenly put up at a meeting between Finance Minister Arun Jaitley and Gujarat Finance Minister Saurabh Patel. Nobody in the finance ministry realized that what Patel had mooted would hugely undermine the GST principle. West Bengal Finance Minister Amit Mitra, who had played a key role in resisting pressure to dilute the GST spirit, had to return to Kolkata and could not stay back for the evening meeting where the 1 per cent tax was agreed upon. Once the idea of the new tax became public, industry was shocked and made presentations before the government to withdraw the proposal. Chief Economic Adviser Arvind Subramanian even went public with his reservations about it. For the Congress, the new tax idea turned out to be a godsend. The Congress upped the ante in its demand for changes in the GST structure as proposed by the BJP. After a few more rounds of consultation, the government agreed to drop the pernicious idea of the 1 per cent tax. That helped the GST Amendment Bill to move to the next stage of parliamentary approval.

What changed the Congress approach in the following weeks, so much so that the Constitution Bill that could not be passed in August 2015 received the assent of the Upper House in August 2016? Deft political management by the BJP leadership and the Congress's realization that it could not take its opposition to the GST beyond a point. A smart move to appoint the finance minister of West Bengal, Amit Mitra, as chairman of the Empowered Committee of State Finance Ministers on GST was made on 19 February 2016. The Committee had been without a chairman for a few months as K.M. Mani, Kerala finance minister, had quit his job in the state in November in the wake of corruption charges against him.

Traditionally, the chairman of the Empowered Committee is always a finance minister from a state ruled by an Opposition party. Thus, it was Asim Dasgupta, finance minister in West Bengal during the Left Front rule there, till 2011. Sushil Modi, finance minister of Bihar, succeeded Dasgupta and continued till July 2013, when he too quit the Committee. Jammu and Kashmir Finance Minister Abdul Rahim took charge of the Committee after Sushil Modi and continued till March 2015. After Rahim came Mani, who left in November 2015.

Mitra's appointment after a gap of about three months was significant as this was seen as a political gesture from the BJP to the Trinamool

Congress, in a bid to win its support for the GST Bill in the Rajya Sabha. Mitra was not at the meeting when the decision to make him the chairman was taken. Finance Minister Jaitley had called Mitra to convey the government's decision to appoint him the chairman. The move did help as the Trinamool Congress supported the bill in the Rajya Sabha vote on 3 August 2016. After the voting, Mitra said: 'What would be the level of tax? The idea is to have a tax that does not result in inflationary pressures on the common people . . . The rate should be such that it is neither too low nor too high.' Months later when the GST Council was busy deciding the rate structure for different products and services, the Trinamool Congress was no longer happy with the GST idea and Mitra began expressing serious reservations about many of the provisions in the GST.

In the run-up to the crucial Rajya Sabha session where voting on the 122nd Constitution Amendment Bill on GST was to take place, the government made a few more politically astute moves. It convened an Inter-State Council meeting in New Delhi on 16 July, where chief ministers of almost all the states were present. Prime Minister Narendra Modi used this opportunity to engage with the regional party leaders on the sidelines of the meeting and seek their support for the GST. A significant headway was made when Nitish Kumar, chief minister of Bihar, decided to extend the support of his party, Janata Dal (United) to the bill. 'The passage of the GST is in the interest of the country. We support GST and have favoured it since the beginning,' Kumar said on 19 July. Even the Rashtriya Janata Dal, led by Lalu Prasad, decided to support the Constitution Amendment Bill, signalling his party's break from the Congress on the question of the GST.

A meeting of the Empowered Committee of State Finance Ministers was held on 26 July and it looked as if Jaitley had succeeded in garnering adequate support from the regional parties. The All India Anna Dravida Munnetra Kazhagam (AIADMK) continued to remain opposed to the GST. But even AIADMK agreed not to oppose the bill in the Rajya Sabha and indicated that it would stage a walkout from the house at the time of voting, which is what it did on 3 August. It was a politically astute move from AIADMK. It registered its protests against the GST by staging a walkout. And yet the walkout helped the government secure the much-needed two-thirds of the votes of members present in the Rajya Sabha, since it was a Constitution Amendment Bill. It is ironical that one of India's most fundamental taxation policy changes was facilitated by some astute lobbying by the ruling party and a politically cynical step from the

AIADMK—on paper it showed its disapproval by walking out of the Rajya Sabha, but in effect it helped the government usher in the GST.

With a few Congress-ruled states now veering round to the view that the GST Bill was not a bad idea, the BJP leadership decided to initiate its next move. Of the three demands, the Congress raised, it agreed to accept two of them—it proposed to abolish the 1 per cent extra tax on interstate supplies, thereby rejecting the demands of manufacturing BJP-ruled states like Maharashtra and Gujarat, and it decided to set up a dispute settlement body in which states would have greater say. Politically, dropping the 1 per cent duty on interstate supplies was a big move as this challenged the arguments that had been put forward by manufacturing states like Maharashtra and Gujarat. Yet, in a bid to win the Congress support, Jaitley went ahead with these two amendments. There was a third amendment as well and this was aimed at reassuring the states that the GST rates to be decided by the Council would be governed by the principle of not allowing states to incur revenue losses on the one hand and hurting consumers on the other.

In about a month from the passing of the Constitution Amendment Bill in the Rajya Sabha, the Modi government began expediting the follow-up measures to launch the GST. The amendments made in the Rajya Sabha were sent back to the Lok Sabha, which approved them on 8 August, and in the next one month the government ensured that as many as twenty-three state Assemblies had introduced and approved the amendment to the Constitution for the launch of the GST. This was a crucial requirement. Article 368 of the Indian Constitution mandates that apart from the two houses of Parliament, all amendments to it must also be ratified by at least half of the state legislatures. On 8 September, President Pranab Mukherjee signed on the GST Amendment Bill. Four days later, the Union Cabinet decided to set up the GST Council and its secretariat and ten days later, the first meeting of the Council took place in New Delhi, ushering in a new phase of India's fiscal federalism.

India looked all set to usher in the GST from the start of April 2017. Industry and trade began preparing for a major disruption that would take place in the way they would pay taxes on the goods they produced and the services they provided. Consumers were a little wary about the likely impact the new taxation system would have on the prices of products and services. However, such fears were not only exaggerated but also baseless. Since its introduction in France in 1954, about 160 countries have adopted the GST, although in different formats. But in none of them did rising inflation after its launch become a problem. According to GST expert Satya Poddar, inflation was not an issue in Australia, New Zealand, Singapore or China. It was only a topic of discussion in Malaysia before politics got the better of the GST there. There is no doubt that the GST triggers a shift in relative prices as prices of some products go up with higher rates and those of others go down with lower rates. But the overall price index is a weighted average of individual product prices and if the GST reform achieves revenue neutrality, the new taxation regime would also be price index-neutral.

Yet, there were fears of an inflation spike after the rollout of the GST in almost all the countries where it was introduced. Such fears are fuelled by the consumer perception that prices of some products or services have gone up, ignoring the decline in other products and services where the rates have been lowered. India was no exception. Indeed, concerns over inflation rearing its ugly head would be so strong that later the government would introduce a unique anti-profiteering provision in the GST laws to deter trade and industry from enriching themselves unjustly by not passing on the gains of the GST to customers in the form of lower prices. India's response too was not very dissimilar to many other countries, where such bodies were also set up to act as a deterrent against any inflationary tendency.

The BJP government soon set up an anti-profiteering authority to force disgorgement of the excess profit any trader or industry may have made. This was a move that became controversial; it went against the spirit of the GST—eliminating the inspector raj—and brought back fears of harassment by the tax authorities. The only saving grace was that the anti-profiteering authority, set up under the law, had a tenure of only two years after which it would cease to exist. In other words, the government's logic of introducing the anti-profiteering provisions was to keep a lid on prices in the first two years after the GST launch.

Between September and the first week of November, the GST Council held as many as four meetings, reflecting the seriousness and speed at which the Union finance ministry and the states got down to the task of framing the rules and setting the rates under the GST. While the first meeting discussed the draft rules of procedures, conduct of business, a timetable for the implementation of the GST, thresholds for exemption, composition for some categories of traders and businesses and a compensation law for states that would lose revenue, the third meeting in October deliberated on the various tax rates on products and services. The fourth meeting of the Council was held on 3 and 4 November 2016 and discussed the GST Network's preparations and the finalized rate bands. It was at this meeting that the four-band rate structure was adopted—5 per cent, 12 per cent, 18 per cent and 28 per cent. An additional cess of up to 28 per cent was also agreed on at this meeting, to be levied on luxury and sin goods, over and above the GST. The revenues to be collected from the cess were to be used for compensating the states for their revenue losses, based on an assumption that their revenues were growing at 14 per cent annually over the base level of 2014–15.

The fifth meeting was to be held on 9 and 10 November. However, the Union finance minister took a decision to postpone the meeting that turned out to be very crucial. The minutes of the fourth meeting of the GST Council noted:

> The Chairperson informed that as the Model GST Law was not yet ready, the proposed meeting of the Council on 9-10 November 2016 would not be held. Instead he proposed that the Council could meet on 24-25 November from 3 pm to 8 pm on both days as this would give sufficient time to complete the work on Model GST Law and to present it for the Council's consideration. The Council agreed to this suggestion.

Was that postponement deliberate? Available evidence does not make it very clear. It is most likely, as events would prove later, that the finance minister, who was the chairperson of the GST Council, knew that his prime minister would be planning an announcement for demonetization on the evening of 8 November. It is, therefore, reasonable to assume that Jaitley wanted to postpone the next GST Council to another date. What he did not anticipate was that the immediate shock and disruption caused by demonetization would be so huge that a postponement of a fortnight would not be enough to absorb and overcome its impact for even the Council members. Eventually, the next meeting of the GST Council was held on 3 and 4 December in New Delhi. And one of the vocal demands made at that meeting was to postpone the rollout date for the GST and ensure that there were higher compensation for the states since demonetization would surely have resulted in higher revenue losses.

There was no immediate decision in response to the demand for a postponement of the rollout date for the GST. It was only by the middle of January 2017 that it became clear that meeting the 1 April 2017 deadline for the GST rollout would be impossible. There were demands from within the government and outside for the rollout to be postponed by a year instead of being launched during the middle of a financial year. But four major factors may have tied down the hands of the government in settling for a launch by July 2017. One, the Constitution Amendment legislation paving the way for the rollout of the GST had mandated that the transition should take place not later than August 2017. The Modi government was in a bind. Two, there was a view that postponing the GST rollout any further and seeking another extension from Parliament for it would mean a loss of momentum and India's tryst with the GST could be deferred indefinitely. Three, there was a strong political reason for the government to rush with the rollout of the GST before the one-year deadline set by the amended law. Delaying it till 1 April 2018 would bring it much too close to the general elections of 2019. The government for good political reasons was not willing to face the instability and disruption that the launch of the GST would, in any case, unleash so close to the next general elections. There was a fourth factor that came in the way of postponing the launch of the GST by a year. The internal view in the finance ministry was that if the GST could not be launched in 2017, it was likely that it would not be launched in the near future. And the BJP government was very clear that it must carry the credit of having launched the GST as a badge of honour for its tenure at the Centre. Thus, the new date for launching the GST was going to be 1 July 2017.

Between December 2016 and July 2017, several meetings of the GST Council were held. The idea of an e-way bill system was discussed in March 2017 to electronically monitor and track the shipment and transportation of goods once they left the factory gates and reached the point of final sale. It did not find any favour at the eleventh meeting of the Council on 4 March 2017, but as the problem of revenue leakage became a big threat for compliance and coverage, the government introduced a modified version of e-way bills from the middle of 2018. Initial dislocation and problems over the e-way bills were there, but soon the trade and industry got used to the idea of being monitored and tracked as the loopholes in the taxation system were being plugged with the launch of the GST.

By March 2017, all the four GST Bills for rolling out the central GST law, the integrated GST law, the Union Territories GST law and the GST compensation law were cleared by the Cabinet and became laws by 29 March after they were passed by the Lok Sabha as money bills. According to India's parliamentary procedures, a money bill does not need to be passed by Rajya Sabha and the approval of Lok Sabha alone is adequate for the bill to become an act of Parliament. This meant that there was no need for securing the Rajya Sabha's concurrence on the four GST Bills. Thus, on 12 April 2017, the President gave his assent to the four GST laws. Simultaneously, the process of getting the law on state GST passed by each of the states began in right earnest. This process took some time, but even here by 21 June, all the states had passed the state GST laws except Jammu and Kashmir, which too passed the law a few days later and, therefore, joined the GST regime later than the national rollout of GST on 1 July 2017.

An important meeting of the GST Council took place in the third week of May 2017. This was the fourteenth meeting of the Council and it was here that the blueprint for the tax slabs of zero per cent, 5 per cent, 12 per cent, 18 per cent and 28 per cent were finalized and the fitment of various product groups—about 1200 of them, under those different rates—was discussed. At that point, over 80 per cent of the goods were either exempted with a nil rate or found themselves in the 5 per cent slab, addressing the fears of inflation arising out of the launch of the GST. A similar slab structure of 5, 12, 18 and 28 per cent tax was approved for services as well. The Council also approved the GST compensation cess amount also at this meeting. This was a big relief. The Centre had already promised the states that it would compensate them in the event of their suffering any revenue loss. The compensation cess rates had to be in place so that there was no fiscal uncertainty in making good the revenue shortfall the states might suffer. Trade and industry were also given the leeway of filing delayed returns under the GST for the next couple of months. In the subsequent months, many more such relaxations would be announced, but the government took care to reassure trade and industry that it would be most accommodative in its approach, facilitating what by all indications seemed to be a difficult transition to the GST.

A final hurdle arose when the initial trials with the GST Network showed that the system was not robust enough to take the load of millions of taxpayers filing their returns or uploading their documents within a given day. Attempts were made to persuade traders and businesses not to wait for the last date for filing the returns. But such exhortations made little impact as human behaviour was difficult to change at short notice. The government on its part had taken a decision as early as in September 2015 to award the contract for running the GST Network to information technology giant Infosys for a period of five years. The size of the contract was estimated then at Rs 1380 crore. While the GST Network officials were engaging with the Infosys to remove the bugs and glitches coming in the way of a smooth rollout of the technical system to support the GST, an unexpected drama unfolded at the finance ministry level. Senior Infosys officials explored the idea with the ministry if the launch of the GST could be postponed by some time so that it got more time to fix the problem. However, the finance ministry did not agree to any postponement and Infosys was persuaded to get the software readied before the launch of the GST on 1 July. Partly for this reason and partly because of the inherent complexities in the new online tax system, there were many glitches, problems and disruptions in the filing of returns, uploading of documents and even payment of taxes for several months after July 2017. But over the months, the system stabilized and the earlier blues got over without much long-term damage. The system stabilized primarily because the compliance procedures were curtailed and simplified. For instance, the requirement of invoice matching was dispensed with and a revised online system of matching was tried on a pilot basis after twenty-one months of the GST rollout. The real problem, according to Poddar, arose not from the procedures, but from a flawed structural design that laid more emphasis on somehow implementing the new tax system instead of reforming it.

By now Modi was clear that he must make the GST rollout a marquee event for his government. He wanted to show to everybody that he had succeeded where previous governments failed. But the Opposition political parties were not ready to play ball and decided to be the spoilsport. Thus, when the midnight event on the night of 30 June at Central Hall of Parliament was planned, Trinamool Congress leader Mamata Banerjee announced just two days before the event that her party would skip the event. The Congress and Left political parties too decided not to attend the inauguration of the GST at Central Hall. President Pranab Mukherjee was perhaps the only leader from the entire Congress party who graced the occasion. He had little option since as the President, technically it was his government which was launching the GST. Finance Minister Arun Jaitley recounted the long journey of the GST and showed magnanimity and grace by giving the credit for the launch of the new indirect taxes regime to the collective efforts of several governments of the past. Modi's speech had a different tone.

When Prime Minister Narendra Modi delivered his address to launch the GST at a midnight function on 30 June 2017 at the Central Hall of Parliament, the symbolism of his act was evident to everyone. Only twice since Independence had the Central Hall been the venue for a midnight function—once on the night of 14 August 1947 when the country's first prime minister, Jawaharlal Nehru, delivered the famous 'Tryst with Destiny' speech and the second time was in 1997 when the then Prime

Minister, Inder Kumar Gujral, marked the fiftieth anniversary of India's
Independence with his address. By using the Central Hall of Parliament
and choosing midnight for the launch of the GST, Modi was showing
the significance he was attaching to his government's indirect tax reform
initiative. Referring to past instances of the use of the Central Hall to
celebrate the country gaining freedom or adopting the Constitution, Modi
said: 'Several years later, this House shall once again go down in the annals
of history as there couldn't have been a more anointed venue than this for
the launch of one of the biggest strengths of our federal structure—the
GST reform.'

Modi cited a few salient point of the GST which deserve to be recounted
here. He talked about the unification of many taxes into a single tax system.
Indeed, as many as seventeen central and state-level taxes were subsumed
in the GST. He talked about how consumers as also the investors would
have the comfort of a uniformity of the tax system across the country and
wouldn't have to wrestle with different tax regimes in different states. He
talked about a new culture of governance where tax terrorism and the
inspector raj would be a thing of the past. He talked about how technology
would be used to administer the GST system and announced that the GST
was also about making India digital. He was conscious of the disruption
it would cause and urged everyone to give the new taxation system
some time before it settled down and benefits started flowing from it. 'I
request those who have fears to dismiss them. You get your eye check-up
done by your regular doctor. He gives you power for your eyes. You get
spectacles made. When you get those spectacles, it takes two-three days
to get adjusted. The crux of the story is that even then the eyes need to
adjust to new spectacles.' Modi's tone was different. The exuberance that
he had displayed while announcing demonetization a few months ago was
missing. Modi was urging trade and industry to cooperate and adjust to
the idea of a new system that he believed was superior to the existing one.

Little did one notice then that Modi as prime minister was embracing
yet another scheme that the previous government had launched. Already,
he had adopted the Aadhaar, a biometrics-based unique identity system,
which was launched by the Manmohan Singh government. And now
he was doing something similar with the GST. As prime minister, he
shed all his opposition to the GST he had voiced as the chief minister of
Gujarat some years ago. Not only that, he took necessary steps so that his
government could own up the new tax system so completely that it would
be closely identified with his regime.

CHAPTER 26

THE AFTERMATH OF THE GST

The launch of the GST altered the indirect tax space in India quite dramatically in a way that was never seen before. Such disruptions do not happen very often. The number of business establishments that got registered within the first few months of the launch of GST showed broad acceptance of the scheme. Just five months after the GST rollout, the number of unique entities registered with the GST rose to 9.8 million. Of this, only 6.4 million establishments were registered earlier either for state VAT (5.8 million) or for service tax (0.6 million) or for central excise (0.01 million). In other words, less than half a year after the launch of the GST, the country saw an increase in the indirect taxpayers' base by almost 50 per cent, or 3.4 million establishments. And the coverage increased after the threshold was kept at Rs 20 lakh annual turnover. For state VAT, this meant the threshold was raised from Rs 10 lakh to Rs 20 lakh, and for excise, the threshold was lowered from Rs 1.5 crore to Rs 20 lakh.

It is true that almost 1.6 million registered establishments under the GST had opted for the composition scheme, which essentially allowed them to pay a flat rate of taxes at fixed rates of 1 per cent, 2 per cent or 5 per cent without claiming any input tax credit and running the risk plugging themselves out of the supply chain of larger manufacturers or suppliers who would obviously find it a disincentive to engage in business with them. Establishments with a turnover of up to Rs 1.5 crore were only allowed to avail themselves of the composition scheme. It is also true that almost 65 per cent of the registered entities were just filing returns, but not paying any taxes. Thus, the government's GST revenues have not been positively impacted by the increase in registrations. But the bigger gain is that a long-term source of revenue has been created and tax coverage has increased which could over time lead to greater tax compliance. Of course, any improvement in compliance would be critically dependent on further digitization of the tax administration, which automatically leads to efficient and effective monitoring of taxable transactions. The other source of improved compliance was the dual GST system, as a result of which the assessment exercise happened at three layers—the Centre, states and the taxpayers—reducing the scope for collusion between taxpayers and the tax administration. 'Collusion is nearly impossible when there are three parties that take part in the assessment process,' said Poddar.[1]

The Economic Survey for 2017–18 pointed out another positive disruption of the GST. It noted that as many as 1.7 million establishments registering themselves for the GST were below the threshold limit of Rs 20 lakh. They were not obliged to register with the GST Network under the rules. Yet, they volunteered to do so because they wanted to be part of the GST value chain and take advantage of the business opportunities that this would generate. Similarly, there were about 1.9 million establishments which could have registered for the composition scheme because of their turnover threshold but chose not to do so. The Survey's conclusion was that the GST regime had clearly wooed them into its network.

The rollout of the GST also had a political fallout for the ruling party at the Centre. The BJP leaders were not tired of pointing out how the new indirect tax regime was a sign of their deep commitment to cooperative federalism. Modi had indeed talked about cooperative federalism before the launch of the GST at various forums, and the GST was now being touted as the proof of that commitment. The idea of setting up NITI Aayog was to encourage the states' participation in policymaking. After the Centre failed to amend the land acquisition law, it had wanted the states to introduce similar laws to make available land for industrial projects. But not too many states came forward to amend their laws. Similarly, labour law rigidities were sought to be relaxed by encouraging states to amend the respective laws. But again only a few states changed their labour laws to make them more flexible. Even the progress on encouraging states to reform their respective laws on agriculture produce marketing was quite tardy.

Under these circumstances, the GST was being presented as the first big reform where the Centre had struck a new relationship with the states, even though it faced many major procedural hurdles and glitches. The GST Council was an example of a forum where decisions were taken after taking on board all states, irrespective of their governments' political affiliation. Jaitley's decision to compensate for the entire loss of revenues that the states might incur for the first five years was a turning point in the negotiations for rolling out the GST. But it also showed that the Centre was willing to be sympathetic towards the states' fiscal concerns. The functioning of the GST Council was also an indication of how the new tax had brought a new equation between the Centre and the states, which only strengthened the federal foundations of the republic. The fact that all decisions at the Council during the first two years after the GST's rollout were taken by consensus was another proof of that positive change in the environment on Centre–state economic relations at least as far as the GST was concerned.

An impact of the GST that most analysts did not anticipate is with regard to direct tax collections. The launch of the GST has certainly improved the coverage of the business establishments under the tax net. This may result in an increase in GST revenue over the years. But an associated gain as a result of GST registrations and the new system of electronic tracking of all transactions is that promoters and business establishments, particularly those in the micro and small enterprises sector, are now coming under the income or corporation tax net. The GST has certainly helped in reducing the incidence of unaccounted transactions, but this has also led to improved direct tax compliance.

The new indirect tax regime has also surprised many public finance analysts in terms of the impact GST was to have on manufacturing and consuming states. It was earlier believed that GST would favour states that consume more than those that have a large concentration of manufacturing enterprises. This is because GST is a destination-based tax, where the final tax is paid and collected at the point of consumption. This had naturally ignited fears of revenue loss among the major manufacturing states. It is also the reason that manufacturing states like Gujarat and Maharashtra had lobbied hard for the levy of a 1 per cent interstate supply tax on GST rate as they feared revenue loss. Fortunately, the country was spared the trauma of such distortions in the GST regime. And now the data shows that the manufacturing states are not doing that badly as regards revenue collections under GST. The tax numbers for Maharashtra and Gujarat, which are largely producing states, show that their tax revenue growth actually went up from 9 per cent and 3 per cent respectively in 2016–17 to 19 per cent and 12 per cent in 2017–18. Haryana also showed a doubling of its revenue growth to 20 per cent and Punjab recorded a trebling of its revenue growth to 13 per cent in this period. In contrast, states like Bihar, Madhya Pradesh, West Bengal and Andhra Pradesh have seen their tax revenue growth declining in this period, in spite of them being known to be consuming states. However, Kerala and Uttar Pradesh are largely consuming states, but they recorded healthy growth in revenues.

Clearly, India's GST experience has questioned the textbook assumptions that it favours the consuming states more than the producing or manufacturing states. The fact that Gujarat and Maharashtra have a strong base of services consumption must be an important factor that should be borne in mind. An increasing segment of GST revenues is now coming from the services and since the manufacturing states are also major consumers of services, their loss on account of revenue from goods appears to have been more than made good by the rapidly growing services sector. There is yet another reason behind the skewed growth pattern. Revenue growth is also a function of the efficiency of tax administration and this is more so with the GST. Thus states that are laggard in collecting taxes and plugging revenue leakages will tend to do worse than those which have beefed up their tax administration apparatus.

Tax experts, however, do not wish to jump to any conclusions on how revenue growth has taken place in the first couple of years after the launch of the GST. They concede that revenues in the producing states have not suffered, but point out that this could be due to the release of the blocked input tax credit refunds for exports and also for domestic industries.

Looking ahead, GST's roadmap seems to have been redefined to address many of the criticisms the original duty structure had attracted for it being imperfect with too many rates and too many exemptions and the procedures being too cumbersome for honest taxpayers to comply with the system without an adverse impact on their ease of doing business. The top rate of 28 per cent is being pruned and will probably remain only for a score of sin or luxury goods like tobacco and luxury vehicles. The need for a compensation cess to continue beyond the stipulated five years may no longer exist. Indeed, this could be phased out even before the end of the five years. It is a cushion that was needed when the GST was launched but now that the states' compensation needs are coming down, the question now is whether the compensation cess should be scrapped. Tax experts are of the view that scrapping the compensation cess is a decision that should be taken only after detailed studies. Most of the tobacco duties were converted into the compensation cess. What will happen to the tax on tobacco if the compensation cess were to be scrapped? There will be similar such questions on the continuation or discontinuation of the compensation cess.

Refunds of claims to GST taxpayers continue to be a problem and the GST Council and the GST Network have their task in this area cut out. India will be among the many countries where prices did not go up hugely after the rollout of the GST. Fearing mainly the inflation that would arise because of this move, the government set up an anti-profiteering authority to ensure that industry and trade did not pocket the entire gains of lower tax incidence on account of the GST and instead passed them on to consumers.

So far, the inflation rate has remained benign, and the anti-profiteering authority has largely existed only on paper. It has a life of two years from its constitution in 2017. The sooner it is wound up the better it is for the sanctity and cleanliness of the GST regime. The bigger challenges for the GST regime lie in the areas of extending it to include petrol, diesel, crude oil, natural gas and aviation turbine fuel. These products have huge revenue implications for the Centre as well as the states. Theoretically, supplementary excise or sales tax can still be levied under the GST on products such as petrol, diesel, crude oil, natural gas and aviation turbine fuel. Thus, the argument that such products cannot be brought under the GST because of revenue implications is fallacious, according to tax experts. Nevertheless, bringing these products under the GST regime, even as excise and sales tax continue to be levied on them, would be a challenge for the tax administration in the future.

The government should also strive hard to avoid the pitfalls of excluding more sectors from the input-tax credit chain. The heart of the GST lies in building a value chain of economic activities, where each producer of goods or provider of services gets a refund of the taxes paid at all the intermediate stages of production or delivery. This helps in removing the cascading of taxes and also improves greater tax coverage and tax compliance. After intense lobbying, the GST Council has succumbed to the pressure of excluding the restaurants and a segment of the housing sector from the input-tax credit chain. In lieu of that, both the sectors now attract a relatively lower tax rate ranging between 1 per cent and 5 per cent. Ostensibly, this has been done to bring down prices of end products and services. However, such exemptions have a long-term deleterious impact on the GST structure as more sectors get encouraged to demand similar treatment. The long-term goal should be to bring every sector under the GST coverage so that the benefits of a VAT system trickle down to all sectors of the economy.

One of the major features of the Indian GST has been its slow and tentative approach to issues. This has turned out to be a uniquely Indian strategy of incremental reforms to make them politically acceptable and their pain for the system more manageable. It has drawn the criticism that the GST regime was imperfect to start with, but its defenders argue that perhaps a slow and gradual process to reform the GST system to make it perfect over a period of time is a more viable and effective option. If the GST regime has survived the huge hue and cry in the early years of its launch, it is because of this slow and cautious approach. GST was disruptive, but its disruption was relatively more measured than in other countries, where the ideal model of the tax system was introduced, unmindful of the adverse consequences such a strategy would result for both the polity and the economy. India may have been spared that trouble. There is an equally convincing counterview to this assessment. International experience of the GST rollout has shown that a major tax reform like this does not usually get better over time. A GST system born with design defects, as the Indian GST system indeed suffers from, has a very remote chance of getting better in the course of its implementation. 'The GST is like a baby that is the prettiest at the time of birth, and gets uglier with age. Of course, if the baby is born premature, a few months in the incubator can make it survive, but the incubator will not help rectify any of its congenital deformities,' Poddar says ominously.[2] On the one hand are countries like New Zealand, Australia, Singapore, South Africa and Canada, which started off with a relatively clean GST and have been able to stay clean. On the other hand, the European Union (EU) VAT system was a partial model with many flaws and compromises. Over the years, no reforms have been possible in the EU and the flaws remain uncorrected. The Indian GST has followed the EU model and the big question is whether India would prove the international experience wrong or fall into the old rut with its flawed GST getting more flawed over time. Already, some changes have been introduced in the GST, like the denial of input tax credits to a few sectors in lieu of lower rates, which have given rise to new anomalies and have compounded the distortions.

The Key Questions

With about two years gone after the launch of the GST, what would the government's report card look like on the question of how successful its biggest tax reform has been? Was the GST a reform or was it just an implementation of a new but flawed tax system? Was it a positive disruption with the potential of huge long-term gains for the economy, tax policy and the taxpayers? Or was it just a disruption in regulated doses, keeping in view the limitations India's political system imposed on any such reforms?

With the Constitution Amendment Bill excluding the petroleum products, alcohol and land, the die was cast for a basic design flaw in the

GST that was rolled out from July 2017. Most modern GST systems in the world, like those in New Zealand, Australia, South Africa or Singapore, had decided to bring them under their coverage as soon as they were launched. The Indian GST excluded them with the provision that some of these products could be included later if and when the GST Council decided to follow such a path. But why weren't these products included under it in the first place? No logic or reason for excluding them was given. The only possible explanation was that their exclusion would keep such transactions below the tax radar in the country. As Satya Poddar would say, 'Their exclusion significantly dilutes the economic benefits of the GST reform.'[3]

The question that crops up is if the government could successfully resist the pressure from some manufacturing states like Gujarat to impose a 1 per cent extra tax on the GST, why could it not muster enough political courage to remove the other imperfections in the new taxation system? Was there a lack of political leadership? Did the leadership of Modi and Jaitley fritter away an opportunity to put in place a flawless GST and instead allowed themselves to be pulled away by popular concerns over the likely disruptions that a modern GST system would have caused, even though such changes would have been for the larger and long-term good of the economy, taxation policy and taxpayers?

Some of the blame for the lack of a forceful and visionary leadership to implement a flawless GST must also be shared by the top officials' team that led the execution of the new taxation system. They had direct access to Modi and Jaitley and if they were convinced of the need to introduce a modern, flawless GST, it was possible they would have got the political leadership's go-ahead for those changes. Could the officials' team have been more receptive and responsive to feedback from tax experts, industry and trade? Such questions also arise because over and above the basic design flaw of the GST, the government also allowed a few imperfections to creep into the system. For instance, the rate structure, with multiple rates, did not look very different from the earlier tariff schedules that would take up hundreds of pages with schedules and exemptions. The denial of input tax credits in a few sectors, an inverted rate structure in some cases and the cumbersome procedures for zero-rating of exports were among the many imperfections that continue to undermine the efficiency of the GST system in India.

The final scorecard for the Indian GST, therefore, is a mix of some pluses and many minuses. It has undoubtedly led to a significant reduction in corruption and collusion between taxpayers and tax officials, thanks to a digital system of filing returns. The efficiency of the tax administration has also seen a commendable improvement as a result of automation and centralized processing through the GST network. The GST system has also seen most efficiency gains in the lower-income states. Compliance procedures have also been simplified in the two years after its rollout. The quarterly filing threshold has been raised to Rs 5 crore, as a result of which almost 93 per cent of the tax return filers are now enjoying the benefits of reduced compliance burden. The smooth introduction of the e-way bill system has plugged revenue leakage without any harassment. The growth in GST collections, a cause for concern in the first year or so after the launch, has also stabilized at a comfortable level in spite of the many rate cuts that were introduced in two rounds in the first two years. Concerns over revenue collections meeting the target have not gone away, but there are early signs of the GST system stabilizing.

However, the design flaws and the imperfections have continued to be a drag on the GST system. The benefits of reduced tax cascading have been limited to only 20 per cent, according to Satya Poddar. In sectors like electricity, agriculture and small and medium enterprises, there has been no reduction in tax cascading. The GST in India has certainly been a disruption. But whether it can reform itself further to address the design flaws and the imperfections is a question that will be answered in the years to come. That will also depend largely on the political will of the government. The safety net for the GST in India is the Constitution amendment that has now made it virtually impossible for anyone to go back to the earlier taxation system. But that is no comfort. The challenge is to move towards a GST that is flawless and has a better design.

CHAPTER 27

INDIA OF THE FUTURE

The disruptions of the future are difficult to anticipate. Disruptions are an outcome of a combination of factors—social, economic and political. Forecasts on future disruptions are also likely to change as and when the objective realities change in the social, economic and political spheres. A disruption that may appear very likely to happen now may not look so a few years down the line or a few years earlier.

Could demonetization happen during the United Progressive Alliance government's rule? Alternatively, could any government other than that led by Indira Gandhi have nationalized banks and triggered the biggest disruption in India's financial sector?

The likelihood of future disruptions is intricately connected with the political regimes in power and economic and social conditions that prevail in the country at a given point in time. With these caveats in place, here is an attempt at forecasting twelve big disruptions that could hit India in the next few years.

India Going Presidential

The makers of India's Constitution decided that India should be a parliamentary democracy. Broadly speaking, Parliament is supreme in a parliamentary democracy, wherein the leader of the government, and indeed every minister of the government, is accountable to Parliament. The leader of the government in a parliamentary democracy is not elected by the people. Members of the political party or a group of political parties that enjoys the majority of the lower house of Parliament elect their leader, who then is invited to form the government. If the leader loses the confidence of Parliament, he or she has to resign.

In contrast, presidential democracy is more personality-oriented, wherein the leader of the government is directly elected by the people and then he is entrusted with the responsibility of running the government made up of people chosen by him. India is often cited as a classic example of parliamentary democracy, just as the United States follows a presidential form of democracy.

It has to be remembered that when India's Constitution was being drafted, the Congress, the leading political party at that time, had several towering personalities who were ideally suited to lead a presidential form of government. Be it Jawaharlal Nehru or Sardar Vallabhbhai Patel or even Subhash Chandra Bose a few years before his disappearance, they all had tremendous mass following across the country and were ideal presidential candidates for any election in a presidential democracy. Yet, the Constitution-makers opted for parliamentary democracy, in the belief that the principles of collective responsibility and accountability are better enshrined and protected in a form of government where the leader is directly accountable to Parliament.

A parliamentary democracy has a natural safety valve built in the system. The supremacy of Parliament is what keeps the necessary checks and balances on a leader of the government. Remember that the leader of the government in parliamentary democracy is elected to Parliament only as a member, and it is only the members of the majority party in Parliament who decide to make him the leader, or the prime minister. Since the leader of the government in a presidential democracy is elected directly by the people, he is relatively less bound by Parliament. Indeed, the leader in such a government can in some cases veto a proposal approved by the legislature.

Strong leaders will, therefore, have a tendency to root for a presidential form of government. In a presidential democracy, campaigning and electioneering also get personalized. Instead of a battle between the values and principles that are espoused by different political parties, presidential elections obviously turn out to be battles between two personalities, their individual popularity and what policies or values they stand for. Institutions matter to some extent, but personalities hold the sway in a presidential democracy.

Indira Gandhi is believed to have entertained ambitions of changing India's Constitution to usher in presidential democracy in lieu of parliamentary democracy. One of her key ministers, Vasant Sathe, had even floated a paper on the subject in the early 1980s. Among Congress leaders who had endorsed her idea of introducing presidential democracy in India, the name of Siddhartha Shankar Ray figured quite prominently. Ray was also among those who helped Gandhi promulgate internal emergency in the country in 1975. Even during the Emergency years between 1975 and 1977, Indira Gandhi did toy with the idea of a change in the Constitution by switching over to a presidential system of government, similar to what prevailed in France. As Kuldip Nayar wrote in *Emergency Retold*, her concern was that the 'parliamentary system was too slow, at times "unproductive", and it never gave a free hand to the person at the top'. A detailed note on the features of the proposed presidential form of government was prepared by Gandhi's close advisers. But as an idea it had few takers in the Congress party at that time and Gandhi dropped the plan.

The general elections in 2014 and 2019 were held almost under circumstances that prevail in a presidential democracy. Narendra Modi was projected as the prime ministerial candidate for the BJP. The Congress projected Rahul Gandhi as their number one candidate. In the end, the general elections in 2014 and in 2019, in many ways, were fought on the issue of whether the voter would like to see Modi as the prime minister or Gandhi. Significantly, even without becoming a presidential democracy, India behaved like one at least as far as the general elections were concerned. This trend has not caught on in state Assembly elections as yet, although in many state Assembly elections, political parties do project their chief ministerial candidates. The idea as well as the effect are the same.

Is a disruption like India becoming a presidential democracy possible? It is likely that general elections fought in a way presidential elections are held may be increasingly favoured in the coming polls. That is also because political parties find it easy to fight the elections where personalities are projected as the eventual leaders of the government. Modi as prime minister between 2014 and 2019 showed that his governance style was more suited to a presidential form of government. But an early change in the Constitution to make India a presidential democracy is unlikely. Such an amendment will have to be endorsed by a simple majority in both houses of Parliament and a two-thirds majority of all members present and voting, in addition to half of the state assemblies approving the change in the Constitution. No national party is expected to have a simple majority in the Rajya Sabha at least till November 2020.

Simultaneous Elections for the Lok Sabha and State Assemblies

This idea too is an offshoot of strong governments and their desire to perpetuate a system where winners can take all. Combining Assembly elections with the Lok Sabha elections also helps strong leaders to gain more mileage from their electioneering and campaign work.

Until 1967, most state Assembly elections were held along with the Lok Sabha polls. It was not done by design, but it happened because state Assemblies normally ran their full tenure of five years, just as the Lok Sabha completed its five-year terms. Thus, 1952, 1957 and 1962 saw simultaneous Assembly polls and Lok Sabha elections. The tenures of neither many state Assemblies nor of the Lok Sabha followed a five-year schedule after 1962. Some of them were dissolved before the end of their term as the government fell or went in for early elections. Consequently, the election schedule for different state Assemblies and the Lok Sabha was spread out over a five-year cycle.

For the Election Commission, this sequence was helpful as the complications and the burden of holding simultaneous elections were rising with the number of electorate, the number of state Assemblies and the number of constituencies growing at a rapid pace. In theory, the Election Commission could have continued holding simultaneous elections for all state Assemblies and the Lok Sabha, but there was no need for it as the polling schedule changed. It is also true that the complexities of holding elections now in India have increased tremendously, with the introduction of verifiable paper audit trails along with the use of electronic voting machines and the security requirements for maintaining law and order and ensuring peaceful elections. The Election Commission, however, seems to be prepared to take on the challenge if such a situation arises.

For quite some time, BJP ideologues have expressed the view that the country need not be held ransom to some election or the other almost every year, bringing to a halt all policymaking processes as governments tended to go slow in taking decisions for the fear of upsetting voters or for the fear of any strictures from the Election Commission. The festival of democracy, according to such BJP thinking, needs to be celebrated only once in five years, and not every year. This is an idea whose implementation can raise many more questions on how the tenure of state Assemblies would have to be aligned with that of the Lok Sabha. What happens to Assemblies where the government falls before its tenure of five years, requiring an early election? Simultaneous elections in the whole country may sound appealing on paper, but will raise many more questions on how the Assembly polls would have to be held without either undermining the spirit of democracy or disrespecting the mandate given by voters.

Even a report was prepared under the leadership of BJP Vice-President Vinay Sahasrabuddhe, who also headed the Indian Council for Cultural Relations (ICCR), and was submitted to Prime Minister Narendra Modi in early 2018. The report stated, 'India and its political environment is perennially in election mode, where normally its electorate votes for around six state assemblies every year. A situation like this adversely impacts its developmental projects and programmes, which ultimately affects the country's governance at large.'

Indeed, the desire to hold simultaneous elections for the Lok Sabha and state Assemblies was at its peak in early 2018. This was when a section of the BJP leadership was toying with the idea of advancing the general elections along with the Assembly elections in states, where the BJP was in power. At the time, five state elections were going to be held later that year. Political expediency was the name of the game. The idea was to fight anti-incumbency in at least three of the states by combining them with national elections, where Prime Minister Modi could use his political capital to the hilt. However, that proposal did not go beyond a point in 2018.

But the idea has not been given up by the BJP. This is particularly so when it fits in well with its other idea favouring a presidential style of elections. The impact of a presidential style of campaigning and elections is far greater on the electorate if it is combined with simultaneous elections. Two things stand in the way of such a disruption. One, the Election Commission has to indicate its logistical capacity to conduct simultaneous elections. Two, there will be a need for legislative changes to make sure that the Lok Sabha and the Assemblies run their full tenures.

An idea that some BJP ideologues have been advocating is to borrow the German model where no government can be defeated on the floor of the legislature unless an alternative alliance stakes claim to form a new government till the end of the specified tenure. That is one method which can ensure the continuity of simultaneous elections for both Assemblies and the Lok Sabha. How likely are simultaneous elections? Quite likely. The idea has grown roots in this country. The BJP's election manifesto for the 2019 elections stated categorically that the party was keen on introducing simultaneous elections in the entire country. The *BJP Sankalp Patra Lok Sabha 2019* stated:

We are committed to the idea of simultaneous elections for Parliament, State assemblies and local bodies to reduce expenditure, ensure efficient utilisation of government resources and security forces and for effective policy planning. We will try to build consensus on this issue with all parties.

Article 370, Article 35-A and Citizenship

Three possible legislative changes can be expected in the coming years, which could fundamentally alter the character of the Indian state. One pertains to the abrogation of Article 370, the second refers to the annulment of Article 35-A of the Constitution and the third change is the amendment of the country's citizenship law.

Article 370 was adopted to define the relations between Jammu & Kashmir and the Centre in line with provisions under the Instrument of Accession that Maharaja Hari Singh of Kashmir had signed with the Indian government. Its essential objective was to protect the rights of Jammu & Kashmir to draft its own Constitution and decide for itself what powers it could extend to the Central government. A.G. Noorani, eminent lawyer and an expert on the Indian Constitution, has noted that Article 370 outlined several specific provisions for Jammu & Kashmir. These provisions ensured that the state remained exempted from the applicability of the Indian Constitution; the Centre's legislative powers over the state were limited to three areas of defence, foreign affairs and communications; and the coverage of other Central laws to the state was subject to the concurrence of the state government as determined by the State Constituent Assembly. A key provision was that Article 370 could be abrogated or amended only by a recommendation of the Constituent Assembly of Jammu & Kashmir. However, according to expert views, after the dissolution of the Constituent Assembly in 1956, changes in Article 370 could be undertaken by the state legislature with constituent powers under the J&K constitution.

Ever since the BJP has been leading the government at the Centre, the demand for abrogating Article 370 has been made with greater force. The BJP's election manifesto, released before the 2019 general elections, revealed the party's plans without any ambiguity. It said:

In the last five years, we have made all necessary efforts to ensure peace in Jammu & Kashmir through decisive actions and a firm policy. We are committed to overcome all obstacles that come in the way of development and provide adequate financial resources to all the regions of the state. We reiterate our position since the time of the Jan Singh to the abrogation of Article 370.

While the 'decisive actions' in the state are debatable and controversial, the manifesto has left no one in doubt about a BJP-led government's intent on abrogating Article 370.

Similarly, there is a strong possibility that Article 35-A of the Indian Constitution could be removed soon by the government in the coming years. Its deletion from the Constitution would alter the way people living in different states of India could migrate to Jammu & Kashmir and acquire property there. Article 35-A was added to the Indian Constitution through a Presidential Order in 1954, as a result of which non-residents of Jammu & Kashmir were barred from holding or acquiring any immoveable property within the state. The rights of non-residents were also restricted as far as getting a job or scholarship or aid from the state government was concerned. Increasingly, the BJP has been demanding that Article 35-A should be annulled. The party is of the view that the move to restrict ownership of property in Jammu & Kashmir only to local residents has come in the way of development in the state and has indirectly sustained the separatist movement there. These are highly contentious claims. But the party's manifesto for the 2019 general elections was quite categorical about the need for doing away with Article 35-A:

> We are committed to annulling Article 35-A of the Constitution of India as the provision is discriminatory against non-permanent residents and women of Jammu & Kashmir. We believe that Article 35-A is an obstacle in the development of the state. We will take all steps to ensure a safe and peaceful environment for all residents of the state. We will make all efforts to ensure the safe return of Kashmiri Pandits and we will provide financial assistance for the resettlement of refugees from West Pakistan, Pakistan-occupied Jammu & Kashmir (POJK) and Chhamb.

Finally, a law to facilitate the acquisition of citizenship by six non-Muslim minority communities entering India as refugees before a specified date could be introduced in Parliament. On 8 January 2019, the then home minister, Rajnath Singh, introduced in the lower house of the Indian Parliament the Citizenship Amendment Bill that was aimed at facilitating the acquisition of citizenship by six non-Muslim minority communities namely Hindus, Sikhs, Jains, Buddhists,

Christians and Parsis, who came from Afghanistan, Pakistan and Bangladesh and entered India before 31 December 2014. The objective of the bill was clearly to help the non-Muslim minorities in acquiring citizenship in India, but it excluded the Muslims from this facility, including those who might have moved from Bangladesh to Assam and did not find their names in the National Register of Citizenship (NRC) prepared by the state authorities in pursuance of a Supreme Court directive. Of the four million residents of Assam, who did not find their names in the first draft list of the NRC, more than half were believed to be Muslims.

Thus, the proposed Citizenship Amendment Bill would have bailed out the Hindus not figuring in the Assam NRC, but not the Muslims. The bill was passed by the Lok Sabha, but before it could be taken up by the Rajya Sabha, controversy over its intent and impact forced the government to drop it in February 2019. However, the BJP did not give up its plans to move ahead with such a bill. Its manifesto for the 2019 general elections made that very clear:

> We are committed to the enactment of the Citizenship Amendment Bill for the protection of individuals of religious minority communities from neighbouring countries escaping persecution. We will make all efforts to clarify the issues to the sections of population from the Northeastern states, who have expressed apprehensions regarding the legislation. We reiterate our commitment to protect the linguistic, cultural and social identity of the people of Northeast. Hindus, Jains, Buddhists, Sikhs and Christians escaping persecution from India's neighbouring countries will be given citizenship in India.

How soon can these legislative changes be brought about? The BJP was re-elected in May 2019 to lead the government at the Centre with a majority in the Lok Sabha that was bigger than what it had got in 2014. Given the huge mandate, the Narendra Modi government could be expected to quickly move ahead on all the three legislative proposals. However, the party's lack of majority in the Rajya Sabha could be a stumbling block, at least till such time it gains a majority in the upper house as well. All legislative changes, other than the money bills entailing financial expenditure from the exchequer, have to be cleared by the Rajya Sabha as well. And the Constitution amendment bills have to be cleared with a simple majority or with a two-thirds majority of all members present and voting in both the houses. The BJP and its alliance partners can hope to get a majority in the Rajya Sabha by November 2020, going by the schedule of elections to the upper house. Thus it is likely that such legislative changes that require the consent of the Rajya Sabha may have to wait till November 2020.

Ram Mandir

There is no doubt that the BJP continues to remain unequivocally committed to the idea of building a Ram temple in Ayodhya, on a piece of disputed land, where the ancient Babri mosque had stood till 6 December 1992 before it was pulled down by a mob of Hindu zealots. More than two decades have passed by since that cataclysmic event, but the movement to build a temple for Ram continues to provide sustenance to the BJP's political agenda. In the first week of May 2019, a five-judge bench, led by the Chief Justice of India, Ranjan Gogoi, set a timeline for the resolution of the Ram Mandir crisis by August. A Supreme Court–appointed mediation committee would indicate by that time how and in what manner representatives of Hindus and Muslims would like this dispute to be settled.

Whatever be the decision of the mediation committee, there is a strong likelihood of the BJP raising the temperature on the Ram Mandir issue. The party's manifesto for the 2019 general elections said:

> We reiterate our stand on Ram Mandir. We will explore all possibilities within the framework of the Constitution and all necessary efforts to facilitate the expeditious construction of the Ram Temple in Ayodhya.

The BJP-led government at the Centre enjoys a majority that is as large as 55 per cent of the total seat strength of the Lok Sabha. Only time will tell how and in what manner such a government would ensure that its political agenda is fulfilled. But as and when the Ram Mandir is constructed, the event would mark yet another disruption in the Indian polity and society, whose consequences for the nation's future would be huge and damaging to the diversity of the Indian society. Of that there is little doubt.

One Country, One Language

This is yet another dangerous disruption that one can think of. It is an extension of a majoritarian mindset that seems to have gripped India's politics, whose consequences can be catastrophic for the country. There are no guesses which language is being promoted as the language that is supposed to be unifying the entire country. It is Hindi. Political memory in India, like public memory, appears to have become very short. A similar attempt was made in the 1960s, when the Indira Gandhi government unsuccessfully tried to impose the use of Hindi on south Indian states. Languages can be emotive issues. They can inflame passion.

Countries are born on the basis of a language movement. The birth of Bangladesh is an outcome of a language movement, a desire to assert one's right to speak and write in one's own language. Far worse consequences can follow if there is an attempt to impose another language on people for whom that is not their mother tongue. In the early years after India's Independence, a sensible policy was adopted. English was allowed to be used for official correspondence, particularly among states. That made English the link language among states that spoke different languages across the country.

Meanwhile, a remarkable cultural change has taken place in the country in the last few decades. The rise of the Mumbai film industry has also meant the increasing popularity of the films it produces in Hindi. The market for Hindi films produced in Mumbai is now virtually the whole country. It is not through an official diktat, but through films made in Mumbai that Hindi has become more popular in many states, where it was hardly being spoken earlier. However, Hindi zealots in north Indian parties, in particular the BJP, have shown tendencies to propagate the use of Hindi as a language for communication among states. Already, some central ministries have begun using sending letters to different departments and even to other state governments in Hindi. It is true that there are many states in the country that have the capacity to communicate in Hindi. But there are quite a few south Indian states like Tamil Nadu, Kerala, Karnataka, Andhra Pradesh and Telangana, and eastern and north-eastern states that would face difficulties if Hindi were to be imposed on them.

The idea of imposing one language on the whole country and strengthen its unity is defeating the very idea of India, which is a celebration of diversity in every respect. Yet, a disruption caused by the imposition of Hindi on the whole country cannot be ruled out, given the current nature of political discourse. The danger is that spreading the use of one language is being managed in phases and almost quietly. But when the implications of the move become clear to the non-Hindi speaking states, the country's integrity as a nation would be put to test. The draft National Education Policy, prepared by the Modi government under the chairmanship of former ISRO chairman, K. Kasturirangan, had initially sought to impose Hindi as one of the three languages to be compulsorily taught in schools across the country. After protests from southern states, the draft was amended to allow schools and states the option of choosing the languages that they wished to include within the three-language formula. Two of the members of the Kasturirangan committee objected to the modification in the draft, leaving nobody in doubt that the long-term project of having Hindi across the country is not likely to be given up.

Delimitation of Electoral Constituencies

Until around 1976, the constituencies—or seats of the Lok Sabha—the Rajya Sabha and Vidhan Sabha (Assembly) were reset after every Census. Thus, the redrawing of the constituencies and the number of seats each state would have for the various forums took place in 1951, 1961 and 1971. This process, however, was stopped in 1976 in the wake of the Emergency that Indira Gandhi had imposed on the whole country a year earlier. This is the brief history of delimitation of constituencies in India after Independence. It was, however, decided in 2001 that the number of seats in the Assemblies, the Lok Sabha and the Rajya Sabha would remain unchanged till 2026. The freeze was decided so that states that had imposed population control methods on their people—like Kerala, Tamil Nadu and Punjab—should not lose many parliamentary seats, compared to states like Uttar Pradesh, Bihar and Rajasthan, which had not kept a similar check on their fertility rate.

It is clear, therefore, that such a delimitation exercise, if held after 2026, would be hugely disruptive. Past delimitations have resulted in a relative strengthening of the representation of mostly north Indian states in Parliament. The outcry after relative marginalization of states that had controlled their population growth and thereby lost the number of representatives in Parliament was somewhat muted then. But when the 2026 delimitation takes place, protests are likely to be louder. Already the decision of the Fifteenth Finance Commission to use the 2011 Census, instead of the 1971 Census, for determining the devolution of resources among states has provoked many south Indian states, led in particular by Kerala, to question why their relative prosperity should be held against them. They may not have much of a case as the use of the 2011 Census may deprive the state of some resources, but the per capita allocation of resources would not become inequitable.

But the delimitation exercise will raise other issues. Already, states like Uttar Pradesh, Maharashtra and Bihar exercise greater influence on national politics because of the relatively larger number of seats they have in both the houses of Parliament. After the delimitation exercise of 2026, these states would start wielding even greater power in terms of the number of representatives they would send to the Lok Sabha and the Rajya Sabha.

It is very unlikely that the 2026 deadline can be postponed. What can be done is to devise a new formula for deciding on electoral representation in Parliament. The criterion of population may have to be expanded to include some other associated parameters. Otherwise, prospects of smaller and relatively well-off states resenting a delimitation exercise that reduces their representation in Parliament look real.

Constituency delimitation would become a difficult disruption to handle, unless the Centre and the states come together and negotiate how to deal with the challenges. There is need for institutions like the Inter-State Council to be entrusted with the task of developing more advanced and evolved criteria for the next round of delimitation if its adverse impact on the country has to be limited. One possible way to minimize the impact of the constituency delimitation exercise, based on population growth, would be to opt for another round of state reorganization. This would give birth to more states. The relative gains in political power from constituency delimitation would be far less if large states like Uttar Pradesh, Maharashtra or even West Bengal were reorganized. Either way, constituency delimitation would be a hugely disruptive exercise.

Bank Privatization

Many governments in the past have tried out this disruption—privatizing banks—but simply failed. Ironically, the challenge of privatizing banks has arisen because of an earlier disruption caused by Indira Gandhi in 1969 when in her bid to exercise greater social control over banks, she nationalized in one stroke fourteen banks in the country. In the late 1990s, the Atal Bihari Vajpayee government had mooted the idea of reducing the government stake in public-sector banks to 33 per cent but allowing them to function as public-sector banks as far as parliamentary supervision over them was concerned. It was a novel idea, primarily aimed at tackling a political problem. So, Vajpayee's finance minister, Yashwant Sinha came up with a scheme where the government stake would be reduced to below 51 per cent, but the government would continue to treat the banks as public-sector banks as far as their employees and other obligations like subjecting the management of banks to parliamentary supervision were concerned. The proposal had to be dropped as too many problems cropped up and many more questions were raised.

The recent crisis in the banking sector, largely because of the growing NPAs of public-sector banks, is now raising the question on whether the time is ripe for considering the extreme option of privatizing them. There are now over a score of these public-sector banks, which account for almost three-fourths of the banking industry in the country. However, the government is in no mood to privatize the banks. One, selling off banks at this stage would be politically controversial for the government. Indeed, any government that undertakes privatization of banks will have a tough political challenge to face. The government has instead promised to pump about Rs 2.11 lakh crore of extra resources into the banks so that their capital base could expand, they could start lending again and, hopefully, be revived. A far bigger question, even if the government were to decide on privatizing banks, would be: Who would buy these banks? With scarce resources available with Indian companies and stringent regulatory norms exercised over bank ownership, any attempt at bank privatization is unlikely to succeed.

It would thus appear that bank privatization is not a disruption whose time has come in India. Instead, what one can expect is a merger of more public-sector banks (already the number of public-sector banks has been brought down from twenty-six to nineteen through mergers between 2017 and 2019), more stringent regulatory norms for public-sector banks and better monitoring of their performance by the government, their majority shareholder.

Corporatization of Indian Agriculture

Can Indian companies do farming in India? Close to seventy-five years after India's Independence, the thought of companies engaged in farming seems to be unacceptable to the country's political class. This is the legacy of India's economic model of the 1950s that left Indian agriculture alone. In the process,

Indian agriculture became dependent on state incentives like minimum support prices, procurement policies and subsidies. Even the idea of taxing rich farmers was considered anathema and a political hot potato. It is not that Indian agriculture has remained completely untouched by the corporate sector. Limited experiments with contract farming have yielded rich dividends for both the farmers and the companies that were engaged in contract farming. There were political risks and a few farmers' protests, but those instances were few and contract farming in India has made some headway.

Manmohan Singh, as finance minister, had mooted the idea of agri-business consortiums, with state support in 1991. The idea had many takers as this had the potential of establishing market linkages with the agricultural produce. Indian farming was likely to have the beneficial impact of a corporate culture and even access to bank finance could increase through the agri-business consortium route. However, the idea of agri-business consortiums has made limited progress and only a few hilly and north-eastern states have encouraged them.

Is the time ripe for allowing Indian companies, to start with, to acquire land and take up farming? The move will require land laws to be changed, which will face huge political opposition. But are the fears over such political opposition exaggerated? More than 85 per cent of India's operational landholdings are of a size less than two hectares or about five acres. Use of technology and better farming techniques can yield results only if landholdings are consolidated. The role of large organized entities in making this happen can hardly be overemphasized. There is need for large organized bodies, if not Indian corporates, to take up farming. And that would be a positive disruption for agriculture, ushering in perhaps the next Green Revolution.

Private Sector in Indian Railways

The operation of the railways in India has always been reserved for the public sector. The industrial policy of 1948, the Industrial Policy Resolution of 1956 and even the New Industrial Policy of 1991 had kept the railways under the exclusive domain of the state. The importance the government attached to the railways could be gauged from the fact that it was retained in the public sector along with just two other sectors—atomic energy and mining. While the operation of railway services continued to remain under state control, a gradual easing of policy has taken place from 1991 onwards to allow the private sector to operate in specified areas within the railways. For instance, the private sector has been involved in redeveloping railway stations.

Foreign investment has been allowed in the building of railway locomotives. But there has been no private-sector involvement or investment in either the building and maintaining of core railway infrastructure like tracks or in the operation of railway services for freight and passengers.

No government so far has mooted privatization of the railways as an idea. There has been an implicit understanding shared by all governments—led by both the Congress and the BJP —that the railways deliver a social service by offering an affordable national transportation network connecting cities and towns across the country. Yes, the railways bear a social cost for these services, a part of which is recovered through cross-subsidization from freight revenues. There have also been demands from within the railways that the central exchequer must compensate them for running these services at a loss. The consequences of raising freight tariff to make good a part of the railway loss on account of uneconomic railway services are adverse for the Indian economy in general. But the policy response so far has been to let the railways bear the burden through freight tariffs, even though it has been losing business to the road sector, making transportation of goods by the railways costlier and often uneconomical for industry.

Privatizing the railways under such circumstances could well be the silver bullet for tackling a variety of problems afflicting the Indian economy. However, this is one proposal that has met with stiff resistance on account of the international experience of privatization of national railways in many other countries not yielding the desired benefits. In the current situation, privatizing railways is an attractive idea with many positive benefits for the entire economy, provided the exercise does not result in the creation of another private-sector monopoly, there is competition among the private operators of freight or passenger services and there is an independent, robust regulatory structure overseeing the sector. But there are not too many takers for such a move within the government system, at least. This is ironical because allowing the private sector in the operation of railways would be a positive disruption, helping it become one of the main engines of India's economic growth.

Universal Basic Income

The idea of a UBI was mooted as an idea within the government by Arvind Subramanian in the Economic Survey he presented in 2017. Subramanian, who was then the chief economic adviser in the finance ministry, had then argued for a new system under which every person would enjoy a right to a basic income to cover his or her basic needs. The Survey cited four principal reasons for adopting the UBI scheme: to achieve the goals of social justice, reduce poverty, ensuring a more efficient system of delivering government benefits to the people and creating new possibilities for jobs by giving individuals the choice on the terms of engaging with the labour market.

A year prior to the presentation of the Economic Survey by Subramanian, Vijay Joshi, eminent economist and Emeritus Fellow at Oxford, had favoured a UBI scheme in India in his 2016 book *India's Long Road to Prosperity*. His arguments were similar to what the government's Economic Survey had made on UBI. Joshi was of the view that UBI would guarantee a minimum income floor for all Indians and also pave the way for replacing the age-old and inefficient system of providing subsidies under various schemes. Joshi conceded that the idea of a UBI was politically difficult, but should nevertheless be promoted as it was a far better system for improving the economic well-being of Indians. Economist Pranab Bardhan has also been pleading for a UBI scheme in India.

But Joshi had also correctly concluded that there was no political appetite for switching over to a UBI system. Finance Minister Arun Jaitley said after presenting his fourth Budget in 2017 that the UBI scheme was an idea whose time in India had not yet come. He cited the lack of political maturity of the Indian system to accept the logic of such a fundamentally different scheme. The big question that bothered the political classes was that a UBI scheme would make the financial burden on the government unbearable if all other existing subsidies were not withdrawn or phased out. In an ideal situation, the launch of a UBI should be accompanied by the withdrawal of all other subsidies. Without that, the UBI would be a fiscal disaster for the government. Yet, no government is willing to bite the bullet by launching UBI and simultaneously withdrawing the various subsidies schemes.

The possibility of a UBI, however, has brightened after Telangana Chief Minister K. Chandrashekhar Rao made an electoral success of the income support scheme Rythu Bandhu for farmers in the state. Rao was returned to power in the Assembly elections of 2018 and one of the reasons cited in his favour was that he had earlier implemented Rythu Bandhu, even though it benefitted only landowners, not landless labourers, and promised to increase the benefit amount by 25 per cent as part of his election manifesto. It appears that other states, too, may explore a UBI scheme like Rythu Bandhu to be launched in the entire country. Indeed, Odisha came out with a basic income support scheme for all its small farmers, cultivators and landless farm labourers, committing an annual expenditure of over Rs 10,000 crore. The Central government, too, announced in its 2019–20 Interim Budget the PM

Kisan Yojana that offered Rs 6000 per year to every farming family holding land of up to two hectares or about five acres. This scheme covered almost 85 per cent of all the operational landholdings in the country and imposed an annual additional expenditure burden of Rs 75,000 crore on the exchequer. In the run-up to the 2019 general elections, the Congress promised that if it was elected to power its government would provide a minimum income of Rs 12,000 per family for about 50 million poorest of poor households, which would cost the exchequer an estimated annual spending of Rs 3.6 lakh crore or 1.9 per cent of the 2018–19 GDP. The BJP manifesto in turn promised to expand the coverage of its PM Kisan Yojana to cover all farmers irrespective of the size of their landholdings, a promise that was fulfilled as soon as the BJP government was formed after the May 2019 elections.

India's political class is already reconciled to the idea of providing income support for at least farmers, which in many ways is a variant of a UBI scheme. The impact of a UBI on the state exchequer would be much bigger. But the disruptive element in the launch of the UBI will be the degree to which the government would withdraw various existing financial incentives and subsidies being given to all Indians at present. As is clear, the launch of a UBI can be financially prudent only if it is accompanied by the phase-out of existing subsidies to make it a fiscally sound and sustainable model. This will require huge financial adjustments to be made by various stakeholders. It seems that the idea of a UBI is growing roots in the Indian government system. In spite of the many disruptive consequences, UBI is one idea that may see the light of the day soon.

Dismantling the IAS

India's premier civil service, the ICS during the British rule and the Indian Administrative Service after Independence, is often described as the steel frame that keeps the country intact and running. Even now, lakhs of young Indians sit for the IAS entrance examinations to gain entry into the coveted service. An IAS officer can hope to climb the administrative ladder pretty fast and can retire as the country's top civil servant—the cabinet secretary—or be selected to head the many regulatory bodies in different fields after retirement. An IAS officer is reputed to have deep knowledge of the way India's political system functions and has the ability and tact to overcome any policy challenge.

When the government is in a bind on any tight economic or even political situation, it relies on the skills of an IAS officer. The latest example was when the government relied on a retired IAS officer, Shaktikanta Das, to be the governor of the central bank, the RBI. Das was a competent bureaucrat and spent many years of his service in the Union finance ministry. But when the government's relationship with RBI Governor Urjit Patel, soured a bit and the latter decided to quit, the only option the government had was to hire a retired IAS officer, who was expected to heal the wounds in the government–RBI relations and prevent any further instability at the top of the country's central bank, which is also the monetary policy authority and the regulator for banks. It is a cosy relationship—the politicians ruling the government need the IAS officers and the IAS officers need the government to administer the system to ensure governance.

Should the IAS be continued as an all-India service or should it be simply scrapped? This idea has often been mooted to address the weaknesses in policy governance, particularly in many departments where domain expertise in the area can be of critical importance. Economic policymaking in the ministries of finance, commerce, industry, power and coal can qualitatively get better if instead of IAS officers the government had the option of choosing experts in specific areas to man these departments. Similar issues crop up with regard to ministries of environment and science and technology, where scientists or climate experts should do a better job than IAS officers, who are generalists, having spent many years in different departments dealing with a diverse set of subjects and issues, before taking charge of these ministries. In the end, policy outcomes are not always as good as they could have been had the policy formulation exercise been steered by experts.

The case for doing away with the IAS is strong. But if the government were to take such a decision, the challenge of policymaking and ensuring governance would become more formidable at least in the short run. An alternative cadre of expert officers from industry and academia would have to be quickly created and nurtured. In the past, the government did try to build such expert cadres to oversee economic policymaking. However, the strong IAS network did not allow such alternative cadres to grow and expand their footprint beyond a point.

Even if the IAS cannot be scrapped for practical reasons, it seems the government can certainly go ahead experimenting with a new set of officers who have expertise in specific subjects and skills. The Modi government has already begun experimenting with the idea of appointing experts in the government. Nine professionals were hired in April 2019 from the private sector to join different central ministries. Can the government go in for a big change like phasing out the IAS? The political class perhaps would, in theory, be in favour of such a shift in the government's hiring policy, but it is also hugely dependent on the continuation of the IAS system. The resistance to a change would also come from the existing IAS officers, who certainly will have a vested interest in furthering the growth and expansion of the IAS. Phasing out the IAS seems to be a difficult change for any government to introduce.

Change in the Financial Year

In 2016, the Narendra Modi government had mooted the idea of shifting the financial year of the government from April–March to January–December. In July that year, it set up a committee under the chairmanship of Shankar N. Acharya, a former chief economic adviser in the finance ministry who played a crucial role in the economic reforms programme launched in 1991, to examine the feasibility of such a switchover.

Acharya submitted the committee's report in the last week of December 2016. The government kept quiet about the contents of the report even as a few media reports had initially suggested that the Acharya Committee had indeed recommended a switch from an April–March financial year to the calendar year as the financial year. However, as clarity emerged on the contents of the report, it became clear that no such recommendations for switching over to a new financial year were actually made in the report.

The government has continued to maintain complete silence over the contents of the Acharya Committee report. Indeed, the report was not even made public. That the government continued to maintain status quo on the question of the financial year was an indication that the arguments put forward by the Acharya Committee against the switchover to a January–December financial year cycle might have been strong and irrefutable. The government, however, advanced the date of presenting the Union Budget by four weeks to 1 February. This seemed to have been done in preparation for the change of the financial year from April–March to January–December. But the government is yet to take the plunge.

Will the idea of changing the financial year gain momentum in the coming years? It is very likely. The Narendra Modi government is not the first to have examined the need for changing the current financial year format. Even the Indira Gandhi government had mooted the idea in the

1970s but did not go beyond just setting up a committee of experts to look into this question. The idea of changing the financial year sounds appealing to any government that wants to leave its own imprint on the governance style. Already, the Modi government has advanced the presentation of the annual Budget by a month. The previous BJP-led government under Atal Bihari Vajpayee had changed the time for presenting the Budget—in 1999, then finance minister Yashwant Sinha chose to present the Budget in the forenoon of 27 February, discarding the 'long-standing tradition of British Raj of presenting the Budget at 5 p.m.'.[1]

Comparatively, changing the financial year is an easy decision to take, even though its disruptive impact on the government system, and indeed on the rest of the economy, will be huge. There were media reports in April 2019 suggesting that changing the government's financial year from April–March to January–December was under serious considerations at the highest level of the government. There were media reports in April 2019 that the revenue department in the finance ministry was keen on switching over to a calendar year, instead of the existing system of an April–March financial year, at least for tax purposes. How this would pan out is difficult to gauge. But an early action on this front cannot be ruled out.

APPENDIX

Twenty-one Steps That Narendra Modi Announced on the Day of Demonetization

1. 'Persons holding old notes of five hundred or one thousand rupees can deposit these notes in their bank or post office accounts from 10th November till close of banking hours on 30th December 2016 without any limit.

2. Thus you will have 50 days to deposit your notes and there is no need for panic.

3. Your money will remain yours. You need have no worry on this point.

4. After depositing your money in your account, you can draw it when you need it.

5. Keeping in mind the supply of new notes, in the first few days, there will be a limit of ten thousand rupees per day and twenty thousand rupees per week. This limit will be increased in the coming days.

6. Apart from depositing your notes in your bank account, another facility will also be there.

7. For your immediate needs, you can go to any bank, head post office or sub post office, show your identity proof like Aadhaar card, voter card, ration card, passport, PAN card or other approved proofs, and exchange your old five hundred or thousand rupee notes for new notes.

8. From 10th November till 24th November the limit for such exchange will be four thousand rupees. From 25th November till 30th December, the limit will be increased.

9. There may be some who, for some reason, are not able to deposit their old five hundred or thousand rupee notes by 30th December 2016.

10. They can go to specified offices of the Reserve Bank of India up to 31st March 2017 and deposit the notes after submitting a declaration form.

11. On 9th November and in some places on 10th November also, ATMs will not work. In the first few days, there will be a limit of two thousand rupees per day per card.
12. This will be raised to four thousand rupees later.
13. Five hundred and thousand rupee notes will not be legal tender from midnight. However for humanitarian reasons, to reduce hardship to citizens, some special arrangements have been made for the first 72 hours, that is till midnight on 11th November.
14. During this period, government hospitals will continue to accept five hundred and thousand rupee notes for payment.
15. This is for the benefit of those families whose members may be unwell.
16. Pharmacies in government hospitals will also accept these notes for buying medicines with doctors' prescription.
17. For 72 hours, till midnight on 11th November, railway ticket booking counters, ticket counters of government buses and airline ticket counters at airports will accept the old notes for purchase of tickets. This is for the benefit of those who may be travelling at this time.
18. For 72 hours, five hundred and thousand rupee notes will be accepted also at

- Petrol, diesel and CNG gas stations authorised by public sector oil companies.
- Consumer co-operative stores authorised by State or Central Government.
- Milk booths authorised by State governments.
- Crematoria and burial grounds.

These outlets will have to keep proper records of stock and collections.

19. Arrangements will be made at international airports for arriving and departing passengers who have five hundred or thousand rupee notes of not more than five thousand rupees, to exchange them for new notes or other legal tender.
20. Foreign tourists will be able to exchange foreign currency or old notes of not more than Rs 5000 into legal tender.
21. One more thing I would like to mention, I want to stress that in this entire exercise, there is no restriction of any kind on non-cash payments by cheques, demand drafts, debit or credit cards and electronic fund transfer.'

ACKNOWLEDGEMENTS

This book would not have been written if Lohit Jagwani had not met me over coffee at the India International Centre one afternoon last summer. Lohit is a persuasive editor. Even though I had no immediate desire to write a book, he had, during that short meeting, succeeded in planting in my mind an idea whose execution in the form of a book is in your hands. As they say, the perspiration is mine, but the inspiration behind the book is Lohit. The credit should go to him for inspiring me with the idea that India's journey as a democratic country could be better understood by analysing a series of disruptions that took place in the last seven-odd decades.

I must also acknowledge my gratitude to *Business Standard*, where I have worked for almost a quarter of a century, for allowing me to undertake this venture. I will remain indebted to T.N. Ninan for his permission to write the book. He has been my editor for the longest period of my nearly four decades of career as a journalist, and he set before me standards in journalism that I have always strived hard to follow. I have had the privilege of discussing with many colleagues and experts the many ideas that have been expanded in this book. The list will be very long if I were to name all of them. But I would be failing in my duty if I do not mention at least some of those who made a signal contribution to a few of the chapters in the book. Deepak Lal explained to me the policy environment that led to India's turn towards statism. Surinder Sud outlined the forces that were at play behind India's Green Revolution. They also went through the chapters that I wrote on the basis of these meetings and made important suggestions. Others who took the trouble of reading the chapters included: Vijay L. Kelkar, Coomi Kapoor, T.C.A. Srinivasa-Raghavan, Mahesh Uppal, Tamal Bandyopadhyay, Arun Kumar and Satya Poddar. All of them made relevant and useful suggestions. Suveen Sinha kindly and very readily agreed to draft a short biographical sketch of mine, a task that I was uncomfortable doing myself, and stayed well within the word limit Lohit had imposed on it. I am grateful to each one of them. Of course, I am solely responsible for whatever shortcomings the book stills suffers from.

I have also benefitted immensely from the wisdom and knowledge of the many authors whose books I had to read while writing this book. I need to record my deep gratitude to each of these authors. A list of the authors and the books is given in the Bibliography section.

I will be failing in my duty if I do not record my deep gratitude to all the members of my family for the support I got from them while I was busy writing the manuscript.

NOTES

Section 2: Partition of India

Chapter 2: A Tryst with Destiny

1. https://www.indiaofthepast.org/contribute-memories/read-contributions/major-events-pre-1950/263-acceptance-of-indias-partition-by-indian-leaders-june-3-1947
2. Ibid.
3. Ibid.
4. Ibid.
5. Ibid.
6. William Dalrymple, 'The Great Divide', *The New Yorker*, 29 June 2015, https://www.newyorker.com/magazine/2015/06/29/the-great-divide-books-dalrymple
7. Ibid.
8. Tai Yong Tan and Gyanesh Kudaisya, *The Aftermath of Partition in South Asia* (London: Routledge, 2000).
9. Vazira Fazila-Yacoobali Zamindar, *The Long Partition and the Making of Modern South Asia: Refugees, Boundaries, Histories* (New Delhi: Penguin Books India, 2008).
10. https://www.indiaofthepast.org/contribute-memories/read-contributions/major-events-pre-1950/263-acceptance-of-indias-partition-by-indian-leaders-june-3-1947
11. http://theconversation.com/how-the-partition-of-india-happened-and-why-its-effects-are-still-felt-today-81766
12. https://www.britannica.com/biography/Mohammed-Ali-Jinnah
13. https://www.britannica.com/event/Lucknow-Pact
14. Khursheed Kamal Aziz, Rahmat Ali: A Biography (Wiesbaden: Steiner Verlag, 1987).
15. https://www.indiaofthepast.org/contribute-memories/read-contributions/major-events-pre-1950/263-acceptance-of-indias-partition-by-indian-leaders-june-3-1947

Chapter 3: Making the Best of an Inevitability

1. Ramachandra Guha, *India after Gandhi: The History of the World's Largest Democracy* (New Delhi: Picador, 2007).
2. https://www.britannica.com/place/India/The-transfer-of-power-and-the-birth-of-two-countries#ref486443
3. Nitish Sengupta, *Bengal Divided: The Unmaking of a Nation 1905–1971* (New Delhi: Penguin, 2007).
4. Ibid.
5. Raghabendra Chattopadhyay, 'Liaquat Ali Khan's Budget of 1947–48: The Tryst with Destiny', *Social Scientist* 16 (June–July 1988).
6. Ibid.
7. Ibid.
8. http://www.asianage.com/india/all-india/141118/the-greatest-indian-after-the-mahatma-why-gandhi-chose-nehru-to-lead-india.html; Rajmohan Gandhi, Patel: A Life (Ahmedabad: Navajivan, 1991).
9. Guha, *India after Gandhi*, https://www.indiaofthepast.org/contribute-memories/read-contributions/major-events-pre-1950/263-acceptance-of-indias-partition-by-indian-leaders-june-3-1947
10. http://www.worldstatesmen.org/India_princes_A-J.html
11. Guha, *India after Gandhi*.
12. http://www.worldstatesmen.org/India_princes_A-J.html
13. https://data.worldbank.org/indicator/MS.MIL.XPND.GD.ZS?locations=IN
14. https://www.indiaofthepast.org/contribute-memories/read-contributions/major-events-pre-1950/263-acceptance-of-indias-partition-by-indian-leaders-june-3-1947
15. Rudranghsu Mukherjee, ed., *Great Speeches of Modern India* (New Delhi: Random House India, 2007).
16. Ibid.
17. Medha M. Kudaisya, *The Life and Times of G.D. Birla* (New Delhi: Oxford University Press, 2003).
18. Ibid.

Section 3: Turn towards Statism

Chapter 4: A New Economic Vision

1. https://bbmb.gov.in/bhakra-project.htm
2. Rudrangshu Mukherjee, ed., *Great Speeches of Modern India* (New Delhi: Random House India, 2007).
3. http://planningcommission.gov.in/aboutus/history/PCresolution1950.pdf
4. http://indiafacts.org/complete-truth-jawaharlal-nehru-forced-john-mathai-resign/

Chapter 5: Nationalization as the New Mantra

1. https://www.epw.in/system/files/pdf/1957_9/3-4-5/socialistic_pattern_of_society_and_the_second_five_year_plan.pdf
2. Rudrangshu Mukherjee, ed., *Great Speeches of Modern India* (New Delhi: Random House India, 2007).
3. Rudrangshu Mukherjee, *Jawaharlal Nehru* (New Delhi: Oxford University Press, 2019).
4. Mukherjee, ed., *Great Speeches of Modern India.*
5. Medha M. Kudaisya, *The Life and Times of G.D. Birla* (New Delhi: Oxford University Press, 2003).
6. https://dipp.gov.in/sites/default/files/chap001_0_0.pdf
7. https://rbidocs.rbi.org.in/rdocs/content/PDFs/90028.pdf
8. https://rbidocs.rbi.org.in/rdocs/content/PDFs/90028.pdf

Section 4: The Food Crisis

Chapter 6: From Ship to Mouth

1. Jairam Ramesh, *Intertwined Lives: P.N. Haksar and Indira Gandhi* (New Delhi: Simon & Schuster India, 2018).
2. https://dbie.rbi.org.in/DBIE/dbie.rbi?site=publications
3. http://www.asianage.com/india/all-india/250517/naxalbari-1967-the-uprising-that-changed-our-politics.html
4. http://www.asianage.com/india/all-india/250517/naxalbari-1967-the-uprising-that-changed-our-politics.html
5. Ramesh, *Intertwined Lives.*
6. https://www.globalsecurity.org/military/world/india/famine-bengal-1943.htm
7. https://www.thehindu.com/todays-paper/tp-opinion/food-as-peoples-right/article2769860.ece
8. https://indianexpress.com/article/opinion/columns/swallowing-the-humiliation/
9. https://www.econ.ucla.edu/lal/Palgrave%20Dictionary%202008.pdf

Chapter 7: A New Experiment by Indira Gandhi

1. Pranay Gupte, *Mother India: A Political Biography of Indira Gandhi* (New Delhi: Penguin Books India, 2009).
2. https://www.thehindu.com/todays-paper/tp-opinion/food-as-peoples-right/article2769860.ece
3. https://dbie.rbi.org.in/DBIE/dbie.rbi?site=publications

4. Ashok Mitra, *A Prattler's Tale Bengal, Marxism, Governance* (Kolkata: Samya, 2007).

5. https://www.downtoearth.org.in/news/agriculture/only-15-landholders-earn-91-of-total-national-income-59505

6. https://indianexpress.com/article/research/five-instance-why-lal-bahadur-shastri-is-the-most-modest-prime-minister-india-has-ever-seen-4870695/

7. Ibid.

8. https://link.springer.com/article/10.1007/s40003-013-0069-3

9. Norman Borlaug, *The Green Revolution Revisited and the Road Ahead*, Lecture to the Norwegian Nobel Institute, Oslo, 2000.

10. http://digitalcommons.unl.edu/cgi/viewcontent.cgi?article=1027&context=envstudtheses

Section 5: Nationalization and More Statism

Chapter 8: The Era of Nationalization

1. Jairam Ramesh, *Intertwined Lives: P.N. Haksar and Indira Gandhi* (New Delhi: Simon & Schuster India, 2018).

2. Medha M. Kudaisya, *The Life and Times of G.D. Birla* (New Delhi: Oxford University Press, 2003).

3. Ramesh, *Intertwined Lives.*

4. https://www.thehindu.com/archives/plan-for-social-control-of-banks/article21665627.ece

5. Ibid.

6. D.N. Ghosh, *No Regrets* (New Delhi: Rupa, 2015).

7. Rakesh Batabyal, ed., *The Penguin Book of Modern Indian Speeches* (New Delhi: Penguin Books India, 2007).

8. https://coal.nic.in/content/historybackground

9. Ibid.

10. https://www.coalindia.in/en-us/company/history.aspx

Chapter 9: Politics of Robin Hood

1. http://www.hbs.edu/faculty/Publication%20Files/Charting%20Dynamic%20Trajectories%202014_f07bc6b5-cb08-4657-8970-08ea4ba53d1e.pdf

2. https://www.dailypioneer.com/2017/columnists/indias-new-privy-purse.html

3. https://www.licindia.in/Top-Links/about-us/History

4. https://dipp.gov.in/sites/default/files/chap001_0_0.pdf

5. https://www.cci.gov.in/sites/default/files/Indicus_20090420152009.pdf
6. https://www.cpcl.co.in/CompanyProfile
7. https://www.nytimes.com/1975/11/28/archives/britains-burmah-shell-oil-due-for-takeover-in-india.html

Section 6: The Oil Jolt

Chapter 10: India's New Disruption

1. https://www.opec.org/opec_web/en/about_us/23.htm
2. https://www.thebalance.com/opec-oil-embargo-causes-and-effects-of-the-crisis-3305806
3. https://history.state.gov/milestones/1969-1976/nixon-shock
4. Ibid.
5. https://www.nytimes.com/1974/01/03/archives/nixon-approves-limit-of-55-mph-states-must-meet-standard-or-lose.html and https://www.washingtonpost.com/news/monkey-cage/wp/2018/10/16/saudi-arabia-hinted-at-a-u-s-oil-embargo-its-not-1973/?noredirect=on&utm_term=.0894e4a29e5d

Chapter 11: The Search for Black Gold

1. https://www.nytimes.com/1974/01/20/archives/india-slow-to-grasp-oil-crisis-now-fears-service-ecomomic-loss-a.htm
2. https://www.imf.org/external/pubs/ft/ar/archive/pdf/ar1974.pdf
3. S.P. Wahi, *Leading from the Front* (New Delhi: Crossbill Publishing, 2013).
4. Ibid.
5. Author's interview with Vijay L. Kelkar.
6. https://dea.gov.in/sites/default/files/BUDGET-1974-75.pdf

Section 7: The Emergency

Chapter 12: Toppled in Court

1. B.N. Tandon, *PMO Diary—I: Prelude to the Emergency* (New Delhi: Konark Publishers, 2003).
2. Ibid.
3. https://indianexpress.com/article/opinion/editorials/july-11-1978-forty-years-ago-ex-lg-kills-self-5254103/
4. Shah Commission of Inquiry: Interim Report I, 11 March 1978.
5. Ibid.

6.   Ibid.
7.   Ibid.
8.   Pranab Mukherjee, *The Dramatic Decade: The Indira Gandhi Years* (New Delhi: Rupa, 2015).
9.   Shah Commission of Inquiry: Interim Report I, 11 March 1978.
10. Tandon, *PMO Diary*.
11. Ibid.
12. Ibid.
13. https://www.hindustantimes.com/india/the-court-verdict-that-prompted-indira-gandhi-to-declare-emergency/story-uaDsy0j3B0vSdiPn2md9WO.html
14. P.N. Dhar, *Indira Gandhi, the 'Emergency', and Indian Democracy* (New Delhi: Oxford University Press, 2000).
15. Mukherjee, *The Dramatic Decade*.
16. Ibid.
17. Ibid.
18. Coomi Kapoor, *The Emergency: A Personal History* (New Delhi: Penguin Books India, 2015).
19. Ibid.

Chapter 13: Why It All Happened

1.   P.N. Dhar, *Indira Gandhi, the 'Emergency', and Indian Democracy* (New Delhi: Oxford University Press, 2000).
2.   Ibid.
3.   Jairam Ramesh, *Intertwined Lives: P.N. Haksar and Indira Gandhi* (New Delhi: Simon & Schuster India, 2018).
4.   Ibid.
5.   Ibid.
6.   https://indianexpress.com/article/opinion/columns/emergency-chronicles-indira-gandhi-5597323/
7.   https://indianexpress.com/article/opinion/columns/emergency-chronicles-indira-gandhi-5597323/
8.   https://www.indiatoday.in/india/story/indira-gandhi-emergency-rule-rk-dhawan-congress-259245-2015-06-23
9.   Kuldip Nayar, *Emergency Retold* (New Delhi: Konark Publishers, 2013).
10. https://www.indiatoday.in/magazine/cover-story/story/19771031-indira-gandhis-arrest-seen-as-janata-partys-first-major-political-blunder-818822-2015-03-25
11. https://www.theguardian.com/world/2015/mar/23/indira-gandhi-india-election-archive-1977

Section 8: The BoP Crash and Reforms of 1991

Chapter 14: A Pound of Flesh

1. https://indianexpress.com/article/explained/janpath-1991-when-snooping-led-to-the-collapse-of-a-government-5418895/
2. Based on the author's conversation with B.P. Verma.
3. Yashwant Sinha, *Confessions of a Swadeshi Reformer: My Years as Finance Minister* (New Delhi: Penguin Books India, 2007) and author's conversation with B.P. Verma.
4. Based on the author's meetings and conversations with Manmohan Singh in 1991.
5. Based on the author's meetings and conversations with Manmohan Singh in 1991.
6. https://www.indiatoday.in/magazine/special-report/story/19880515-bofors-inquiry-joint-parliamentary-committee-report-reveals-more-than-it-conceals-797272-1988-05-15
7. https://www.business-standard.com/article/beyond-business/two-months-that-changed-india-111070200041_1.html
8. Ibid.
9. Ibid.
10. https://www.indiatoday.in/magazine/cover-story/story/19910715-narasimha-rao-election-as-prime-minister-heralds-return-of-the-old-congress-guard-814537-1991-07-15#ssologin=1#source=magazine; Based on author's meeting with Manmohan Singh a day after the swearing in

Chapter 15: An Anatomy of the Crisis

1. http://documents.worldbank.org/curated/en/999451468260069468/pdf/multi0page.pdf
2. https://rbi.org.in/Scripts/BS_PressReleaseDisplay.aspx?prid=18556
3. https://www.indiatoday.in/magazine/special-report/story/19910831-under-attack-narasimha-rao-govt-lowers-hiked-fertiliser-prices-compromises-on-critical-issue-814754-1991-08-31#ssologin=1#source=magazine
4. https://www.indiatoday.in/magazine/cover-story/story/19910715-bjp-emerging-as-a-major-party-was-the-biggest-surprise-in-electio ns-1991-814590-1991-07-15 and https://www.indiatoday.in/magazine/cover-story/story/19910715-exit-poll-rajiv-gandhi-assassination-resulted-in-distinct-swing-in-favour-of-congressi-814550-1991-07-15

Section 9: Reservation and Mandir

Chapter 16: The Game of Life and Death

1.   https://www.history.com/this-day-in-history/iraq-invades-kuwait
2.   https://indianexpress.com/article/india/india-others/sunday-story-mandal-commission-report-25-years-later/
3.   P.V. Narasimha Rao, *Ayodhya: 6 December 1992* (New Delhi: Penguin Books India, 2006).
4.   Ibid.
5.   Based on the author's interaction with Ram Mohan Rao.
6.   https://www.business-standard.com/article/politics/communal-forces-cannot-and-should-not-be-in-govt-sitaram-yechury-119030200570_1.html
7.   http://www.ncbc.nic.in/Writereaddata/Mandal%20Commission%20Report%20of%20the%201st%20Part%20English635228715105764974.pdf
8.   B.G. Deshmukh, *A Cabinet Secretary Looks Back from Poona to the Prime Minister's Office* (New Delhi: HarperCollins, 2004).
9.   Ibid.
10. Rao, *Ayodhya.*

Chapter 17: The Politics of the Mandir

1.   P.V. Narasimha Rao, *Ayodhya: 6 December 1992* (New Delhi: Penguin Books India, 2006).
2.   B.G. Deshmukh, *A Cabinet Secretary Looks Back from Poona to the Prime Minister's Office* (New Delhi: HarperCollins, 2004).
3.   Rao, *Ayodhya.*
4.   Ibid.
5.   https://www.epw.in/engage/article/jats-patels-and-marathas-want-quotas-but-do-they-deserve-them
6.   http://www.ncbc.nic.in/Writereaddata/Mandal%20Commission%20Report%20of%20the%201st%20Part%20English635228715105764974.pdf
7.   https://www.telegraphindia.com/india/concern-and-questions-over-creamy-layer/cid/1670411

Section 10: The Telecom Bump

Chapter 18: In Search of a Landline

1.   Indian Telecommunication Statistics 2002, Ministry of Communications, Government of India

2. https://www.nytimes.com/2007/02/01/opinion/01iht-edtharoor.4431582.html
3. http://dot.gov.in/national-telecom-policy-1994

Chapter 19: The Fallout after 1994

1. Ashok V. Desai, *India's Telecommunications Industry History, Analysis, Diagnosis* (New Delhi: Sage, 2006).
2. Maruthi P. Tangirala, *Telecom Sector Regulation in India: An Institutional Perspective* (Abingdon, Oxon: Routledge, 2019).
3. http://dot.gov.in/new-telecom-policy-1999
4. https://www.ndtv.com/india-news/2g-spectrum-scam-some-highlights-of-cag-report-439416
5. https://www.indiatoday.in/india/story/2g-spectrum-verdict-what-happens-now-to-122-cancelled-telecom-licenses-1113292-2017-12-21
6. https://www.livemint.com/Companies/rPju0LUcHUizRBbXH7ecdL/How-Mukesh-Ambanis-Reliance-Jio-shook-up-Indias-telecom-ma.html

Section 11: Twin Shocks of NPAs and RBI Autonomy

Chapter 20: The Genesis and Rise of NPAs

1. https://www.livemint.com/Opinion/arQr1ZUW9EI51qwmF7lqJN/The-status-of-public-sector-banks-in-India-today.html
2. https://www.businesstoday.in/moneytoday/stocks/invest-companies-fccbs-due-redemption-caution-returns/story/21869.html
3. Raghuram G. Rajan, *I Do What I Do* (New Delhi: HarperCollins, 2017).
4. https://www.iimb.ac.in/sites/default/files/2018-07/WP_No._505.pdf

Chapter 21: Recognition, Recapitalization, Resolution and Reform

1. https://www.livemint.com/Politics/Tio5Driwfu8UkEyvuiCkBM/SC-to-hear-challenge-to-RBIs-circular-on-bad-loans-on-28-No.html
2. https://www.financialexpress.com/economy/arun-jaitleys-big-message-to-defaulters-ibc-instilling-fear/1363934/
3. http://legislative.gov.in/sites/default/files/A2018-17.pdf

Section 12: Demonetization

Chapter 22: Shock Therapy or a Boomerang?

1. https://www.ndtv.com/india-news/pm-modi-to-meet-military-chiefs-today-to-review-security-after-september-surgical-strikes-1622649 and

https://indianexpress.com/article/india/india-news-india/narendra-modi-chief-of-army-staff-navy-air-force-pakistan-ajit-doval-4364124/

2. https://www.bbc.com/news/world-asia-37531900
3. https://twitter.com/sgurumurthy/status/1036157975570743298
4. https://dea.gov.in/sites/default/files/Promo_PaymentsMeans_Card_Digital_0.pdf
5. Raghuram G. Rajan, *I Do What I Do* (New Delhi: HarperCollins, 2017).
6. Ibid.
7. https://www.hindustantimes.com/business-news/rajan-preferred-other-ways-over-demonetisation-to-tackle-black-money/story-vlTbd6oixy6M4DnH65dWxI.html
8. Author's interview with Arun Kumar.

Chapter 23: The Hand of the RBI and Modi

1. https://rbi.org.in/scripts/BS_PressReleaseDisplay.aspx?prid=37259
2. https://www.jagran.com/uttar-pradesh/kanpur-city-now-two-thousand-note-possible-14937251.html and https://www.hindustantimes.com/india-news/journalist-broke-story-about-currency-demonetisation-a-fortnight-back/story-3OpgtR5ehdzkRRrwQITLgK.html
3. https://www.livemint.com/Industry/kPPjdrUjWrqfryG8bwgv9M/RBI-and-demonetisation-An-insiders-account.html
4. Minutes of the 56st meeting of the Central Board of Directors of the RBI.
5. https://rbidocs.rbi.org.in/rdocs/Publications/PDFs/RBIA1934170510.PDF
6. Minutes of the 56st meeting of the Central Board of Directors of the RBI.
7. https://www.livemint.com/Industry/kPPjdrUjWrqfryG8bwgv9M/RBI-and-demonetisation-An-insiders-account.html
8. Arvind Subramanian, *Of Counsel: The Challenges of the Modi–Jaitley Economy* (Gurgaon: Penguin Random House India, 2018).
9. http://mospi.nic.in/sites/default/files/press_release/nad_PR_31may18.pdf
10. http://mospi.nic.in/sites/default/files/press_release/FRE%20of%20National%20Income%2C%20Consumption%20Expenditure%2C%20Saving%20and%20Capital%20Formation%20For%202017-18_0.pdf
11. https://www.cmie.com/kommon/bin/sr.php?kall=warticle&dt=2017-07-11%2011:07:31&msec=463
12. https://www.business-standard.com/article/opinion/seasonal-adjustment-is-not-a-simple-mechanical-task-117111501699_1.html
13. https://indianexpress.com/article/business/economy/cmies-mahesh-vyas-says-3-5-million-jobs-lost-due-to-demonetisation-5357295/
14. https://www.cmie.com/kommon/bin/sr.php?kall=warticle&dt=2018-12-17%2012:47:23&msec=093

15. http://phdcci.in/live_backup/image/data/Research%20Bureau-2014/
    Economic%20Developments/paper/Study%20on%20Impact.pdf

16. https://www.business-standard.com/article/economy-policy/5-
    million-men-lost-their-jobs-after-demonetisation-says-swi-2019-
    report-119041700386_1.html

17. https://www.business-standard.com/article/economy-policy/
    unemployment-rate-at-five-decade-high-of-6-1-in-2017-18-nsso-
    survey-119013100053_1.html

18. https://www.business-standard.com/article/economy-policy/
    unemployment-peaked-to-4-year-high-during-demonetisation-govt-
    survey-119011001329_1.html

19. http://epaper.financialexpress.com/2057957/Delhi/March-07,-
    2019#page/1/2

20. https://www.indiatoday.in/india/story/demonetisation-what-india-
    gained-and-lost-1327502-2018-08-30

21. http://www.arthakranti.org/news-events/159-what-was-arthakranti-
    proposal-to-pm-narendra-modi

22. http://www.newindianexpress.com/opinions/columns/s-
    gurumurthy/2016/jun/22/Rajan-The-exit-that-was-inevitable-883797.
    html

23. Minutes of the 561st meeting of the Central Board of Directors of the RBI
    on 8 November 2016.

24. Rajan, *I Do What I Do*.

25. https://indianexpress.com/article/india/india-news-india/demonetisation-
    of-rs-500-rs-1000-notes-pm-modi-bear-pain-for-50-days-then-punish-
    me-4373933/

26. https://www.thehindu.com/news/national/ministry-withdraws-note-ban-
    report/article25608445.ece

27. https://www.bjp.org/en/manifesto2019

Section 13: GST: Widening the Tax Net

Chapter 24: One Country, One Tax

1. https://www.nipfp.org.in/media/pdf/books/BK_39/Reform%20Of%20
   Domestic%20Trade%20Taxes%20In%20India%20Issues%20And%20
   Options.pdf

2. Ibid.

3. http://gstcouncil.gov.in/brief-history-gst

4. Yashwant Sinha with Aditya Sinha, *India Unmade: How the Modi
   Government Broke the Economy* (New Delhi: Juggernaut Books, 2018).

Chapter 26: The Aftermath of the GST

1.   Based on the author's interview with tax expert Satya Poddar.
2.   Ibid.
3.   Ibid.

Section 14: Disruptions Ahead

Chapter 27: India of the Future

1.   https://www.indiabudget.gov.in/ub1999-2000/bs/bs1.htm

BIBLIOGRAPHY

Batabyal, Rakesh, ed. *The Penguin Book of Modern Indian Speeches*. New Delhi: Penguin Books India, 2007.

Desai, Ashok V. *India's Telecommunications Industry: History, Analysis, Diagnosis*. New Delhi: Sage, 2006.

Deshmukh, B.G. *A Cabinet Secretary Looks Back from Poona to the Prime Minister's Office*. New Delhi: HarperCollins, 2004.

Dhar, P.N. *Indira Gandhi, the 'Emergency', and Indian Democracy*. New Delhi: Oxford University Press, 2000.

Fotedar, M.L. *The Chinar Leaves: A Political Memoir*. New Delhi: HarperCollins, 2015.

Ghosh, D.N. *No Regrets*. New Delhi: Rupa, 2015.

Guha, Ramachandra. *India after Gandhi: The History of the World's Largest Democracy*. New Delhi: Picador, 2007.

Gupte, Pranay. *Mother India: A Political Biography of Indira Gandhi*. New Delhi: Penguin Books India, 2009.

Kapoor, Coomi. *The Emergency: A Personal History*. New Delhi: Penguin Books India, 2015.

Kudaisya, Medha M. *The Life and Times of G.D. Birla*. New Delhi: Oxford, 2003.

Mitra, Ashok. *A Prattler's Tale: Bengal, Marxism, Governance*. New Delhi: Samya, 2007.

Mukherjee, Pranab. *The Dramatic Decade: The Indira Gandhi Years*. New Delhi: Rupa, 2015.

Mukherjee, Rudranghsu, ed. *Great Speeches of Modern India*. New Delhi: Random House India, 2007.

Nayar, Kuldip. *Emergency Retold*. New Delhi: Konark, 1977.

Rajan, Raghuram G. *I Do What I Do*. New Delhi: HarperCollins, 2017.

Ramesh, Jairam. *Intertwined Lives: P.N. Haksar and Indira Gandhi*. New Delhi: Simon & Schuster India, 2018.

Rao, P.V. Narasimha. *Ayodhya: 6 December 1992*. New Delhi: Penguin Books India, 2006.

Sezhiyan, Era, ed. *Shah Commission Report: Lost and Regained*. Chennai: Aazhi Publications, 2010.

Sinha, Yashwant. *India Unmade*. New Delhi: Juggernaut, 2018.

Subramanian, Arvind. *Of Counsel: The Challenges of the Modi–Jaitley Economy*. Gurgaon: Penguin Random House India, 2018.

Verghese, B.G. *First Draft Witness to the Making of Modern India*. Chennai: Tranquebar, 2010.

Wahi, S.P. *Leading from the Front*. New Delhi: Crossbill Publishing, 2013.

Zamindar, Vazira Fazila-Yacoobali. *The Long Partition and the Making of Modern South Asia: Refugees, Boundaries, Histories*. New Delhi: Penguin Books India, 2008.